IS GOD A RACIST?

THE RIGHT WING IN CANADA

'God is a racist' – so goes a statement published in the literature of the Western Guard, a white-supremacist, anti-Semitic group in Toronto. It is one of a number of racist organizations that have sprung up in Canada since the Second World War. Stanley Barrett points out in this disquieting study that although many of the principles of such organizations are offensive to the vast majority of Canadians, these groups represent a growing part of a broader political phenonemon that has recently surfaced in numerous nations.

In examining the rise of right-wing extremism in Canada, a nation traditionally known for its tolerance, Barrett considers a wide range of political convictions, from those of confessed Fascists to those of essentially ordinary, law-abiding, but highly conservative individuals who are deeply concerned about the future of Western Christian civilization.

Barrett's study, grounded in a scientific tradition that has regularly exposed racial myths, is guided by humanistic values that celebrate individual worth. It sheds new light on a growing phenomenon that threatens those values.

STANLEY R. BARRETT is a professor in the Department of Sociology and Anthropology, University of Guelph, and author of *The Rebirth of Anthropological Theory*.

STANLEY R. BARRETT

Is God a Racist?
The Right Wing in Canada

UNIVERSITY OF TORONTO PRESS
Toronto Buffalo London

© University of Toronto Press 1987
Toronto Buffalo London
Printed in Canada

ISBN 0-8020-5758-6 (cloth)
ISBN 0-8020-6673-9 (paper)

Canadian Cataloguing in Publication Data

Barrett, Stanley R., 1938-
  Is God a Racist?

  Bibliography: p.
  Includes index.
  ISBN 0-8020-5758-6 (bound)   ISBN 0-8020-6673-9 (pbk.)

  1. Racism – Canada.   2. Canada – Race relations.
  3. Right and left (Political science).
  I. Title.

  FC104.B37 1987   305.8'00971   C87-094345-6
  F1035.A1B37 1987

For Julius Uzoaba and his family

Contents

Preface

God is a racist. At least, that is the claim of the Western Guard, a white-supremacist, neo-Fascist organization that reached its zenith in the mid-1970s in Toronto. The slogan 'God Is a Racist' appears at different places in the Western Guard's literature (it also was painted on the side of a Toronto church in 1977), and goes to the heart of an organized, growing, and often violent movement in the Western world to save the beleaguered white man from domination and eventual extinction – the inevitable products, the racists contend, of interracial mixing and the evil machinations of Jews.

Who are these people who have taken on the task of rescuing the white man, and what precisely do they want? The impression one gains from newspaper reports and from the statements of our political leaders is that the right wing consists of thugs and nut-cases, poorly educated and mentally disturbed people who hardly need to be taken seriously. Certainly that type exists, but much more numerous are those who can be described as solidly middle class – reasonably well-educated, often well-travelled, intelligent and thoughtful, but racists none the less. In other words, these people are not so different from the average Canadian citizen.

The more benign members of the right wing are disturbed by big government, creeping socialism, high taxes, homosexuality, pornography, and the drug scene. They are concerned about unsettling changes in society, and dream of a bygone age when life was simpler and the moral order was intact. Some of them think that Canadians, by which they usually mean white (Anglo-Saxon) Canadians, are getting the short end of the stick, and they argue for an end to Canada's 'insane' immigration laws, and for a return to what they euphemistically refer to as 'the proper and traditional ethnic balance in Canadian society' – in other words, a Canada with a British flavour.

The more extreme members of the right wing want nothing less than a totally white society. They contend that blacks and whites can never live together in harmony, that interracial marriage is more dangerous to civilization than the atomic bomb, and that a time will come when the world will erupt into a gigantic race war where one's battledress will be the colour of one's skin. Nor are they very favourably disposed towards Jews, which brings us to an important point. When I began this study, I was mainly concerned with the white supremacists' attacks on blacks, largely because of the several years I had spent in West Africa in anthropological research and with CUSO. Yet it soon became apparent that the principal targets of the right were Jews. As it is sometimes said, racists want blacks 'in their place,' but want Jews to stop existing. Blacks are considered despicable, but too feeble-minded to pose a threat to whites. Jews are thought of as clever, dangerous, amoral vermin, conspiring to gain control over the world. The point cannot be stressed too much that the single most important theme running throughout the various radical-right organizations is anti-Semitism, not a little of which has its roots in the image of Jews as the killers of Christ. It would be a mistake, however, for blacks to be unconcerned with organizations like the Western Guard (which sometimes has been the case). Indeed, the attack on blacks is doubly negative: they are regarded by white supremacists not only as a different species, but also as too inferior to defend themselves.

This study tells the story of the Canadian right wing, but it is not an exposé. My purpose has not been to search for incriminating evidence. Instead, it has been the conventional academic one of identifying patterns, converting raw data into abstractions, and probing at deeper levels in order to uncover contradictions and bring to the surface the kinds of insights that will help us to understand white supremacism, anti-Semitism, and the right wing in general. For this reason, I shall only use the names of individuals whose identities are already public knowledge. At the same time, however, this is not a neutral work, and certainly it has not been a labour of love. Concentrated research and writing on racism – regardless of its importance – is debilitating. With the experience of this study behind me, I now understand more than ever before why so many scholars who belong to minority groups steer clear of the subject of racism: the topic is simply soul-destroying. There is, indeed, a great deal of truth to the adage that racism harms everyone. Those academics and activists who do grapple with it are sometimes said to be half-neurotic, spotting racists around every corner. While this statement often tells us more about the accuser than the accused, in some cases it is an accurate assessment: racism can consume even its most sophisticated opponents, reducing their humanity accordingly. Nor do the white supremacists themselves escape unscathed. The more interviews I conducted, the more I began to see that some of them – even those tragic individuals who had drifted into the radical right almost accidentally, consumed by anger over communist take-overs of their natal lands, or frustrated by a world that did not unfold according to their expectations, and whose lives had previously been conventional and correct – exhibited a sort of moral rot, their principles potted and decayed. That could hardly be otherwise. A person cannot spend his time despising half of mankind, searching for conspiracies in every walk of life, and feeding off the flaws in human nature and human institutions without paying the price. The capacity of racism to deplete one's humanity may help to account for one feature of this project that has left me disturbed: although in the course of conducting my research I met a great many people dedicated to eradicating racism, only rarely did I meet a man or woman whose perspective clearly surmounted the interests of his or her own ethnic group. Possibly that is too much to ask. Yet what impressed me was the handful of outstanding men and women who courageously confronted racism year after year and still retained a capacity for wisdom.

Perhaps not surprisingly, on numerous occasions I asked myself how I got involved in this project. Certainly, there was little in my background to lead me inevitably to the topic. I grew up in a small village in rural Ontario, heavily Protestant and conservative. I can still remember vividly two of my boyhood 'cultural' experiences. One was when a friend of the family visited from the enormous metropolis of Toronto. She was a Catholic, something I had never seen up close before, and she had to drive several miles from our village to attend mass. The other was when my brothers and I visited the home of some new kids in the village to trade comic books. We were ever so alert and not a little apprehensive: the new kids were Jews. With the passage of years, my experiences broadened. As a teenager during summer holidays, I always was thrilled to work at a construction site with an immigrant from Italy, Turkey, or wherever, no doubt romanticizing ridiculously the wonders of those enchanted lands. When I first entered university as an undergraduate and began to meet Africans and other Third World peoples, and to appreciate the unfair world into which they were born, I always wondered why not every single one of them was a revolutionary. Yet I have never been politically active, and I do not consider myself a Marxist. If anything, I am a middle-of-the-road Canadian, or more grandly, a liberal humanist. Liberal humanism combines social conscience with the critical attitude. Sustained scepticism and agnosticism in all earthly things, tempered by the goal of human amelioration, are its tools. Dogmas are its foes, from racism itself to inflexible versions of Marxism and science. Yet during the course of this project, I have had to face the question whether liberal humanism, which draws from but is not overwhelmed by Marx's vision, is a defensible position for someone opposed to racism. Socialist regimes as they exist today may be as remote from attaining Marx's Utopia as Christian-dominated nations are from living up to the precepts of Christ. Moreover, it is far from proven that racism and anti-Semitism evaporate when socialism triumphs. Nevertheless, racism is essentially a tool of power, a mechanism of sustaining privilege, and it is difficult to reject the socialist's argument that anything less than a fundamental realignment of the social order will fail to eradicate it.

For many of us, the opposition to racism needs no elaboration. Racism is by definition pernicious. Yey some people – and not just members of the right wing – will regard this evaluation as dogmatic. After all, I have already stressed that many white supremacists and anti-Semites are well-educated and intelligent. Sometimes they do correctly identify contemporary social problems; there *is*, for example, substantial racial strain in the modern world, the denial of which does little to promote the anti-racist cause. White supremacists are fond of pointing out that there are two sides to every story, and that their only sin has been to have had the courage to examine both the liberal and racist interpretations of the world scene, which in their view makes them the truly educated. How does one respond to all this? Let me first say that the educated person, in my lexicon, is one who has a tolerance for ambiguity and a capacity to countenance a multitude of viewpoints. The white supremacist does not belong to this category. In all my interviews I never met a single committed racist who had anything but a superficial knowledge of the massive scientific literature that exposes racial myths. That is not surprising: true believers want their prejudices confirmed, not disturbed. Their argument, thus, that they have merely examined the issue from all sides, is baseless. But there is an even more important objection, which racists themselves and their covert admirers in the wider society would do well to consider. After several years of research and reflection, I began to see that the radical right is most vulnerable to criticism on moral-philosophical grounds. The radical right is a philosophy for old men (not necessarily age-wise), for the jaded. Its perspective degrades humanity. The radical right attempts to build a social order that exploits human weaknesses. It latches on to what in essence are flaws in the human condition, but rather than trying to surmount them, it drives the wedge in deeper, as in the case with racism itself. Those who attempt to resolve racial problems and promote understanding may never fully succeed. But at least they do not diminish the human spirit as does the radical right. It is the overwhelming misanthropic thrust to the philosophy of the radical right that makes me positive about the future, despite the plausible prophecy of one expert (Rex 1970: 161) that racism will continue to plague the planet for a long time ahead. The fund of human goodness runs too deeply and is too irrepressible to give in to a philosophy shot through with paralysing negativity.

Acknowledgments

The research and writing that went into this project stretched over a period of seven years, beginning in January 1980. I did not, however, work on it continuously, partly because I took time out to write another book (*The Rebirth of Anthropological Theory*), and partly because of teaching and administrative responsibilities. Over the course of these years, numerous individuals in academia, libraries, and anti-racist organizations helped me with this study. I am particularly grateful to Ben Kayfetz, and wish also to acknowledge the assistance of Alan Shefman and several individuals at the Ontario Human Rights Commission. For the vast majority of clergymen, the suggestion that 'God is a racist' will be blasphemous, and I record here the vigorous opposition of many of them to organizations like the Ku Klux Klan, including Rev. Robson who kindly agreed to talk to me about the Riverdale Action Committee Against Racism (RACAR). In Vancouver, Maurice Saltzman, Mark Silverberg, Jean Gerber, Charan Gill, and Paul Winn gave freely of their time. In Alberta, the perspectives provided to me on the Keegstra affair by Herb Katz and R.K. David were particularly valuable. Several knowledgeable journalists, including Neil Louttit, Terry Glavin, and Ross Henderson, kindly agreed to share their expertise with me. In my own university, David McKinney was a constant source of support, and other academics such as Wilson Head, Frances Henry, Evelyn Kallen, Cyril Levitt, and David Millett all helped me to understand the phenomenon of racism. I owe a special debt to Gerald Hinbest who was my research assistant on the project for one summer. Numerous other individuals who provided me with the data and insights on the right wing, wittingly or unwittingly, must go unnamed, including members of the right wing themselves, infiltrators, and ordinary Canadians (from the well-heeled to the penniless) whose racist inclinations set me on the trail in the first place.

Finally, I am especially grateful to the Secretary of State, Multiculturalism Directorate, for the initial research grant that made this study possible, to the University of Guelph Research Board for providing me with grants along the way, and to the Canada Council's leave fellowship during 1985-6 when this book was written. The book has been published with the help of a grant from the Social Science Frederation of Canada, using funds provided by the Social Sciences and Humanities Research Council of Canada. The views expressed in this study are my own, and do not necessarily reflect those of the numerous individuals who have helped me, or the position and policy of the agencies that provided financial support, including the Government of Canada.

PART ONE
INTRODUCTION TO THE RIGHT WING

1

The Study

Do you think the country is going to the dogs? Are you concerned about falling morals and rising prices? Does life seem unfair, corrupt, and bewildering? Do you sometimes wonder if the world has been swept out of control, and only a drastic overhaul will put it back on an even keel? If so, somebody wants you: the radical right and the radical left. Both share the view that Western society is in a state of crisis and that the revolution is imminent. Each is determined to emerge from the anticipated anarchy in firm control of the political apparatus. That is about all they have in common. The radical left wishes to build a new social order, one in which egalitarianism will thrive and privilege will perish. The radical right wants to turn the clock back, to recapture a mythical golden age, where élitism and privilege will prevail, especially on a racial basis.

At the level of political action, the radical right probably cannot be fully comprehended independent of the radical left, and in a theoretical work a comparative analysis would be feasible. This study, however, with the exception of a brief section in the final chapter, focuses almost entirely on the Canadian right wing for the simple reason that very little research on the subject has been done, and my task has been to present a comprehensive picture. This itself has been a big enough job. Despite the celebrated trials of James Keegstra and Ernst Zundel, and the flash-flood of Ku Klux Klan activity in the early 1980s, many Canadians probably still are not aware of the extent of the right wing's presence in the country. In the 1920s, the Ku Klux Klan was a virulent force, and in the years preceding the Second World War, Fascist and Nazi parties sprang up across the land. While this book is informed by a historical dimension, my interest is primarily in the contemporary era. As we shall see, since the Second World War there has been a slow but steady trickle of organized right-wing activity, and within the last two decades the dam has broken. In the chapters that follow data are presented on more than one hundred right-wing organizations in Canada, and on almost six hundred members. These numbers are not insignificant, but it would be a mistake to conclude that Canada has been unusually receptive to the right wing's message. In recent decades the right wing, including its most extreme proponents, has raised its head in most nations of the industrialized Western world. In terms of both its capacity for tolerance and its susceptibility to the politics of hate, Canada is decidedly unexceptional.

ARGUMENTS

Although this study is primarily an ethnography, a descriptive account of the right wing, it is guided by three overarching questions. The first: how can the right wing, and especially white supremacism, exist in Canada, a country that has enjoyed an enviable reputation for tolerance? What is the relationship, if any, between the right wing and the wider society? My argument, which reaches its climax in chapter 11, is that racism – quite apart from any of the formally organized right-wing groups – has been institutionalized into Canadian society since the country's beginning. The right wing, including the most extreme racists and anti-Semites, simply represents a more crystallized and overt form of a broader phenomenon. Indeed, I regard the right wing as a laboratory in order to study more readily the institutionalized, often covert, racism of the wider society. Neil Louttit, a journalist who infiltrated the Ku Klux Klan in Toronto (*Toronto Star*, 9–19 July 1981), concluded his story with the comment that what frightened him most was not the Klan itself, but the realization that a segment of Canadian society was susceptible to the Klan's message. In a more detailed study, another journalist (Sher 1983: 211) observed: 'Far from being an aberration in a supposedly just and equal society, the Klan arguably is more of a reflection – however exaggerated – of the racism endemic in that society.' Referring to the Fascist parties in Canada in the 1930s, the eminent sociologist Dennis Wrong (1959: 53) stated, 'anti-Semitic violence and political demagoguery are nearly always the outward and visible signs of milder antipathies that have deep roots in the population.' All of these comments support my contention that it would be an unfortunate mistake to regard white supermacists, anti-Semites, or their less radical confrères as foreign entities on Canadian soil, a bizarre and atypical form of life clinging to the edges of the social structure.

The second question: why does the right wing exist from the perspective of the members themselves? What causes people to join the right wing, and especially to embrace the politics of racism? Although several factors are involved, my contention, elaborated in considerable detail in chapter 12, is that the 'God is a racist' theme underlies the motives of right-wing individuals. That is, from the point of view of these people, their protest has an essential religious component. This view is reflected specifically in the belief of extreme racists that religion – the Christian religion – condemns blacks and other coloured peoples to an inferior, subhuman level, and identifies Jews as the children of the Devil. But what I mean by the religious dimension is something more general and more vague. White supremacists see intrinsic links between Western civilization, Christianity, and the white 'race.' Civilization, they believe, is the special prerogative of white people, for only they have been blessed by God with the moral and creative capacity to attain it. Their call to the battle lines is based on the assumption that there exists today a massive, insidious, and relentless campaign by Jews and non-whites to attack the very foundation of Western Christian civilization. The contention of white supremacists is that if they lose the battle all mankind will suffer, for without the white man's leadership the world will descend into barbarism.

The third question: why do the right wing, racism, and anti-Semitism exist from the anthropologist's (theoretical) perspective? Although there is considerable overlap among these three phenomona, the right-wing resurgence in recent years is specifically an expression of deep-rooted problems within the capitalist system, as well as a reaction against the Western world's steady drift over the past centuries towards liberalism, egalitarianism, and universal brotherhood. Anti-Semitism, while pre-dating Christianity (Trachtenberg 1943: 6), cannot in its contemporary form be understood apart from the Christ-killer theme, nor can the fading away of the taboo against Jew-baiting – a taboo which has existed since the Second World War – be ignored. Racism, particularly in the context of black-white relationships, is often portrayed as universal and natural, not just by white supremacists, but also by some scholars. Yet that is not true. I am prepared to argue that ethnocentrism, the tendency to view one's own group as the centre of the universe and to disparge other groups, has been with us since the beginning of recorded time. But that is not what is meant by racism. Racism constitutes an elaborate and systematice ideology; it acts as a conceptual tool to rationalize the division of the world's population into the privileged and the deprived. It is inherently a political phenomenon. Racism in this sense is a relatively recent thing. It did not exist, according to Snowden (1970, 1983), in ancient Greece and Rome. Most specialists agree that it emerged with the advent of the colonization of the Third World by

European nations, and thus coincided too with the development of capitalism. This explanation resonates clearly with the Marxian perspective, and for very good reasons. Any account of racism that fails to entertain the roots of the phenomenon in colonialism and capitalism, or to highlight its political dimension, is bound to be inadequate.[1] Yet, as I explain more fully

1 Not everyone would agree with my argument that racism is a relatively recent phenomenon, tied specifically to the advent of colonialism and capitalism. Jordan (1968: 7), for example, points out that long before Englishmen had contact with blacks, the colour 'black' was loaded with negative symbolism. Ardener (1953–4) asserts that the preference for a light skin among the Ibo (or Igbo) in Nigeria pre-dated colonial contact. Samuels (1969–70), referring to colour sensitivity among people of Japanese origin in Hawaii, contends that the high value placed on having a light skin was indigenous to Japanese culture. Yet even if these claims are correct, the colour factor could only at the most have constituted one of the facilitating conditions that led to the eventual emergence of systematic racial ideology.

    There also is the biblical source of racism as revealed in Genesis. After the Flood, Ham looked on his father's nakedness, as Noah lay drunk in his tent. God then cursed Ham, his son Canaan, and all their descendants (assumed to be Africans), condemning them to servitude. Yet as Jordan (1968: 18) points out, the curse visited on Ham and his posterity did not become a pronounced Christian theme until the sixteenth and seventeenth centuries, again coinciding with colonialism and capitalism.

    Finally, one of the publisher's anonymous readers for this study referred to the concept of 'the purity of blood' that existed in the Iberian peninsula at the time of the Christian reconquest. 'Old Christians' were apprehensive that 'New Christians' (Jewish and Moorish converts) would contaminate the faith, and the latter were denied some rights and privileges enjoyed by the former. The concept of 'the purity of the blood' accompanied the eventual Portuguese colonization of Brazil (see Freyre 1963), where it became fused with the religious (especially Catholic) and class criteria that separated the masters from the slaves. While the Iberian case would seem to be a clear example of racial ideology that pre-dated the later era of widespread colonization, before concluding that it annihilates my argument two qualifications should be considered. First, the Iberian case itself grew out of an era of colonialism in its own right, in which the militarily and culturally advanced Moors invaded the Iberian peninsula; in a sense, it can be said to foreshadow the later, more extensive colonial era, and thus to be consistent with my thesis. Second, there is no single, specific date when one can say that colonialism (and thus racism) began. History does not unfold that neatly or discretely. Just as capitalism as an organized endeavour emerged unevenly in time, place, and degree, and there were individual capitalists long before capitalism as a system of rational economic pursuit was clearly established, racism as a massive and systematic ideology only gradually (and then non-uniformly) took shape, and prejudice-inclined individuals preceded it.

    In summary, if we distinguish between racism and anti-Semitism, and appreciate the difference between ethnocentrism and racism, I believe that my arguments stand up. Nevertheless, I wish to emphasize that I am much more familiar with the relevant anthropological and sociological scholarship than with the historical literature addressed

in chapter 12, I part company with those Marxists who favour an 'economistic' explanation, conceiving of racism as a mere mechanism that props up the class system, and thus as something to be explained entirely in class terms. No major social phenomenon is unidimensional. Not only has racism in the past century ventured beyond its economic cage, so that today it possesses a semi-autonomous political dimension, but it has also become criss-crossed by a range of factors including deep-seated psychological ones.

CONCEPTS

Before proceeding any farther, we need to define a few basic terms. There are literally dozens of definitions of racism, with little to choose between them. Banton (1970: 18) suggests that 'racism is the doctrine that a man's behaviour is determined by stable inherited characteristics deriving from separate racial stocks, having distinctive attributes and usually considered to stand to one another in relations of superiority and inferiority.' Social scientists usually distinguish among racial prejudice, racial discrimination, and racial ideology. The first refers to attitudes or mental predispositions normally (but not necessarily) of a pejorative nature towards individuals or groups independent of and unresponsive to actual contact and experience. The second refers to behaviour. Here we are not dealing simply with what people think about others, with stereotypes and distortions, but instead with concrete acts involving differential treatment according to perceived racial differences. The third concerns the general institutional framework of society. Racial ideology is part of the elaborate sets of ideas and beliefs that rationalize, legitimize, and sustain patterns of inequality. Racism in this sense is embedded in the structures of society, reflects the overall relations of power, and to a large extent is relatively unmotivated; that is, it exists on its own momentum, and is reproduced generation after generation by virtue of the continuity of the social system itself.

Further useful conceptual distinctions have been made by Patel (1980). He classifies the various scholarly approaches to racism as the deviant-individual, social-forces, and institutional-structural perspectives. The first

---

to the pre-colonial era, and it is always possible that my lack of knowledge has led me to errors in fact and interpretation. One final remark: while racism and anti-Semitism are overlapping but nevertheless distinctive phenomena, when I refer to both of them simultaneously I shall often, for stylistic purposes, only use the term 'racism,' subsuming anti-Semitism within it. The context of the prose should make it clear when I am employing racism as a general category and when I an using it in a narrower sense.

classification refers to seemingly random racial incidents, such as attacks on members of visible minorities in the subway. The underlying assumption is that such acts are committed by inadequately socialized individuals. Thus, it is not society itself that must be addressed to remedy the situation, but instead those scattered individuals who deviate from its norms. The second connects outbreaks of racism to assumed temporary social ruptures, such as a sharp increase in immigration or unemployment. Once again, racism is seen as an aberration, generated by atypical circumstances, rather than as an integral feature of society. The third perspective contains quite a different implication: racism is a structural product of the institutional framework, a manifestation of the pattern of social relationships which meshes with and reinforces the overall system of stratification. It will be obvious that institutional-structural racism and racial ideology are different sides of the same coin. Together they constitute a master concept in the investigation of rate relations, subsuming prejudice and discrimination, and the deviant-individual and social-forces perspectives as well.

In this study I shall often deal with racist extremists or fanatics. But what do these terms mean? Spoonley (1981: 100) defines extremism as deviance from the political norm and the tendency to occupy the poles of the ideological scale. Yet this definition doesn't seem satisfactory, for it is tantamount to stating that morality is no more than what the majority of people think it is, no more than what exists. Moreover, the political norm is not static. For example, today's North American conservatives are essentially reproductions of nineteenth-century liberals, promoting individual freedom, private enterprise, and small government. Similar confusion surrounds the concept of fanaticism. One of Canada's prominent racists told me that a fanatic (like himself) is merely someone who is quite sincere in his beliefs. A member of the radical left suggested to me that there is good and bad fanaticism: the truly dedicated socialist and the die-hard Fascist. The implication is that fanaticism is in the eye of the beholder. Nor can the term be restricted to the racial and political realms. Some people are 'fanatics' about fishing, and what about workaholics: aren't they, too, fanatics? George Santayana once defined the fanatic as a man who redoubles his efforts when he has forgotten his aims. In a general sense, that comes pretty close to what I mean by the term. However, I would add one specific characteristic, at least with regard to right-wing fanatics. These people, in my view, are those who are prepared to move from the level of argumentation to that of violence. The right-wing fanatic is ready to pave the route to the new Jerusalem with the corpses of its opposition.

We now come to the final and perhaps most critical distinction made in this study: that between the radical right and the fringe right. Before elaborating on these terms, let me make two points clear. First, the fringe right is 'moderate' only in relation to the radical right; if the latter did not exist, or was not the implicit measuring rod, the fringe would look much less benign. Second, some readers may disagree with the distinction I draw between the radical and fringe right (and what for want of a better term might be labelled legitimate politics), but *everybody* who thinks about political matters draws the line somewhere, either clearly or vaguely. This is inevitable by virtue of the basic permise that to think is to classify and categorize. To a member of the far left, the bad guys start with the NDP and the Liberals and everybody else to their right (and perhaps with other radical-left organizations that do not share their interpretation of Marx and Engels, or look to Albania rather than to China for inspiration!). To a member of the right wing, the rot starts with the 'pink' conservatives and everyone to their left.

As the field-work for this project progressed, I began to realize that somehow a distinction had to be made between those individuals who were committed racists and anti-Semites and those who were extremely conservative but not on the same level as the Ku Klux Klan. Other writers have faced the same dilemma. Westin (1964: 242), for example, states that the John Birch Society is located between the 'hate' right and the 'semi-respectable' right. The Overstreets (1964: 20) remark that it is exceptionally difficult to draw the line between the radical right and the fringes of legitimate conservatism. Their solution is to define extremism (both on the right and on the left) in terms of the methods employed – violence and terror. My own approach is to combine the criterion used by the Overstreets with the actor's perspective. By the latter I mean how individuals define themselves and their organizations. It must not be thought that members of the radical right generally attempt to conceal their commitment to extreme politics. Virtually all of the 'open' as opposed to 'secret' members of organizations such as the Ku Klux Klan and the Western Guard proudly proclaim that they are racists and Fascists. These people themselves often allude to what distinguishes them from less radical members of the right wing. A common term used by members of the radical right to identify themselves is 'the hard line.' Included here, they argue, are only those individuals who are true racists and committed anti-Semites. All others, they contend, are merely 'kosher conservatives.'

In this study, the 'radical right' will refer to those individuals who define themselves as racists, Fascists, and anti-Semites, and who are prepared to use violence to realize their objectives. The 'fringe right' will refer to people who share the view that the Tory party is controlled by socialists posing as conservatives, who oppose Third World immigration, foreign aid, homosexuals' rights, and the changing sexual norms of society, but who at the same time do not condone physical violence and reject all accusations that they are Fascists, racists, and anti-Semites.

There are, obviously, some flaws in these definitions. For example, while *all* of the organizations that I place in the radical-right camp are *potentially* violent, the amount of *actual* violence in Canada carried out by them has been considerably less than that perpetrated by comparable organizations in the United States. Of course, one could stretch the definition of violence to include conceptual issues, such as public pronouncements that Third World peoples are dirty and inferior, or the pasting of racial slogans on construction hoardings – neither of which is done very often by members of the fringe right. There also is the problem of deception. While in my experience most active members of the radical right openly admit they are racists, not all do, sometimes because they have sensitive jobs in the outside world or have decided to try their hand at contesting public office, and don't want their pasts to stand in the way. Whenever my data strongly indicated that people were indeed racists, despite their denials, I placed them in the radical-right category. Occasionally, these included some members of the fringe right who for one reason or another had decided to sing their Nazi songs in private.

Another flaw concerns the considerable diversity among the organizations placed within each of my two main categories. The radical right ranges from the openly racist and violent Ku Klux Klan at one end to the Canadian Anti-Soviet Action Committee (CASAC) at the other. The fringe right stretches from Ron Gostick's Canadian League of Rights to groups much closer to the political mainstream such as Young Americans for Freedom and the National Citizen's Coalition. While, at the extremes, it is reasonably easy to separate the organizations belonging to each category, the point where they meet is a great deal more fuzzy. For example, although I have put CASAC in the radical-right category, and the Canadian League of Rights in the fringe right, one could plausibly argue for the reverse. CASAC, after all, is a recognized student organization at the University of Toronto, and Gostick has been long regarded as an anti-Semite by some commentators. Yet my decision has been based on what I know about these organizations and their leaders, including the company they keep. Geza Matrai, the force behind CASAC, is undoubtedly a sincere foe of communism, but he also is the man who once attacked former premier Aleksei Kosygin on a state visit to Ottawa, and his associates have included some of the most prominent racists in the country. Gostick, on the other hand, whose views appear to have softened in recent years, cavorts with people who point their cannons at issues like foreign aid, and promotes his solutions to communist subversion and totalitarianism in legion halls, hotels, and school auditoriums across the country. Of course, the obvious solution here would be to establish another category between the radical right and the fringe right specifically for groups like CASAC and the Canadian League of Rights.

Although this study focuses almost entirely on the political space to the right of the established parties, a word of clarification about the line between legitimate conservatism and the fringe right is in order. We cannot, as in the case of the distinction between the radical and fringe right, draw upon a relatively straightforward criterion such as violence. Indeed, it might be thought that the dividing line between the political mainstream and the fringe right is simply in the eye of the beholder, merely reflecting currently accepted notions of legitimacy based on little more than the status quo. Yet there still is the actor's perspective. The individuals whom I have placed in the fringe-right category – even the least radical among them – tend to see themselves as different from those in the Progressive Conservative party; they often regard themselves as the 'real' conservatives, and the others as closet socialists who are leading the country down the road to ruin. There also is a difference in terms of the public-private dimension. Whereas some ordinary Canadians, and perhaps even the odd member of our established political parties, may privately hold unpopular views about issues such as homosexuality, foreign aid, and immigration, members of the fringe right are much more prepared to promote their beliefs on the public stage. Had these differences not existed, there would have been little reason for the members of the fringe right to attempt to establish alternatives to the mainline parties in the first place.

Finally, there is the wide variety of organizations within the fringe-right category – some standing within shouting distance of the political mainstream and others miles away. Just as it was suggested that another category could be inserted between the radical and fringe right, the same could be done – let us label it 'neo-conservatism' – to represent the space between legitimate conservatism and the fringe right. Although in my judgment the radical-right and fringe-right categories, albeit crude, are adequate for the purposes of my analysis, I have no objection to readers who wish to place the milder organizations dealt with in this study – including most or all of those in chapter 10 – into the neo-conservative category, but I would insist that the majority of them are lodged more to its right than to its left. Some readers will welcome the suggestion that a few of the organizations in this study straddle the neo-conservative and fringe-right categories, but before they begin to applaud they may wish to consult John McMurtry's stimulating and provocative paper (1984), in which a strong case is made for equating Hitler's Fascism and current neo-conservatism (including the Reagan and Thatcher varieties) in the Western World.

METHODOLOGY

One does not just wake up in the morning and decide to undertake a study of white supremacists. Many factors led me in this direction, both personal and academic. The brutal attack on a Tanzanian immigrant in Toronto's subway, leaving him with two broken knees, started me thinking. A short while later a friend from Nigeria was set upon by several white youths. These and similar cases suggested that racism was becoming increasingly overt in the country, and possibly crossing the line from verbal abuse to physical confrontation, and I decided to embark upon a study in its general area. But what should be the focus? It was at that point that certain scholarly arguments came to bear upon my decision. Anthropology as a discipline has changed considerably since the Second World War. Primitive societies are virtually a thing of the past, and many of us argue that the discipline, if it is to survive, must prove its mettle by grappling with the fundamental issues of the contemporary world, including those in highly industrialized societies. In recent years there also has emerged the argument that research is subversive, and that we no longer should concentrate our efforts on the poor and deprived, but instead equally on the powerful and wealthy. As Nader (1972) put it, anthropologists should start 'studying up,' focusing on élites. Regarding racism, Carmichael (1971: 174) has suggested that white scholars concerned about the issue should investigage the victimizers rather than the victims, and focus on white-dominated institutions that generate racism. An identical position has been adopted by Schwartz and Disch (1970: 63) who complain that whites almost always concentrate upon blacks as if it is the latter who hold the keys to racial reform, but rarely examine white society itself. All these arguments struck me as persuasive, and I decided to approach the subject of racism from 'the other end' – looking at whites and victimizers, rather than their dark-skinned victims. Yet the focus was still too vague. At that point I could have embarked on dozens of projects ranging from immigration policy to housing, education, and the police. As often is the case, the final decision, to examine the right wing in Canada, came about mostly by accident. Two of my students in the university where I taught wrote essays in my classes on the Western Guard, an organization that very definitely fell into the category of the white victimizer. Intrigued, and with the full realization that my own ascriptive characteristics would be an advantage – my skin colour, my Protestant and small-town background, and my age – I decided to take a crack at investigating that organization. Little did I suspect that before the project was finished, I would end up with data on more than one hundred right-wing groups.

From the outset, two questions had to be answered before the project could begin. First, was the research feasible? Would white supremacists agree to talk to me, and would it be safe to interview them, given their reputation for violence? My procedure was to seek advice from several organizations and individuals possessing specialized knowledge in racist matters. These included the Ontario Human Rights Commission, the Canadian Jewish Congress, prominent black Canadians, and academics with experience in race and ethnic studies. The consistent message was that white supremacists would readily grant me at least initial interviews under tolerable conditions.

The second question concerned the potential social value of the research: would a study of the extreme right wing do more harm than good? There are two dangers in focusing on groups like the Ku Klux Klan. One is that it gives them free advertising. This charge is often laid against the media. The Klan and other extremist organizations thrive on media exposure, and in symbolic fashion the media thrives on them. Moreover, would a study of white supremacists grant them a degree of legitimacy, by putting them in the academic curriculum? Or does ignoring them amount to tolerating them? There is no easy answer to these questions, just as the issue of whether laws should be established, regardless of their infringement on freedom of speech, to ban organizations like the Klan can be argued convincingly from both sides. As it often is said, organizations like the Western Guard and the Ku Klux Klan create a Catch-22 situation: to confront them may exaggerate their importance, but to ignore them may be tantamount to condoning them. Not surprisingly, anti-racist groups concerned with the increasingly bold Ku Klux Klan in the early 1980s were divided down the middle on how to confront it. The other principal danger is that a focus on white supremacists diverts attention from more subtle but ultimately more significant forms of racism – that which is part of our everyday experience, institutionalized into the school system and the courts, and reflected in the relative lack of employment opportunities for visible minorities.

The question of whether or not the research should be done was put to the same anti-racist individuals and organizations mentioned above. With one exception, everyone I consulted argued strongly that the research was of the utmost significance. What they opposed was a quickie job, a superficial approach, which did not adequately analyse and criticize the various racist organizations. Nevertheless, let me make it clear that I do not personally consider the subject of this book – organized forms of racial extremism and milder versions of right-wing expression – to be as important as more mundane issues such as the intrusion of racial criteria into employment and housing. I do believe, however, that studies such as mine are necessary in order to educate the populace about the precise nature of the attack against minority groups in this country, and to deliver a clear message to these groups that the views and actions of racists are unacceptable. Such a perspective, I would assume, along with the explicit effort to interpret white supremacism and anti-Semitism (and more benign right-wing beliefs) in the context of the racism institutionalized into the wider society, enhance the significance of the study.

Having been given the green light to undertake the project, I had to decide precisely how to go about it. Most studies of the radical right are based on archival research, and that was part of my methodology. An attempt, happily successful, was made to collect all available primary materials on the right wing, including newspaper clippings and more importantly the various in-house journals produced by the organizations themselves. Some of this material was found in public archives and libraries, some was provided to me by members of the right-wing organizations, and the remainder came from a variety of sources such as anti-racist organizations and individual citizens who had over the years amassed collections of right-wing publications.

As crucial as this material was for the study, I was not satisfied to rely upon it solely. I decided to proceed as anthropologists generally do and conduct face-to-face interviews with the right-wing members. This was a much greater challenge than the archival research, but at the same time it has provided a depth to the project that otherwise would not have been achieved. From the outset I was faced with the problem of how to go about establishing contact. For several weeks I was guilty of the normal failing among field-workers, busily engaging myself in all kinds of sideline activities in order to put off the initial entry into the field. In my case, these activities included repeated visits to various anti-racist organizations and long spells in the library. Finally, I took the plunge and arranged by telephone to meet the leader of the Western Guard at a public library in Toronto. John Ross Taylor, a Fascist and committed anti-Semite who was associated before the Second World War with Canada's most infamous Fascist, Adrien Arcand (see Betcherman 1975), had become the leader of the Western Guard in 1976. Taylor's first question was whether I was a Jew. After being assured that I was not, he questioned me about my racial background and my curiosity about his organization. Apparently satisfied with my explanations, he proceeded to outline the ideology and goals of the Western Guard. For more than four hours he talked almost non-stop, seemingly unaware of the two men sitting nearby whose interest in us was rather obvious. I never found out who these men were. They might have been Western Guard members who had tagged along to make certain their leader was in no danger; or possibly they belonged to one of the country's police agencies, and were keeping tabs on who the Western Guard man was meeting.

I went into the interview openly as an anthropologist. Any other approach, such as posing as a potential member, would have been too difficult to maintain, probably beyond my personal capacity to play roles, and anyway easily uncovered simply by making inquiries and possibly attending some of my introductory-level lectures at the nearby university where I was employed. Much to my surprise, the fact that I was an anthropologist was held in my favour. Taylor had a great admiration for physical anthropology, which he believed had firmly demonstrated the existence and inequality of independent races. As we shall see in chapter 12, there is a not inconsiderable body of literature labelled 'scientific racism' that people like Taylor draw upon to argue the validity of their views.

For each of the interviews that I conducted, I tried to play a role that I thought would be appropriate for the individual. Taylor was a man in his late sixties. With the anthropologist's knowledge of the harmonious relationships between alternative generations, I decided to approach him with the idea that he was a grandfather in the classificatory sense. For a couple of hours prior to the interview, I concentrated on the grandfather-grandson relationship, psyching myself up in order to act out the role when the interview began. Such careful preparation, which I followed in most other interviews as well, was absolutely necessary, otherwise my own anti-racist values would have made it impossible to do the research.

At the outset of the project I had anticipated the difficulty I would have in arranging interviews with the racists, but I was quite unprepared for another problem: depression. After each of the initial interviews, I was severely depressed, to such an extent that I wondered whether I could continue with the research. The depression was partly a consequence of my approach. In order to conduct the interviews, I had to act a part completely foreign to me, and to sustain it for an average of three to five hours. When the interviews were completed and I returned to reality, I was emotionally exhausted. The depression also was a reflection of the fact that never in my life had I talked to people who were committed racists; they stood for every-

thing that I personally opposed, and I felt soiled in their company. Sometimes after concluding an interview, I would see a black man on the street,
and would want to say something to him, to express the repugnance I felt
for what I had listened to during the interview; and often I purposefully ate
in a Jewish restaurant, as if that would remove the grime. As the months
went by, the severe depression and soiled feeling lessened, only to recur with
the occasional individual whose views were particularly peculiar and evil.
No doubt this was partly because I began to grow accustomed to the racists
and their beliefs; another reason was that many of those interviewed later in
the project were less bizarre and misanthropic than those I had contact with
at the beginning, which brings us to an important point. If racists as a category all wore horns, the battle against them would be a great deal easier.
But this is not the case. Many of them were indeed thoroughly despicable
characters. Yet others were in many ways high-principled men who also
happened to be racists. A few were humorous individuals who liked to tilt at
windmills, or lost souls who could just as easily have found comparable ful-
filment in a religious sect. The type that chilled me most, in fact, was not the
hard-nosed bully who wanted to kick somebody's teeth in, but rather the
highly educated man, wealthy and sophisticated, who sat sipping his cognac
while elaborating on the nobility of the white race and the necessity of excis-
ing the 'mud people' from our midst.

While occasionally I met members of the right wing in their homes, most
interviews were conducted in a public place – libraries, restaurants, bars. I
did not use a tape recorder, nor did I take notes during the interview.
Instead I followed a system of memorization that I had developed during
previous research in a closed community in Africa when it had become clear
that I could not work openly with systematic techniques. Immediately after
the interviews, which lasted, on average, three to five hours, I would write
down what I had memorized. Usually this comprised about twenty to
twenty-five pages of notes; occasionally more than fifty pages were produced from a single interview. Sometimes a member of the extreme right
would ask whether I had a tape recorder concealed in my jacket or brief-
case. I would always invite him to check me thoroughly. Ironically, the only
time when I did use a tape recorder – in two long interviews with James
Keegstra – the batteries went dead half-way through the second meeting.
The fact that I did not use a tape recorder fostered an informal, relaxed
atmosphere, during which most of those who were interviewed talked at
length and freely. Almost without exception the interviews were successful.
As time went by, I became a more familiar figure in right-wing circles, and
in order to prevent any misunderstanding, I periodically reminded the

people with whom I associated that I had no interest in joining their organizations, that my only interest was academic. In other words, I constantly tried to maintain that delicate balance between conveying that I was interested in learning about the extreme right wing yet at the same time was an outsider.

When an anthropologist does field-work in a small community, the aim is to become sociologically invisible, to slip smoothly into the normal flow of life. But in one-shot interviews, the situation that characterized this project, the procedure is different. One tries to do nothing less than 'capture' the interviewee for a period of three to four hours, to project one's personality and role so seductively that the person will talk as if he has known the researcher all his life. At the same time, however, there must be a clear understanding that the relationship is between researcher and interviewee, not between fellow members, otherwise one cannot raise the analytical questions that are necessary. On a few occasions, I was taken to meet members of the right wing by individuals who had infiltrated organizations. Almost always, the interviews were unsuccessful. There simply was too much role-ambiguity. The interviewee was confused about whether to treat me as an anthropologist or as a potential member, and I in turn was inhibited from probing analytically. What was missing from these interviews was the hour or so monologue during which the subject tells how and why he became involved in the right wing, explains his beliefs in great detail, and reflects on these beliefs and activities as they related to his past life.[2]

There was a definite and qualitative difference in the interview situation between the radical-right and the fringe-right members. Much less mental preparation was needed by the interviewer with the latter; they did not exude the air of fanaticism and moral decay that was sometimes shown by radical-right members, and the research was much easier. This was the case, for example, when I spent several weeks in Alberta working on the Keegstra affair. Actually, about 75 per cent of Keegstra's supporters and opponents initially refused to let me interview them, mainly because they had been hounded by reporters for several months. After I explained the nature of my study, and made the point that I was an anthropologist rather than a

---

2 Anyone writing in the 1980s must be sensitive about the choice of masculine and feminine pronouns. Since it seems to me to be awkward to continuously use 'he' and 'she' simultaneously, and since I object to the form 's/he' on stylistic grounds, I more often than not have retained the traditional masculine term. In this study the choice is not as inappropriate as it often is in others, because the vast majority of right-wing members are male.

reporter, almost all of them eventually agreed to meet me. Indeed, four individuals – two in the Keegstra camp and two adamantly opposed to him – made available their elaborate files on the Keegstra affair, including private letters. Part of the problem in the Alberta phase of the project was that my initial contact with most people was by telephone. It is much more effective to show up at one's office or home in person; in the case of individuals crucial to the project, such as Keegstra himself, I always did exactly that. Occasionally, a supposed member of the fringe right would turn out to be secretly a committed racist and anti-Semite; when that happened, as it did when I was investigating the Keegstra case, I was clumsy and ineffectual, mentally unprepared to cope with the situation.

One of the peculiarities of anthropology is that the field-worker has no meaningful, logical criteria that indicate when the job is done; in fact, if full knowledge, truth, and understanding were the measuring rods, anthropology would be a graveyard strewn with uncompleted projects. What happens instead is that the field-worker wraps up a project when the conventionally accepted time period has elapsed – formerly a couple of years in the field, now a year or so. Or the field-worker simply becomes jaded, and through his or her clumsiness begins to alienate the subjects. The latter describes my own initial signs of withdrawal. After almost five years of sporadic research I found it increasingly difficult to play the roles necessary to conduct interviews with white supremacists. I began to argue back with some of them, out of a strong urge to attack their misanthropic views. By that time, too, I had begun to lose the will-power to withstand the various forms of subtle intimidation that inevitably exist in a project such as this one. For example, one radical-right member, suspicious of my motives, talked incessantly in my company about making bombs and blowing up people. Another, equally suspicious, developed the habit of referring to 'our' combined writings in the cause of the white-supremacist movement. On one occasion a far-right organization managed to obtain a copy of my research proposal for the project, and for a while considered ways of manipulating me or feeding me false information. Whether it was true or not, I was informed rather ominously by a rather unbalanced man that the right wing now knew all about me, for some of them had attended one of my large introductory-level classes. About the police's interest in my activities there was no doubt: the dean of the college at the university where I taught was contacted by them, and I was personally visited by a gentleman involved in the intelligence line. In both Vancouver and Ottawa I was asked to meet police officials, and on one occasion, largely as a result of my own clumsiness in connection with a very sensitive situation, I was put through the hoops by an inquisitorial team from the RCMP. Ironically, on more than one occasion, right-wing members suspected that I myself was an undercover RCMP agent.

Somewhat more humorously, but still with the intent to intimidate me, a letter was sent anonymously to the chairman of my department; it contained a copy of questions about my project that had been submitted for discussion to parliament by a Conservative MP who apparently saw my research as a threat. Ironically, around that same time a Liberal party functionary contacted me with a list of Conservatives whom he claimed were far-right members, and suggested that I look into their cases; managing to keep a straight face, I politely declined the invitation. A different kind of invitation was presented when I interviewed a particularly virulent member of the right wing. He was in the habit of showing up with not one but two female companions; the subtle message was that I could take my pick. My interpretation that the women were bait, involving an attempt to compromise and thus control me, may have been mistaken – perhaps it was merely a friendly gesture; in either case it certainly was a gross misjudgment of my character. Occasionally, a man or woman would attack me verbally in an aggressive manner, but curiously that occurred with the fringe right much more often than with the radical right. The explanation, I suppose, is that members of the fringe right were always apprehensive that I would see them as closet racists and Fascists, whereas the radical-right members brought with them to every interview an implicit resource: their reputations for violence. Because that resource was never far in the background, radical-right members could afford to be affable.

The accumulated effects of these various incidents began to slow me down, and the end of the field-work phase came rather suddenly when a man reputed to be a police informer found himself in a menacing situation and contacted me to try to save his skin. At that time I was planning to embark on a series of highly structured interviews (or schedules) in order to gather quantitative data. However, when this individual turned to me for help in negotiating with the organization that had threatened him, I decided that was enough. The only important research I conducted thereafter was with the Keegstra affair, but in comparison to some of the rough water that I had come through, the research in Alberta was like paddling downstream.

2

Organizations and Members

This chapter presents an overview of the various groups and members that make up the Canadian right wing. Let me stress that the focus here, and indeed throughout the study with the exception of chapter 11, is on the *organized* right wing. The latter, of course, is not the sole source of right-wing expression in Canada, and does not include such right-wing elements as those that are blended into our various institutions. There have been several distinct stages of organized racism and right-wing activity in Canada: the Ku Klux Klan in the 1920s; the Fascist phase of the 1930s; the incipient Nazi thrust of the 1960s; followed by the full-blown neo-Fascism of the 1970s and 1980s. Although my research was concentrated on the contemporary era, especially the last two decades, it is important to appreciate the historical context in which the phenomenon developed.

BEFORE THE SECOND WORLD WAR

The Ku Klux Klan was not the only openly racist organization in Canada in the 1920s – the White Canada Association, for example, was founded in Vancouver in 1929 – but its range and support were extensive. As I shall explain in more detail in chapter 6, the American Klan has gone through three main phases: the period after the American Civil War when the Klan was founded in Tennessee in 1865; the period beginning in 1915 when a significant revival took place and the target became not only blacks, but also Catholics, Jews, communists, and labour unionists; and the period from the mid-1950s to the present as the black civil-rights movement in the United States gained momentum. Winks (1971: 320) suggests that the original Klan of the 1860s may have had some followers in Ontario, although the facts are not conclusive. What is certain, however, is that the U.S. Klan's second phase swept over the border into Canada. In 1921 solicitations for Klan membership[1] appeared in newspapers in British Columbia (Henson 1977) and a klavern (or den) was established in Montreal (Calderwood 1973).

During the 1920s, there were three separate Klan organizations in Canada: the Ku Klux Klan of Canada, the Kanadian Ku Klux Klan, and the Ku Klux Klan of the British Empire. The Klan's presence was particularly pronounced in Ontario, British Columbia, Alberta, and Saskatchewan. Promoting anti-Catholic sentiments, the Klan in Ontario established local units in several towns and cities, including St Thomas, Sault Ste Marie, Belleville, Kingston, and Ottawa. One newspaper estimated the Toronto Klan alone to have 8,000 members (Sher 1983: 27), no doubt a gross over-estimate. In the town of Barrie, St Mary's Roman Catholic Church was bombed by a Klansman, and in Oakville the Klan held a parade and burned a cross on the main street. A pastor from a Hamilton church took part, and Hamilton itself was the scene of cross-burnings (Sher 1983: 27).

In 1924 a Klan klavern was established in Vancouver (Winks 1971: 286). The BC Klan claimed a membership then of more than 10,000 (again, the figure is probably grossly exaggerated), including five MLAs (Killan 1978: 161). In that province the Klan merely latched on to the strong anti-Asian sentiments, and the demand that East Indian, Chinese, and Japanese immigrants be repatriated. The target was different in Alberta. Immigrants from Central and Eastern Europe were singled out, as well as French-Canadian settlers, and, as was the case in Ontario, anti-Catholicism became the Klan's rallying cry. Of course, an anti-Catholic organization was already firmly rooted in Canada – the Orange Order – and it made life much easier for the Ku Klux Klan. As Palmer (1982: 106) has put it: 'Klans sprang up in areas where the Orange Order, with its long tradition of anti-Catholic sentiment and anti-French feeling, had been established. Without en-thusiastic support from Orangemen, it is doubtful that the Alberta Klan would have achieved any significance.' According to Calderwood (1973: 106), the Orange Order performed a similar role for the Klan in Saskatchewan, the province in which the infamous organization achieved its greatest success. Again riding on a platform of anti-Catholicism and anti-immigration, with an undercurrent of anti-Semitism, the Saskatchewan Klan in the late 1920s boasted a membership of at least 40,000 (Henson 1977). Even if Kyba (1964, 1968) is correct that the membership was more in

---

1 The Klan membership forms in British Columbia required allegiance to the Constitution of the United States, not Canada's (Henson 1977).

the range of 15,000, it still was quite remarkable. Equally so were the number of Protestant ministers[2] who had joined the Saskatchewan Klan (at least twenty-six), and the Klan's impact on the political scene, especially the 1929 election. As Kyba (1964: 27) remarks, it was thought by some people that the KKK had become in effect a radical wing of the Conservative party. Sher (1983: 53–6) points out that the Klan worked hand in hand with the Conservatives to help defeat the ruling Liberal administration. Nevertheless, it must be stressed that the Klan also had its appeal to Liberal supporters (Anon. 1928: 600). As Calderwood (1975: 164) has remarked, no single political party in Saskatchewan had a monopoly on Klan memberships. Indeed, the prejudices activated by the Klan's presence transcended even the barriers of party politics.

The Ku Klux Klan adventure in Canada was as short-lived as it was dramatic, and by the 1930s it was a spent force. Yet there was little time to celebrate, for as the Klan shrunk a Fascist and Nazi movement grew. Quebec had the largest and oldest Canadian Jewish community in the 1930s, and it was there that the most virulent Fascist organization took root (Betcherman 1975: 4). This was Adrien Arcand's Parti National Social Chrétien. Prior to the 1930s, anti-Semitism in Quebec certainly was present, but was not overt or politically organized. All that changed as Arcand broke onto the political scene in 1930 as editor of three weekly newspapers in Montreal, published by a man called Ménard, and espousing an anti-Semitic message. Arcand portrayed Hitler as the champion of Christianity. He also advocated Fascism as the solution to the world's problems, and contended that liberal democracy was merely the dictatorship of money powers. In his words (1938): 'Liberal democracy ... is an internationalist-minded Jewish invention which was imposed on France in 1789 and spread by Napoleon throughout France.' By 1937 Arcand claimed that in Montreal alone he had more than 80,000 followers (Edwards 1938: 10). While this certainly was a wild exaggeration, he nevertheless was not standing alone. His membership lists for that year (Betcherman 1975: 89) revealed the names of 700 card-carrying members. One of his most important subalterns was a medical practitioner named Dr Lambert, whose claim to fame was the compilation of the pernicious tract *The Key to the Mystery*. This document, a diatribe against Jews, continues to be distributed today by John Ross Taylor, the current leader of the Western Guard. Arcand, who once recom-

---

2 Protestant ministers were admitted without paying membership fees (Anon. 1928: 594). According to Calderwood (1975: 156), the majority of those who joined the Klan were ministers in the United church.

mended that Canadian Jews be resettled near Hudson Bay, had close links with the Conservatives and the Union Nationale. In 1934 he was a paid publicist in R.B. Bennett's Conservative party in Quebec. A year later he was, according to Weinfeld (1977: 24), minister of labour in Duplessis's Union Nationale; he was also the editor of one of its semi-official publications, *L'illustration Nouvelle*.

On the brink of the outbreak of the Second World War, Arcand attempted to expand his organization beyond Quebec. In Ontario the organization was to be called the National Christian Party of Canada, although in later years it became known as the National Unity Party. Initially Taylor, then only twenty-four years old, was chosen as the leader of the Ontario branch. However, his tenure was short-lived. Within a few months Joseph Farr had replaced him, and Taylor went on to join the Canadian Union of Fascists, originally established in Manitoba as a branch of Mosley's British Union of Fascists. Betcherman (1975), a source for much of this background on the pre-Second World War Fascists, does not clearly explain why Taylor was dropped, but Taylor told me in 1982 that it had nothing to do with rumoured ill-feelings between himself and Arcand, whom Taylor described as the greatest citizen Quebec has ever produced. Instead, Taylor claims, it was a matter of religion. Arcand's organization and movement was almost entirely Catholic. At the time, Taylor was a Christian Scientist, although since then he has converted to Catholicism.

Until 1938, when Hitler's expansionist policies became clear, Arcand enjoyed a great deal of success. Newspapers outside Quebec began to pay attention to him, and often were laudatory in their evaluation. *The Globe and Mail* (2 December 1937), for example, referred to Arcand as 'the brilliant young French Canadian.' Even commentators in the United States became aware of his stature in Quebec. Arcand made a trip to New York in 1937 and spoke at a rally staged by the German-American Bund. *The Nation, Foreign Affairs,* and *Life* published articles about him. Perhaps even more significantly, a magazine such as *Country Guide* (1938) in Canada was prepared to give Arcand space to outline his own interpretation of Fascism. Clearly there is a significant difference between the political climate then and now, for while the media today often bend over backwards to report on the activities of organizations such as the Ku Klux Klan, and quote verbatim from its members without accompanying editorial comment, they do not act as outlets for right-wing publication per se.

Immediately prior to the Second World War, Arcand was in communication with Fascists in other countries, such as Mosley in Britain, and according to Betcherman (1975: 12) he received financial backing from sympathetic Fascists abroad. That underlines an important point: despite the emphasis upon nationalism in Fascist movements, their international links are often substantial. Ironically, the long string of successes enjoyed by Arcand frayed and snapped at the very point in time that his hero, Hitler, emerged as the dominant force on the world scene. With the outbreak of the Second World War, Arcand and other Fascists such as Taylor were interned in concentration camps.

Although Arcand was the most prominent and influential Fascist in Quebec, there were other organizations in that province with similar goals, such as Les Jeune-Canada and the Fédération des Clubs Ouvriers (Betcherman 1975: 34–6), as well as the *achat chez nous* movement, a campaign against Jewish goods and businesses. However, it must not be thought that Fascism was confined mostly to Quebec. As Betcherman (1975: 45) has stated, Fascists in other provinces, especially Ontario, were even more numerous and better organized than in Quebec. As was true in that province, organized anti-Semitism had not been pronounced in English-speaking Canada before the 1930s (Speisman 1979: 117). But in Toronto swastika clubs began to emerge, leading to the notorious Christie Pits incident in 1933, when members of the Balmy Beach Swastika Club and other Gentiles clashed with Jewish students and factory workers organized in self-defence clubs (Glickman 1985), Jewish shops along Bloor Street in Toronto were vandalized and Jews in nearby neighbourhoods were randomly assaulted. Taylor, still active in the radical right today, had begun to promote the cause of the Canadian Union of Fascists, but the dominant Fascist at that time in Ontario seems to have been Farr. He had been a sergeant-major in the British Army, and was a member of the Orange Order. He first gained prominence as the head of the Swastika Association of Canada, and later of the Ontario-based Canadian Nationalist Party. The latter party was closely associated with one bearing the same name in Western Canada, led by William Whittaker. Eventually the National Unity Party was founded, amalgamating Arcand's Parti National Social Chrétien with the Ontario and Western branches of the Canadian Nationalist Party. Curiously, one of the most prominent right-wing organizations in Canada today is the Nationalist Party, although it has no direct link with its predecessors.

A somewhat different phenomenon was the Brownshirt Party, formed in Kitchener, Ontario, which was explicitly Fascist and anti-Semitic, and the Deutscher Bund, or German League, established in Waterloo in 1934. The first was basically the design of one man, Otto Becker, who came to Canada from Germany in 1929, and the second was organized by a Nazi agent, Dr Karl Gerhardt (Betcherman 1975: 55). Betcherman (1975) argues that the

Fascist recruiters attracted to Kitchener (formerly called Berlin) by its large German population (then 53 per cent) met with little success. Yet as Wagner (1981: 68) points out, by 1937–8 membership in the Deutscher Bund had grown to about 2,000 across the country, close to 100 of whom were German Nazi Party members. Wagner also insists that there was little overlap or communication between the Deutscher Bund and Arcand and other Canadian Fascists. The Deutscher Bund was principally a movement initiated by German Canadians intent on establishing pristine national socialism on Canadian soil.

AFTER THE SECOND WORLD WAR

The years following the Second World War have been justifiably described as 'the sanitary decades' (Raab 1983: 14). Fascism had become a dirty word, and the world had had enough of racism and anti-Semitism. Nevertheless, it would be a mistake to assume that the right wing had dropped off the face of the earth. From the late 1940s through the 1950s and 1960s, there was a small but steady trickle of organized right-wing activity in Canada, leading eventually to the flood in the 1970s. Arcand, for example, in the wake of his release after the war from a New Brunswick concentration camp, attempted to reassert his political presence. Under the banner of the National Unity Party, he ran for office in the 1949 federal election, placing second with 5,590 votes (*Globe and Mail*, 15 November 1965). In 1965, the same year that a banquet in his honour was held to mark the twenty-fifth anniversary of his internment, he published *A Bas La Haine* (Down with Hatred), a book which purportedly denounced the growing campaign at that time against hate literature; in effect it was a restatement of his anti-Semitic and Fascist beliefs (*Toronto Daily Star*, 10 September 1965). Arcand, who had been provided by Duplessis with translating and editing work after being set free in 1945, died in poverty in 1967; but his National Unity Party, led now by a man called Lanctôt, continues to exist today.

In the late 1940s Ron Gostick, whose story I tell in chapter 8, established Canadian Intelligence Publications, and quickly gained a reputation for anti-Semitism. By the late 1950s, John Ross Taylor, the irrepressible Fascist, had embarked on a new venture: a right-wing mail-order business called the Natural Order. There also at that time was the White Canada Party in Toronto, run by a self-styled genius called George Rolland (Toronto *Telegram*, 23 November 1960) who made his living as a watch-maker. He preached about the biological inferiority of blacks and advocated a policy of white purity and racial segregation. Although the White Canada

Party was a one-man show, it would be wrong to dismiss it as totally insignificant. For example, during the 1950s, Rolland ran for public office year after year; contesting a position on the Toronto Board of Control, he managed to win 4,000 votes in 1955, 5,500 in 1956, and 5,633 in 1957. In 1960 in Toronto there was as well the Canadian League, a pro-white group opposed to the peace movement. One of its founders was Derek Sones, formerly a member of Chesterton's League of Empire Loyalists in England. Of course, the Orange Order continued to exist, albeit with less clout. While there had apparently been about 250,000 members across Canada before the First World War, fewer than half of that number exist today, although most of its strength remains in rural towns and villages. In 1980 an information meeting for the Orange Association of Metro Toronto held in a high-school auditorium drew only about sixty people (*Globe and Mail*, 6 October 1980). Occasionally current members of the radical right talked to me about the continuing importance of the Orange Order, but I only know of one of them (formerly associated with both the Western Guard and the Ku Klux Klan) who belongs to that organization.

There was, thus, a sporadic right-wing presence throughout the 1950s in Canada, but it was not until the 1960s that the public began to take note of it, possibly because of its more rapid growth, or perhaps simply because it made a lot of noise. By 1963, Gostick's Christian Action Movement, a forerunner of today's Canadian League of Rights, existed, and a curious collection of social-credit enthusiasts, some advocating monetary reform and others more interested in reviving Hitler's political program, began to gather around Neil Carmichael, a Toronto-based coin and stamp dealer. Before the decade was out, other organizations had appeared on the scene, such as the Friends of Rhodesia Association, the Canadian Nazi Party, and the Edmund Burke Society. These last two groups, founded in Toronto in 1965 and 1967 respectively, were clearly the noisiest. The first was brazenly Fascist and racist; in 1967 it was converted into the National Socialist Party, with its headquarters in London, Ontario. The second was part of the fringe right, founded by highly conservative individuals, some of whom eventually moved on to become full-blown Fascists.

The Nazi phase of the 1960s, plus the appearance of the Edmund Burke Society, may have been a shock to many Canadians, but they were simply a prelude of things to come; in the 1970s and 1980s there was a virtual explosion of right-wing activity. Among the most important organizations to emerge then (see the Appendix) were the Western Guard, the Nationalist Party, the Ku Klux Klan, the Aryan Nations, Concerned Parents of German Descent, and CASAC; Campus Alternative, Alternative Forum, and Citizens for Foreign Aid Reform (C-FAR); and a host of lesser groups such as the British People's Party, the Black and Red Front, Catholics against Terrorism, and Young Americans for Freedom (YAF). Significantly, all of these organizations emerged at a period when the memory of the atrocities of the Second World War and Hitler's anti-Semitism had begun to dim, when major changes in Canada's immigration laws were introduced, and when unemployment and inflation were rampant. In conclusion, while there have been distinct waves of racism, anti-Semitism, and right-wing activity in Canada, at least some such activity has been continuous since the Second World War itself.

Many observers have remarked that Quebec, once the home of a vigorous Fascist, anti-Semitic movement, is today relatively free of organized right-wing activity. Ontario, Alberta, and British Columbia – not Quebec – have been the settings of the Ku Klux Klan meetings. Why should this be so? One reason may be Quebec's nationalism; this cause has overshadowed all others, and left little room for unrelated issues to take root. Another factor is language. No organization can hope to make headway in Quebec today unless it can communicate in the French language. Despite the fact that there is a thriving right wing in France, and an available literature in French produced by men like Paul Rassinier and Robert Faurisson, the language of racism in North America is English, and the main Canadian organizations such as the Western Guard, the Nationalist Party, and the Ku Klux Klan have almost entirely been confined to English Canada.

It would be a mistake, nevertheless, to conclude that anti-Semitism and the right wing are now non-existent in Quebec. For example, twenty-five of sixty-three anti-Semitic incidents in Canada in 1982 occurred in that province; only Ontario, with thirty-four cases, enjoyed the dubious distinction of being the leader in this respect (*The Review of Anti-Semitism in Canada*, 1982). Moreover, Arcand's National Unity Party was revived in the postwar years, and three other Fascist organizations existed (at least on paper) in the 1960s in Quebec: the National Socialist Party of Canada, led by Bellefeuille; the National Socialist (Nazi) Party, led by de la Rivière; and the Union of Fascists (Canada), led by Dieskau. Bellefeuille, a part-time Department of Transport employee in Sorel, Quebec, at the time, claimed 1,500 to 2,000 members (Toronto *Telegram*, 1 November 1960), and once appeared on a CBC television show with the leader of the American Nazi Party, George Lincoln Rockwell (*Globe and Mail*, 31 October 1960). De la Rivière claimed a membership of about three hundred for his party, which he said had no connection with Arcand's group (Toronto *Telegram*, 8 May 1967). There also is an extreme conservative Catholic organization, the

Michael, based in Quebec, but with some activity beyond that province. The Michael advocates conducting services in Latin, and preaches about the evils of the international bankers. Another right-wing religious group in Montreal is called the Young Canadians for a Christian Civilization, a Catholic organization that originates from Brazil and is better known as TFP (Tradition, Family, and Property). In Montreal there also is a branch of the World Anti-Communist League, and at McGill a new student newspaper, *McGill Magazine*, was founded in the early 1980s to act as a vehicle for conservative opinion on campus. As far as I know, there was no organized protest against it at McGill University, possibly because students in general are now more conservative, and also because there appears to have been nothing explicitly racist or anti-Semitic in it. Indeed, almost half of the advertisements in one issue of *McGill Magazine* were from Jewish sources, such as the promotion of the kibbutzim in Israel. Finally, the Montreal branch of the League for Human Rights has a document that focuses on the Mouvement Québécois pour combattre le rasism (MQCR), founded in 1978 by a man who was then president of the teacher's union. This man, according to the League for Human Rights (a B'nai B'rith organization), preaches 'a racist doctrine equating Zionism with racism.'

ORGANIZATIONS SINCE THE SECOND WORLD WAR

When I began this project in early 1980 it was with the intention of examining a single organization – the Western Guard – but by the time the research was finished I had material on 161 groups: 79 on the radical right and 82 on the fringe right. In the following analysis, those organizations that predated the Second World War have been excluded, as have several that are simply different names or branches of existing groups, some small one-issue groups, and U.S. organizations with only a modest presence in Canada; an example of the latter is the National States Rights Party, which established a post-office box in Toronto in 1981, although it had been banned by the postmaster general of Canada in 1965.

Some of the characteristics of the remaining 130 organizations (listed in the Appendix) – 60 radical right and 70 fringe right – are summarized in table 1. What must be stressed from the outset is that the sheer number of organizations gives an exaggerated impression of the strength of the right wing in Canada. Only 30 of the 130 organizations can be considered to be major ones. The vast number of fringe-right groups (80 per cent) were minor, and fully 28 per cent of the radical-right ones were front organizations – changes of names usually done to cover the tracks of those involved

TABLE 1
General characteristics of organizations (130)

	Radical right		Fringe right	
	n	%	n	%
Category	60	46	70	54
Importance				
major	18	30	12	17
minor	25	42	56	80
front	17	28	2	3
Religious status				
secular	44	73	54	77
Christian	14	23	16	23
anti-Christian	3	5	0	–
Focus				
multi-issue	54	90	41	59
single-issue	6	10	29	41
Location				
Canada-wide	4	7	11	16
Ontario	43	71	45	64
British Columbia	7	12	7	10
Alberta	2	3	4	6
Other provinces or beyond Canada	4	7	3	4
When founded				
before 1945*	2	3	2	3
1945–60	1	2	2	3
1961–70	12	20	9	13
1971–80	30	50	47	67
1981 on	15	25	10	14

*Before 1945 means founded then but still in existence after the Second World War.

in racist activity or to create the impression that radical-right groups were sprouting up everywhere. Unlike the radical right, which tended to focus on a whole range of issues, such as white supremacy, anti-Semitism, communism, immigration, and homosexuality, almost one-half of the fringe-right organizations came into existence in order to confront a single issue, such as freedom of speech, gay rights in the educational system, and foreign aid. For about one-quarter of both the radical- and fringe-right organizations, Christianity was their raison d'être; their right-wing positions were merely a secondary product of a dominant theocratic world view. Yet it can be said that almost all the 'secular' organizations were involved in trying to turn the tide against what was viewed as a massive attack on Western Christian civilization. Even the three anti-Christian organizations, as we shall see in chapter 12, were themselves religious groups whose members believed that Christianity was alien to white people, a spiritual form of Marxism, or simply too inadequate to fight the white man's battle.

A number of the organizations – especially on the fringe right – claimed a nation-wide membership. It is correct that some like the Ku Klux Klan and the Canadian League of Rights had clout in several provinces, but for the most part the vast majority of the organizations were concentrated in one or two provinces. Indeed, 88 (68 per cent) of them were located in Ontario. This concentration may partly be a result of the size of the population and immigration patterns in Ontario, or it may simply mean that I have better data for that province. The two other provinces with fairly extensive right-wing activity – even more so than reflected in the number of organizations – are British Columbia and Alberta. As I suggested earlier, there have been various waves of organized right-wing activity in Canada, dating back to the country's foundation. But since the Second World War it has been in the 1970s and 1980s that the phenomenon has escalated. Indeed, during that period fully 102 (78 per cent) of the 130 organizations made their appearance for the first time.

Finally, almost all the radical-right organizations were anti-Semitic, anti-black, anti-communist, anti-immigration, anti-foreign aid, anti-world government, anti-egalitarian, anti-homosexual, anti-feminist, and anti-abortion; they also firmly believed in a Jewish conspiracy, supported nuclear armaments, and were violence-prone. Most of the fringe-right organizations also were anti-communist, anti-homosexual, anti-abortion, and anti-egalitarian. Unlike the radical right, however, there was not uniform agreement among members on other issues, and indeed there was overwhelming rejection of anti-Semitic and anti-black beliefs (at least the deliberate brand), and of violence as well.

MEMBERSHIP SINCE THE SECOND WORLD WAR

An immediate word of qualification must be offered about the following numbers: they should be treated as more or less crude approximations of existing reality. From several sources I was able to learn the identities of 586 right-wing members: interviews with high-profile members, newspaper accounts, and lists that periodically came my way from anti–right-wing organizations, infiltrators, undercover agents, and paid informers. Certainly I make no claim that my ultimate count of 586 is complete, and if the reader laments the lack of exhaustive material on education, occupation, ethnic origin, and so on, I do too. But my resources were not those of the RCMP, and I have had to be satisfied with less than perfect data.

As shown in table 2, not only did the vast majority (448) of the 586 individuals belong to the radical right, but also most of these (75 per cent) lived in Ontario, the province which also hosted the highest proportion of fringe-right members (69 per cent). White supremacists often claim that increased contact among races does not result in greater understanding and tolerance, but instead in heightened racial tension; they regard the cities, to which new immigrants often are drawn, as the battleground of the future. Over 80 per cent of the 586 members lived in urban centres, with little difference existing between the radical and fringe right. As far as gender is concerned, it is hardly surprising that men greatly outnumbered women, but two aspects are worthy of comment. First, the Ku Klux Klan, and similar white-supremacist organizations, usually claim that about one-third of their membership is female. Yet my data show a figure of 13 per cent for the radical right overall. Furthermore, I can confidently assert that the number of prominent female members in these organizations is very small indeed. One day in Toronto, for example, while interviewing a woman who belonged to a major white-supremacist group, I mentioned the names of about half a dozen women. Those, she said, pretty well exhausted the high-ranking women in the movement.

The other aspect worth noting is that the proportion of women in the fringe right is even smaller than in the radical right. At first sight, this may seem puzzling, because one might assume that the greater relative legitimacy of the fringe right would render gender less relevant as a criterion for membership. But the explanation has to do with another difference between the radical and fringe right – the balance between leaders and followers. In table 2 the right-wing membership is broken down into three categories: leaders, active followers, and supporting members. The difference between the second and third categories is that active followers are usually public, visible members of the organizations in question, the people who attend regular meetings, paint racist slogans on walls, or can be counted on to show up at rallies and help distribute posters. Supporting members are those behind the scenes, people who whole-heartedly agree with the organi-

TABLE 2
General characteristics of members

	Radical right						Fringe right					
	Ont	BC	Alta	Other*	Total	%†	Ont	BC	Alta	Other	Total	%
Place of residence	338 (75%)	72 (16%)	10 (2%)	28 (6%)	448	100	95 (69%)	15 (11%)	17 (12%)	11 (8%)	138	100
Sex												
male	297	56	10	27	390	87	90	12	16	11	129	93
female	41	16	–	1	58	13	5	3	1	–	9	7
Urban rural dimension												
urban	264	69	7	19	359	95	68	12	6	10	96	86
rural	13	2	2	2	19	5	6	–	10	–	16	14
Total	277	71	9	21	378	100	74	12	16	10	112	100
Unknown	61	1	1	7	70		21	3	1	1	26	
Position in organization												
leader	22	9	2	7	40	9	21	2	2	5	30	22
active follower	131	12	7	3	153	35	36	3	2	2	43	31
supporting member	173	50	1	18	242	56	38	10	13	4	65	47
Total	326	71	10	28	435	100	95	15	17	11	138	100
Unknown	12	1	–	–	13	–	–	–	–	–	–	–

*'Other' means provinces other than Ontario, British Columbia, and Alberta, or beyond Canada.
†In tables 2, 4, and 5, percentages are calculated in terms of known cases.

zation's position, subscribe to its publications, and often donate funds, but who are not prepared to do so openly. Most of the radical-right organizations have at least two kinds of membership (in addition to the leadership), one for open and another for covert supporters. What is interesting is that while only 9 per cent of the radical-right members occupy leadership roles, 22 per cent of the fringe right do. This fact partly explains the greater proportion of men in the fringe right; despite the feminist movement, leadership opportunities in Canadian society in general are still more numerous for men than for women, which by definition is even truer in right-wing circles.

The higher proportion of leaders to followers in the fringe than the radical right also throws light on an important difference between them. The radical right consists of a concrete package, with clearly demarcated lines between its organizations and members and the rest of society; it is, in other words, a closed social entity. The mode of operation in the fringe right, in contrast, is to establish definite organizations but to leave the line between members, potential members, and the rest of society blurred and fluid. A viable fringe right does not so much need a large formal membership as it does an adequate number of leaders to hold meetings and distribute materials, plus a long mailing list. While this may help to explain the high proportion of leaders in the fringe right, it also reflects the difficulty of estimating its membership. Certainly the figure of 138 members is highly artificial. The fringe-right audience, if anything, is immensely larger than the radical right.

Table 3 indicates the organizational affiliation of right-wing members. Some of them were involved with more than a single organization (the average number of organizations to which radical and fringe members belonged was 1.38 and 1.22 respectively), which explains why the total number of affiliations (789) exceeds the total number of members (586). On the radical right, the Klan had the greatest number of members across the country, and Ontario had the most members overall, although once again I caution that my data may simply have been better for that province. It was also the Klan that had the most members of any organization in British Columbia (actually there were several different Klan organizations there, as explained in chapter 6), but the Nationalist Party had more members than any other organization beyond Ontario, British Columbia, and Alberta, including a couple of short-lived branches in the United States. This table indicates an important difference between Alberta and the two other provinces with the most pronounced right-wing presence. In Alberta the fringe right is stronger than the radical right; whereas only 2 per cent of the

TABLE 3
Organizational affiliation

	Radical right						Fringe right					
	Ont	BC	Alta	Other	Total	%	Ont	BC	Alta	Other	Total	%
Radical right												
Klan	146	62	3	7	218	35	3	–	–	–	3	1.8
Nationalist party	129	7	–	15	151	24	–	–	–	–	–	–
Western Guard	95	1	–	4	100	16	1	–	–	–	1	0.6
Canadian Nazi party	21	–	–	–	21	3	–	–	–	–	–	–
Other radical right	52	7	8	7	74	12	–	–	–	–	–	–
Fringe right												
EBS	32	–	–	1	33	5	35	3	1	2	41	24
Fromm-linked org.	5	–	–	–	5	0.8	18	1	–	1	20	12
Gostick-linked org.	1	–	–	–	1	0.2	5	6	3	3	17	10
Social Credit	11	–	2	–	13	2	9	–	4	–	13	8
Other fringe right	4	–	–	–	4	0.6	45	9	13	7	74	44
TOTAL	496	77	13	34	620		116	19	21	13	169	
%	80	12	2	5	99		69	11	12	8	100	

radical-right affiliation is located in that province, 12 per cent of the fringe right can be found there. As we shall eventually see, the Alberta scene, to a greater extent than in other Canadian provinces, is dominated by a rural-based Christian fundamentalism, represented by James Keegstra and that province's provincial branch of the federal Social Credit party. Having said that, however, it must be pointed out that extreme and violent organizations like the Aryan Nations show every sign of increasing their footholds there.

One final point: fifty-six members of the radical right were also members of or closely associated with fringe-right organizations. Of these, thirty-three had previously belonged to the Edmund Burke Society. When that organization folded in 1972, these thirty-three either continued in its radical-right successor, the Western Guard, or joined other far-right organizations. The reverse condition, fringe-right members with a foot in the far right, was much more rare; I know of only four cases of this sort. As we shall eventually see, it is a gigantic leap from the fringe to the extreme right. And once it has been made, very few people ever climb back down and march to a more moderate tune.

We now move on to some more dubious figures. Although I have data for only 250 cases (see table 4), the fringe-right members tend to be older than their radical-right counterparts; most of the latter are between twenty and forty years old, with a number of teenagers as well. As far as education is concerned, at least based on my limited data, we are in for a surprise. Often the right wing – especially the extreme right – is dismissed as the

TABLE 4
Birth

	Radical right		Fringe right	
	n	%	*n*	%
before 1920	17	8	9	18
1921–30	26	13	9	18
1931–40	25	12	8	16
1941–50	62	31	16	32
1951–60	49	24	4	8
1961–70	20	10	4	8
1971 and over	1	0.5	–	–
TOTAL	200	99	50	100
Unknown	248		88	

gathering ground for the ignorant and uneducated with the assumption that if only we could get them back to school they would see the error of their ways. Yet 62 per cent of the ninety-three radical-right cases analysed (see table 5) had attended university, college, or technical school. Moreover, I suspect that this percentage would be the same for all 448 radical-right members, and perhaps slightly higher. It is probable that my ninety-three cases consist of the most visible members of the radical right, including leaders, active members, and those whose names have got into the media. The two sectors most unrepresented are likely the young, hit-and-miss members (people who hang around organizations like the Nationalist Party for a while and raise hell), and the 'secret' supporting members who remain in the background. Some of the former run into trouble, get arrested, are written up in the media, and then find their way into my files. That is certainly not the case with the supporting members. Often they remain anonymous *because* they are well-educated, economically secure, and don't want to jeopardize their positions. Supporting members constitute the largest of the three categories, and it is possible that if all of them were included, the educational level of the radical right would even be higher than I have reported. This argument can be strengthened by breaking the educational level of the ninety-three known cases down into the three main categories of members; what we find is that there is almost no difference between leaders and active followers in terms of higher education; 25 per cent of the leaders and 27 per cent of the active followers had attended university, and the same proportion in each case had attended college or technical school (they did differ at the lower educational levels, with the remaining 50 per cent of

TABLE 5
Education

	Radical right		Fringe right	
	n	%	*n*	%
Elementary	4	4	2	4
Secondary	31	33	7	12
Technical or college	26	28	6	10
University	32	34	42	74
TOTAL	93	99	57	100
Unknown	355		81	

the leaders having gone to secondary school, while only 35 per cent of the active followers had done so). The glaring difference was between these two categories and the supporting members; fully 50 per cent of the latter could boast university training, and 31 per cent of the remainder had some other form of post-secondary educational experience.

So far, I have only been dealing with the educational attainments of the radical right. Not too surprisingly, those of the fringe right are even more impressive. Forty-two (74 per cent) of the fifty-seven for which I have solid data were university educated, and a further 10 per cent had technical or college education. One thing, therefore, is certain: we may question the quality and type of education that these individuals have received, but to see education per se as the panacea for the crippling problems brought on by racism is simplistic and superficial.

Finally, there is the crucial matter of occupation. Since there is usually a fairly high and stable correlation between education level and occupational attainment, we should not be shocked to find that the right wing – again, especially the radical right – is not concentrated at the bottom rung of the ladder. Working with data on 141 members of the radical right and 79 members of the fringe right, I organized the various occupations into four categories: professional (such as medical doctor, lawyer, architect, clergyman, engineer, teacher, industrialist, senior civil servant), white collar (small businessman, owner of small store, nurse, journalist, office manager, real estate agent, laboratory technician, electrician, computer programmer, junior civil servant), blue collar (clerk, security guard, secretary, taxi driver, labourer, hospital orderly), and student.

The data in table 6 tell the story. Almost 60 per cent of the radical right were either in professional or white-collar jobs. These included five clergymen (a couple connected to small sects), five teachers, two medical practitioners, and two lawyers. Other occupations that were represented included those associated with real estate (5), journalism (3), taxi driving (4), and security-guard positions (8). As regards the fringe right, 85 per cent were professionals or white-collar workers. Included among these were seven teachers, six clergymen, five journalists, four senior civil servants, three lawyers, and two doctors. The occupational attainments of the far right may seem impressively high, but the fact remains that they are significantly lower than those of the fringe right. Yet I suspect that the gap would narrow if it were not for two factors. First, as I carried out this research I learned that numerous individuals in the radical right were employed in jobs far below their educational qualifications; that situation, indeed, was one of the prices they paid for their racist activity. Second, there again is the ques-

TABLE 6
Occupation

	Radical right		Fringe right	
	n	%	n	%
Professional	25	18	37	47
White collar	58	41	30	38
Blue collar	46	33	4	5
Student	12	8	8	10
TOTAL	141	100	79	100

tion of the supporting members, who probably had attained much higher levels of education than the remainder of the extreme right. Had data been available on all the supporting members, it is probable that the proportion of professional and white-collar workers among the radical right would be higher than I have indicated.[3]

It would be useful to have precise information on dimensions such as ethnic origin, marital status, family background, and divorce, but my data for those areas are too spotty and unreliable to present statistically. For what it is worth, however, I can report that there were two dominant sectors in the radical-right membership. One was Eastern European. Their involvement stems from their concern about communism, and often a more or less deep-rooted anti-Semitism which they or their parents have carried with them to Canada. The other sector was British, or more broadly those who identified things Nordic with superiority. These people, part of the Canadian establishment, see the rampant changes in society as a threat to their social position, and lament the dilution of the British flavour brought about by Third World immigration. On the basis of names alone, there appeared to be a significant difference between the ethnic origin of the radical right in

3 A recent landmark study by Hamilton (1982) found that there was a direct correlation between the wealth of an electoral district in Germany and the degree of voting support for the Nazi party, which contradicts the prevailing wisdom that Hitler's support came mostly from the lower middle class. My data on the educational and occupational attainments of the Canadian right wing are consistent with Hamilton's, and cast serious doubt on the assertion, often made by the media and politicians, that the radical right in particular is solely a lower-class movement.

Ontario and that in British Columbia. A great many of the former were Eastern European, whereas most of those in British Columbia were British. Similarly, a higher proportion of the radical-right members in Ontario were not born in Canada as compared to their counterparts in other provinces.

The white supremacists often talked to me about the toll their beliefs and activities had taken. As one man said, no marriage can withstand the pressure brought to bear upon it when the media and organizations such as the Ontario Human Rights Commission and the Canadian Jewish Congress swing into action. The vast majority of the leaders of the radical right were either divorced, separated, single, or living in a common-law relationship. Then, as well, numerous members of the right wing came from broken homes. Yet is would be too facile to conclude that family disruptures and divorce account for their right-wing activity. These social problems are endemic in society at large, and yet most people don't go out and join the Ku Klux Klan. Finally, related to the question of religion, the vast majority of those for whom I have data were Protestants (including a sprinkling of clergymen), plus a few Catholics (including two priests). Astoundingly, there even were some Jewish members. One was an articulate spokesman for (and sometimes critic of) the Edmund Burke Society. Another was formerly married to a member of the Ku Klux Klan, and given the task of tapping her Jewish contacts for information about the 'enemy.' Then there was a now-elderly woman with a long history in the radical-right movement, as well as an underground character who took part in the Klan's abortive attempt to overthrow the government of Dominica. Even more stunning was the case of a handicapped individual who apparently blamed his father for his appearance, and in a bizarre psychological twist turned against his Jewish faith.

I suppose it is also worth indicating that many members of the radical right (including at least 50 per cent of the leaders) had been arrested at one time or other, sometimes repeatedly, as had a handful of fringe-right members, especially those who formerly belonged to the Edmund Burke Society. In addition, several members of both the radical and fringe right had run for public offices, such as the mayorship of Toronto; again, the same individuals tended to be candidates on repeated occasions, especially the leaders. Yet what is most important to remember, I believe, is the educational and occupational profile of the right wing, plus the sheer number of individuals involved. The popular image of the far-right members as nuts and thugs isn't entirely wrong. Hanging around most of these organizations are a handful of 'heavies,' often young, poorly educated people who find it easier to fight than to think. What many people do not realize is that it only takes a half-dozen such individuals to create a crisis in a country. Another mistake is to assume that education and occupational attainments are insulators against wanton violence. One does not have to be an unemployed school drop-out to go off the deep end.

As regards the number of people who belong to the right wing, it will be noted that there are only an average of 4.5 members for every organization. The implication is that there has been a great flurry of organized activity with few warm bodies to back it up. It is a fact that many of the organizations have been one-man shows, ephemeral, or fronts. However, I have no doubt that the figure of 586 members is a gross underestimate. Not only does that figure represent only the actors whom I have identified, but it also excludes a host of other individuals: the 700 card-carrying members of Arcand's Fascist organization before the Second World War; the several thousand Ku Klux Klan members in the 1920s; the nearly 100 German Canadians in Canada who at the outbreak of the war were members of Hitler's Nazi Party; the rank and file of the Canadian League of Rights, and various small but right-wing social-credit organizations, and members of groups like Renaissance; and, finally, those individuals who are reputed to have been racists and anti-Semites but who did not formally belong to right-wing organizations – civil servants and politicians like Frederick Charles Blair and Ian MacKenzie portrayed by Abella and Troper (1982) and Sunahara (1981). Had all these been included, we would be talking in the range of thousands of individuals, and not a mere 586.

3

Forerunners: The Canadian Nazi Party and the Edmund Burke Society

At sixteen he wept when his mother showed him pictures of Dachau and Auschwitz. At twenty-four, with his Hitler-style hair and moustache, raised-arm salute, and exaggerated goose step, William John Beattie, a former boy scout, who in 1965 became the leader of the Canadian Nazi Party, was said to be the most hated man in Canada (*Toronto Star*, 5 February 1973). The appearance of that organization, and of the less radical Edmund Burke Society two years later, clearly marked the end of the sanitary decades in Canada. The Canadian Nazi Party was soon converted into the National Socialist Party, and the Edmund Burke Society eventually produced the white-supremacist Western Guard plus a host of highly conservative groups. Together they paved the way for the rush of right-wing organizations that would march across the nation in the decades to follow.

THE CANADIAN NAZI PARTY

Beattie may have been the most prominent Fascist in the mid-1960s, but he was not the first one to step into the limelight at that time. Preceding him was a Scarborough secondary-school student who pricked the public's curiousity when the media reported (*Toronto Daily Star*, 18 September 1963) that a young Canadian had been convicted in Alabama for inciting a mob to riot and for throwing a brick at a policeman during a racial confrontation. David Stanley, then only eighteen years old, had ended up in Alabama after spending the summer hitch-hiking across the United States. In Birmingham, he met Dr Edwards R. Fields, head of the anti-Semitic National States Rights Party, and was provided accommodation in the party's dormitory.

According to Stanley's widowed father, a Toronto accountant, his son was just an ordinary teenager and had never shown any interest in racial matters. Yet this statement was not borne out when Stanley returned to Canada (a condition of his suspended sentence). He began to promote a number of organizations which existed mostly on paper, but which nevertheless achieved the end he desired: forcing the public to take notice of his racist message. One organization was the National White Americans Party. A flyer with this banner, indicating that Jews were to be executed or sterilized (Stanley preferred the latter), was mailed to Toronto residents by 'Col J.P. Fry,' a pseudonym used by Stanley. While still in high school he founded the Canada Youth Corps and advertised for recruits between the ages of fourteen and twenty-one to be trained in the use of weapons and explosives (*Globe and Mail*, 21 December 1964). Canadian Action was another name that he used for his organization, and on a return trip to Alabama in 1964 he made himself leader of the World Service, an anti-Semitic organization that originated in Germany.

Stanley also promoted the available racist literature such as *The Key to the Mystery*, and wrote his own version, *The Red Rabbi*, which labelled Rabbi Abraham Feinberg a communist. His favourite tactic, however, was to distribute leaflets carrying messages such as 'Communism Is Jewish' and 'Hitler Was Right'; this he did with great energy: stuffing them into apartment mail-boxes, scattering them around shopping malls, dropping them from the tops of buildings, and on one occasion depositing them in various cities across Western Canada en route by bus to Vancouver, giving the false impression of a rapidly accelerating Nazi presence in the country. As early as age eighteen, it was evident that Stanley already possessed a sound grasp of the radical-right liturgy: blacks were supposedly intellectually inferior; all civilizations had been created by Aryans; and Jews were conspiring to gain control of the world by manipulating international finance, fostering communism, and promoting interracial marriage, pornography, and moral degeneracy in general. Stanley's perspective was certainly sensational, and a pliable media granted him the forum he sought. In 1965, for example, he appeared on the CBC's 'This Hour Has Seven Days' (*Globe and Mail*, 18 January 1965).

Stanley's mission for the white man brought him into contact with several other committed Fascists, including William John Beattie, who became his lieutenant. A rallying point for the right wing in the early 1960s was the headquarters of Neil Carmichael, the Toronto coin and stamp dealer. Carmichael, the creator of anti-Semitic comic books, had run for political office four times under the Social Credit banner. He eventually was kicked out of that party because of his anti-Semitic pronouncements, and in 1963 formed the Social Credit Action Party, to be followed by his Credit

Jubilee Party. In attendance at Carmichael's headquarters were a range of individuals of varying Fascist persuasion. One of them was an elderly Scandinavian who believed that white people had been duped by Jews into becoming Christian, which in his view was a Semitic religion. A follower of Odin, a right-wing religious alternative to Christianity originating in Nordic mythology, this former seaman printed his own anti-Semitic newspaper, *Whiteman's Mission* (Toronto *Telegram*, 25 August 1964). Another man whom Stanley met was John Ross Taylor. After the war, Taylor had established the Natural Order, a mail-order business for right-wing literature. Obviously impressed by the older man, Stanley joined forces with Taylor and the Natural Order. That marked a turning-point in Stanley's right-wing career. The Canadian public was becoming increasingly concerned about hate propaganda, and two government committees emerged to deal with it. One was the House of Commons Standing Committee on External Affairs; the other was the advisory committee established by the minister of justice, chaired by Maxwell Cohen, an ex-dean of the McGill Law School (former prime minister Pierre Trudeau was a member of this committee).[1] The climate that produced these committees also led to the postmaster general's action in 1965: both Stanley and Taylor lost their mailing privileges.

By 1965 Stanley had moved to Vancouver. For a while he continued to represent Taylor's Natural Order, and to distribute hate literature. However, in a turn of events which I have not seen paralleled for any other member of the radical right in Canada, Stanley dropped out of the movement apparently after reading Hoffer's *The True Believer*, in which he saw himself portrayed. He denounced Beattie and the Nazi Party and apologized to Canadian Jews (especially Rabbi Feinberg) for his past activity. This recantation did not occur, however, until after he had coached Beattie in Fascist principles. Up until that point, Stanley, although two years Beattie's junior, had clearly been the leader of the two. But as Stanley's enthusiasm dwindled, Beattie's grew. As Taylor once remarked, Stanley had created Beattie only to lose control of him (*Globe and Mail*, 24 August 1965).

Beattie was born in Saint John, New Brunswick, in 1942. His adolescent years in Toronto seem to have held few pleasures. His parents were divorced, and the constant quarelling between his father and stepmother often drove him onto the streets. At Osgoode Hall, which he sometimes

---

1 The Cohen Report, entitled the *Report of the Special Committee on Hate Propaganda in Canada*, was published in 1966.

visited, he noted that the rich and poor seemed to be treated quite differently in court. His walks through the opulence of Forest Hill only served to make him more resentful of the life of misery led by his mother. How much all of this led him to the right wing – and why not to the left wing – is difficult to say. At any rate, the youth who cried when he saw pictures of Nazi camps seems to have gravitated readily towards radical politics. It apparently had been Beattie who had pushed Tommy Douglas at an NDP rally in 1963 at Maple Leaf Gardens (Sypnowich 1964). He lost his first job as a clerk for Massey-Ferguson after reading a sixty-nine–point manifesto at Toronto City Hall, outlining how to save Canadian society. A little while later when he was hitch-hiking, a generous man not only gave him a lift, but also an issue of Gostick's *Canadian Intelligence Service*. Beattie took this publication to one of Carmichael's meetings. As he read it to the assembled group, someone in the audience asked him if he knew to whom the repeated references to 'they' referred. As Beattie has recounted, it suddenly hit him: 'they' were the Jews. With this in mind, perhaps it was appropriate that it was also at the Carmichael headquarters in 1965 that Beattie, along with two teen-aged supporters, all wearing swastika arm-bands, stood up and announced the formation of the Canadian Nazi Party. That apparently was too much even for Carmichael, who promptly kicked them out.

One can almost sense the glee with which Beattie embarked on his Fascist spree. Affecting Nazi mannerisms and littering his home (which served as party headquarters) with swastikas, he declared to an outraged public that only Christ had been a greater man than Hitler, and only the Bible was superior to *Mein Kampf*. (Taylor, incidentally, advised Beattie not to use Nazi symbols, arguing that the Canadian public wasn't ready for them.) Whereas Stanley had a penchant for slipping Fascist literature under doors, Beattie was more attracted to the podium. His auditorium, or more precisely his arena, was Allan Gardens in Toronto, where his outdoor rallies, two in 1965 and another in 1966, set off a staggering reaction. Crowds of nearly 5,000 people, most of them there to protest against Beattie, mauled, punched, and hauled him to the ground; on each occasion he was rescued by the police and escorted to safety. On some occasions individuals who just happened to be in the wrong place at the wrong time, such as a handful of men from Northern Ontario in Toronto looking for work, were attacked on the presumption that they looked like Nazi supporters. Once a minister was mauled by the frenzied crowd. His case was sympathetically reported by the media, but he was not simply another innocent bystander. Rather, he was a friend of Beattie's, prone to the same Fascist line, and actually had been seen leaving the Nazi Party headquarters prior to the rally. This man, then twenty-eight, had attended a seminary in Saskatchewan, and although not ordained, presented himself as a Pentecostal Holiness preacher.

Not all the protest against Beattie was unorchestrated. More than a dozen organizations sprang up to do battle with the Canadian Nazi Party. These included the Canadian Organization for the Indictment of Nazism (COIN), the Association of Survivors of Nazi Oppression, and the Ward 8 Anti-Nazi Group (in the ward where Beattie's headquarters was located), consisting almost entirely of non-Jewish members. The best-known organization, however, was N3 Fighters against Racial Hatred, named after Newton's third law that for every action there is an opposite and equal reaction. Curiously, one of its vice-presidents, Norman Gunn, emerged in later years as the president of the John Birch Society in Canada, and as a friend of the fringe right in general.

N3 was clearly out for blood, and its aggressive counter-attack led to accusations that it was contributing to the success of the Nazis, providing them with the advertising that they craved. Its approach contrasted sharply with that of the Joint Community Relations Committee (JCRC) of the Canadian Jewish Congress and B'nai B'rith. In a letter dated 8 June, 1965, addressed to 'Dear Friend,' the JCRC stated that because the volume of hate propaganda had become so large, it was no longer effective to apply the 'quarantine technique'; instead, those involved had to be confronted and exposed. At the same time, however, the JCRC accused others (such as N3) of irresponsibly inflaming people's emotions, and stated: 'We must above all exercise that restraint and self-discipline that is absolutely indispensable if we are to avoid the climate of terror, mob-rule and intimidation which can only serve the purposes of the neo-Nazis.' This split between the 'moderates' and the 'radicals' within the Jewish community on how best to deal with blatant anti-Semitism has resurfaced in subsequent years, notably in connection with the Zundel case.

Throughout 1965 Beattie was in contact with George Lincoln Rockwell, then the leader of the American Nazi Party, telephoning him to crow about his most recent exploits against Jews. Rockwell had urged Beattie to visit him below the border, but Beattie lacked funds for the trip. Eventually the two men, each barred from entering the other's country, met at the centre of the Queenston-Lewiston bridge, midway between the Canadian and U.S. immigration posts. By that time the Canadian Nazi Party had reached its zenith. It is true that Arcand (*Toronto Daily Star*, 10 September 1965) dismissed it as an irrelevant organization 'consisting of two or three lunatics from Toronto,' whom Gostick (*The Canadian Intelligence Service*, February and June 1965) referred to as Nazi spooks created by the media. Yet when Stanley announced his resignation in August 1965, he said he had a mailing list of about 1,000 names – about half of them 'Canadians' and the other half European immigrants – 250 of whom lived in Ontario. The number of active members, however, was much lower. One infiltrator (Garrity 1966) estimated about a dozen young men ready for violence; another dozen older men, mostly German or other European immigrants whom Beattie had met at Carmichael's; and perhaps 100 further supporters in the background, including Beattie's 'Oshawa group,' consisting of three German-born Hitler enthusiasts.

Rockwell was initially reluctant to grant formal recognition to the Canadian Nazi Party, which led Beattie to reorganize it, in an attempt to render it respectable. Some of the younger members were pushed aside (seven of those on trial in 1965 for unlawful assembly at Allan Gardens were males and mostly in their teens), and an eight-man executive was created. This group included a real-estate dealer, a successful artist, an owner of a small factory (who provided Beattie with duplicating facilities), a clerk, and an undercover investigator; the latter, an infiltrator, was the organization's security chief! For a few months the membership also included at least three other infiltrators, all univerity students at the time. Among other members were a printer and a laboratory technician, plus two behind-the-scenes supporters – a geologist and his wife – who gave Beattie money and employed him at $60 per week to label rock specimens (Garrity 1966). The reorganization obviously removed any reservations harboured by Rockwell, for in 1966 he accepted the Canadian Nazi Party as an affiliated branch of the World Union of National Socialists. He also apparently sent Beattie a list of 279 Ontario residents who had contacted or contributed funds to the American Nazi Party.

The future must have looked pretty rosy to Beattie at that time, but the fact is that his days of glory were clearly numbered. Following his first appearance at Allan Gardens in 1965, he had been convicted and fined $150 for causing a public disturbance (he didn't have a speaker's permit). In 1966, he held another rally, this time with a permit, claiming that top communist leaders were Jewish and calling for the execution of former Israeli premier David Ben Gurion; again there was a riot, as the frenzied crowd screamed anti-Nazi slogans and fought the police in order to get at Beattie (*Toronto Daily Star*, 20 June 1966). By 1967 Beattie was in prison, serving six months for conspiring to commit public mischief; he had stuck swastika emblems into the lawns of prominent Jews. When he was released, his life was changed. For a while he lived in London, Ontario, where the Canadian Nazi Party had been reborn as the Canadian National Socialist Party.

Beattie became its national leader, and the man who supported him financially and gave him a place to live, Martin Weiche, became its national party chairman (today Weiche is the leader). In 1968, Beattie returned to Allan Gardens, this time under the auspices of the new organization, but by then few people seemed to care. He and Weiche had set up a recorded telephone message, stating among other things that blacks were being manipulated by Jew-communists.[2] Jacob Prins, then Beattie's bodyguard, and a man who never was far from the Fascist action in the next decade, delivered some of the messages for which he was eventually taken to court (*Toronto Daily Star*, 19 June 1969). From London, Beattie moved to Sault Ste Marie, where he worked in a motel. Perhaps not accidentally, Sault Ste Marie, Sudbury, and even Wawa were centres of sporadic Nazi activity, produced by a few European immigrants in the area. While in Sault Ste Marie, Beattie had agreed to become a police informer, seduced into the role by a couple of bottles of rum and a few dollars a week. His targets were the Western Guard, the Liberty League (a splinter group from the former), and a radical branch of the Social Credit. Beattie himself had previously been a member of the Social Credit party, and later joined the Conservative party (formerly in the Canadian reserves, he also belonged to the Canadian Legion). He eventually resettled in Toronto, after having briefly left Sault Ste Marie to try his luck in Halifax.

Perhaps with the example of David Stanley before him, Beattie claimed that he had wanted to drop out of the right-wing movement after his prison term had expired, but said he had not been allowed to do so by other right-wing members or by the police, who had continuously sought information from him. He also complained that society was un-Christian: it would not accept that he had paid for his crimes, and nobody would give him a job. By then his wife, who had supported him with her job as a clerk before his prison term, had left him, taking their children (he remarried in 1975). By 1972 Beattie announced publicly that he had reformed (*Toronto Star*, 27 December 1972). His Nazi activity, he remarked, was just a form of protest, adding that had he been born ten years earlier he would have ended up in Rochdale (a former left-wing hang-out). He referred to his past career as a Nazi as 'a form of mental illness' and 'as an excuse not to work – a nice soft life to run down other people' (Toronto *Sun*, 10 November 1974). By 1974, supposedly with the help of a former member of the Jewish Defence League (Toronto *Sun*, 10 November 1974), he had entered a BA program at the

2 By 1975 Beattie again had a recorded telephone message in connection with yet another organization. He also eventually ran for mayor of Toronto.

University of Toronto, with the intent of eventually obtaining a law degree. During these years his reputation within the radical right plummeted. The word had spread that he had been a paid informer for the Ontario Provincial Police (*Toronto Star*, 27 December 1972). He was considered not only unreliable but also partially mad (even his mother, who had died the year the Canadian Nazi Party was formed, apparently once inquired about having him put into a mental hospital). It was rumoured that while in prison his mind had been altered by drugs or hypnosis. On one occasion he stood in front of Zundel's residence shouting that Zundel was a Fascist. At a 'White Confederacy' meeting in Cleveland in the mid-1970s, Beattie was one of several individuals singled out for exposure and condemnation.

Unlike Stanley, Beattie underwent only a temporary conversion from the politics of hate. He gave up his university studies, and by the mid-1970s had re-emerged as a royalist, with union jacks stitched to his clothing and painted on his house, promoting the British People's League, the British Canada Party, and the United Anglo-Saxon Liberation Front. As he remarked (Toronto *Sun*, 24 November 1975): 'The British spirit is still here in Toronto, and I want to appeal to the average working guy, not the Empire Club types. I want to spread the British ideas in the pubs.' His choice of venue was not inappropriate. Unlike Stanley, who neither drank nor smoked, Beattie had a reputation as a man who rarely turned down a drink. While he dismissed his Nazi past as a mistake, something that was the private concern of Germans, this did not mean that he had relinquished his racist beliefs. It merely reflected his commitment to his own racial (or ethnic) roots. As Beattie told me during a meeting in 1982, for whatever reason he is a racist and will never change. He could never become a lawyer, he stated, because he would be forced to deal with Jews and blacks, which would be impossible for him. By 1980, Beattie was considered by other members of the radical right to be a misfit, a man who sat around watching airplanes circling over his house, said to be sent by Queen Elizabeth to protect this future leader of the country. His prospects for reclaiming a prominent position in the movement seemed to be small, and yet as we shall later see, it was Beattie who arose from the ashes of the demolished Ku Klux Klan in the 1980s to temporarily rally the right-wing forces to meet their presumed God-inspired destiny.

THE EDMUND BURKE SOCIETY

'The only thing necessary for the triumph of evil is for good men to do nothing.' These were the words of Edmund Burke, the famed eighteenth-century British parliamentarian (Bredvold and Ross 1977), and they provided inspiration to an unusual collection of young Canadians in the late 1960s who had no doubt about what was evil and who were the good men. Those were the years of radical campus politics, generated in part by opposition to the Vietnam War and by disillusionment about the moral basis of capitalist society, and characterized by an adventurous disregard for tradition and a willingness to embrace revolutionary measures that would transform the social order. Yet out of the sharp swing leftward on Canadian campuses emerged a curious political animal: a small group of staunchly conservative individuals, enthusiastically capitalistic and vehemently anti-communist, and equally at ease with the street demonstrations and violent confrontations that had hitherto been the province of the radical left.

Origin
In February 1967 three young men sat around a counter at a coffee shop in Toronto's Lord Simcoe Hotel. They had just attended a meeting of the Canadian Alliance for Free Enterprise (CAFE), an organization inspired by the conservative writings of Ayn Rand. The shared view of the three men was that CAFE was a 'talk' group. They believed, in contrast, that the danger of communism and the disintegration of Western society demanded action. The upshot was the decision to establish a new organization, one that would canalize 'militant conservative activism.' In this way was born the Edmund Burke Society.

The three founding members were Donald Andrews, Paul Fromm, and Leigh Smith, at the time public-health inspector, University of Toronto student, and secondary-school teacher, respectively. Although all three were solidly middle class, their backgrounds were quite different, as were their eventual right-wing careers. Andrews, born in Yugoslavia, came to Canada under circumstances that can only be described as poignant. His father, a partisan during the Second World War, had been killed by German soldiers. His mother married a Canadian serviceman and emigrated to Canada, leaving behind her son, whose whereabouts were unknown. Finally, she located him, with the help of the Red Cross, and at the age of about ten Canada became his new home. Fromm, whose father was an accountant for an oil company, was born in Colombia, although his ancestry is French Canadian and German. Only Smith was born in Canada, the youngest of a large family in Quebec.

As Andrews tried to adjust to a new way of life in North America, he grew increasingly negative about the society he had left behind in Yugoslavia, to the point where communism became a phobia. It was his hatred of communism, and not racism, that spurred him on during the early years of the Edmund Burke Society. By the mid-1970s, however, he had emerged as perhaps the dominant figure in the Canadian radical right, the leader of the Western Guard, and a confessed Fascist. Fromm, an effective orator and writer, had by then occupied an equally prominent position in the fringe right. Smith, a deeply conservative man, but the least radical of the three, faded out of the right-wing picture soon after the Edmund Burke Society had been established. This was not, Fromm explained to me, because Smith disagreed with the organization's philosophy, or because he was simply shunted aside. Instead, he had moved away from Toronto in 1967, taking up residence in Ottawa, where he remains today as a teacher.

Because the stories of Andrews and Fromm are threaded throughout the following chapters, my comments here will be confined to Smith. At the time of my interview with him in 1984, he was extremely upset that a recent book (Sher 1983) had referred to the Edmund Burke Society as a 'racialist' organization. The organization, he insisted, had originally the laudable goals of opposing communism and moral degeneration, and he deeply resented the implication that he had once been part of a racist group. His reaction to the increasingly radical turn to the Edmund Burke Society, eventually leading to the Western Guard, renders his defence plausible. In a letter of resignation from the organization on 7 April 1972, which was printed in Countdown (vol. 1, no. 1, June 1972), he stated: 'This letter is to inform you of my resignation, of this date, from the Edmund Burke Society, now called the Western Guard. My resignation, long overdue, simply formalizes growing disagreements that I've had for a long time over the methods used, which seem to take no account of the former stance on law and order.' In 1984, Smith told me that he totally disagrees with Andrews's racism. He also had little patience with anti-Semitism. The radical right, he insisted, fails to appreciate that Israel is a bastion of democracy and capitalism, and thus an ally. Smith also distanced himself from some of Fromm's views, such as those concerning immigration. Fromm, in Smith's opinion, had been too greatly influenced by Andrews during their years together with the Edmund Burke Society.

The right wing (typical of any organization catering to true believers) does not look kindly on its defectors, and Smith's unflattering appraisal was reciprocated. In an article in Straight Talk (vol. 7, no. 2, n.d.), first, the Edmund Burke Society's periodical and later continued by the Western Guard, it is stated that a lot had been expected of Smith when the Edmund Burke Society was founded, but it soon was discovered that he was a 'blowhard.' A hard-nosed woman associated with the Ku Klux Klan in the early

1980s told me she had attended a meeting in Ottawa organized by Smith, but was totally put off by his mild 'liberal' politics. From the point of view of a Marxist-Leninist, such a description of any member of the Edmund Burke Society would be ludicrous. Moreover, as we shall soon see, even before the Edmund Burke Society was converted into the Western Guard, incipient racism and anti-Semitism had become increasingly apparent. Nevertheless, Smith probably represented a considerable number of the original Edmund Burke Society members – highly conservative, adamantly anti-communist, and yet basically decent people who would knowingly embrace white supremacism and violence only under the most exceptional circumstances. The only inkling that I had of a true believer under Smith's public mask was his highly emotional reaction to Sher's (1983) study of the Ku Klux Klan. He repeatedly said that he was extremely upset about Sher's accusation, and in fact he had lodged his protest openly in a letter to the editor of *The Globe and Mail* (17 March 1984). Possibly his spirited reaction was inspired by his suspicion that his teaching career had been unfairly damaged by his past association with the Edmund Burke Society. Or maybe it was simply that hardly anyone likes to be called a racist – perhaps especially those who are only a few steps removed from being one.

It would be wrong to leave the impression that with Smith's departure in 1967 for Ottawa, his right-wing activity came to a complete stop. There was at that time a branch of the Edmund Burke Society at Carleton University. In later years he ran an 'Ottawa Forum'; Fromm, with whom he retained some contact, once was the guest speaker. As I discovered in the course of my interview with Smith, he also knew personally some of the more important right-wing people in Ottawa, and even was aware of some of the recent covert political moves of the Toronto-based Fascists.[3] Yet by 1984 he was very definitely a peripheral figure – a man who couldn't accept the transformed society in which he lived, and yet could not go along with those who were bent on grafting a racist social order onto a resuscitated past, by means violent and otherwise.

Membership
Fromm claimed that the Edmund Burke Society had 1,000 members, half of them in Toronto (*Varsity*, 13 November 1967). Andrews (Miller 1971) esti-

---

3 None of this, of course, implicates Smith in the activities of these organizations, other-wise some of the country's police forces, with similar knowledge, would belong there too. Let me reiterate that all the available evidence suggests that while Smith was, dur-ing this period, a highly conservative individual, he was not a racist.

mated about 800 to 900, and both Ayre (1970) and Levy (undated) suggested a Canada-wide figure of about 500 to 600. In a retrospective article on the Edmund Burke Society that appeared in issue 57 of *The Nationalist Report* (the Nationalist Party's organ), Bob Smith referred to 'its dedicated hard core of sincere and articulate intellectuals teamed with husky street fighters and supported by anti-red East Europeans.' That is a fairly accurate generalization, although it omits the inactive supporting members behind the scenes. The 'intellectuals' were mostly students led by Fromm at the University of Toronto. The street fighters tended to gather around Andrews, who was himself the intellectual equal or superior of most of those on campus. The East Europeans were located both on and off campus.

About one-third of the members, according to Andrews, were students, and the remaining two-thirds lower-middle class or working class, with a sprinkling of those from the middle and upper-middle classes. The average age was between fifteen and forty (Miller 1971), and about 14 per cent were women (Toronto *Telegram*, 26 September 1970). My own data on seventy-four former members indicate a somewhat higher social standing. Most of these (sixty-seven) lived in Ontario, had a college or university education, and professional or white-collar occupations.

The East European presence, anti-communist refugees from the Ukraine and Baltic, was significant. The Edmund Burke Society itself (*Straight Talk*, vol. 2, no. 6, March 1970) estimated that about 25 per cent of its membership across Canada, and as many as 40 per cent of its downtown Toronto cadre, was East European. A former editor of *The Varsity* claimed in an interview that Fromm purposefully went to the International Students Organization at the University of Toronto to obtain lists of groups and individuals and to seek support from the Baltic and German groups. Joseph Genovese, who had joined the Edmund Burke Society at its first public meeting in March 1967, said the organization 'quickly cemented alliances among Toronto's ethnic communities. Latvians, Estonians, Lithuanians and Yugoslavs, among others, were very receptive to our strong anti-communist position. They welcomed us at their meetings and they came to ours' (*Straight Talk*, vol. 7, no. 2, n.d.). In another issue of *Straight Talk* (vol. 3, no. 5, January-February 1971), the Burkers saluted 'our many friends and allies in the Lithuanian and Estonian communities' on the occasion of their celebrations of their independence anniversaries, although both are 'slave states in the communist slaughterhouse of nations.' In 1971 Edmund Burke Society members held a memorial ceremony with members of Toronto's Czech and Slovak communities to commemorate in sorrow the

1968 Soviet invasion of Czechoslovakia (*Straight Talk*, vol. 4, no. 1, September 1971). In 1972, the organization again extended its 'sincere greetings and best wishes' to the Lithuanian and Estonian communities 'celebrating the anniversary of their short-lived independence' (*Straight Talk*, vol. 4, no. 5, February 1972). Genovese claimed that the Edmund Burke Society had provided a vehicle to unite the various East European communities in Toronto, whose numerous historical grievances had previously prevented them from joining together in a common anti-communist front (*Straight Talk*, vol. 7, no. 2, n.d.). This claim was confirmed by two prominent East-European Canadians, who said that the Edmund Burke Society had given new life to the ethnic anti-communist groups (Levy, n.d.). One of the two, Kastus Akula, born about 1925, was a moderately successful Belorussian novelist. The other, Gil Urbonas, born about 1921, was a Lithuanian who will be focused upon later in connection with his periodical, *Speak-Up*.

By 1969, the Edmund Burke Society consisted of two types of members: active members and supporting (or associate) members. The former were divided into the leaders, who occupied a nine-man council, and the followers, or possibly brain and brawn. The nine-man council, in turn, was split into two categories. The three founders were permanent members, and the remaining six positions were elected. The chairmanship was supposed to rotate among the three founding members, but since Smith was out of the picture, it passed back and forth between Fromm and Andrews. Eventually Genovese emerged as its occasional chairman. There had been an attempt to establish two separate chapters in Toronto, one on the University of Toronto campus and the other the Toronto City Chapter. This division may explain why at times both Andrews and Fromm simultaneously held the position of chairman (for example, in 1969 Fromm was listed as chairman of the University of Toronto branch, and Andrews as chairman of the Edmund Burke Society council), but my impression was that this was mostly a paper distinction. Edmund Burke Society leaders claimed they had chapters in Windsor, Montreal, Ottawa, Edmonton, and Vancouver, and there were formal chapters at York University, Sir George Williams University (now Concordia), Carleton University, McGill University, and on at least one occasion booths were set up at Scarborough College.

There is little doubt that the college campuses, especially the University of Toronto, were the centre of Edmund Burke Society activity, and that the man of the hour was Paul Fromm. As far back as 5 September 1967, *The Varsity*, the student newspaper, printed a letter from Fromm in which he complained about the Marxist orientation of Canadian students, and stated that he was 'inclined to agree with a pamphlet being circulated by the Edmund Burke Society on campus to the effect that the University of Toronto withdraw from the Canadian Union of Students.' A cute move on Fromm's part, since he was the organization's main figure on campus. On 30 October 1967, *The Varsity* carried an article by Fromm about the Edmund Burke Society's demonstration against Vietniks at an anti-war parade in Toronto, and in early 1968 (*Varsity*, 22 January 1968) it was reported that fifteen members of the organization picketed a model UN General Assembly on campus, handing out pamphlets proclaiming the UN as a tool of communism and a danger to freedom.

None of these activities could have done much to ingratiate Fromm with the politicized student body at the time. Yet Fromm not only won an election in 1968 as a representative of St Michael's College on the Student Administrative Council, but he even received more votes than any of the others elected, including Bob Rae (of NDP fame) and Mark Nakamura (a high-ranking figure today in the Ontario Human Rights Commission). As Genovese observed several years later, Fromm won simply because he was a curiosity. Another Edmund Burke Society member, Joanus Proos, also managed to get elected, but by acclamation. In a sense, that was Fromm's high point in student politics. A few months later (*Varsity*, 4 October 1968), a report circulated that students at St Michael's College had initiated a petition to impeach him. Shortly after that, Fromm lost in his bid to get elected to a four-member student commission on university government to investigate and possibly reorganize student affairs. One of his successful opponents was Rae (*Varsity*, 11 February 1970). Fromm's days as a 'big man on campus' were clearly over. Yet what was surprising was that he and his small group of followers could have had such an impact at all, especially at the polling booth. The simple explanation, I suppose, in addition to the normal dose of apathy that almost always is present, is that the Edmund Burke Society was so visibly out of step with the vast majority of students at the time and created such a racket that it could not be ignored. Or perhaps its election successes were attributable to little more than the undergraduates' notion of a bad joke.

Beliefs and Goals
From what has already been said, it will be evident that the driving force behind the Edmund Burke Society, which defined itself 'as a political *movement* and not a political party' (*Straight Talk*, vol. 4, no. 1, September 1971), was its anti-communism. The organization itself set out its beliefs and goals on a number of occasions. For example, on the front page of all

the early issues of *Straight Talk* was the message: 'The Edmund Burke Society is a conservative organization unaffiliated with any political party. We are dedicated to the principles of individual freedom and responsibility, free enterprise, and firm *action* against all tyrannies, especially Communism and its manifestations in Canada and abroad.' In one issue of *Straight Talk* (vol. 3, no. 8, May 1971), it is stated that the Edmund Burke Society believes in: '1 / Individual rights and freedom with *responsibility* as the necessary other side of the coin. 2 / Keeping the government limited and close to the people; thus, we support local government in preference to a large federal bureaucracy. 3 / Aid to Canada's *true* allies (for example, Nationalist China). 4 / The liberation (and active steps to bring it about) of *all* the "captive" nations, dominated by international communism. 5 / The free enterprise system of economics.' At the same time the organization was opposed to: '1 / One world government. 2 / Pornography, drugs and "the new morality" – trends which tend to erode the fibre and spirit of Western Christian civilization. 3 / Corrupt business practices (for instance, usurious interest rates or trade with the reds).'

An even more elaborate statement appears in the next issue of *Straight Talk* (vol. 3, no. 9, June 1971), repeating the emphasis on anti-communism, individual freedom, free enterprise, Christian values, local government, and moral degeneration (drugs, pornography, abortion, etc.). The three founders, it is said, 'were profoundly disturbed by the continuing success of communism; by the official toleration of communism and socialism by Canada's "establishment"; and by the threat, everywhere present, to the fundamental moral and political values of Western Christian Civilization.' The statement goes on to argue that 'basic Christian values *must* be taught in our schools along with a compulsory course in good citizenship, stressing the incredible successes and advances made by Western Christian Civilization.'

To sum up, the Edmund Burke society was pro–United States, pro–Vietnam War, pro–South Africa ('a bastion against communism'), pro–Rhodesia, pro–Nationalist China, and pro–Biafra.[4] The list of things it

4 The Edmund Burke Society's support for Biafra (the secessionist Igbos of Southeastern Nigeria) was probably a result of the fact that the federal Nigerian forces had the backing of Britain's Labour government and Russia. Also playing a part may have been the reputation of the Igbo for being highly individualistic, entrepreneurially oriented, Westernized, and Christianized – a microcosm of the values the Edmund Burke Society sought to promote in Canada.

  The Edmund Burke Society established links with several organizations in addition to the Canadian Friends of Biafra: the Friends of Rhodesia Association, which provided

opposed is much longer. The organization was anti-'peace creeps' and American draft dodgers ('to all the draft dogers and deserters cluttering up our country, may they have a justly rotten Christmas'); anti-immigration (one article in *Straight Talk* refers to 'the criminal permissiveness of Canada's immigration policy'; another, entitled 'Immigration: That Forbidden Topic,' asks: 'Is it right to import a racial problem, which will ultimately result in misery for Canada, misery for the coloured immigrants, and profit only to the communists and people planners?'); anti-sex education (the organization often presented a film on the subject); anti-welfare (its slogan: 'I'm fighting poverty, I work for a living'); anti-homosexuality (an affront against God); anti-women's liberation ('a not-so-secret front for lesbians'); anti-abortion (as Fromm wrote: 'And why is abortion genocide? It is *our* people that they are killing. Abortion is the premeditated murder ... of thousands of our descendents – of those who will preserve and refurbish our Civilization'); anti-Canada Council grants to Marxist subversives; anti-excessive taxation and big government; and anti-drugs (the Edmund Burke Society's interpretation was that Russia and China were behind the drug scene as a means of destroying the moral fibre of Western civilization). The organization even had its own 'anti-drug squad.' Fromm (*Straight Talk*, vol. 4, no. 2, December 1971) argued that anyone arrested more than twice for a hard-drug offence should receive the death penalty.

The Edmund Burke Society was particularly hostile towards Trudeau, who was referred to as 'the communists' man in Ottawa' (*Straight Talk*, vol. 4, no. 2, December 1971). One article (*Straight Talk*, vol. 1, no. 7, May 1969) was entitled 'Pierre Loves Mao.' In another, there is a list of Trudeau's 'horrors' and 'errors' since his election in 1968, including the plan to recognize Red China and to establish Medicare ('a vicious monopoly'). Somewhat comically, the Edmund Burke Society originally came out in strong support for Trudeau's War Measures Act against the FLQ (*Straight*

---

the Burkers with funds (*Straight Talk*, vol. 7, no. 2, n.d.); Canadian Chinese Nationalists, with their shared hatred of Mao; the Canadian League of Rights (Gostick's organization); Breakthrough, a Detroit group; Tradition, Family and Property; the Anti-Bolshevik Youth League, located in Alberta; the National Front in Britain; the Falange of Bolivia, a 'para-military, political movement' with anti-communist aims (*Straight Talk*, vol. 4, no. 2, December 1971); the Social Credit party in Ontario, which at one point the Burkers successfully infiltrated and dominated (see chapter 10); finally, the Edmund Burke Society expressed a desire to interact with 'real' conservatives in the Progressive Conservative party (*Straight Talk*, vol. 1, no. 4, January 1969), which in its view was dominated by 'pink' conservatives such as Stanfield, a man who in the Burkers' view was soft on communism (*Straight Talk*, vol. 3, no. 10, July-August 1971).

Talk, vol. 3, no. 3, November 1970), but by the next issue of *Straight Talk* (vol. 3, no. 4, December 1970) argued that his actions were a complete sham: 'Trudeau's move was dramatic and colourful – troops in Ottawa; troops in Montreal; a sweeping dictatorial law. Excellent public relations ... Trudeau can't stop the F.L.Q. because he doesn't want to!'

Finally, characteristic of extremist politics, both on the right and on the left, is a belief in some sort of conspiracy, and the Edmund Burke Society was no exception. In one issue of *Straight Talk* (vol. 3, no. 5, January-February 1971), there is a two-page reading list at the end, followed by the statement: 'Don't expect to find these books in your library or local book store. They're not allowed to stock them for fear that you might start asking some questions and learn the truth.' In another issue there is a comment on the Bilderbergers, 'a group of extremely powerful men in banking, business, politics, communications, and the universities, who meet once a year ... The press is usually excluded ... The discussions are strongly secret ... most of the participants are ... leftists' (*Straight Talk*, vol. 3, no. 10, July-August 1971). In an article written by Fromm, entitled 'The Conspiracy in Canada' (*Straight Talk*, vol. 4, no. 1, September 1971), he begins: 'When EBS started out four years ago, most of us were just plain anti-communists.' He goes on to ask why our political and business leaders are soft on communism, and states: 'the only coherent explanation of the history of the last 30 years is one that holds that a small group of highly powerful men have worked and manipulated to reach an accommodation with communism; to set up a one-world super state of socialism, which they control.'

Activities

The Edmund Burke Society repeatedly stressed that what made it special as an anti-communist organization was its dedication to action, not just talk. For the most part, action consisted of attempts to broadcast its message in as many ways as possible, and in what were referred to as counter-demonstrations. With regard to the first, one of the organization's most important steps was to establish its own publication. In 1967 two issues (labelled volumes I and II) appeared of *The Edmund Burke Society Bulletin*. In 1968 the publication was renamed *Straight Talk*, and for the duration of the organization's existence, and after it became the Western Guard, ten issues of *Straight Talk* were published annually. Among the organization's activities was a letter-writing campaign. There even was what was referred to as a 'letter-writing squad' which bombarded the daily newspapers; in an early issue of *Straight Talk* (vol. 2, no. 3, December 1969), members were not only advised to write their MPs, but also *how* to write letters: short, to the point, and ending with a question; the latter, it stated, usually assured a reply. Members also were advised to write letters to local newspapers, avoiding 'length and verbal overkill.' Another method used by the organization was bumper stickers, such as: 'Trudeau – Canada's Greatest Mistake'; 'Go to College and Learn to Riot'; 'Would You Give Blood to the Viet Cong?'; 'Socialism, Cancer of Liberty, Never Worked.' Books, pamphlets, postcards, and films were distributed, and *Straight Talk* was sold on street corners. There was an Edmund Burke Society bookstore-headquarters, which featured lectures on Saturday mornings and Monday evenings. Prominent members such as Fromm and Andrews appeared frequently on radio and television, and dozens of talks were given at secondary schools.

Two of the organization's most controversial publications were *The Sour Grapes of Cesar Chavez* and *East Wind over Ottawa*. The Edmund Burke Society mounted a sustained drive to discredit the man who was fighting on behalf of Mexican-American workers in California, dismissing him as a communist agitator whose only familiarity with grapes was at the table. The other publication caused a mild storm in Canada, since it was a direct attack on Trudeau and his alleged communist sympathies; one former Burker stated that in the long run it may have hindered the right wing's prospects, for it provided fuel to those who were intent on passing anti-hate laws. In addition to these publications, the Edmund Burke Society manned an anti-communist display at the Canadian National Exhibition, where passing visitors called them Fascists and Nazis.

Some of the organization's other efforts brought them closer to physical confrontation with their opponents: distributing leaflets that denounced Mao in Toronto's Chinatown, and compiling intelligence files on as well as infiltrating left-wing groups. These activities led directly to the organization's specialty: the counter-demonstration. Andrews once remarked (Toronto *Telegram*, 26 September 1970): 'I guess we have counter-demonstrated every major leftist demonstration in Toronto in the last three years.' One of the first counter-demonstrations occurred in April 1968 in front of the U.S. Consulate in Toronto. According to the report of an Edmund Burke Society participant (*Straight Talk*, vol. 7, no. 2, n.d.), about 1,000 Viet Cong supporters, members of the CNFL (Canadians for the National Liberation Front, Viet Cong), marching to protest the U.S. war effort, were met by about 150 Burkers. A bloody brawl followed, eventually broken up by Metro's mounted police. In October 1967, Edmund Burke Society members followed an anti-war demonstration to Queen's Park, and there, to the horror of the peace marchers, they hung in effigy Ho Chi Minh. In May

1970 the Burkers counter-demonstrated against 'the last of the big Communist anti–Vietnam war demonstrations in Toronto' (*Straight Talk*, vol. 7, no. 3, n.d.). The ensuing violence resulted in widespread damage to property, numerous injuries, and almost one hundred arrests, 90 per cent of them supposedly left-wingers, the remainder Edmund Burke Society supporters. In later years, it was revealed that the rampaging demonstrators and the destruction actually were precipitated by Edmund Burke Society infiltrators into the left-wing ranks. The purpose was to discredit the anti-American peacenik movement. The celebration of Lenin's hundredth birthday at the North Toronto Memorial Gardens was the occasion for another violent episode. Edmund Burke Society members had quietly purchased tickets for the occasion. When the master of ceremonies, surrounded by diplomatic representatives from Cuba and Czechoslovakia, attempted to toast Lenin, someone yelled, 'May he rot in Hell!' As *The Toronto Daily Star* (4 April 1970) reported, the Burkers spat at, insulted, and threw eggs at the guests. Tables were overturned, a smoke bomb was hurled, and one Edmund Burke Society member apparently was stabbed, although the police – more than sixty strong – said he was probably cut by broken glass.

Convocation Hall at the University of Toronto was the setting for two further donnybrooks. The first occasion was a visit by William Kunstler in June 1970, described in later years by a Western Guard member as 'the noted Jewish communist lawyer ... defender of the famous "Chicago Seven" ' (*Straight Talk*, vol. 7, nos. 5–6, n.d.). In one version, Kunstler, disturbed by hecklers in the audience, invited Fromm to the podium to present his viewpoint. Before Fromm could speak, the lawyer emptied a pitcher of water over his head. In another version, Fromm spilled or poured a glass of water over the lectern, prompting Kunstler's action. Whatever the chain of events, one thing was clear: Fromm was knocked cold, and another fight was in progress (*Guerilla*, vol. 1, no. 3, 3 July 1970; *Globe and Mail*, 24 June 1970). Edmund Burke Society members obtained two warrants for the arrest of Kunstler on assault charges, but he had already left Canada. Thirty Ontario lawyers eventually offered to defend him. He chose Clayton Ruby as his lawyer, and was acquitted.

The second Convocation Hall battle took place almost a year later. Quebec labour leader Michel Chartrand and lawyer Robert Lemieux, referred to later by a former Burker (*Straight Talk*, vol. 7, nos. 5–6, n.d.) as FLQ communists, were the targets. As the *Toronto Daily Star* (29 March 1971) described it, Edmund Burke Society members hurled a stink bomb, threw stones through windows, and sprayed the hall with a mace-like substance. The building caretaker had to be treated for temporary blindness, and a Toronto *Telegram* reporter also was hospitalized after being kicked in the head and abdomen. Two Burkers carried away another member, and five others had twelve charges levied against them, although apparently all were later dismissed. Unlike the Kunstler battle, in which the greatly out-numbered Edmund Burke Society soldiers had to withdraw to lick their wounds, the second battle at Convocation Hall was a great success, at least from the perspective of the Burkers.

What has been described in later years by Western Guard members as the 'greatest event of them all' (*Straight Talk*, vol. 7, nos. 5 and 6, n.d.) and one of the 'highlights' (*Straight Talk*, September 1977) was actually the ac-tion of a single man. In 1971, a Hungarian immigrant, Geza Matrai, leaped on the back of Premier Aleksei Kosygin as he walked on Parliament Hill in Ottawa. Instantaneously he became a hero to the right wing (on the cover of *Straight Talk*, vol. 4, no. 2, December 1971 – 'Geza Matrai: Man of the Month'). However, the establishment took quite a different view. Matrai was found guilty of assaulting Kosygin, and was sentenced to three months in the Guelph Reformatory, and two years' probation, during which he was forbidden to engage in any political activity. Matrai's attack on Kosygin had more immediate consequences than the eventual court case. Kosy-gin was due to visit the Ontario Science Centre in Toronto; police raided the homes of about a dozen Edmund Burke Society members, as well as their bookstore-headquarters. At the latter, they found a pig, on which the Burkers were planning to paint 'Kosygin,' to be paraded at the Ontario Science Centre (Toronto *Telegram*, 27 October 1971). At least two members were arrested for the possession of restricted weapons. From all accounts, the demonstration that took place at the Science Centre was chaotic and violent, as right- and left-wing forces clashed, although the Marxist *Guerilla* (vol. 2, no 21, 3 November 1971) declared: 'As expected, the demonstra-tion was mostly Slavic and right wing.' Blood flowed that day, and many held the police responsible, accusing them of using more force than was necessary (*Toronto Star*, 19 November 1971).

Violence
That the Edmund Burke Society's 'militant conservative activism' could at times stretch into violence was evident in relation to the 'counter-demonstrations.' As Ayre observed (1970: 22), the Burkers 'are ironically becoming more and more like their enemies, the Maoists and the New Left-ists, aggressively intolerant and unmanageable.' Elsewhere (*Toronto Daily Star*, 19 October 1971) it was stated: 'The right-wing Edmund Burke Society has always played a semantic game with the word violence. In their lexicon,

as filled with strident slogans as that of the left they so bitterly oppose, the operative word is counter-violence.' How did an organization devoted to 'law and order' end up in street brawls? Well, as Edmund Burke Society members themselves claimed: 'The only language the violent left understands is no-nonsense counterviolence' (*Straight Talk*, vol. 3, no. 2, October 1970). After one bloody clash with the left, *Straight Talk* (vol. 3, no. 7, April 1971) carried this account: 'Our members distinguished themselves as true sons of Western civilization: when attacked, *Strike Back*! None of the cowardly turn-the-other-cheek rubbish thrown at us by the liberal moralists of today. It's amazing what a beating the reds took.' Elsewhere a *Straight Talk* writer (vol. 3, no. 6, March 1971) asked how many anti-communist organizations can claim they are actually feared by their enemies? The Edmund Burke Society, he gloated, can make such a claim. As one of its slogans went, 'The ones they smear are the ones they fear,' referring to left-wing attacks (*Straight Talk*, vol. 3, no. 4, December 1970). One organization, the Communist Party of Canada, (CPC) made several formal overtures to the Toronto City Council, the chairman of the Metro Toronto Police Commission, and the attorney general of Ontario, complaining about Edmund Burke Society hooliganism, and especially attacks on Bookworld, the CPC's bookstore. The Bookworld manager summarized various Burker activities such as threats to bomb a Unesco-approved book exhibit, the use of mace at a United church where a discussion of civil liberties in Quebec after the War Measures Act of 1970 was taking place, disruption of a meeting of East Asians to discuss the Ugandan crisis, and pouring glue into typewriters used by students at the *Varsity* offices; the Edmund Burke Society also was accused of breaking into Bookworld, stealing important files, turning tapes on and flooding hundreds of books (including the works of Lenin), blasting Bookworld's display window with a shot-gun, and putting a sticker on the store window that read: 'Have you killed a Communist today? Do it now!' Bookworld also fingered the Edmund Burke Society for setting fire to the headquarters of an organization called Praxis in 1970. In one issue of *Straight Talk* (vol. 3, no. 5, January-February 1971), Praxis is described as 'a private corporation, founded in 1968 by a like-minded crew of about a dozen leftist academics roosting on the faculties of the Universities of York and Toronto ... Praxis attracts university professors, CBC employees, social workers, sociologists, as well as a very small percentage of businessmen.' Elsewhere (*Straight Talk*, vol. 3, no. 1, September 1970), the Praxis Corporation is said to have 'the avowed aim of taking over our society and moulding it to the Socialist pattern.' The Burkers certainly did not look on Praxis people as comrades in arms, but they did not claim responsibility for the fire. In fact, in a later issue of *Straight Talk* (vol. 3, no. 6, March 1971), Andrews stated that a Maoist group was spreading 'the vicious lies that Edmund Burke Society is responsible for the burning of the premises of the Praxis Corporation.'

No doubt the Burkers, who saw themselves as saviours of the Western world and the Christian, capitalist way of life, would argue that they had no choice but to do battle with the opposition. As one member put it (*Straight Talk*, vol. 2, no. 5, February 1970), 'while we cannot condone senseless hooliganism ... can we, in good conscience eschew all force, everywhere and under all circumstances.' Ron Haggart, a well-known journalist, once described the Burkers (Toronto *Telegram*, 12 May 1970) as 'hoodlums ... shouting Nazi slogans ... right-wing thugs.' Harsh words, perhaps, and yet it is clear that, to use Spoonley's (1984) felicitous phrase, the Edmund Burke Society more and more was turned on by 'the ecstacy of confrontation.' By 1971, just a year away from its transformation into the militant, extremist Western Guard, these words appeared in *Straight Talk* (vol. 3, no. 9, June 1971) in relation to the adoption of the Celtic Cross as its new symbol: 'The Celtic Cross, well known to the New Right in Europe, is the mark of a new, muscular, Western dedication. It is a warning to the communists, creeps, perverts, usurers, pornography peddlers, drug pushers and to all those who aid and abet communism and its brother-cancer, socialism, that Their Day Has Come. A New Right Is On The Rise!'

Racism and Anti-Semitism

It will be recalled that one of the founders of the Edmund Burke Society, Leigh Smith, took strong objection to Sher's (1983) charge that the organization was racist. The fact is that at the beginning very little attention was paid to racial matters; the main issue, instead, was communism. More than one member of the radical right in the 1980s remarked to me about how naive they had been about the race issue in the days of the Edmund Burke Society. A teach-in organized by the Edmund Burke Society and the Friends of Rhodesia Association (FORA) showed a poster depicting a black and white handshake. Armand Siksna, later to attain notoriety (and a prison sentence) for participating in KKK leader McQuirter's plan to kill another Klansman, once wrote that he could never vote for George Wallace because of his racial policies; in an article several years after the Western Guard had emerged (*Straight Talk*, vol. 7, no. 3, n.d.), one writer, commenting on Siksna's eventual transformation into a committed racist, remarked: 'You've come a long way, Armand!' This same writer said that in the Edmund Burke Society days, most of them did not even understand the race question, adding that some of them 'thought that the only difference between Negroes and Whites was the amount of exposure to the sun.' A similar attitude prevailed regarding Jews. Both Fromm and Smith, two of the Edmund Burke Society founders, told me that there were Jewish members at the beginning, and I have names of some of them (I also was told that there were black members, but have not been able to confirm this). Fromm said that Andrews actually supported Israel during the 1967 war, and in fact in the second volume of *The Edmund Burke Society Bulletin* (July 1967), the Edmund Burke Society came out completely on the side of Israel for the simple reason that Russia backed the Arabs.

As the years went by, however, there was growing evidence of a turn to racism in the organization, although for the most part such messages were sporadic and indirect. In statements supporting Rhodesia, it was claimed that only 'a generation ago, the African people were completely primitive ... and thus not ready for Western democracy' (*Straight Talk*, vol. 1, no. 3, December 1968), and that all black Rhodesians preferred white to black rule (*Straight Talk*, vol. 2, no. 2, November 1964). South Africa was referred to as a bastion of democracy, a valued ally. In one article, Andrews claimed that the press always reveals the racial identity of whites involved in crimes, but covers up the racial identity of blacks (*Straight Talk*, vol. 4, no. 3, November-December 1971). References were made, with an underlying air of pleasure, to Rocky Jones's 'Negro racism' (Jones was a vocal and talented black leader in Nova Scotia at the time, with a nation-wide profile), to Eldridge Cleaver's 'poisonous piece of racism' in *Soul on Ice*, and to black organizations that according to the Edmund Burke Society expressed reverse racism. There was an article extolling the 'strong stand on the race issue' taken by Britain's National Front (*Straight Talk*, vol. 3, no. 1, September 1970), and members were urged to read *Spearhead*, one of the National Front's publications.

For the most part, references to Israel and to Jews were consistently negative, rather than blatantly anti-Semitic, but a swing in the latter direction also began to emerge. One article criticized Jews in Toronto for only condemning Soviet oppression of Jews, rather than of all people under its domination (*Straight Talk*, vol. 3, no. 3, November 1970). An article attributed to Fromm (*Straight Talk*, vol. 3, no. 2, October 1970) stated: 'While Nazism was certainly a totalitarian state, was the Soviet Union not the greater menace?' Fromm continued: 'The economic slavery and religious persecution suffered by many peoples of the Soviet Union made Hitler's misdeed seem amateurish.' One could argue that this peculiar interpretation of history was a logical product of the overwhelming concern of the

Edmund Burke Society with communism, next to which all other issues paled. And yet in the same article Fromm remarked: 'Some allege that Hitler killed six million Jews.' Allege. It would appear that Fromm's comments about Hitler and Nazism may not have been so innocent after all. Indeed, in an earlier issue of *Straight Talk* (vol. 1, no. 3, December 1968) we find: 'Racism was a personal abberation of Hitler's and is not true of fascism.' Elsewhere (*Straight Talk*, vol. 4, no. 3, November-December 1971), Fromm expressed his preference for Hitler over Trudeau, stating that while Trudeau was 'leading us down the road to a communist dictatorship,' Hitler 'was at least anti-communist.'

There was a growing reluctance to regard Israel as a friend of democracy and the West, and the Arab world as part of Russia's orbit. One article stated: 'Before falling over oneself in defending socialist Israel as the bastion of western democracy, any objective reader should try to recall the last time he heard an anti-communist utterance from Golda Meir' (*Straight Talk*, vol. 3, no. 1, September 1970). In another issue of *Straight Talk* (vol. 2, no. 9, July-August 1970) there is a reference to the Red Rabbi, the label given to Rabbi Abraham Feinberg by David Stanley. Elsewhere (*Straight Talk*, vol. 3, no. 4, December 1970) Israel is said to be soft on communism, rather than a bulkhead against it. At the same time, however, *Straight Talk* printed a letter by a man who may himself have been Jewish (he was a member of the Edmund Burke Society and a regular contributor to the periodical), in which he accused the author of an earlier article on the Middle East of being misinformed and prejudiced against Israel. For the most part, though, the perspective of the Edmund Burke Society on Israel was one-sided and negative, which is precisely, but in opposite terms, what the organization seems to have thought about the information made available to the Canadian public (*Straight Talk*, vol. 3, no. 1, September 1970): 'due to the fact that no politician owes his election to the Arab vote and due to the fact that Arabs do not control the advertising revenues or mortgage loans of newspapers, there is a distinct possibility that the Canadian public may be deluged with propaganda from one side only.' While the accusation here that it is the Jews who control the media and manipulate politicians was only veiled, the case was put more forthrightly later (*Straight Talk*, vol. 3, no. 5, January-February 1971): 'If we might be so bold, we would like to suggest to those self-confessed persons seeking to save us from foreign domination that they look into the degree of control and influence exercised by the state of Israel in the internal affairs of Canada.'

Of particular interest was the reaction of the Edmund Burke Society to the Jewish Defence League (JDL). As a dedicated opponent of the Soviet

Union, the JDL should have been regarded by the Burkers as a friend. However, in an article written by Fromm entitled 'The Jewish Defence League – Kosher Conservatives?' (*Straight Talk*, vol. 3, no. 5, January-February 1971), it is stated that the JDL suffers from Hitlerphobia and that its only concern is with anti-Semitism. The article concludes: 'we should be skeptical before we welcome them wholeheartedly as anti-communist freedom fighters. Their motivation seems to be that of narrow Jewish chauvinists, interested exclusively in themselves ... They are in fact not *anti-communists* but anti–anti-Semites. In other words, while their harassment of Soviet diplomats may get them labelled in the press as "anti-communists", their scope of concern is so narrow as to render them almost useless as allies.' Obviously influencing Fromm's appraisal of the JDL was his realization that Rabbi Meir Kahane, the former New York–based head of the JDL, was not very favourably disposed towards organizations like the Edmund Burke Society. Appearing in *The Globe and Mail* (25 November 1971) were these words by Kahane: 'My greatest fear is that the wave of the future in this country – for worse, not for better, for worse – is the white ethnic. For the most part he's anti-Semitic, anti-black, and capable of doing a lot of bad things.' These words were reprinted verbatim in *Straight Talk* (vol. 4, no. 3, November-December 1971).

THE MEDIA

The Canadian Nazi Party and the Edmund Burke Society brought into focus many of the issues that were to loom on the horizon in the next two decades, and in the remainder of this chapter I shall take a closer look at three of them: the media, freedom of expression, and the police.

'Just think,' Beattie once said (Garrity 1966), 'three or four kids, that's all we were, and we had the country up in arms.' On another occasion he remarked (*Toronto Star*, 9 May 1977): 'There never was a Nazi Party. Just 6 or 7 kids I conned into it. It existed because of the news media and the circus in the park.' Stanley said (*Toronto Daily Star*, 18 October 1966) that newspaper publicity was the only thing that kept the Nazis in business. It was, he remarked, the *publicity* about hate literature, not the literature itself, that made the hate campaign a success. The Nazi's approach to the media was succinctly put by Beattie (Garrity 1966): 'Tell 'em anything if it's going to get your name in the paper.'

A similar attitude was taken by the Edmund Burke Society. Fromm's appearance on the television program 'Under Attack' in 1969 was described as a 'real break' (*Straight Talk*, vol. 2, no. 2, November 1969). Later

Andrews was a guest on the same program, and Fromm on the Pierre Berton show. Newspaper coverage was referred to as proof of the organization's success. Even the apparent set-backs had a silver lining, as long as they resulted in media attention. One article (Toronto *Telegram*, 26 September 1970) claimed that the Burkers regarded the Kunstler trial as a 'publicity bonanza.' Certainly, they crowed (*Straight Talk*, vol. 2, no. 9, July-August 1970) about all the good media coverage that ensued from Fromm's prone figure – coverage not only in Canada, but also in the United States and as far away as Switzerland. The organization publicly expressed great indignation in connection with the police raids on the homes of members and its headquarters, where the 'Kosygin' pig was seized. But privately they were delighted, for at 'last someone was taking them seriously' (Miller 1971). Referring to the disruption of a peace rally, a *Straight Talk* writer said (vol. 3, no. 3, November 1970):

We successfully dominated news coverage of the event. A report on news coverage is appropriate. For the newspapers, the *Globe and Mail* afforded us the best coverage. Some of our signs were photographed and we were referred to without any of the usual pejorative adjectives. (e.g. 'ultra-conservative' or 'far-right'). The coverage in both the *Star* and *Telegram* was passable. Even the University of Toronto *Varsity* rendered an unbiased account. The hippie organ, the *Guerilla*, ignored the march and termed it a waste of time. Both Channel 9 and Channel 6 (CBC) covered this event on both the local and national news. Channel 9 sent a reporter ... Radio coverage was extensive, although somewhat hostile. All in all, we did extremely well.

A similar gush of pleasure followed a protest by fifteen Burkers (*Straight Talk*, vol. 3, no. 9, June 1971) against a cinema in Toronto showing 'filth': 'excellent coverage on the night news on both Channel 6 and Channel 9 T.V. and Edmund Burke Society was mentioned on radio stations C.H.U.M. and C.F.R.B. The news coverage, then, was highly successful.'

As we shall see later, most right-wing organizations are ambivalent about the media. On the one hand, the media are regarded as the vehicle to put the organizations on the map, and thus media attention is absolutely essential. On the other hand, the media are seen as strongly slanted towards liberals and the left. Some Edmund Burke Society members were surprised and hurt by the hostile reaction of the media. Why, they wondered, did people oppose them when all that they were doing was confronting communism and standing up for capitalism and the values of Western Christian civilization? The answer that many of them eventually arrived at was not just the socialist inclinations of the government, but more critically the presumed Jewish control of the media.

FREEDOM OF EXPRESSION

Is freedom of speech unlimited? Should people have the liberty to say (and think) what they wish, as long as they don't act upon their words? Anyone who followed the Zundel and Keegstra trials, or the determined reaction against the Klan in the 1980s, will know that the issue of freedom of speech was never very far beneath the surface; they may be less aware that it has figured prominently in previous situations, such as the Stanley-Beattie era. Organizations like N3 declared that the Nazis should not be allowed to speak in public. The United Jewish People's Order declared that the sacred right of free speech stops short of the advocacy of genocide. James Mackey, then Metro Toronto's chief of police, wrote to Mayor Philip Givens requesting that Beattie not be granted further permits to speak in any city park. Rabbi Gunther Plaut (*Globe and Mail*, 5 May 1965) affirmed his strong belief in freedom of speech, but declared that when mass violence is advocated, the line has been crossed.

The press itself more often than not had taken the position that freedom of speech overrules all other considerations. Frank Tumpane (Toronto *Telegram*, 8 June 1966) probably expressed the general attitude of journalists when he wrote that while he finds the Nazi philosophy repugnant, except in times of national peril there is no valid reason to deny its spokesmen the right to free expression. We are stuck, says Tumpane, with protecting people like Beattie. A more sensitive reaction was provided by Robert Fulford (*Toronto Daily Star*, 8 May 1965). Unlike other journalists, Fulford attempted to understand the perspective of the victim, reporting that non-Jews fail to appreciate the horror that the term 'Nazi' conjures up for Jews, who make the reasonable assumption that nobody else is going to stand up for them.

The right wing has usually parroted the media's general orientation. Taylor, for example, called the 1964 mail ban on *The Thunderbolt*, the organ of the National States Rights Party, 'a complete denial of the freedom of the press.' The Edmund Burke Society regarded Bill C-3 (the so-called 'hate' bill) as anathema, claiming that the Canadian Jewish Congress was behind it. To quote from *Straight Talk* (vol. 2, no. 3, December 1969): 'this bill provides a political weapon to harass people who dare discuss controversial matters of race and religion.' Gostick, the man who emerged as a prominent right-winger after the Second World War, interpreted the Beattie-Stanley Nazi phase as an orchestrated media event set in motion to assure the passage of 'hate' legislation. In his words (*The Canadian Intelligence Service*, vol. 15, no. 6, June 1965): 'Our information is that the whole "Nazi" show is a fraud and a hoax, created and promoted by the very elements decrying "hate" for the purpose of creating the right climate to assure passage of restrictive legislation respecting speech and the mails.' In the same vein, the Edmund Burke Society dismissed the neo-Nazi menace as non-existent, and observed: 'Free speech is a Canadian tradition. In fact during the last war, this was one of the four basic human rights that our government told us that we were fighting to preserve. Many of our fathers and brothers paid the highest penalty – their lives – to defend this right ... The censorship advocated in the "hate bill" will restrict the rights of *all* Canadians.'

These words of the Edmund Burke Society have echoed down the years as other groups such as the Ku Klux Klan also have made impassioned pleas for freedom of speech. The innocent reader can hardly be blamed for thinking that not all can be rotten in such organizations, devoted as they are to defending a freedom most of us hold so dearly. And yet not all is as one-sided as it might seem. The Edmund Burke Society, for example, took the position that cinemas 'which profit from the undiluted trading in human flesh' should be put out of business (*Straight Talk*, vol. 3, no. 9, June 1971). Following the Kunstler débâcle, Edmund Burke Society members went to the U.S. Consulate to complain that the famous lawyer should not have been allowed into Canada. The organization also opposed entry to Black Panther leader Huey Newton and to the well-known revolutionary Abbie Hoffman. Elsewhere, it demanded that red agitators such as Hoffman or FLQ supporters should be denied the use of public facilities such as universities. All this reveals a characteristic of the freedom-of-speech issue that is usually not appreciated. Even those organizations that so strongly defend it, such as the Edmund Burke Society, draw the line where their opponents are concerned. In other words, the boundaries of freedom of speech are both flexible and finite, set by the vested interests of the organizations in question.

POLICE

Where do the police fit into the right-wing picture? Are they, as the radical left claims, part of the right wing, the state's instruments in maintaining the status quo for the benefit of the privileged? Are they as a collectivity more racially inclined than other segments of society? It is clear that in the United States policemen have always been attracted to the Ku Klux Klan, but what is significant about the membership of the Canadian right wing is that it has included hardly any policemen, at least to my knowledge. This does not mean that the police have not been involved in other ways. The RCMP used wiretaps to keep tabs on the Canadian Nazi Party (I have copies of some of the tapes), and as we shall soon see, the police appear to have infiltrated the Edmund Burke Society in a very peculiar manner.

In the eyes of the members of the Canadian Nazi Party, the police were friends. Beattie was in the habit of praising their efforts to protect him at Allan Gardens. In one of his recorded telephone messages in 1969 for the National Socialist Party, he said: 'Support your local police. The police are your best friends. Teach this to your children.' The Edmund Burke Society was even more enthusiastic about the police; they were regarded as allies, part of the framework in which order and morality would prevail, a silent partner in the organization's program. From almost the beginning, the Burkers distributed bumper stickers with the slogan 'Support Your Local Police.' In an article about accusations by a black organization of police brutality, *Straight Talk* (vol. 1, no. 10, August 1969) came out firmly on the side of the police, referring to their 'fine performance.' The courteous Edmund Burke Society normally sent letters to police administrators announcing their intention to counter-demonstrate, and assuring the police complete co-operation in maintaining law and order. One can almost sense the anguish, and disbelief, among the Burkers as experience, in the form of arrests and surveillance, taught them that the police were not very eager to return the admiration. After two members were arrested, a writer commented (*Straight Talk*, vol. 3, no. 8, May 1971): 'Being a cop used to be a job one could be proud of. It was an institution to be looked up to. In too many cases, it has degenerated to the level of a highly organized street gang. However, the answer to bad cops is not no cops but better cops.' Elsewhere we read (*Straight Talk*, vol. 3, no. 1, September 1970): 'The constable who exceeds his authority, who violates the legal rights of citizens, who outrages public decency by his language and conduct, who employs violence needlessly and who is gratuitiously brutal, who takes bribes or behaves otherwise in an improper manner, is obviously a menace to the good order of the community and a disgrace to his fellow constables.'

After the police crack-down on the Burkers following Matrai's attack on Kosygin, a *Straight Talk* writer cried (vol. 4, no. 2, December 1971): 'Political Police! This is the only description that fits the actions of the leadership of both the Metropolitan Toronto Police and the R.C.M.P. I realize that it is quite a step from this statement to our public image as a movement known for its "Support Your Local Police" slogan.' The article concluded by stating that it is necessary for anti-communists to 'reassess their previously rather uncritical view of the police,' who were accused of discriminating against the Christian Edmund Burke Society in favour of the

JDL. Further along in the same issue we find: 'Every cop protects his buddy. Have you ever seen a policeman with enough integrity to give evidence against a fellow-cop in a court of law?' Referring to the débâcle at the Ontario Science Centre on the occasion of Kosygin's visit, in which charges of police brutality were levelled, the Edmund Burke Society expressed hope (*Straight Talk*, vol. 4, no. 4, January 1972) that a subsequent attorney-general's inquiry would 'give the Metro police a much needed slap-on-the-wrist to humble their high-handedness and arrogance, and to remind them that they are public servants.'

At the height of this volte-face regarding the police, *Straight Talk* (vol. 4, no. 3, November-December 1971) published a very significant article by Kastus Akula, who had lived under both Hitler and Stalin. Akula began by stating that Edmund Burke Society members who spread the idea that Canada is a police state have no idea what they are talking about. Describing a real police state, Akula wrote: 'just imagine carrying your passport inside your own country every day. Image being watched by local henchmen of the "ministry of love." Imagine applying for a police permit to take, let's say, a trip to Winnipeg; undergoing police scrutiny when applying for a job; informing on others and they, in turn, informing on you; having no rights to demonstrate, keep arms, or take your children to church.' After this sobering message, Akula concluded by saying 'let's stop calling Canada a police-state and take some action to prevent it from becoming one!'

I now turn to a rather sensitive issue: the possible involvement of the police in establishing the Edmund Burke Society. In 1982 while carrying out research in British Columbia, I came across a document that threw quite a different light on this organization. According to the document, the Edmund Burke Society was actually set up as an instrument for Canada's security services in order to draw out the left wing and crystallize its right-wing opposition. The kingpin behind all this was supposedly a military man, trained at one point by a CIA anti-subversion squad, who had been active in university-campus security for the armed forces in the late 1960s. Working along with him was a 'red squad,' a common term in police circles for a group of people organized and trained to infiltrate organizations, act as *agents provocateurs*, and generally undermine the left wing by various 'dirty tricks.'

How serious should one take these charges? At the outset it must be pointed out that most of the information in the document consists of the speculations of a man who had been fired from the Central Housing and Mortgage Corporation for allegedly showing a cabinet document to the Native Council of Canada (he later won a court case for wrongful dismissal). It could reasonably be argued that this man had no reason to love the state bureaucracy. And yet, there is a great deal of circumstantial evidence that lends plausibility to his accusations. There are, for example, newspaper reports of his dismissal and trial, as well as the military man's role in campus security. Several of those said to belong to the 'red squad' were, indeed, members of the Edmund Burke Society. Moreover, I know for a fact that at least two of them have over the years been police informers. Finally, the document itself was submitted to an inquiry about the RCMP by a Progressive Conservative MP. If the charges in the document are fanciful, the person who prepared it should be congratulated for his imaginative powers. However, if the RCMP and other police agencies did *not* control the Edmund Burke Society behind the scenes, perhaps there will be someone in the top echelons asking: why not?!

CONCLUSION

It is apparent that the Canadian Nazi Party and the Edmund Burke Society were simply ahead of their times. They anticipated the swell of white-supremacist organizations that swept over the landscape in the 1970s and 1980s, and the swing to the right in general of the politics of Western industrialized nations. The Canadian Nazi Party was certainly more radical in its views, but the Edmund Burke Society's significance should not be underrated; it provided the training ground for the two principal figures who were to dominate the scene during the years ahead: Andrews on the far right and Fromm on the fringe right. The Burkers themselves did not seem to appreciate that their organization had become double-barrelled: the one chamber containing bird-shot, the other buckshot. As one member put it (*Straight Talk*, vol. 3, no. 6, March 1971): 'Let's face it: we in the Edmund Burke Society are the shock force of the pro-Western counter-revolution; but we're still gentlemen.' That is the way they saw themselves: high-principled people with the courage to confront the forces that were eroding the country. Yet there always had been a deep contradiction within the organization: how to defend the Western, Christian capitalist way of life and still remain part of the establishment, rather than going off the deep end and becoming outright racists. For make no mistake about it, although racism and anti-Semitism were only occasionally revealed by the Edmund Burke Society, they constituted a submerged strain that constantly threatened to come to the surface. The polarization of the membership in 1972, with part of it siding with Andrews's Western Guard and the remainder following Fromm, was merely the almost inevitable maturation of that long-fermenting contradiction.

PART TWO / THE RADICAL RIGHT

4

The Western Guard

'Hitler was a softy on the Jew question.' So spoke John Ross Taylor (Crysdale and Durham 1978: 130), the leader of the Western Guard when I began this project in 1980. The sentiment expressed in Taylor's words pretty well captured the spirit of the organization that was to dominate the right-wing scene throughout the 1970s. The decision to convert the Edmund Burke Society into the white-supremacist Western Guard had been made at a council meeting on 23 February 1972. A formal announcement to that effect appeared the next month. One of the reasons offered for the change (*Straight Talk*, vol. 4, no. 6, March 1972) was simply that many people often confused the Edmund Burke Society with the John Birch Society, an American right-wing organization which by 1972 had crossed the border into Canada. A second reason was that Edmund Burke was no longer considered to be an adequate figure-head for the anticipated bloody battle against the foes of Western civilization.

The emergence of the Western Guard was a clear sign that the radicals in the Edmund Burke Society had won out over the more moderate sector, and a direct consequence was the resignation of several members, notably Paul Fromm. Although Fromm eventually went on to establish a variety of organizations that paralleled the philosophy of the moribund Edmund Burke Society, he remained a member of the militant Western Guard for almost three months after the council decision had been taken to create it. At a banquet held in Toronto in April 1972, attended by a leading member of the Ku Klux Klan from Michigan, Fromm gave the opening address (Toronto *Sun*, 1 May 1972). In that same month, he spoke to a group of high-school students in Arnprior under the auspices of the Western Guard (*Straight Talk*, vol, 4, no. 7, April 1972). The announcement of the name change had appeared in the March issue of *Straight Talk*, but in the April issue Fromm was still listed as the editor. It was not until the next issue (May-June 1972) that he ceased being the editor, and a note appeared announcing his resignation. No other comment was made then, but in the July issue there was a lengthy report on his resignation, revealing that it had been a very bitter affair. Apparently there had been an agreement whereby Fromm would remain editor of *Straight Talk*, which would cease to be connected solely to the Western Guard; in return, Fromm would promise not to establish another right-wing organization, nor would he announce his resignation from the Western Guard to the press. However, Fromm did in fact give a press release, and Western Guard officials were of the opinion that he was trying to reconstruct the Edmund Burke Society, and to retain *Straight Talk* as its organ (Fromm had the mailing list for subscribers). Moreover, they claimed that Fromm had made off with $400 from the Western Guard treasury. The parting shot was the accusation that he had arranged to have a female member of the right wing arrested at one of his meetings in June 1972. This was a friend of Geza Matrai, the man who attacked Kosygin in 1971. She had been sought by the police in connection with the disruption of a homosexual forum at St Lawrence Hall in Toronto about a month earlier.

When I undertook the research for this project in the early 1980s, I discovered that there still was considerable hostility towards Fromm within the radical-right organizations. Some people, intent on smearing his reputation, said that he actually did understand the real issues, such as the threat of Jews, but was too cowardly to make his views public. Others stated that he was nothing more than an ineffectual intellectual, satisfied to talk about the issues rather than act upon them. When I related these accusations to Fromm, he rejected them, and remarked that there is nothing so vicious as a family feud, for in a sense when he had departed from the Western Guard, he had left his 'family.'

The official line in *Straight Talk* appears to have been that Fromm resigned because a council vote had gone against him. Andrews added (Crysdale and Durham, 1978: 150) that Fromm had dropped out because he had been unable to work alongside lower-class whites. Fromm himself has explained his actions. In the first issue of *Countdown*, an organ he founded to replace *Straight Talk*, it was reported that he pulled out because of 'irreconcilable differences over tactics' and the 'lack of security in screening members' which has allowed 'a number of highly unstable and undesirable people' to join and harm the Western Guard (*Countdown*, vol. 1, no. 1, June 1972). In the second issue of *Countdown* (vol. 1, no. 2, July 1972), Fromm replied to the accusation that he was guilty of 'theft, trickery and being a police informer,' and of having resigned because a council vote had gone against him. He justified his resignation as follows:

1 / The growing lack of security in the Western Guard, which allowed disreputable people and informers easy access to private information ... 2 / The alliance with a U.S. group [the National Youth Alliance in Washington, led by Dr William Pierce, a prominent racist in the United States at the time], which, whatever its merits or demerits in the U.S., can only give our enemies more to smear us with. 3 / A growing 'rule it or ruin it' attitude to other rightist groups. Plans were seriously considered ... for severely embarassing the public meetings of the John Birch Society in Toronto. 4 / A growing dedication to violence. Don't get me wrong: I'm no pacifist. However, there was less and less effort to spread *our* very real ideas and proposals and more and more reliance on purely negative violence ... 5 / A refusal by the majority on the Council to plan a programme of goals and action. The Guard was drifting from crisis to crisis.

Finally, an intriguing explanation for the emergence of the Western Guard, as well as for Fromm's resignation, concerns the alleged involvement of some of Canada's police agencies in establishing the Edmund Burke Society in the first place. According to the document about this matter referred to in the last chapter, a faction of the Edmund Burke Society eventually rebelled against the police agencies' close control over its activities. This faction expelled Fromm and the principal (undercover) police agent, and founded the Western Guard. The latter, of course, was to be free from police influence, but the document in question states that some members of the 'red squad' remained in the Western Guard. Moreover, by 1975, an *agent provocateur* had worked his way into the organization, eventually playing a crucial role in putting Andrews behind bars. I suppose it could be argued that the determined actions on the part of the police to imprison Andrews merely confirmed that they had earlier been in control of the right-wing organization, and were miffed when the Western Guard shunted them aside. That, however, strikes me as far-fetched. Somewhat more plausible evidence of the involvement of the police, but still far from concrete, was Fromm's own statement that he resigned partly because of the 'growing lack of security in the Western Guard.' Indeed, at a Social Credit meeting at the end of February 1972, members of the newly formed Western Guard reportedly informed the Socreds that the change had been made 'as a move to purge police spies and other undesirables' who had managed to infiltrate the Edmund Burke Society (*Globe and Mail*, 28 February 1972).

MEMBERSHIP

Fromm was not the only prominent member who decided to leave the Western Guard. Leigh Smith had resigned a month earlier. Gil Urbonas left to promote his own publication, *Speak-Up* (*Toronto Star*, 18 May 1972), and two prominent writers in *Straight Talk*, Kastus Akula[1] and Patricia Young, joined Fromm's *Countdown* (vol. 1, no. 1, June 1972). Also part of Fromm's new team was Jeff Goodall, who had resigned from the Edmund Burke Society as far back as 1970.

Although decimated, the fledgling Western Guard was still a force to be reckoned with. As indicated in chapter 2, at least thirty-three of those who had previously belonged to the Edmund Burke Society continued as members of the Western Guard. In addition, the newly named organization began to attract others who shared its commitment to the goals of white supremacism. Men like Taylor, Prins, and Weiche who had been closely associated with Beattie's Canadian Nazi Party and the National Socialist Party swung their support behind the Western Guard. During the next few years, many of the most notorious figures of the radical right in the 1980s had joined the Guard. Wolfgang Droege, imprisoned in the 1980s for his part in the attempted KKK overthrow of Dominica, was a Western Guard member by 1975 (*Straight Talk*, vol. 7, no. 8, n.d.). Marion McGuire, jailed for severl months in Dominica for her role in that caper, was referred to in *Straight Talk* (vol. 6, no. 4, n.d.) as the 'newest and most stirringly eloquent addition.' Bob Smith, a man saddled with possibly even more personal problems than McGuire, joined the Western Guard in 1972. By 1976 he had become the editor of *Straight Talk*. Other members included Siksna, listed as the chairman of the East Toronto Committee in the mid-1970s; Leo Jutting, later a mainstay of Andrews's Nationalist Party; Eric Thompson, who was eventually to become Zundel's lieutenant; and Proos and Genovese. The latter two had been Fromm's principal followers at the University of Toronto during the heyday of the Edmund Burke Society. Yet they led the attack against him when he resigned. Reporting on a speech given by Andrews at Latvian House on white Canada, Proos (*Straight Talk*, vol. 5, no. 1, September-October 1972) stated that only the really committed had attended, while Fromm's cowardly, 'responsible' anti-communists huddled behind closed doors, gossiping and licking stamps. Genovese became even more prominent in the Western Guard than he had been in the Edmund Burke Society. He was the Western Guard's chairman in the early years, and later became head of the Department of Order, responsible for security. He also was briefly the president of the Ontario Social Credit Association. This man, a graduate in business from the University of Toronto, eventu-

---

1 A decade later Akula was still around, as evidenced by a letter to the editor with an anti-communist message (Toronto *Sun*, 15 June 1982).

ally became a computer programmer for an insurance company, and dropped out of the movement. The reason, Taylor lamented to me in 1982, was that Genovese had married, a fate Taylor said that has ruined the right-wing careers of many good men.

Andrews claimed that the Western Guard had about 300 members around 1975, with *Straight Talk* going to about 1,500 people (Crysdale and Durham 1978: 13). Yet an RCMP infiltrator (*Globe and Mail*, 23 November 1977) put the figure at 40 to 45. I myself have data on exactly 100 members of the Western Guard, almost all of whom lived in Ontario. About 50 per cent of the membership, claimed Andrews (*Toronto Star*, 18 June 1984), consisted of new Canadians who 'find themselves down in the economic scale,' and dwell next to Afro-Asians in the poor downtown areas of Toronto. Elsewhere Andrews has said (Crysdale and Durham 1978: 13–14) that about two-thirds of the members were 'Anglo or Canadian' and the remainder European, with a fair proportion of Germans, Hungarians, and Balkans. They also fell into two age groups, those about 20 to 25 years old, and those about 45 to 65 years old; the younger people were the activists; the older ones provided funds and undertook the research to sustain the organization's racist philosophy. About one-half of the members, Andrews stated, worked with their hands, and the other half was middle class, including lawyers, nurses, office workers, and teachers, with approximately eight men to every woman.

Although the membership was basically confined to Ontario, there was a handful in other provinces such as British Columbia. The Western Guard even claimed to have members in the U.S. Armed Forces and as far away as South Africa. For a brief period there also were branches of the Western Guard in Georgia and New York State (*Straight Talk*, vol. 7, nos. 2, 4, 5, and 6, n.d.). The latter involved a union between the Western Guard and the Buffalo-based National Guard Party, but it only lasted for about a month.

Unlike the Edmund Burke Society which was seen by its members as a political movement, the Western Guard was meant to be a political party. One year after the Western Guard emerged, the name was changed to the Western Guard Party. Andrews was the leader, ruling over an executive council, which included the secretary, the treasurer, the head of the Department of Information, and the chief of security. Shortly after the Western Guard was established, the category of 'supporters' was created for people who did not want to be publicly identified. By 1973, Andrews stated (*Straight Talk*, vol. 5, no. 5, n.d.) that there were three kinds of members: party member, party supporter, and party guard member. The last apparently consisted (at least on paper) of a special cadre prepared to accept party discipline and bear the main responsibility for carrying out the organization's activities, such as distributing leaflets, painting racist messages on buildings, and harassing blacks and Jews. By the summer of 1975, the Western Guard had been organized into a cell system (*Straight Talk*, vol. 7, nos. 5 and 6, n.d.). Among the cells was one for the 'beer drinkers and motorcycle riders' and another for those who wanted to 'sit around all the time and have a nice conversation and drink sherry' (Crysdale and Durham 1978: 20).

THE ANDREWS ERA (1972-6)

With Fromm out of the picture, Andrews emerged as the kingpin in the Western Guard, and remained solidly in place until a court case dislodged him in 1976, allowing the ambitious John Ross Taylor to seize control of the organization. The remainder of this chapter is divided into the Andrews and Taylor eras, each of which had its own special character.

Beliefs

It would be a mistake to assume that with the name change to the Western Guard there was an immediate and massive shift towards the ideology of white supremacism. On the contrary, the early issues of *Straight Talk* under Western Guard control were no more radical (and Fromm's eventual *Countdown* no less radical) than that publication had been in the last couple of years of the Edmund Burke Society. In the first issue of *Straight Talk* after the Western Guard had emerged (vol. 4, no. 6, March 1972), there was an article concerning the organization's opposition to a Jewish painter and a Toronto art gallery. While stating that he did not plan to be frightened off by being labelled anti-Semitic, the writer disclaimed any intent of anti-Semitism. The artist was not being attacked because he was a Jew, but because his work was a perversion of Western Christian culture. Admittedly, even that disclaimer smacks somewhat of anti-Semitism, but the very fact that it was made would be unheard of in later years. Other articles dealt with Social Credit and Governor George Wallace's victory in a Democratic primary. The perspective was certainly right of centre, but no more so than in earlier issues. Fromm remained the editor, Akula the associate editor, and Patricia Young, a syndicated columnist from British Columbia, continued to contribute articles.

The April issue contained another article about Social Credit, and one on abortion. The latter stated that abortion is one of the most dangerous

threats to the Western world: 'It is clear that the target of the abortion campaign is Western Civilization. We, who are the most productive, most creative, and most able to help the backward nations, are being asked to kill
ourselves off.' Strong stuff, but not different from what appeared during
the Edmund Burke Society days. The same was true of the May-June issue,
but by then there were signs of an imminent change of direction. That was
the issue in which Fromm's resignation was reported. Neither he nor Akula
appeared as editor (they were replaced by Andrews and another man), and
it was there that we learn of the pact made with the racist American
organization.

Issue 9, the July issue, was taken up for the most part with Fromm's resignation, but for the first time in *Straight Talk*'s history there was an article
by John Ross Taylor, a veiled account of Jewish involvement with usury
and international finance. There also were references to two books promoting the racist position, and reprinted articles by two prominent American
white supremacists. It was not, however, until the August issues, more than
a half a year after the Western Guard emerged, that the race factor barged
onto the centre of the stage. On the cover of that issue (*Straight Talk*,
vol. 4, no. 10, August 1972) appeared in large type the words: 'Do We Need
a White Canada?' From then until when Taylor took over in 1976, there
were thirty-three further issues of *Straight Talk*, and twenty-five of them
carried explicit racist messages (the others were slogans such as 'Vietnam
Betrayed' and 'Reds at City Hall'). Some examples: 'Race Is the Real
Issue,' 'White Power,' 'Mongrelization of Toronto,' 'Negroes Massacre
Whites,' 'Race Pollution Is Forever,' 'Canada – a White Man's Country.'

From 1972 to 1976, the attack on blacks (and the accompanying claim
that whites had become second-class citizens in their own countries, sold out
by white race-traitor politicians) was relentless. The television show 'All in
the Family' was said to be degrading. Archie Bunker expressed prejudices
felt by most whites, the Western Guard claimed, and then was made to look
stupid as a result. Britain, it was observed (*Straight Talk*, vol. 5, no. 1,
September-October 1972), 'once sent forth men to conquer a world empire,'
but has 'degenerated into little Asians complete with garbage-filled streets
and babe-draped Indian mothers defecating in the gutters.' Over and over
again, it was argued that blacks are an inferior race, that race-mixing is
unnatural and unworkable and that interbreeding is the most dangerous
threat to the white man that exists. The quality of care in Canadian hospi-
tals by black nurses was compared to 'the hit and miss days of bone-nosed
witch doctors' (*Straight Talk*, vol. 6, no. 6, n.d.). Blacks were said to be
disproportionately involved in violent crime. Literature was handed out

indicating that 'a strange tribe of two-toed people who can run like the wind' had been observed in East Africa. One article (*Straight Talk*, vol. 7, no. 8, n.d.) stated; 'You cannot blame or hate the negro for wanting to be with a White woman but you sure can blame this kind of "white women." A white race traitor, man or woman, the fruits of thousands of years of racial segregation, will destroy the seed in one selfish, lustful union.' The expulsion of Asians from Kenya in 1967 served as proof to the Western Guard that the Indians and Africans can't coexist (*Straight Talk*, vol. 5, no. 1, September-October 1972). This, incidentally, is precisely the kind of 'evidence' that the racists gleefully seize upon. What are racial crises to others are heaven-sent 'proofs' to the white supremacists.

Perhaps the overwhelming theme during Andrews's years at the helm was immigration. It used to be 'an exotic treat,' ruminated one writer (*Straight Talk*, vol. 5, no. 9, n.d.), to see a Negro or an Indian with a turban, but now you can't get away from them. Another article (*Straight Talk*, vol. 5, no. 1, September-October 1972) stated: 'If present immigration trends are allowed to continue ... racial conflict on the American and British models is inevitable – in fact, it is as predictable as a mathematical equation.' In the organization's 'Green Paper Brief on Immigration,' apparently submitted to a special parliamentary committee on the topic in 1975, three recommendations were made: 1 / stop all coloured immigration completely; 2 / repatriate non-whites; 3 / give $1,000 to white families on birth of each white child. Elsewhere it was contended that blacks would never think of emigrating to a black- or brown-run country, and that nowhere do whites try to settle in coloured nations (*Straight Talk*, vol. 8, no. 2, n.d.). All this, of course, reflects a remarkable ignorance about population movements in the Third World, and more to the point it conveniently ignores the long history of white colonialism.

We come now to the peculiar perspective of the white supremacist. Race riots are occasions to rejoice. First of all, they may indicate that the white man is finally waking up. Second, they are perfectly 'natural' manifestations, 'natural' confrontations between different species. For example, a racial clash between whites and blacks in Toronto's Regent Park was described as an expression of the whites' territorial instinct, and a perfectly natural hatred between two species. The writer in *Straight Talk* (vol. 8, no. 3, n.d.) stated: 'The Western Guard tried to point out [to white youth] that is is pointless to hate negroes per se – that there is nothing wrong with being a God-created negro. What is wrong is that these negroes have been allowed, through White treason, to invade the Whiteman's living space.' Another article discussed a racial confrontation in Washington, DC, where blacks supposedly beat and stabbed about 1,000 whites: 'The blacks were only doing what comes naturally to them. They were only expressing the natural and healthy hostility of one kind of animal towards a different kind' (*Straight Talk*, vol. 7, nos. 5 and 6, n.d.). The Western Guard also expressed pity for blacks, claiming it is not their fault they can't keep up with whites – they simply don't have the same intelligence. It is partly on this basis that the white supremacists argue that the separation of the races is not only beneficial to whites, but to blacks as well: their supposed genetic inferiority would not then be a handicap. It was in this context that Andrews said (*Straight Talk*, vol. 6, no. 7, n.d.) that he doesn't hate blacks, and in fact thinks it is unfair to turn them loose in white nations because they lack the capacity to survive. There is, according to the racists (*Straight Talk*, vol. 5, no 7, n.d.), one dimension in which whites are inferior: 'No other race is infected with the capacity for such unnatural masochistic self-hatred as Whitey directs towards himself. No other race has the capacity for such concern towards other races. There are no Marches for Millions in India or Africa for flood relief in Mississippi.' The members of the Western Guard, obviously, did not put much faith in the argument that the Third World's poverty is largely the consequence of the Western world's capitalist excursions.

Another peculiar twist to the Western Guard's perspective concerned its enthusiastic attitude towards a handful of other perceived races. The Chinese are said to be admirable because they 'prefer to keep to themselves and treat the rest of us with neither love nor hate.' Even the Jews, usually portrayed as vermin, are worthy of praise in one respect: they are, in the Western Guard's view, 'the strongest racists' of all (*Aryan* WG Universal, Winter 1977–8, WGU 1). Similarly, praise is heaped on one segment of the black community: those who share the Western Guard's vision of a totally segregated world. Taylor claims that fruitful discussions were once carried out with U.S.-based Black Panthers; closer to home, a black group, the New African People's Alliance, said to oppose interracial marriage and to promote black racial pride (*Straight Talk*, vol. 5, no. 5, n.d.), supposedly worked actively to support a Western Guard member's election campaign for public office. Native peoples, who also were regarded as 'good racists' in their own right, were singled out for special attention. They were to be the beneficiaries of a system modelled after South Africa's Bantustans – separate territorial units for Indians and Eskimos. When a group called the Toronto Warrior Society attacked the racist position of the Western Guard, the latter's members seemed genuinely surprised, remarking (*Straight Talk*, vol. 7, no. 2, n.d.): 'Our attitude towards North American Indians has always been amicable.'

Finally, there is the question of race versus nation, and the peculiar position that the 'true' Aryans occupy within it. The names of several of the right-wing organizations – Nationalist Party, National Socialist Party, National Front – reflect the central focus on nation. Yet some white supremacists argue that Hitler himself outgrew nationalism, replacing it by the transnational race concept. Similarly, in *Straight Talk* (vol. 7, no 4, n.d.) we read: 'To meet our goals, we must think in terms not of a White Canada, but of a White Family of Man.' The other point concerns the racist's definition of Aryan. As Chalmers (1981) has pointed out, in the 1920s the Ku Klux Klan in America was opposed to Greeks, Italians, and Balkans. Even in more recent times, some white supremacists refer to people of Slavic, Italian, or Greek descent as 'white niggers' or 'semi-Jews.' Some of the people whom I interviewed who traced their ancestry to Germany, Holland, or Scandinavia commented that they were the 'purest' Aryans. This attitude has been a source of considerable animosity within the movement. In an article entitled 'Is Hungary an Aryan Nation?,' one author concluded that it is; he was himself a Hungarian. Andrews, a Slav, has been particularly agitated about the issue. Germany, he once remarked (*Straight Talk*, vol. 7, nos. 5 and 6, n.d.), 'would never have lost the war if it hadn't been for German chauvinism alienating millions upon millions of fellow White men: namely the Slavic populations of eastern Europe.' He went on to complain that some people think they should be leaders of the movement 'solely on the basis of their belonging to a particular sub-stock of the White race.' He concluded by declaring that ability, not pedigree, should be the criterion for leadership. Coming from a man who has prejudged the majority of the world's population to be inferior on the basis of pedigree alone, his complaint contains not just a little irony.

Anti-Semitism

Whereas anti-communism had been the focal point for the Edmund Burke Society, it was only a peripheral issue for the Western Guard during the Andrews era. The overwhelming focus was racism – specifically, the pernicious attack against blacks and the Third World. Anti-Semitism itself was only a secondary concern of the white supremacists, although its profile grew larger as the years went by. Terms like the 'jewdicial' legal system became more common, and people like Lubor Zink, Barry Goldwater, and William F. Buckley, Jr, were referred to as 'kosher conservatives' who smear white nationalists. Organized crime in America was said to be run by Jews, as were the banks and the media. The usual denial of the Holocaust was made, and Jews were blamed for ushering in the modern liberal thought that has eroded white racial pride. In one article (*Straight Talk*, vol. 8, no. 1, n.d.), kosher slaughter practices were labelled inhuman; words became action when the window of a kosher meat and fish store in Toronto was smashed, and swastikas and slogans were scribbled, such as 'Buy Aryan, Boycott Jewish Business' (*Toronto Star*, 8 March 1976). The attackers signed themselves the National Socialist Underground, almost certainly a Western Guard front (*Globe and Mail*, 23 November 1977).

Again, there were the peculiarly radical-right interpretations of the world scene. The vast majority of Jews were said to be descendants from the Khazars in southern Russia, who converted to Judaism in the ninth century, and thus have no claim to Palestine at all. Golda Meir, it was argued (*Straight Talk*, vol. 5, no. 2, November-December 1972), actually 'forced' Arab commandos to kill the Jewish athletes at the Munich Olympics in order to create martyrs. Jews, it was claimed, not only have the liberty of leaving the USSR whenever they wish, but actually are in control there. Communism and capitalism, rather than being at loggerheads, are merely twin programs controlled by Jews to take over the world. With all this in mind, Jews can hardly be blamed for being sceptical about the Western Guard's claim that it was 'the best friend the Jews have' (*Straight Talk*, vol. 5, no. 7, n.d.).

Actions

A large part of the Western Guard's efforts still went into the publication of *Straight Talk*. In late 1972 Burke's words, 'The only thing necessary for the triumph of evil is for good men to do nothing,' remained on the cover page. By early 1973, that slogan was replaced with the following: 'The Western Guard is dedicated to preserve and promote the basic social and spiritual values of the White People. Under the symbol of the Celtic Cross, we fight for our Christian moral values, our European heritage, and the spiritual and cultural rebirth of our people.' A few months after the Western Guard had been established, two fictitious men – Attila Marschalko and Emilio De Bono – were listed as the editors of *Straight Talk*. As Taylor explained to me, that had to be done in order to provide a semblance of continuity, because there was at the time such a great turnover in membership. Another fictitious character was Anton Degrelle, who often claimed credit on behalf of the organization for acts of violence such as disrupting a homosexual rally.

By 1973, the Western Guard had established its own white-power recorded telephone message. For several months it ceased to operate, but when it was reinstated in 1975, Bob Smith, later to succeed the fictitious editors of *Straight Talk*, delivered the message. The bookstore that had been established by the Burkers continued to operate until the middle of 1972, but then was replaced by several 'bookrooms' in private homes, which probably meant the venture was dead. Western Guard members gave speeches for several Sundays in a row at Beattie's old stamping-grounds, Allan Gardens; acted as guards at the Nationalist Chinese celebrations in Toronto; sold copies of *Straight Talk* on the streets (it also was available in a Toronto smoke shop); and threw their support behind a number of 'sincere P.C. candidates' in a federal election (*Straight Talk*, vol. 5, no. 1, September-October 1972). They also found time to celebrate the birthdays of Hitler and Mussolini.

One of the Western Guard's favourite tactics was to distribute leaflets and to paint slogans on buildings and at construction sites. The latter had become so extensive by the mid-1970s that the Toronto Department of Public Works, Permit Services Branch, had a form sheet for 'Report on Racial Slogans, Signs, et cetera.' I have thirty-five of these reports for April 1975. Some of the slogans were as follows: 'White Power'; 'Racism Is Not Evil'; 'Hail Don Andrews'; 'Kill Communist Pigs – White Power'; 'More Niggers, More Crime – Kill Racial Mixers'; 'Happy Birthday Adolph [*sic*] Hitler.' In 1976 Bethune College at York University was sprayed with swastikas and slogans such as 'Communism Is Jewish' and 'Adolf Hitler College.' The Western Guard even had an 'Action Group' which specialized in such activity. There also was a 'Defence Group Don Andrews' consisting of members who provided the organization's brawn, plus the Western Guard vigilantes who took it upon themselves to patrol Toronto's subway so as to protect white commuters.

Violence was no stranger to the Western Guard. In 1974 (*Globe and Mail*, 8 April 1974), a group called 'the White People's Vigilantes' (again almost certainly a Western Guard front) showed up at a meeting at the University of Toronto organized by supporters of the liberation of Mozambique. Chairs were turned over, the glass doors were smashed, and people were sprayed with mace and with a fire extinguisher. In that same year, on a CITY-TV program ironically called 'Free for All,' Western Guard members went on the attack. A nine-year-old boy was slapped in the face, and a black trumpet player was hit with a piece of aluminum piping. On another occasion, Charles Roach, a prominent black civil-rights lawyer in Toronto, was the recipient of a one-dollar bill on which was written: 'This is to help pay your way back to Africa.' 'White Power' also was stamped on it, and the letter contained a swastika. The window of Roach's law office was smashed, and his furniture and files were splattered with paint (*Toronto Star*, 18 November 1977).

The Western Guard's reputation notwithstanding, it once applied to various Metro Toronto boroughs for a grant to study the effects of non-white immigration on the white population of the country. Both Mayor Crombie and Metro Chairman Paul Godfrey said they would oppose any move to provide the organization with funds. Three members of the Western Guard – Taylor, Prins, and Zapparoli – actually did appear before the Grants Committee of North York Borough Council to argue their case for a $10,000 grant (it was turned down). The Western Guard also tried its hand in the election arena. Andrews ran for mayor of Toronto in 1972, 1974, and 1976, gaining 1,958 (1 per cent), 5,792 (4.6 per cent), and 7,129 (5.3 per cent) votes. Others such as Taylor, Smith, Siksna, Prins, and several lesser-known members ran for alderman and for positions on the board of education. With the exception of Andrews, who placed second both in 1974 and 1976, most of these candidates came in last. Occasionally Western Guard members also ran for public office under the Social Credit banner.

Confrontations with Police
Although the Western Guard, like the Edmund Burke Society before it, promoted slogans saying 'Our Cops Are Tops' and 'Support Your Local Police,' there never was much delusion that the police were allies. In one issue of *Straight Talk* (vol. 8, no. 2, n.d.), it is remarked that these slogans are a source of mirth for the police, who can barely conceal their contempt for the organization. Certainly, police surveillance of the Western Guard, leading to numerous arrests and convictions, was extensive. In 1972, Geza Matrai was sentenced along with his female companion to sixty days for spraying a gas substance at a homosexual meeting at St Lawrence Hall in Toronto. Another Western Guard member was placed on probation for fifteen months for possession of a dangerous weapon and for assault on a 'professional poverty spokesman' (*Straight Talk*, vol. 5, no. 1, September-October 1972). Siksna and another man, who were accused of painting slogans on construction hoardings, became the first Canadians to be charged under Canada's new anti-hate laws (*Straight Talk*, vol. 6, no. 2, n.d.). They were acquitted, as were several others later charged with the same offence. A man closely associated with Weiche in London, Ontario, was sentenced to twenty-eight days in jail for 'assaulting a Jew, an East Indian and a White race-traitor' (*Straight Talk*, vol. 6, no. 9, n.d.). Another man, whose association with the radical right increased after he was arrested on a weapons charge (he testified on behalf of the defence in the Zundel trial), was sentenced to two consecutive nine-month terms. Droege, the man who spent time in an American prison for his part in the

attempted KKK overthrow of Dominica, was jailed for fourteen days for writing white-power slogans at Toronto's St Lawrence Market (*Toronto Star*, 28 October 1975). He also was placed on probation for two years for painting 'White Power' on construction hoardings. In 1976 he was convicted for assaulting a reporter and fined $100 (Toronto *Sun*, 29 April 1981). Not all the opposition to the Western Guard came from the police. In 1974, Andrews's home was gutted by fire, the result he believed of deliberate arson. Around 1976 a member of the Jewish Defence League planted a bomb on the porch of Andrews's house. Andrews gave chase and caught the man, who was eventually charged in court. An article entitled 'Open Season on WGP' (*Straight Talk*, vol. 8, no. 3, n.d.) revealed that in 1976 there were five attacks on the organization, including the fire, the bomb attempt on Andrews's home, and another on his car.

By 1975, Andrews himself had been charged with various offences on at least four occasions, but as it was pointed out in *Straight Talk* (vol. 7, no. 2, n.d.), he had won every case. In 1972, a charge that he had allegedly threatened to murder a former member of the Edmund Burke Society was thrown out of court. He also was acquitted of the charge of common assault on a 'Jewess' (*Straight Talk*, vol. 5, no. 7, n.d.) following a movie about Hitler's last days. His court appearance for his part in the CITY-TV fracas also ended in an acquittal. I suppose that had his various court appearances continued to have had such happy results, the right wing would have soon begun to suspect that he was a police agent. The fact is, however, that by mid-1976 his luck with the legal system ran out, partly because of the efforts of a genuine undercover informer. Andrews and two other men were charged with an arson plot, planning to disrupt an Olympic soccer game at Varsity Stadium involving an Israeli team, illegal possession of weapons and explosives, and mischief; the latter concerned window-smashing and painting swastikas and racial slogans on synagogues and other buildings. Andrews and a follower called Dawd Zarytshansky were eventually found guilty and sentenced respectively to two years in federal penitentiary and eighteen months in provincial reformatory. They were, however, found not guilty, because of lack of evidence, of plotting to disrupt the soccer match, and for the same reason the third man was acquitted entirely. During the trial, Andrews testified (*Globe and Mail*, 21 December 1977) that in the party's organ blacks were described as 'human and organic garbage,' and admitted to a 'general dislike of Jews.' Zarytshansky, a large man who liked to be called 'Tarzan,' reportedly admitted (*Globe and Mail*, 20 January 1978) to writing an unmailed letter to the *Canadian Jewish News* inviting its editor to soak up heat in a solar oven, and police found a speech by Hitler in his home. They also discovered chemicals, smoke bombs, and a book instructing how to make bombs and other weapons under a garage used by Zarytshansky. Obviously, this young man, then only twenty-two years old, had come to embrace a variety of beliefs beyond the anti-communism that he said had originally attracted him to the organization.

The man whose testimony in court led to putting Andrews behind bars was a thirty-two–year–old RCMP paid informer from the Maritimes named Robert Toope. Toope was an appropriate candidate for the job, having been previously identified as an anti-communist during a factory strike. From May 1975 until July 1976 (Toronto *Sun*, 25 November 1977) he was an active Western Guard member, receiving a total of $7,339.40 (tax-free) for his efforts. The RCMP, believing that the Western Guard might attempt to carry out a terrorist attack against the Israeli soccer team (which Toope later confirmed was planned), had decided to place an informer inside the organization. Had they not done so, it is improbable that Andrews and his subaltern would have been convicted. Yet there always is the risk that the planted informer will go overboard and become an *agent provocateur*. That is precisely what seems to have happened with Toope. He said in court (*Toronto Star*, 24 November 1977) that he broke the law more than a hundred times. When his RCMP contact cautioned him not to commit illegal acts, he desisted, but found that his information dried up. One evening he was caught by police while putting up racist posters on private property. His 'handler' had told him that should that happen, there would be no problem, and in fact the charge of mischief was finally dropped after he had appeared in court several times.

Toope testified (*Globe and Mail*, 21 December 1977) that Andrews rarely was directly involved in illegal activities, but gave orders to others to carry them out. In the radical right's view, it was Zarytshansky who in the end sold Andrews out. He gave the Crown a signed statement implicating both of them. As the *Nationalist Report* (issue 43) later commented: 'One can only wonder what grand promises were made to him by the cops, and shake one's hand, a stiff lesson learned from betrayal of one's comrades.'

Andrews, interestingly enough, had been interviewed by two students from York University (Crysdale and Durham 1978: 114) on 13 June 1976, just over a month before he was arrested on 19 July 1976. During that interview he had brought up the topic of police informers and said: 'We have police agents.' It is doubtful, however, that he had known about Toope. In a lengthy post mortem on the Toope affair some years later in Andrews's *Nationalist Report*, the impression given was that Toope had taken everyone by surprise. That article, incidentally, made the point that Toope himself had initiated the various illegal acts, thus unfairly giving the Western Guard a lawless character. Undoubtedly he was at the centre of things. Yet to conclude that in his absence the Western Guard would have confined its activities to rantings and ravings in private meetings is not plausible. With or without Toope, the Western Guard was on a collision course with the legal system of the country.[2]

THE TAYLOR ERA (1976-PRESENT)

I suppose one could see John Ross Taylor's rise to the leadership of the Western Guard in 1976 as the successful culmination of his long and arduous devotion to Fascist politics. In my view, however, it was simply the last hurrah of a desperate man saddled with a disintegrating organization.

Born in 1913, Taylor apparently had enjoyed a privileged upbringing. His English-born grandfather, a Toronto alderman at the turn of the century, had been a wealthy manufacturer, the owner of a soap factory. His father, a successful lawyer, had won a gold medal on graduation from the University of Toronto in political science. Taylor himself never attended university; he told me he decided not to after an interview with a university official who said he was only interested in patching up the holes in society, not transforming it. Taylor, an only child, described his mother as a Boston 'beauty' from a prominent and wealthy family. When his father died, he moved to Boston at the age of six with his mother, where he said he went to an élite school and won honours in public speaking. One of his election leaflets, however, indicates that he attended John Ross Robertson Public School and North Toronto Collegiate Institute in Toronto. The Group of Seven, Taylor claims, were frequent visitors to his family's home. His mother's portrait by Harris apparently hangs in the National Gallery. Taylor contends that his family was on very friendly terms with Vincent Massey, whom he once visited abroad. All this suggests the classical profile of the right-wing radical as described by Lipset and Raab (1970): a clear case of downward status mobility, from the grandeur of his grandfather's status as an industrialist and his father's as a lawyer to his own position over the years as a salesman – Taylor's stated occupation when he has not been involved full-time in right-wing politics.

Taylor once told me that had he not become a Fascist he would have been a clergyman or a healer. In his later years he had converted to Catholicism;

---

2 Zundel told me that several years later the former RCMP informer once delivered a parcel to his office, taking off immediately when he realized where he was. Andrews said he knew where Toope lived, and could reach him any time he wished.

that did not, however, prevent him from criticizing the Jesuits, whom he thought were part of the conspiracy. Earlier he had been a Christian Scientist, and for a while he flirted with the Baha'i faith. Taylor is a vegetarian, drinks alcohol moderately, but does not touch tap water, for the fluoride in it is 'rat poison.' He rarely watches television because of the subliminal messages intended to weaken the will and moral fibre of the white race. Like many right wingers, sexual matters, especially homosexuality, preoccupy him. During one interview, he went on at length about the wife of a very prominent politician whom he said had exposed her private parts in a public place. He also remarked (approvingly) that it was quite possible that Hitler had never consumated his marriage.

Taylor said during an interview that his view had crystallized by the time he was twelve years old. In one of his articles, it is revealed that he formally joined the right wing in 1933. Four years later he was briefly the Ontario leader of Arcand's Fascist party. In that same year he ran for alderman in the largely Jewish riding of St Andrews in Toronto, wearing a swastika on his lapel and giving the Nazi salute; he pulled out before the election actually took place. After being interned at Petawawa for fifty-three months during the Second World War, he worked as a salesman in Saskatchewan. During the late 1940s and 1950s he kept a low profile, mostly because Fascism was then a dirty word among Canadians. Another reason concerned his family. He had three children, two from his wife's previous marriage, and was busy trying to make a living. In 1962 he separated from his wife, and a few years later was divorced. Apparently he has many relatives in Ontario, but said it has been years since he has seen any of them. By the early 1960s, his right-wing views were reactivated. Living in Haliburton, he established his mail-order business. The emergence of Stanley and Beattie drew him farther back into the Fascist camp. In 1963 he again ran in St Andrews riding for the provincial legislature, collecting 102 of nearly 10,000 votes. In 1972 he was a candidate for alderman in Ward 11 in Toronto, finishing in last place with 323 votes. Taylor personally told me that these various election efforts were merely 'token.' He never expected to win; the purpose was to take advantage of the public platform in order to broadcast his Fascist message.

If the Nazi era in the mid-1960s was a sign to Taylor that the climate inhibiting Fascism had thawed, the transformation of the Edmund Burke Society into the militant and racist Western Guard must have seemed like a sunny day in spring. There was no doubt, of course, that Andrews was in charge, but Taylor's profile gradually became more prominent. As early as 1972 his first article in *Straight Talk* was printed. In the August issue of that year, another of his articles, entitled 'Jews and Communism,' appeared.

His agrument was that anti-Semitism was non-existent in the Soviet Union: indeed, the 'privileged' Jews were the only ones who had the option of emigrating, if they wished to do so. From 1972 to 1976, Taylor published several other articles in *Straight Talk*, ranging from an argument that abortion has been foisted on the Western world as part of a communist plan to destroy the white race by encouraging a decline in its birth rate and the mongrelization of its racial stock, to the view that Canada had deliberately fomented war in the Middle East by allowing Canadian Jews to send millions of dollars to Israel. By 1973, Taylor had become a member of the Western Guard executive. By the end of that year he was listed as the chairman of the Propaganda Committee. Shortly after, he became the head of the organization's Department of Truth, and was responsible for the publication of the party organ and other literature.

On 18 July 1976, the day before he was arrested, Andrews resigned from the Western Guard. This was duly reported in *Straight Talk* (vol. 8, no. 4, n.d.): 'The well-liked Don Andrews has resigned from the leadership of – as well as from membership in – the Western Guard Party and has severed every connection with the Party. All persons who were closely connected with him have also resigned.' This undoubtedly was the opportunity for which Taylor had been waiting, because he quickly assumed control over the organization, and embarked on a crusade to belittle Andrews's previous contributions. By the fall of 1977 (*Straight Talk*, October-November 1977), Andrews was being referred to as the *former* leader of the Western Guard. In that same year, Taylor told two student interviewers from York University that the Andrews period was not only irrelevant, but also not nearly 'hardline' enough (Crysdale and Durham 1978: 127). When I interviewed Taylor in 1980, he stated that Andrews's new organization, the Nationalist Party, was unimportant, while the truth was that it had basically eclipsed the Western Guard.

Part of the court order against Andrews was that he terminate all association with the Western Guard. Yet apparently when he was released from prison, Taylor and his deputy, Jacob Prins, were waiting at his home for him. The horrified Andrews, so I have been told, ordered them to leave at once, saying he would secretly contact them (in another version, I was told that Taylor met Andrews outside the prison). At any rate, Andrews's perception was that Taylor was intent on getting him into hot water with the police in order to maintain his leadership of the Western Guard. There is no doubt that Taylor was apprehensive that Andrews would somehow regain control over the organization. On 30 March 1977, Taylor addressed a letter to 'All public media and All White Nationalists throughout the world' accusing Andrews of falsely giving the impression to a Toronto newspaper that he still led the Western Guard. He said Andrews saw his formal resignation in 1976 'only as a cheap trick to appease the authorities until such time as his legal complications would be over.' He claimed that since Andrews was released on bail in August 1976, 'he has done everything in his power to reassert his authority over the Guard or its members and disauthorize and isolate its present leadership.' Taylor continued: 'The Don Andrews that returned from jail has proven himself to be very different in his attitudes towards our party.' While Taylor did not spell it out in the letter, he told me that he believed that Andrews's mind had been warped by drugs and hypnosis while in prison. Taylor concluded his letter by delcaring: 'The party executive has accepted his resignation from the party as permanent and final. There is no place for dictatorial personality cults in the service of our Race and Nation.' The last is certainly a strange comment coming from a Hitler-worshipper, and no doubt attested to the fact that Taylor was running scared.

It must not be thought that Andrews was taking all this lying down. He continued to lure Western Guard members to the new organization that he had founded, the Nationalist Party, with the clever slogan: 'Those who leave the party are the party.' He also accused Taylor of being a police informer. What happened, apparently, was that Siksna went to Prins and said Taylor was an agent. Taylor accused Andrews of being behind the affair, stating (probably correctly) that Siksna would never have done it on his own. Significantly, from a completely different source I found evidence that at one point a prominent Western Guard member may have been informing on a rival right-wing organization to the police.

Beliefs

Although blacks had been the main target during the Andrews era, after Taylor took over anti-Semitism soon dwarfed all other issues. At his direction, the following was inserted into the Western Guard application form: 'I affirm that I am not a Jew by race or religion nor an adherent of Communist doctrines.' Of course, Taylor saw communism and Judaism as inseparable. He once told me that he had done his best to educate Andrews about Jews, but the latter had been a slow learner. On another occasion, he said that Andrews is not ideologically pure. He used to be anti-German, partly because his father had been killed by Germans and partly because of Hitler's attitude towards Slavs. Taylor asked me if I had looked at Andrews's lips. Andrews, he said, is from Eastern Europe, and his racial origin is similar to the Khazar Jews; Taylor cautioned me that it would be wrong to conclude that Andrews *is* a Jew, but left open the possibility.

In Taylor's view, the only legitimate position in the movement was what he referred to as 'the hard line.' That, in essence, meant a no-holds-barred opposition to Jews. All Jews, he said, not just the leadership, are potentially dangerous; Anne Frank's diary is a fake; the Holocaust is a lie; a cure for cancer has been known for years, but has been suppressed by Jews; Canada is the centre of the world (as forecast in the Bible – signs like 'Canaan' for 'Canada'), and Moscow gets its orders from Canadian Jews, who control both countries; the CN Tower in Toronto was built as a communications facility for Jew-Communists to maintain contact with Russia; since the Second World War, German soldiers have been living underground in Antarctica, where they skirmished with Admiral Byrd, and will soon emerge to re-establish Hitler's program. In 1980, Taylor told me that every one of us is a number on a computer controlled by the emerging world government, run by Jews, which would take over in 1984. In June 1982, he said what he had consulted a psychic, and found out that the revolution would take place the next month.

These were not the only bizarre views embraced by Taylor. According to him, for the past several years Canada was embroiled in a fierce but secret civil war. The two principal antagonists were the Anglo Freemasons and the Jewish Freemasons. The former were under the control of Britain and Queen Elizabeth, and the latter were under the control of Jews, supported by Trudeau in co-operation with Lévesque; France and Russia also were in league with the Jewish Freemasons. Lévesque supposedly brought in paratroopers from France in 1978, and there were two waves of Russian invasion. In 1980, 20,000 Russian troops swept across Western Canada. Defeated by the Anglos, 12,000 of their numbers were killed. Taylor asked me if I remembered all the forest fires in Western Canada at that time. They were deliberately set, he said, to cover up the battle with the Russians. The Mississauga train disaster in the 1970s also supposedly was a front. Taylor claimed there was no train accident at all; that was just a ruse to clear out the population so that Anglo troops could march against the enemy. Those who got in the way, he said, were simply killed off. Included here were Brezhnev, Diefenbaker, and John Robarts.

The second Russian invasion supposedly occurred in May 1982 in Ontario. Again it was repulsed by the Anglos. Since then there was, said Taylor, a skirmish at Yonge and Eglinton in Toronto, where twelve Russians were killed. He added that three homosexual Jews had their throats slit by the Anglo Freemasons who were determined to rid the country of such 'scum.' Taylor said in the summer of 1982 that within five weeks there would be a complete Anglo Freemason take-over in Canada; when that occurred, the seat of government would move from Ottawa to Queen's

Park in Toronto. As further proof of the secret war, Taylor once remarked that one only has to look at the age profile of the Toronto police force. There were, according to him, very few policemen between the ages of twenty-five and forty. Why? They had been killed fighting the Russian invaders. He also once asked me if I had noticed that in newspaper advertisements the union jack had begun to appear more frequently. The implication? The Anglo Freemasons were moving in! When they did, he added, people like Andrews and other prominent white supremacists would be as surprised as anyone else, and might actually cause more trouble than the Jews, because their quest for power would have been usurped. All these claims about the secret civil war are, of course, decidedly far-fetched, and there always is the possibility that Taylor was simply pulling the anthropologist's leg. Yet the same claims were made elsewhere, such as in his recorded telephone messages of 12 October and 20 November 1979.

Not surprisingly, the members of the radical right generally defended Taylor to the hilt when addressing the wider public, but within the movement there often was a different reaction to his various bizarre beliefs. On one occasion when I was interviewing two of the most prominent Canadian Fascists, they burst into laughter when I put some white sugar in my coffee. As they explained, it was Taylor's belief that white sugar made one a homosexual. These two men also claimed that Arcand had not dropped Taylor as leader of his Ontario wing before the Second World War because he was not a Catholic, but instead because it soon had become apparent that Taylor was mentally unbalanced. Their evaluation of the man was neatly summed up in their following comment: Taylor, they said, has absolutely no judgment about the issues; he argues with the same fervour about the goals and direction of the right wing as he does about the quality of a plate of spaghetti.

Actions
Although in Taylor's eyes the most important phase of the Western Guard had begun with his leadership in 1976, the fact was that the organization had entered the stage of decline. This was reflected clearly in regard to the organization's principal publication, *Straight Talk*. By the spring of 1976, Taylor still was listed as the director of the Department of Truth (*Straight Talk*, vol. 8, no. 1, n.d.). By the next issue the two fictitious editors, Marschalko and de Bono, had been replaced by Bob Smith. By the late summer of 1976 the announcement of Andrews's resignation appeared, and by the fourth issue (vol. 8) Smith's name no longer appeared as editor. That marked the virtual end of *Straight Talk*. One further issue with the same

volume identification (*Straight Talk*, vol. 8, no. 5, n.d.) followed, but it contained nothing but a long report on a White Confederacy Congress in Cleveland, rather than the usual articles and notes about white supremacy and its adherents. There were, in addition, two other issues bearing the *Straight Talk* label (but with a differnt volume identification: September and October-November 1977). One contained nothing except reprinted newspaper articles and White Power telephone messages, plus a single page about Andrews's trial. The other consisted of little more than a two-page summary of the various phases of the movement since the Edmund Burke Society days.

As *Straight Talk* wound down, Taylor began to promote another publication, *Aryan*, as its successor. Actually, *Aryan* had already been established as a parellel publication to *Straight Talk*, and thus was not new (there also, incidentally, had been a publication called *Aryan* put out by East Indians in Vancouver at the turn of the century). At any rate, the first issue under Taylor's command appeared in 1977–8, but this publication too soon folded. Just as *Aryan* was to be a successor to *Straight Talk*, a new organization called the Western Guard Universal was founded. Its stated aims were to fight Jewish-Freemasonic-Communist world-destroyers everywhere. Taylor made much of its forty-four–point program, but it was simply a copy of the Western Guard's Toronto Manifesto that had been prepared during the Andrews era. There also was a pretentious reference to a forty-four–member World Council of the Western Guard Universal; the executive consisted of Taylor, Prins, and Norm Saxon – the last mentioned having a particularly felicitous name for an Aryan leader!

Other Prominent Members
When Taylor succeeded Andrews as head of the Western Guard, a man who had been closely involved with the radical right for several years (he was a member of a small U.S.-based Klan organization) rose in importance. Jacob (Jack) Prins's claim to the nickname 'Tarzan' may have been even more warranted than Zarytshansky's. At 6 feet 6½ inches and 270 pounds, and with a background in boxing, wrestling, and judo, this man sometimes was referred to as Taylor's bodyguard (a role he had earlier performed for Beattie). Born in the Netherlands in 1922, where he may have trained for his country's decathlon team, Prins apparently studied engineering at the University of Hague. During the Second World War he was captured by the Germans, but eventually came to realize that he was on their side. He married a German woman, lived in Palestine briefly, and immigrated to Canada in 1955, where he has worked as a maintenance mechanic for a large grocery chain. Now divorced, he has four children by his previous marriage.

Prins joined the Western Guard in 1972. He ran for alderman in 1972 and 1974 in Ward 2, finishing in last place both times. Along with several others, he was charged with assault in connection with the mêlée at CITY-TV in 1974. Although never as prominent as Taylor, Prins had been appointed head of the Western Guard's West Toronto Committee during the Andrews era. When Taylor took over in 1976, Prins became membership secretary, co-ordinator of Western Guard Police, and international ambassador. Although these were basically paper titles, they do show that the man's star had begun to rise, at least within the organization itself. Taylor, who once remarked to me that Prins has a first-class mind, gradually relied on him more and more. By 1980, Prins had become the organization's deputy leader.

Another prominent figure was Dr George Zapparoli, who supposedly had a PH D in international law from Yale University. Born in Italy in 1927, with his roots in the nobility of Lombardy, he was forced to leave that country because of his efforts to divide the north and the south and create a 'Germanic' state in the former. He regarded Mussolini as a 'standard and an inspiration to the Western Guard Party' (*Straight Talk*, vol. 8, no. 3, n.d.). Zapparoli, whom Taylor said spoke seven languages and was a direct descendant of the kings of Lombardy, published *Ward 3 News* (two pages in Italian and two in English), a bimonthly for the Italian community. He once ran for alderman in Ward 3 under the Western Guard banner, finishing fifth place in a seven-man race, with 426 votes (3.3 per cent). It was Zapparoli who compiled the Western Guard's 'Green Paper on Immigration.' He also wrote the 'Constitution for the White Confederacy' which was held in Cleveland, Ohio, in the mid-1970s, and prepared the report on the Western Guard's application to the North York Council for a $10,000 grant. Zapparoli had been a member of the Social Credit Association of Ontario, and the deputy leader of the Western Guard. A Catholic, he died in 1977, survived by his wife and five children.[3]

I only learned about one prominent woman who apparently was associated with the Western Guard during the Taylor era. In my first interview with Taylor, he referred to her as an expert on Fascism. Later he said she was absolutely brilliant, possibly the world's leading authority on Hitler. Such was Taylor's high estimation of this woman that he included her name in an affidavit dated June 1980, indicating certain steps to be followed in the event that he was imprisoned. In short, he authorized Jacob Prins to take him to a hypnotist after release to determine if he had been brainwashed, and added that it was to be done in the presence of the woman in

3 See his obituary in *The Toronto Star*, 5 July 1977.

question. One high-ranking Klansman held quite a different opinion about the woman; she simply was too clever, he observed, to be what she appeared: a true believer in the movement's goals. Two female Fascists spelled out their doubts more clearly; it was their firm belief that the woman was an undercover police agent. I had written to this woman in 1982, indicating that Taylor had urged me to contact her. In her reply, she stated that she fully supported Taylor's right to freedom of speech, but added that they had 'had a falling out some time ago concerning his unauthorized use of my name as editor of a publication I did not support.' By that year, her association with the Western Guard, which may have loomed larger in Taylor's mind than in reality, had been terminated.

Taylor in Court

'You can't kill an idea by putting its author in jail.' A pretty good line, no doubt, and it was spoken by none other than John Ross Taylor when it became apparent that the immediate future might find him behind bars (*Toronto Star*, 15 June 1980). With the Western Guard membership decimated and *Straight Talk* virtually finished, Taylor had turned to another outlet: white-power recorded telephone messages. These probably constituted his most effective activity as leader of the Western Guard, but they ultimately brought about his downfall.

In June 1979, the Canadian Human Rights Commission, responding to complaints from the Canadian Holocaust Remembrance Association and other concerned parties, held a tribunal to evaluate Taylor's white-power messages. Just as Taylor had the dubious honour (along with David Stanley) to be the first person in Canada to lose his mailing privileges, he also was the first person to be brought before a tribunal with respect to the legislation on discriminatory telephone messages.[4] Taylor's messages were publicized by cards bearing a maple leaf symbol and a telephone number, and by a notation in the telephone book about 'White Power.' The tribunal, held 12–15 June 1979, raised such thorny questions as: what are the limits of free speech? does it matter that people voluntarily dial the telephone number? and is truth a defence? As the tribunal's report stated (p. 39): 'Strange as it may sound, the establishment of truth is not in issue in this case.' That was because Parliament's position was that the use of a telephone for such discriminatory messages was so basically wrong that no justification could exist. The tribunal's conclusion, after examining thirteen of

---

4 See the Canadian Human Rights Act Human Rights Tribunal, presided over by J. Francis Leddy, Sidney N. Lederman, and Rose Volpini, 12–15 June 1979.

the messages recorded from 1977 to 1979, was that the complaints against the white-power messages were substantiated. It did not have the power to levy fines or impose a prison sentence, but it could issue a cease-and-desist order, which is precisely what it did on 22 August 1979.

Taylor apparently had indicated that he would change the messages, and the one on 29 June 1979, immediately following the tribunal, stated that the Western Guard has not discriminated against Jews. Yet it then went on to say that it has 'proved' communism was founded and funded by Jews, the Holocaust is a hoax, the Anne Frank diary is a fraud, there is a conspiracy of 'certain international money powers ... for the purpose of erecting a Communist-world-slave-state,' and 'race-mixing is more dangerous than atomic war.' Not surprisingly, Taylor found himself in federal court on 19 February 1980.[5] Representing himself in the defence, he read a long diatribe which essentially regurgitated the anti-Semitic and racist line in the telephone messages, plus providing the audience with an unusual review of the history of treason. Some radical-right members later remarked to me that Taylor's defence had been ridiculous. The presiding judge concurred, and Taylor was convicted of contempt of court for disobeying the tribunal's order to terminate the racist telephone messages. He was sentenced to one year in jail and fined $5,000, but was given a suspended sentence on the condition that the messages stop.

In June 1980, a warrant for his arrest and for the Western Guard to pay the $5,000 fine was issued by a federal-court judge because the taped messages, with little modification, continued. Taylor initially went into hiding, but finally turned himself in to the authorities in April 1981. He spent eight days in jail before bail was arranged pending his appeal of the sentence, which he lost. After 243 days behind bars, he was released in March 1982. On 21 June 1982 the Western Guard's white-power message resumed (*Toronto Star*, 22 June 1982). Taylor, who remained head of the Western Guard while in prison, told me that he didn't want to make Andrews's mistake of appointing a temporary replacement who might take over permanently. This certainly was ironical, because that was exactly how Taylor himself had grasped control of the organization in 1976.

When Taylor emerged from prison in 1982, he did not follow through with the plan in his affidavit of being taken to a hypnotist by Prins, in the company of his talented female follower. As Taylor told me, all this was unnecessary because he had not been subjected to mind-altering practices in prison, and the food had not contained drugs. Yet the fact was that the peo-

5 I attended that court hearing, and it was there that I first met Taylor.

ple in question were no longer with him. The young woman had switched allegiance to the fringe right, and Prins had deserted the Western Guard for McQuirter's Ku Klux Klan. The break with Prins, according to Taylor, had been particularly emotional, but he rationalized that Prins had 'always been with McQuirter.' He also said that Prins was not reliable, and that despite his size he always backed away when the going got tough. Prins, Taylor stated, had his cottage up north, and that was all he really cared about. With Prins gone and Zapparoli dead, Taylor's Western Guard had been essentially reduced to a one-man show. Curiously, the man he then turned to for mutual support was John Beattie. Just a couple of years earlier, Taylor had repeated to me the general comments within the right wing about Beattie: the man was untrustworthy, a police informer, partly insane. Yet by 1982 Taylor was referring to Beattie as a possible future saviour of white Canada. It was mainly from Beattie, whom Taylor said was much more sound regarding his attitude towards Jews than Andrews was, that Taylor put together his information about the supposed secret civil war in the country. Taylor and Beattie were by 1982 both pariahs in the right wing, and their common position brought them together.

As the years passed, Taylor became engaged in a variety of sideline activities, such as a submission to the Human Rights Committee of the United Nations, contending that he had been 'a true political prisoner.' To a large degree he was still a figure of derision within the right wing. Yet that critical judgment had been softened as a result of his jail sentence, and by the mid-1980s there was an increasing tendency to regard him as 'the grand old man' of the Canadian radical right.

5

The Nationalist Party

What does the immigrant think as he steps foot on Canadian soil? What are his dreams and fears and prospects? Does he know that the receiving line may include members of the Western Guard and the Ku Klux Klan? And what about the children? How many of them are set adrift in their new country, helpless and vulnerable, slated never to rise beyond the level of second-class citizens? Consider the case of Vilim Zlomislic. A victim of the Second World War, with his father dead and his mother remarried to a man he had never seen, he arrived in Canada about the age of ten or eleven, forced by circumstances beyond his control to adapt to a new land that was far from completely hospitable. No doubt this boy was only one among thousands to share such a fate, but what makes his case exceptional is that he was none other than Donald Andrews himself. The white supremacists constantly contend that heredity explains all, but if ever there was an example to demonstrate the overwhelming significance of environment, Andrews is it.

FROM COMMUNIST TO FASCIST

Vilim Zlomislic was born in 1942 in Yugoslavia. From the outset life was cruel and grim for him. By the time he was a year old, his father had been killed by Nazis and his mother had been shipped to Germany for factory work. Vilim, a Serbian, was put into an orphanage. Blessed with above-average intelligence and charm, the boy apparently thrived; by the time he was seven he had become an outstanding member of the Young Pioneers, a Yugoslavian communist youth group, and was rewarded with a vacation at a camp on the Adriatic. In the mean time his mother had married a Canadian working in a German displaced persons' camp and eventually began a new life in Canada. Although told after the war that her son had been killed in an air raid on the orphanage, she persisted in her search, and with the help of the Red Cross she located him in 1952. In March of that year he arrived at Toronto's Malton Airport. 'Are you my Mum?' he apparently asked his mother in Russian (*Globe and Mail*, 1 October 1979); she hugged him so hard he began to cry.

Thrust into a new country, Donald Clarke Andrews, as his mother renamed him, soon learned English. However, his adjustment was hampered by a severe injury to his thigh that he had incurred at the youth camp on the Adriatic. In Yugoslavia he had spent almost a year in a hospital. After his arrival in Canada he developed osteomyelitis (a bone disease). Between the ages twelve and fourteen, he was confined to a hospital and his home with a leg brace. His leg injury merely compounded his differences from his peers. He was a foreigner, brought up in a socialist country, and unable to join in with his new friends in sports or similar activities. Curiously, it is a background like that which often creates social scientists: one stands on the sidelines, so to speak, observing and analysing, but not participating. Andrews himself, it appears, became a voracious reader. He excelled in school, but because money was scarce he did not go to university. Instead he enrolled in a public-health course at Ryerson Polytechnical Institute, the only institution that provided him with a grant. For about fourteen years he worked as a public-health inspector, a job he lost after spending eight months in jail in 1978. His marriage (he has one child) ended in divorce. Until he was twenty-one he was a member of the New Democratic party (Miller 1971). Weiche told me that Andrews left that party simply because he was ignored, but Andrews himself has said it was as a result of his reading, especially concerning the history of the Second World War. He went through a period of rethinking and re-education which led him to despise all forms of totalitarianism, including the communist variety. As I have stressed earlier, it was not racism or Fascism, but instead anti-communism, that originally drew him to the Edmund Burke Society. Within a few years, however, he had discovered the racist literature (he said Rockwell's *White Power* had a great influence on him), and was openly proclaiming that he was a Fascist. Indeed, the presiding judge in the court case that sent Andrews to jail in 1978 described him as the master-mind behind organized racist attacks in Toronto. I have been told, nevertheless, that he continued to vote for the NDP, assuming that its victory at the polls would be disastrous for the country, and accelerate the revolution in which white nationalists would assume power.

When released from prison, Andrews reapplied for his former position as a health inspector, but was turned down. As an alternative source of livelihood, he decided on the taxi business. The Metro Toronto Licensing Commission, however, refused him a licence because of his 'actions and words against racial minorities' (*Toronto Star*, 24 August 1979) and its doubt that he would treat all passengers without discrimination (Toronto *Sun*, 20 March 1979), or act as a goodwill ambassador for the city. This was somewhat ironical since a number of radical-right members, including some with university degrees, were already making their living driving taxis. Nationalist Party members pointed out that in his capacity as a public-health inspector Andrews had always comported himself in a professional manner (which probably was basically true), and thus there was no reason to deny him a taxi licence. One member asked: 'Would the Commission dare ask Rastafarians if they hate Whites, or Jews if they hate Palestinians ... ?' Curiously, four year later the Licensing Commission changed its mind and granted Andrews a taxi licence (*Contrast*, 17 June 1983).

In addition to the taxi business, Andrews had several other sources of income. He apparently worked for a while for one of his relatives, selling insulation for houses. He also, I have been told, was in the escort business, and one of his rival leaders of the Canadian right wing claimed he augmented his income by acting as a money-lender. Probably his major source of funds was real estate; he owned several rooming-houses in the city, and the capital they generated allowed him to invest in businesses such as a coffee enterprise in the Caribbean. At one point in the 1980s, Andrews and eleven other members of the radical right worked in a Toronto hospital (one person was a volunteer), including Alexander McQuirter, who went on to lead the Canadian Knights of the Ku Klux Klan. Some of them, Andrews among them, were eventually fired for drug-related charges – trumped up, the white supremacists claimed, to conceal the real reason: their political beliefs.

Despite Andrews's demonstrated commitment to the radical-right cause, he was somewhat of an enigma within the movement, and the reaction to him varied considerably. Taylor, for example, was not the only person who held him in low regard. Another prominent Fascist repeated to me Taylor's charge that Andrews was anti-German, and that his mind had been altered by drugs or hypnosis while in prison. Numerous individuals remarked that it was never clear whether Andrews was in the right wing because he genuinely believed in its goals or because it provided tenants for his rooming-houses. Andrews himself once justified his landlord role to me as not just a source of income (although that was important to him), but also as an opportunity to supply a haven for white nationalists visiting Canada or on the run. The accusation that Andrews was manipulative was made time after time. One Fascist, himself a German, referring to the alleged money-lending role, said that it was Andrews's Slavic mentality that if people don't know how to budget their finances they deserve to be taken for a ride. More than one person claimed that Andrews was hungry for the limelight, and couldn't stand to have talented followers around him. They pointed out that many of those who left the Nationalist Party later excelled in other organizations such as the Ku Klux Klan. His supposed manipulative character also was reflected, according to reports, in the manner in which he treated one of his loyal followers. This man, I was told, had to give up his paycheque to Andrews, who allowed him just enough money to become inebriated. Finally, quite a number of Andrews's fellow Fascists claimed that by the early 1980s he had lost heart in the movement, possibly because of his prison term. There were rumours that he was planning to liquidate his assets and resettle in South America. It was said that the time had come when he wanted to enjoy the good things in life: the company of women, pleasant conversation, and economic security. Andrews himself told me that his immediate goals were to become economically and socially secure. I am not certain what he meant by the latter, but as a result of his various business ventures there is no doubt that he was in a better financial position than most others in the movement.

In my interviews with Andrews, it became perfectly evident that he did crave the centre of attention. Whereas portraits of Hitler hang in some of the homes of Canada's Fascists, Andrews's home apparently was adorned with his own portrait (Crysdale and Durham 1978: 113). Andrews had a habit of addressing those around him in an aggressive tone, demanding their attention. Yet as some of his fans remarked, that merely confirmed his capacity for leadership. One of these admirers, referring to the man whose paycheque supposedly ended up in Andrews's pocket, provided a different perspective. That member, he said, was a walking zombie. If it were not for Andrews, the man wouldn't wash, shave, or even get dressed. It was Andrews who tried to keep him functioning as a human being. Still others remarked that Andrews was the most intriguing man they had ever met, and declared that he stood head and shoulders over all other right-wing leaders in the country.

The reaction to Andrews outside the right-wing movement was more consistently negative, but even there we find exceptions. For example, a black health inspector, originally from Jamaica, who worked with Andrews in Scarborough, reportedly said (*Globe and Mail*, 1 January 1979) that while he was opposed to Andrews's politics, and regarded him as a manipulator, he nevertheless liked him as a person. The same was true of one of Andrews's former secondary-school teachers. According to him, Andrews, whom he referred to as 'one of the most tragic failures of his career,' had been a truly brilliant student, with a consuming interest in all topics. He said Andrews got along well with his fellow students and displayed absolutely no signs of being violence-prone. He lamented the fact that Andrews had never gone to university, where his wits would have been sharpened by a sustained critical atmosphere. Instead, Andrews became largely self-taught, and to the chagrin of his teacher, whom Andrews continued to visit after graduating from high school, latched onto the simplistic solutions of the right wing.

In a telephone interview in 1984, this man, then retired from the teaching profession, remarked that Andrews was too intelligent to believe 'all that John Birch stuff.' He contended that the fundamental fact about Andrews was his anti-communism, which he would attack by any means available. At one point he had tried to persuade Andrews to go the university, but the young immigrant had too much pride to depend on his stepfather for what financial support could be offered. Significantly, the teacher said he once approached some friends in the Canadian Jewish Congress to obtain funds for Andrews's university education; apparently the funds could have been made available, but the plan fell through, possibly again because of Andrews's pride. When I told him that Andrews again was likely to be taken to court, this time for spreading hatred through *The Nationalist Report*, he remarked that the Jews must be behind it, and pointed out the irony that the Canadian Jewish Congress had almost financed Andrews's education.[1] This man was prepared to dismiss the racist, anti-Semitic, and violent history of the Western Guard and the Nationalist Party, at least as they involved Andrews, as peripheral features lacking deep roots. Several times he asked me to tell Andrews that he was quite prepared to give him a character reference, or testify on his behalf, in relation to the imminent court case. As he observed, Andrews was simply a victim of the circumstances in Europe from which he emerged, and the subsequent neglect by his mother and stepfather in Canada. He went on to state that in Canada we do little to help immigrants like Andrews. When we leave our workplaces, we shut our doors. Immigrants are simply brought in to the country and set adrift.

My own view of Andrews is similar to his former teacher's, but with one important difference. I concur that Andrews is highly intelligent, with a flair for leadership, and that a great deal of his life has been the tragic consequence of circumstances beyond his control. However, at some point over

---

1 I have not been able to confirm this offer of funds by the Canadian Jewish Congress. Ben Kayfetz (personal communication) was sceptical that it had been made.

the years he went sour. That is, while driven at the beginning by his opposition to communism, his eventual involvement with racial hatred changed him. Like so many others who have spent part of their adult lives searching for reasons to despise the majority of their fellow human beings, he has become a flawed individual, warped by the very beliefs he has embraced.

MEMBERSHIP

Because Andrews had been forbidden by court order to associate with the Western Guard, he decided to establish a new organization. In early 1977 he founded the National Citizens Alliance. In June of that year it was renamed the Nationalist Party. *Straight Talk*, of course, remained in the hands of Taylor's Western Guard, and as a substitute Andrews introduced *The White Nationalist Bulletin*. That was in February 1977, and by the next issue it had been renamed *The Andrews Report*, which in turn became *The Nationalist Report* in 1978. The two earlier publications were modest affairs, mostly two pages in length, but *The Nationalist Report* grew from two to six pages to a solid ten to twelve pages, and signified that the Nationalist Party had become firmly established.

Many former Western Guard members followed Andrews to his new organization. The membership figure usually given to the news media was about 300 in the Toronto area (Toronto *Sun*, 4 March 1979). Andrews told me in 1982 that he had only about 20 really committed members. From my own data on 151 members, I identified 31 who regularly attended party meetings and participated in the organization's activities. Their average age was between twenty-five and thirty-five. Four were women, only two of whom had a high profile. Four of the men had university degrees, eight others had attended college or technical school, an even dozen had only completed secondary school, and one man, then in his fifties, had not gone beyond the primary level (I lack data for the remaining people). One of the thirty-one members worked as a professional, thirteen had white-collar occupations, three were skilled tradesmen, four were blue-collar workers, and three others were unemployed at the time. The following includes some of the occupations held by the Nationalist Party members: manager of a cafeteria, taxi driver, arborist, university professor, tavern owner, bailiff, clerk, manager in a fast-food outlet, computer programmer, research assistant, small-business owner, secretary, nurse's aide, motel owner, house painter and real estate agent.

Fourteen of the thirty-one activists were born in Eastern Europe, and four in Britain. The remaining thirteen were born in Canada, but most of them traced their ancestry back to Britain. Five of the thirty-one were reputed to be police informers – two supposedly a part of the 'red squad.' Almost half of these people had been arrested at some time or another, mostly for acts such as painting slogans on buildings. Two were considered 'heavies' (one was a former boxer), people who served as bodyguards for the leaders and could be counted on in a scrap. At least three were alcoholics, and the same number were considered unreliable and mentally unbalanced. These thirty-one regulars included at least one (covert) Jew, plus a reputed homosexual who had been sporadically involved in the radical right for several years. By 1984, seven of these thirty-one individuals had either formed or joined other organizations, including four in the Ku Klux Klan. At one of the regular meetings of the Nationalist Party in 1979, about twenty-five to thirty people attended. These included a graduate from the University of Toronto who had lived in Mexico for several years, a salesman, an underworld character (possibly a Jew), a cafeteria manager who was born in Ireland, an owner of a motel, an arborist, a businessman, and a teacher. The Nationalist Party, like the Western Guard, was organized into a cell system. In one cell in 1980, there were at least six members. Three were of Eastern European origin, and the others had British roots. In another cell, the ethnic breakdown was the same.

Remarking on the relative absence of female members in his organization, Andrews observed that women posed a problem for the right wing. They often inhibited their husbands and lovers from becoming fully involved. Those who joined only seemed to stay for a few months, partly, Andrews explained, because men were not prepared to take them seriously, and were threatened by women who were strong-willed and intelligent. He referred to organizations like the Red Brigades and the PLO where women were prominent, and lamented that the same was not true for the Nationalist Party. Women, he added, provided a facility very important to the fortunes of the organization: sex as a source of recruitment. He explained that part of the success of a rival organization was that a shapely, promiscuous woman had become a member, in turn attracting several men. A few years ago several young girls – street waifs – stayed at his houses, and the number of men drawn to the organization dramatically increased. If only he could persuade a hundred young women to join, he said, his organization would become an awesome force.

In addition to the cell system, the Nationalist Party was organized into a central or executive committee and an advisory committee. The former was supposed to be anonymous (*Nationalist Report*, no. 27), but Bob Smith, the party secretary, was referred to in the party organ (no. 42) as one of its members. Others probably included Andrews, who had the title of leader; Ladas, who was listed as director (her case is described more fully later); and the position of treasurer, held by the third man who had been charged in connection with the Israeli soccer team at Varsity Stadium. In 1980, the members of the executive and advisory committees included nine well-known members, among them, apparently, the leaders of each cell.[2] In 1979, both McQuirter and Siksna, shortly before they switched to the Ku Klux Klan, were on the executive. Wolfgang Droege, another prominent Klansman, was for a while the official BC organizer of the Nationalist Party.

BELIEFS

By 1977 the fourth phase of the movement that had begun a decade earlier had been reached. The first was the Edmund Burke Society, the second its transformation into the Western Guard under Andrews, the third the Taylor take-over of the Western Guard, and the fourth the founding of the Nationalist Party. For the most part, the beliefs and goals of the latter were identical with those of the Western Guard, as shown in the following sampling of the content of *The Nationalist Report*: Third World immigrants are flooding the 'hard-pressed cities' and getting government jobs and subsidized housing; Mayor Sewell should resign because he appeared on a platform with homosexuals at a gay rally; 'queer power' is taking over Toronto; whites by the year 2100 will consist of less than 1 per cent of the world's population, and will be on the verge of extinction; blacks are disproportionately involved in crime; non-whites are hired first, forcing whites themselves to turn to crime; organized crime is run by Jews, not Sicilians; most feminist leaders are Jewish; 'super-powerful Jews' are taking over the media and the nation's finances; the Zionist Occupation Government (ZOG), reflected in Taylor's imprisonment, is just around the corner. There also was the usual opposition to abortion and drugs. Nevertheless, abortions were not unheard of among radical-right members, and their involvement with drugs did not seem to be any less than that of the wider society. One man once asked me if I liked pot, and some others were regular users. Despite the racial policy, a member of one organization had a reputation of preferring Chinese girl-friends; whether true or not, I heard that for a while he even had a black female companion.

---

2 In 1982, I deduced from a conversation with Andrews that there were five members of the executive committee.

While the message of *The Nationalist Report* was much the same as its predecessor, there was a difference in tone and style. The language of *The Nationalist Report* was less inflammatory, and the content somewhat more sophisticated. This difference may have come about as a result of Andrews's imprisonment, and his hope of avoiding a further sentence. In one issue it was contended that Islam, unlike Christianity, was basically incompatible with communism, and thus the fear that the Arab world would go communist was groundless. This interpretation, of course, removed an obstacle in the way of siding with the Arab world against Israel. Andrews, on behalf of the Nationalist Party, had even contacted Iran, and in *The Nationalist Report* (no. 22) a letter was printed from the Ministry of Foreign Affairs, Islamic Republic of Iran, thanking Andrews for his earlier letter of congratulations on Khomeini's victory. In chapter 3 it was pointed out that not all anti-communists were embraced as comrades by the right wing. The Edmund Burke Society, for example, dismissed the Jewish Defence League as 'anti–anti-Semites,' not straightforward anti-communists. Similarly, the Nationalist Party regarded the Moonies as strictly 'neo-conservatives,' and contended that their unpopularity in the Western world is accounted for by the fact that so many young Jews have joined that religious sect (*Nationalist Report*, no. 41). In the same way, the potentially embarrassing common ground with anti-communist Vietnamese refugees was avoided by declaring that their real duty was to remain in Vietnam and fight the communism there, and that most of the refugees were just 'non-political economic opportunists' (*Nationalist Report*, vol. 2, no. 5, p. 16).

A periodic complaint among white supremacists is that nobody appears to appreciate them. Thus, in *The Nationalist Report* (issues 37 and 38) we read: 'For the last ten years, White Nationalists have battled minority thugs of varying hues and political persuasions in defence of White folks ... Have we received kudos, testimonials and editorials in our favour from the establishment and its various institutions? Emphatically, *no*.' The article goes on to say that the main opposition has actually come from whites themselves, 'the diseased element' of the race. This state of affairs led the organization to redefine its direction and policy. For example, in a later issue of *The Nationalist Report* (no. 46), it is declared: 'we have come to realize that valuable time has been wasted attempting [to persuade] those who are really racial by birth and not by attitude.' The writer concludes: 'Sooner or later, all elements of the White Nationalist Movement will come to realize that it is only those who are the racially aware and informed of their people who will be able to rise to the leadership.' The implication of all this is intriguing: 'white' translates here into an attitude; only whites with the correct racial consciousness are worthy of attention. In other words, a huge hole has been knocked in the white supremacist's assumed 'natural' racial order. Race is no longer biologically defined: it is a state of mind!

ACTIONS

The Nationalist Report consumed a good deal of the energies of the organization. In issue 42 it was claimed that 4,000 pieces of white-nationalist literature had been distributed in recent weeks, and in issue 18 *The Nationalist Report*'s press run was supposedly 5,000 copies. Pride was taken in its appearance in Alberta at the height of the Keegstra affair. A Toronto high-school student spread copies of the publication around his school. The next day he telephoned the principal of the school, pretending to be an outraged minority student, and then contacted the local newspaper to report a racial outbreak in the school – all in order to advertise the white-nationalist position. The well-worn tactic of painting slogans on buildings continued (there even was a 'postering squad'), and front groups like the National Socialist Alliance appeared. Andrews had a capacity to stand back from the fray, in order to analyse the steps necessary to realize his organization's aims. A good example was provided in his powerful article (*Nationalist Report*, no. 28) entitled 'Securing the Future: A Proposal.' There he observed that whites in Canada are living under a Zionist occupation government (ZOG). The solution he suggested was to obtain power. But how? By liberating a piece of territory. He went on to argue that if only 25 people were to move into a small town, and if only 25 more – newcomers and local recruits – would join, then in a town of 250 they would constitute 20 per cent of the population. 'Taking into account children, the very aged, most women and those weak of will, we could control that town.' He added: 'Would it be impossible to relocate that many men and women? – into trailers, rented rooms and apartments, or purchased rural property? Especially if we had pre-existing contacts to ease the way? Some commuting to work by an inter-state, others on Social Security; even dedicated White Nationalist pen-sioners could relocate and help build something worthwhile.' That was only to be the first phase. The second was 'to set up safe zones in other countries ... either by buying property or by taking over territory.' Apparently Andrews's proposal struck a welcoming chord in right-wing circles, drawing responses from South Africa, South America, and Europe (*Nationalist Report*, no. 30.)

A considerable amount of the Nationalist Party's efforts involved broad-casting its message by open and legitimate means, such as letters to editors.

In the Toronto *Sun* (7 February 1977), Andrews had the 'Letter of the Day' in which he publicly requested permission to appear before an inquiry into racial tension headed by Walter Pitman (see Pitman 1977). His request actually was granted, and was greeted by the Nationalist Party (*Nationalist Report*, issue 45) as the first major victory for the rejuvenated white movement after Andrews had been forced by legal rule to terminate his association with the Western Guard. A rather mild letter to the editor by Andrews also appeared in *The Toronto Star*, (18 February 1977) stating that Canadian sanitary standards are far superior to those in other (Third World) countries. Another of his letters in the same newspaper (19 November 1977) argued that if half a million East Indians showed up in Peking demanding jobs and housing, there would be a massacre. Other members also were successful in getting letters published in the major newspapers, sometimes under pseudonyms.

The Nationalist Party made a major effort to contest various elections. There never was any delusion that its members would gain office. The purpose was to force the electorate to confront 'the real issues facing Canada today, which the phony major parties refuse to discuss – sensitive issues such as immigration, the future racial composition of this country and the powerful minority with anti-Canadian interests who controls the finances and economy of Canada.' The latter, obviously, was a reference to Jews. Nationalist Party members were candidates for the board of education and for alderman; when Andrews ran for mayor of Toronto in 1976 it was actually under the short-lived National Citizens Alliance. A few years later, Siksna also ran for mayor, finishing in sixth place with 870 votes, under the banner of the Ku Klux Klan.

In 1977 the Nationalist Party embarked on a drive to obtain 10,000 signatures necessary to qualify for tax exemption as an officially registered political party. However, the Commission on Election Contributors and Expenses rejected its application on the grounds that many of the 13,000 or so names were signed by the same people. As a direct result of the Nationalist Party's application, the rules on party status were changed. Previously all that had been required was a signature of the person willing to support a party's application for official status. Now there had to be a witness to each signature, and the address and telephone number of both the person signing the form and the witness had to be included. One of the attractions of being formally registered as a political party is that there is a partial rebate of election expenses if parties win at least 15 per cent of the popular vote in a riding (*Globe and Mail*, 22 February 1979).

Andrews insisted that the approximately 13,000 signatures that had been obtained were genuine. He added that it was true that people often didn't know what they were signing. For example, if one of his workers knocked on the door of a 'Chink,' he wouldn't spell out exactly what the party stood for. Andrews said that as a result of the government's rejection of the Nationalist Party as a formally registered party, he no longer intended to play the game politely. It was that rejection, he remarked, that led him to adopt the cell system, and to engage in clandestine activities. Some of his followers apparently had opposed the reorganization of the Nationalist Party into a cell system. They said that Andrews had done it not because of the signatures crisis, or for security reasons (those were just convenient excuses), but instead in order to reduce the chances that he would be overthrown internally. By dividing the membership, he was better able to control it.

Finally, in 1980, a few months after the Ku Klux Klan's dramatic appearance, discussions were held concerning a proposed amalgamation of that organization and the Nationalist Party. Both Droege, by then McQuirter's lieutenant with the Klan, and Andrews confirmed that the merger was imminent (*Vancouver Sun*, 10 September 1980). The Klan supposedly would convert into a federal political organization under the name of the Nationalist Party, and the existing Nationalist Party would be confined to an independent Ontario branch, retaining its current executive. The proposed union soon ran out of steam. As Bob Smith stated (*Toronto Star*, 5 November 1980): 'Any previously reported rumors of mergers between the party and the Klan are merely that – rumors, and have not been and shall not be consummated.' The official explanation for the breakdown in negotiations concerned differences in tactics and ideology. The more probable reasons, however, were first that each organization intended to take over and control the other, and second the animosity between Andrews and McQuirter, the principal rivals at the time for the leadership of the white-supremacist movement in Canada.

OTHER PROMINENT MEMBERS

In the early 1980s I began to hear rumours that one of Andrews's members was challenging him for the leadership of the organization. What was interesting was that the challenger was a woman. Anne Ladas had originally joined the Western Guard after finding some of its campaign literature on her doorstep. She switched along with many others to the Nationalist Party when it was established. An only child, she was born in Greece about 1955, but brought up in Canada. Now divorced, she had trained in secretarial school for two years, and when I met her she was working as a secretary; she said that her superiors knew about her political views, but did not bother her.

Although reasonably intelligent, her biases and limitations stood out clearly. She affirmed the old-fashioned view of women as naturally emotional, family-oriented, protective, and most fulfilled when in the home. Had she not become involved in the movement, she remarked, she would never have been well-educated; now, she told me, she can tell what is propaganda and what is truth in the newspapers. As often is the case with right-wing individuals, sexual issues appeared to be emotionally charged for this woman, although in her case possibly their only real significance was that they suggested the moral decay of society. She referred often to loose women and the permissive sexual contacts of today. Homosexuality was in her view especially evil. In a letter to the editor (*Toronto Star*, 29 October 1980), she wrote: 'If nature's intention was for men to love themselves and for women to love themselves, we would not have any civilization; you and I would not be here ... It does not take a genius to realize that homosexuality is not right.' She remarked during our interview that homosexuality is abnormal, a mental disease, but unknowingly contradicted herself by stating that if there were no laws or customs against homosexuality, we would all engage in such behaviour. Defectors from the movement, she said, often are accused of being homosexuals, even if it was not true, because that was about the worst thing one could say about somebody.

Ladas said that her father was left wing, and totally opposed to her association with the Nationalist Party. Nevertheless, it had been him, she insisted, who had initially alerted her to the Jewish problem – not overtly, but in little ways. Most Europeans, she stated, are aware of the nature of Jews, but that is not necessarily true among North Americans. In fact, she added, it is quite possible that many Canadian Jews actually believe that six million people died in the Holocaust. When I asked if she knew any Jews personally, she said she formerly worked with a Romanian Jew. She even liked him. But she argued that he wasn't typical, and moreover was himself ignorant about the insidious Jewish conspiracy.

Ladas gave her views about why so few women belonged to the right wing. Women, she stated, aren't prepared to put up with the scandal that accompanies membership, plus the economic insecurity and the potential danger. She revealed that her house (then Andrews's too) was bombed in 1976, and that over the years she often has received threatening telephone calls, claiming, for example, that letter bombs had been mailed to her. While she said she did not dwell on the danger aspect, it was always behind her mind.

Ladas, who had run for a position on the board of education in 1980, finishing in last place with 3,801 (19.5 per cent) votes (her strong showing earned her a front-page photograph in issue 30 of *The Nationalist Report*), was eager to impress upon me that not all members of the right wing are 'kooks.' She insisted that she herself was not simply a one-dimensional political fanatic. Previously she had kept her distance from the Greek community in Toronto, but had started to become more involved (she ranked her interests in this order: white nationalism, the Greek community, and womanhood). When I met her in 1982, she was involved in an effort to elect a Greek Canadian as alderman under the Progressive Conservative banner. She remarked that the Progressive Conservative platform defied her own political views, and that the people connected to that party were so boring compared to those in the Nationalist Party. Yet she insisted that it was not simply the drama and excitement that attracted her to the far right.

Of the handful of prominent female members of the radical right about whom I learned, Ladas was the least unbalanced and fanatical. In an interview a few years ago (*Globe and Mail*, 19 April 1978), she remarked that just because she and her fellow members 'had certain views,' that did not mean they were white supremacists or out to put people down. The really committed racists do not bother with such qualifications. This woman also stated that she sometimes wondered if the cause was worth it, if the white people who are so unreceptive to the message are worth saving. I formed the impression that somewhere down the road she might gradually withdraw from the movement. Yet initially I was completely wrong. It was rumoured that as Andrews's zeal for political action was waning, hers was expanding. When I interviewed her, she became perturbed only once; that was when I remarked that there was talk that she had taken over the organization. As she explained, there was no single leader. Instead, the organization was run collectively by the executive. Nevertheless, when I mentioned that I would like to meet a specific individual, she said she would arrange it; she did not say that she would have to consult Andrews or other members of the executive. Another rumour was that Ladas was determined to go on a new signature drive in order to register the Nationalist Party as an official political party. About the same time she and another man were apparently playing around with the idea of establishing a new political party, possibly funded by an American group involved in anti-Semitic activity. The plan was to attract people not previously identified as neo-Nazis, although her partner, a German-Hungarian in his late twenties, apparently was a Nazi fan (I was told that his father had been in the SS during the Second World War). Despite all these signs of radical-right fervour, by 1983 it did indeed appear that Ladas's commitment to the cause was declining. She was chosen as the delegate for the Conservative party representing the Beaches-Woodbine riding in Toronto (*Nationalist Report*, no. 44) to attend that party's convention in Winnipeg at the time when Joe Clark was clinging to power. A document produced by the Canadian Jewish Congress (21 January 1983) alluded to the Conservative party's 'long and honourable record of opposition to all forms of racism,' and regretted its failure to recognize that Ladas was an unsuitable candidate. By the following year, Ladas was working as a volunteer in a former journalist's election campaign, and my sources, correct or not, indicated that she had pretty well cut her ties with the neo-Nazi movement.

On one occasion in a downtown hotel in Toronto, I met several members of the Nationalist Party. One of them, a short, dark, thin man with glasses, a moustache, and drooping black hair, was nervous and uncommunicative and I wondered at the time if he was an alcoholic or drug addict. A few months later I interviewed this same man, Robert Smith. Apparently he had joined the Western Guard after moving into one of Andrews's rooming houses. Over the years he had risen to the position of party secretary and editor of *Straight Talk*. He later became editor of *The Nationalist Report*. He ran for a position on the board of education in 1972, 1976, and 1980, and for alderman in 1974, finishing with less than 5 per cent of the vote each time except in 1980, when he placed sixth out of nine candidates with 8.5 per cent of the vote. In 1980 he also was secretary of the Canadian Anti-Soviet Action Committee.

Smith, a somewhat scholarly-looking man, about thirty years old when I interviewed him, and of Irish-Polish background, had been brought up in Toronto. His father died when he was about eighteen, and his mother two years later. He has a sister who is a nurse, but had lost touch with her. As he pointed out, he did not have any family ties that might have interfered with his political life. Smith studied journalism at a community college. At times he came across as a frustrated novelist. He told me he would like to write screen plays, and professed an interest in television quiz programs, reflecting a fascination with language. His actual occupation at that time was a low-level position in the same hospital where Andrews had been employed. Smith said that he had never been political until he joined the Nationalist Party. He gave me three reasons why he became a member. First, he was disturbed by Kruschev's declaration that communism would bury America. Second, he was abhorred at Marx's intention of going against nature to create a new (unnatural) social order. Third, he was immensely impressed by Andrews. My own interpretation is that the last reason was the fundamental one. Ruminating about his youth in Toronto, Smith lamented the fact that everything was changing, that there no longer was any tradition. Toronto, he claimed, had become the New York of the north – the centre for muggings, rapes, and racial clashes. He declared that his political beliefs – especially those dealing with race – came first in his life. His view was that the white race must mount an enormous campaign to prevent its disappearance, and that if the battle is lost, all of mankind will be finished, for it won't be able to survive without its creative force – the Caucasoid race.

If Ladas represents the kind of right-wing member who was reasonably normal and mentally well-balanced, Smith represented the lost-soul type. An epileptic alcoholic, unmarried and with no family ties, he was precisely the kind of 'loser' that some people claimed Andrews purposefully sought as members. Certainly, Smith did not have a strong personality, and one could never conceive of him being a threat for the position of leader. The expression 'Andrews's clones' was heard often in the movement, and in my experience nowhere did it fit so well as with Smith. He affected Andrews's style of talking, even using the same distinctive phrases that were part of his leader's practised spiel. From different sources I heard that this unfortunate man once tried to drop out of the radical-right movement. For a while he just disappeared. When Andrews finally located him, he found an inebriated, unkempt, barely functioning human being. He also, apparently, found an article Smith had written for future publication: 'How I Escaped from the Jaws of Fascism.'

The next member about whom I shall talk will remain anonymous, because he is not a publicly known Fascist and racist. Yet his story is important because of his middle-class background and its potential for racial politics, and because of the manner in which he was converted to the Fascist line. He was born about 1955 in Northern Ireland where he lived for the first seven years of his life. An only child (he wishes he had siblings), his parents live in Toronto and vote NDP. His father once saw some of his son's neo-Nazi books, and was very angry, warning him not to get mixed up in that nonsense. His mother works as a clerk in a large organization, and his father in a similar capacity on the city's periphery. With his brownish curly hair and moustache, this young, slightly overweight bachelor presents himself as a very average young Canadian. He remarked that he has always been easy-going, just one of the boys, with lots of friends. He used to play hockey, and when I met him still played on a baseball team at the institution where he was employed as a manager. Like Smith, he said he never had been a joiner of clubs or political groups, and the Nationalist Party was the first organization to which he had committed himself. The turning-point in his life came when Andrews got a job in the same institution. At first, he said, he hated Andrews. The latter, who had begun as a dishwasher, eventually was appointed assistant superintendent, and almost succeeded in getting the former's job. In the view of these strains and animosity, how, then, was the man converted? It began, he told me, when Andrews started to present him with 'hard facts' rather than mere propaganda about the biological differences among the races, and especially the insidious but largely unappreciated 'Jewish problem.' He said that even before he had met Andrews, he didn't like 'niggers,' but had been ignorant about the menace posed by Jews. Andrews, he remarked, opened his mind. It could be reasonably concluded that this man had been prone to racism, but the key factor in his conversion was probably his leader's charismatic personality. He stated that Andrews was the most intriguing person he had ever met. He claimed that the Nationalist Party leader could have excelled in any endeavour, and had he entered establishment politics he would have been a famous Canadian today. Yet that, he added, was what was so admirable about Andrews: he would not go against his beliefs and principles simply to achieve fame.

This man said that as a result of his conversion to the racist line, he was beginning to lose his old friends. Just a week or so before I met him, a friend whom he had known since a boy had kicked him out of his house in sheer disgust. The same thing, he said, had begun to happen at parties. It was so unfair, he insisted, because underneath all his friends were racists too. He added that there was absolutely no chance that he would replace his old friends with new ones within the Nationalist Party. With the exception of Andrews and a couple of others, he said, there was hardly anyone to whom he could talk. He described the membership as crude, rough, uninformed, unsophisticated, and low class (at one point he remarked that he couldn't even talk about hockey to most of them). There was definitely, he observed, a class difference between himself and most other members. This worried him in two respects: first, because he had put himself in a situation where he had to associate with such crude people; and second, because he was aware that his class biases were interfering with his commitment and contribution to the cause.

This man's remarks about the social-class basis of membership do not really clash with what I have stated earlier, although they do accurately describe a portion of the membership. Referring to a man who was considered half-crazy, Andrews once said that there are dozens like him in the movement. Many of those whom the Nationalist Party attracted, he remarked, were simply looking for a home. They were misfits, had suffered major setbacks in life, financial or otherwise, and saw the movement as their salvation. Some typical examples: a young man from a broken home who said he joined the Nationalist Party for 'social' reasons – he rarely held a job, and drank heavily; an older alcoholic of Dutch origin, who lived in one of Andrews's rooming-houses, and apparently hit the bottle hard after each pay day; a woman, also an alcoholic, with a reputation for promiscuity; a wealthy man who was considered even by other members to be unpredictable and scatter-brained. Yet these cases were balanced by others such as a suave individual who has been active in right-wing circles since he was about sixteen, and who managed to live a life of leisure on the basis of his wits alone. Then there was a young woman, attractive and intelligent, raised in a solidly middle-class family, whose privileged upbringing featured plays in New York and travel abroad. In addition, many of the members of the Nationalist Party who were referred to by our middle-class character as low class, unsophisticated toughs were actually his equals or superiors in terms of education and class background. But as I have pointed out earlier, sustained participation in the politics of white supremacism takes its toll. By the early 1980s, many of Andrews's followers had been involved in the right-wing movement for a decade or more. For some of them, even the pretence of responding to the conventional norms of social conduct had become too much of an effort.

CONCLUSION

For perhaps the majority of the right-wing organizations, their fortunes rested on the skill and drive of a specific person, and that was certainly true with regard to the Nationalist Party. Individuals of talent like McQuirter and Droege may have been temporarily associated with it, and Ladas may have for a while caught the leadership bug, but the bottom line is that without Andrews there would not have been a Nationalist Party. Several milestones in his life that led to his eventual right-wing position stand out: first, his birth in Yugoslavia, a socialist country; second, his being a victim of the Second World War, with his father dead and his mother remarried and living in a foreign country; third, his severe leg injury, which hindered his adjustment to a new way of life in Canada; fourth, his lack of funds for a university education. None of these, of course, inevitably led him to the right wing, but they profiled that option in his vision. Perhaps the key factor complementing these 'structural conditions' was the man's personality. Andrews, blessed with superior intelligence and a gift for leadership, seems to have needed recognition, even off-centre recognition. Furthermore, some individuals do not seem to be able to exist without a total ideology to sustain them. When their commitment to one belief system (be it communism, Catholicism, or a scholarly paradigm or school of thought) is broken, it must immediately be replaced by something new. Andrews appears to be one of these persons. All available information suggests that as a boy he was a true believer in communism (he himself remarked that had he remained in Yugoslavia he would have been an important communist leader today). His current commitment to Fascism is the flip side of the coin. Despite the various signs that he has lost his zeal for the white-supremacist cause, I remain sceptical. First, he has already demonstrated his tenacity; indeed, not even a prison sentence could slow him down. Second, in many respects he is locked into the radical right. The movement has become his way of life. It is to some extent his source of livelihood. It also is his last source of self-respect. If he were to pull out of the movement, where else could he achieve comparable recognition? What would he do? Who would want him?

6

The Ku Klux Klan

Violence is the last resort of the incompetent. An interesting proposition, and in this case an ironical one, because these were the words of James Alexander McQuirter (Csanji 1981), who ended up in prison on a series of charges including conspiring to overthrow the Caribbean country of Dominica and to murder one of his fellow Klansmen. Violence and incompetence may have come together in these bizarre episodes, but before they did McQuirter had proved himself anything but incapable. Indeed, with little else to draw on except the Klan's sensational name and his own talents, he became a media celebrity overnight, generating more heat from less fire than perhaps any other member of the right wing in recent memory.

HISTORY OF THE KU KLUX KLAN

On Christman Eve, 1865, in Pulaski,[1] Tennessee, six former Confederate soldiers established what apparently was originally intended as a social club. The name 'The Merry Six' had been considered (*White Racism in the 1980s*, n.d. p. 6), but one of the men who had studied Greek suggested 'kuklos,' which means band or circle in Greek; the final rendition was the Ku Klux Klan. The early Klansmen saw themselves as a moral force, upholding law and order, but as Forster and Epstein (1965: 13) have stated: 'The Klan's chief aim was to intimidate the Negro into absolute submission, to drive out the "carpetbaggers" and to destroy every vestige of Negro political power in the Southern states.' The defence of the moral order translated into propping up the status quo, which brought the Klan the implicit support of the white majority. Throughout 1866, bands of nightriders dressed in white

---

1 The town was named after a Polish hero of the American Revolution.

robes terrorized the black population, as well as whites who did not toe the line. At a convention during the following year, a former Confederate Army general, Nathan Bedford Forrest, was elected as 'Grand Wizard' or leader. By the fall of 1868, the estimated membership was about 550,000. In that same year, Forrest, stating that the Klan's purpose of protecting the South had been fulfilled, claimed he had disbanded the organization (Anti-Defamation League of B'nai B'rith, 1982: 72). In reality, a remnant of it continued to exist until the turn of the century, finally dying out partly because of government legislation that made hooded nightriders illegal, and partly as a result of infiltration by government agents.

In 1915 there was a robust revival of the Klan, led by William Joseph Simmons. Whereas the original Klan had been primarily anti-black, the second wave was also opposed to Catholics, Jews, organized labour, communism, and foreigners. It was during this period that the intimidating practice of cross-burning (Klansmen prefer the expression 'cross-lighting') was introduced, as well as a woman's auxiliary section called 'Kamelia.' Largely as a result of efforts by two capable publicity agents, who pocketed a percentage of the membership fees, by the early 1920s the Klan had grown to over one million members. In 1923 a Texas dentist named Evans succeeded in wrestling power from Simmons. Under his leadership, Klan growth was even more remarkable. An estimated three million to six million people joined up (Lipset and Raab 1970: 21), or 15 to 20 per cent and 25 to 30 per cent of the total adult male population and the Protestant population, respectively. During that period, the Klan had not only spread beyond the South, but also had become as much an urban as a rural phenomenon. Leading citizens and businessmen were members (Lipset and Raab 1970: 124), as were a disproportionate number of policemen and clergymen. In many states, and at all levels of public office, the Klan exercised influence. Indeed, three former presidents of the United States supposedly have been Klansmen: Warren G. Harding, Woodrow Wilson, and Harry S. Truman; the latter, according to King (1980), 'was known to quote scripture purporting to show the inferiority of blacks, and ... used the epithet "nigger" until the day he died.'[2]

In Canada, where there was around that time a comparable sharp climb in membership, especially in Saskatchewan, prominent individuals were not lacking. In chapter 2 I indicated that a number of Protestant clergymen

---

2 Truman's alleged connection to the Klan has long been public knowledge. Even the *Toronto Star* (7 November 1982) referred to it, indicating that he only remained in the organization for a brief period.

became Klan members, and that the Klan was implicated in the election arena. It has been reported (Henson 1977: 6) that David Mullin, a farmer who became minister of agriculture in Alberta when the Socreds were in power, once was a member of the Ku Klux Klan. More controversial is former Prime Minister John Diefenbaker's alleged connection. McDougall (1981: 5) states outright that Deifenbaker was a Klansman in Saskatchewan in the late 1920s. However, Robin Winks (1971: 324), the leading scholar on Canadian blacks, puts the case much less forcibly. According to Winks, a Liberal candidate in Prince Albert accused his Conservative opponent, Diefenbaker, 'with being hand in glove with the Klan.' If that was true – and in my judgment there is considerable reason for being sceptical – he was only one among numerous politicians who saw the Ku Klux Klan as an asset in their election campaigns.

The Klan membership in the United States fell as rapidly as it had climbed, and by 1926 there were only about 350,000 members. In 1944 the organization was officially dissolved after the U.S. Bureau of Internal Revenue had ordered it to pay more than one-half million dollars in back taxes. A similar quick decline occurred in Canada, but partly for a different reason. In 1927 two professional organizers, Lewis A. Scott and Finlay Hugh Emmons, whose combined efforts had accounted to a large extent for the Klan's growth in Saskatchewan, absconded with the membership fees.

In 1954 the U.S. Supreme Court's ruling on school desegregation became law. That momentus event, along with forced school busing (referred to by a Louisiana Congressman in the *NAAWP News* as an act of 'liberal fascism'), and the general stimulus given to the Civil Rights Movement, paved the way for a third Klan outbreak. By the late 1970s, there were an estimated 10,000 hard-core Klan members, plus an additional 100,000 active sympathizers – people who contributed funds, subscribed to Klan publications, and attended rallies (Anti-Defamation League of B'nai B'rith, 1982: 23). Over the years, efforts had been made to unite the various Klans into a single organization, but never with much success. By the 1970s, more than three hundred autonomous Klans existed in the United States. The three best-known were the United Klans of America, Inc., led by Robert Shelton; the Knights of the Ku Klux Klan, led by David Duke; and the Invisible Empire, Knights of the Ku Klux Klan, headed by Bill Wilkinson. Shelton's organization, with an estimated 3,500 to 4,000 members was the largest of the three. Duke's, while only half that size, stood out for two reasons. First, it was the most openly anti-Semitic of all the major Klans. Second, it supposedly represented the 'new' Klan, with its members dressed in business suits, and violence and crude 'negative' racism, as opposed to 'positive' racism, relegated to the past. Whereas other Klans has women's auxiliaries (the Kamelia), Duke proudly pointed out that in his organization women were full members with the same rights as men (*U.S. News and World Report*, 23 June 1975). Of course, the pronounced anti-Semitic element in Duke's 'modern' Klan was not accidental. While the earlier Klans were mainly opposed to blacks, today's Klan regards blacks as the pawns of Jews bent on destroying the white race. Duke himself, born about 1951, epitomized the image that he attempted to promote. A history graduate of Louisiana State University, well-groomed, handsome, and intelligent, he was a frequent guest on talk shows and university campuses. In the mid-1970s, he ran for the Louisiana Senate, capturing one-third of the vote. He also, as we shall see, had a major influence on the Canadian scene. In 1980, Duke left the Klan to promote a new organization, the National Association for the Advancement of White People (NAAWP), a take-off on the NAACP. His successor was Don Black, who later became implicated in the plan to overthrow the government of Dominica.

Wilkinson had joined Duke's Knights of the Ku Klux Klan about 1974, but a year later quit to form his own organization, which grew to about 2,000 to 2,500 members. This former electrician and Navy veteran claimed he had members in South America, South Africa, Australia, and Europe, including 500 in Britain alone (*Patterns of Prejudice*, vol. 3, 1977: 16), which he visited in 1978. My sources indicated that in the early 1980s there was in fact a branch of his organization in British Columbia. Included among the new generation of Klansmen were Vietnam veterans; one report (*Nordwest Zeitung*, 26 May 1981) suggested that there were more than 1,000 Klansmen in West Germany, with most of them on U.S. military bases. Wilkinson took a special interest in the Klan Youth Corps, which he saw as an alternative to the Boy Scouts (*New York Times*, 13 September 1981). The irony is that his organization was considered to be the most violent of all. In recent years, Wilkinson's reputation has suffered somewhat as a result of the widespread knowledge that he was an informer for the FBI.

There were, in addition, a number of smaller Klan organizations of some importance. The National Knights of the Ku Klux Klan, now almost defunct, was led by James Venable, an elderly Atlanta attorney. Venable's family once owned all of Stone Mountain in Georgia, where the 1915 rebirth of the Klan took place. An Indiana organization, led by William M. Chaney (Confederation of Independent Orders of the Invisible Empire, Knights of the Ku Klux Klan), had about 1,500 members, and another 500 or so people belonged to independent groups like the Ohio Knights and the Adamic Knights.

While it can be assumed that over the years there have always been a few Canadian members in the American Klans, the Klan presence on Canadian soil during the 1950s and 1960s was certainly not organized or overt. In 1965 at Amherstburg, Ontario, a village with approximately three hundred blacks and four hundred whites, a fiery cross was burned, and blacks were threatened by individuals who identified themselves over the telephone as Klansmen (Winks 1971: 449). It was never proved that they were genuine Klan members. Venable supposedly had members in Canada at that time (Forster and Epstein 1965: 10), and Jacob Prins, who later joined McQuirter's Canadian Knights of the Ku Klux Klan, had apparently been a member of the Adamic Knights when the Western Guard emerged in 1972. That same year also saw the establishment of a Klan organization in Alberta which even other Klansmen like McQuirter considered bizarre (especially when a black man joined it). When the Alberta Klan made friendly gestures towards the Conservative party, the president of the Medicine Hat federal Conservative Association reportedly said he wouldn't seek the Klan's support, but would accept it if offered (*Calgary Sun*, 31 August and 9 September 1972).

Canada was not totally unaffected by the Civil Rights Movement in America (there were some signs of black power in Halifax and elsewhere), but what finally stimulated Klan growth in the country were the changes in immigration regulations in 1967, which removed most of the earlier racial criteria, and the official policy of multiculturalism. Canada has always been regarded by American racists as fertile ground for recruits. It was American promoters who had boosted the Canadian Klan membership in the 1920s. Rockwell, the late leader of the American Nazi Party, claimed as far back as 1960 (*Globe and Mail*, 31 October 1960) that he had a branch in Canada. He also once remarked (Toronto *Telegram*, 13 March 1963) that by 1972 he would be the president of the United States, at which time he would annex Canada. The man who had the most impact on Canada was David Duke. Sher (1983: 87) states that in 1974 Siksna had contacted Duke with the intent of organizing a branch of the Knights of the Ku Klux Klan in Toronto. Two years later, Duke claimed to have affiliated branches in Toronto, Montreal, Calgary, and Vancouver. As he observed (*Globe and Mail*, 22 March 1976): 'We are growing faster in Canada than in the U.S. because we hardly had anything there before.' Metro Deputy Police Chief Jack Marks, it was reported, said that the Klan had been in Toronto since about 1977 (*Globe and Mail*, 28 June 1980). That was the year that Duke visited Toronto. Referring to Canada as 'the last bastion of white supremacy because it was already too late to save the U.S.,' he requested a meeting with

Attorney General Roy McMurtry whom he accused of denying free speech to white Canadians opposed to non-white immigration (*Toronto Star*, 14 March 1977). In that same year, James Alexander McQuirter, accompanied by John Ross Taylor and Wolfgang Droege, made a trip to New Orleans to meet Duke.

Duke was especially enthusiastic about the prospects for white supremacism in British Columbia. In a telephone interview with a reporter (*Vancouver Province*, 9 January 1978), he boasted that there were hundreds of Klan members in the Vancouver area. In his organization's publication, *The Crusader* (issue 50: 11), it was claimed that the western provinces in Canada were at the top of Klan growth in the world. There also was a two-page spread devoted to the Klan in Canada, and an article on Droege. Duke visited Vancouver in 1980. He was eventually expelled on the grounds of his criminal record in the United States (for inciting a riot), but not before he appeared on local talk shows. In January 1978, the Klan got headlines in newspapers (Toronto *Sun*, 22 January 1978) when Jim Alexander (McQuirter's first two names) was invited by a teacher to speak at Cardinal Newman High School; the principal cancelled the talk. In December 1979, an interview was given to the Toronto *Sun* by a man identified as Bruce March, who claimed that the Klan was growing rapidly in the city. It was not, however, until the summer of 1980 that the Klan burst openly into the public. Alexander McQuirter, one of whose aliases was 'Bruce March,' announced the Klan's presence, and set about to put things right in the country. Much to the chagrin of Canadians none of this went unnoticed below the border. An article in *The Washington Post* (16 August 1980), reporting on the resurgence of the Klan among their Canadian neighbours, remarked that their 'long-held beliefs that their racial practices are superior to those of their American neighbours' is open to doubt.

JAMES ALEXANDER MCQUIRTER

The Ku Klux Klan organization that rolled into the limelight in 1980 was above all else a propaganda vehicle, and in terms of media coverage and public reaction it penetrated to some degree every province in the country, plus the Yukon. However, its presence was most pronounced in Ontario and British Columbia, which will be the focus of this chapter. In order to capture the character and make-up of those who led the organization, a specific individual from each of these two provinces will be singled out for detailed attention. For Ontario the choice was obvious: James Alexander McQuirter.

'I can honestly say,' McQuirter said in an interview recorded by an infiltrator, 'that about 95 percent of the people that I know would probably rather not be in the Klan. I can tell you that I would rather not be in the Klan, I would rather be enjoying myself in a happy and racially untroubled society but unfortunately I can see what's happening.' How was it that this young man, only about twenty-two when the Klan surfaced in 1980, began to see the world through racist lenses, and assumed responsibility for saving the nation's white population? One of his close associates pointed out that McQuirter was raised in subsidized Ontario housing in an area surrounded by wealthy Jews; it was that background, he argued, that gave birth to McQuirter's racist inclinations. Yet in my view that could not have been any more than a contributing factor. In the world of scholarship, deterministic theories, one-blow knock-out explanations, are always seductive, and it would be convenient if we could come up with one for McQuirter's case. But the fact is that there was little in his background that led him inevitably to the politics of racism, and certainly nothing comparable to Andrews's past. McQuirter, the eldest of five children, was brought up in Toronto in what he described as a middle-class, liberal family. His roots are basically British, and he was raised as an Anglican. He has described his religious convictions as much the same as those of the average church-goer, but one of his young members told me he was not religious at all. His parents, who were not happy with his politics, were separated and living in different provinces. McQuirter's own marriage ended quickly in divorce.

McQuirter served in the Canadian militia for four years, during which he became an instructor. He once said to me that he wished circumstances had unfolded differently so as to allow him to become a teacher (one of his aunts taught Latin in a town near Toronto). When he was fourteen, he was, he claims, a Marxist. He used to frequent left-wing bookstores, but came to the conclusion that most of the literature was beyond the comprehension of the ordinary citizen. He decided not to go to university because graduates whom he met did not impress him. Moreover, they all spouted one-sided liberal-socialist propaganda. His only lament was that in some people's eyes he lacked the legitimacy that a university degree would have conferred. While still in high school, he joined the Western Guard. When he was seventeen, he became a member of the Ku Klux Klan; his membership form is dated 12 August 1977; it is probable that he joined the Klan after visiting Duke's headquarters in New Orleans that summer (another document indicates that in that same year McQuirter received an honorary Doctor of Divinity from the American Fellowship Church). By 1979 he was a member of the Nationalist Party as well. He once received a formal letter from

Andrews congratulating him for placing third in a competition within the Nationalist Party to obtain the 10,000 signatures enabling it to qualify for official party status in Ontario.

In 1980, McQuirter, with Armand Siksna and Wolfgang Droege as his lieutenants, emerged as the self-proclaimed leader of the Canadian Knights of the Ku Klux Klan. Why did he do it, and why in particular the Ku Klux Klan, an organization that was bound to rally the anti-racist forces against him? In McQuirter's view, men like Taylor and Andrews spent most of their time preaching to the already converted. His worry was that he too would be ignored by the wider public. The moment that he publicly announced the formation of the Klan, he became a media sensation. As he himself remarked, whereas previously nobody paid any attention to him, he was at once flooded with so many invitations to be interviewed and to appear on talk shows and television that he could not keep up with them. The Ku Klux Klan label, *because* of its notoriety, was exactly the eye-catcher that he had been searching for.

No doubt there was another factor contributing to his media success: the man's personal characteristics and talents. Over and over again, there were media reports about his attractive personal appearance (he was, indeed, tall, handsome, and well-groomed), and the calm, reasonable manner in which he explained the Klan's goals: 'he looks like an Ivy League College student'; 'he speaks with the lofty ideals of a Boy Scout councillor' (Canadian Press, 5 December 1980) – these were the repeated descriptions of the leader of the Ku Klux Klan. McQuirter was certainly not unaware of the impact of his appearance. In one interview recorded by an infiltrator, he said: 'Always take the wind out of their sails by dressing up the direct opposite that they would expect. Don't look like a hillbilly and if you can, diet and be reasonably thin, that's good. Make sure you put on a good appearance, somebody you would like to look at, talk to and listen to and that you would feel you would like to have at your living room table to eat and meet your family.' In a letter that I accidentally came upon, sent by McQuirter while in prison to one of his Klan followers, he remarked: 'I go out early each morning because then I can grab a shower. I do this in the morning so as to look clean for any visits or jail officials.' As far as his racist message was concerned, McQuirter divorced himself entirely from the orientation of men like Taylor, whom he considered out of date and defeatist, waiting for the Jews to take over the world so he could then say he told us so. Although not well read, McQuirter was articulate, and displayed a poise in front of the media cameras far beyond his years and experience. This man, who modelled himself after the sophisticated David Duke, also had a flair for the quotable quote. He had, he said, always been an ecologist – saving the white man was simply an extension of saving the whale. And elsewhere (Csanji 1981): 'If they can put people on the moon, we can put the negroes back in Africa.'

As in the case of Andrews, there were widely divergent views about McQuirter within the radical-right movement, but for quite different reasons. Whereas Andrews was considered by some people to be overbearing, manipulative, anti-German, and perhaps not even fully committed to the cause, McQuirter was generally regarded as pleasant and likeable. Why, then, the diversion of opinion about the man? One reason was simply jealousy: McQuirter was getting all the attention. Some people, especially those who had been around the right-wing scene for several years, dismissed him as a pretty boy. They said he had the makings of a good PR man, but lacked substance. Taylor once said that McQuirter was a nice young man, but completely ignorant. Another right-wing leader remarked that McQuirter is in love with himself, and can't stop gazing at his image in the mirror. But there were other reasons as well. Quite a number of people thought McQuirter was an undercover police agent, or at least a police informer. The leader of one organization explained to me that the police had inside knowledge that the Klan was going to be formed. They decided to put in their own man – McQuirter. As this other man commented, the police often tried to recruit their agents among those who had some military experience; as a former militia officer, McQuirter was perfect for the job. A leader of a different organization, who also believed McQuirter was a police agent, remarked that it was extremely unusual for a white supremacist to get the widespread media coverage enjoyed by McQuirter. The latter's reputation was not enhanced by his actions of aiding police to get the goods, in the form of a tape-recorded statement, on a man who had threatened to kill a prominent politician. McQuirter, fearful that the man would commit violence and in that way jeopardize the prospects of the right wing, contacted the police, and with a tape recorder pack provided to him, tricked the man into making a confession. One might have expected that after McQuirter was sentenced to several years in jail all thought of him being a police agent would have evaporated. But that was not the case. One wealthy man closely associated with the Klan remarked to me that the jail sentence was the perfect ruse, the stroke of genius. McQuirter, if he was in fact working for the police, would be given an early discharge, and would then be in a perfect position to dictate and undermine the fortunes of the radical right.

Finally, there was the issue of the man's sexuality. Hardly an interview went by without someone claiming that McQuirter was bisexual (and sometimes homosexual, or a transvestite), or else asking me what I had heard and what I thought. Even a gay spokesman in Toronto remarked that he had wondered about McQuirter. One rumour was that there had been a plan to compromise a prominent politician in a health club, with McQuirter playing the role of seducer. Nevertheless, the people who knew McQuirter best were of the opinion that he was not homosexual or bisexual. They did state, however, that McQuirter appeared to be afraid of women, and never formed lasting relationships with any of them. This viewpoint was even expressed by one of his fond admirers who had joined the movement because she had found the man so attractive.

To sum up, McQuirter, like a few others in the Canadian radical right, was a man of many talents, which makes his devotion to a flawed philosophy even more lamentable. While he did not match Andrews's incisive analytic capacity, he was more imaginative, always able to come up with new ideas for promoting the cause. McQuirter liked to wear the mask of the boy next door, just an ordinary, reasonable person with a normal concern about the world's problems. He once remarked (*Ottawa Citizen*, 8 July 1980): 'We're not a lunatic fringe – in many ways we could be the racial minorities [sic] best friend.' He repeatedly denied that the Klan was prone to violence, and said that he himself was a completely non-violent person. Yet McQuirter was also the man who casually conspired to murder one of his own members.

AL HOOPER

Could a boy who marched in peace rallies and sang in church choirs grow up to become a member of the Ku Klux Klan? Well, in the case of Al Hooper, the Grand Kleagle or chief organizer for British Columbia, the answer is yes. Several Klan members in that province could have been singled out for detailed analysis, such as Farmer, Droege, and Cook,[3] but for two reasons I have selected Hooper. First, like McQuirter he was born in Canada, and it is important to stress that not all members of the right wing are transplants from Eastern Europe, Germany, or Britain. Second, the manner in which he was converted to the racist cause, in the process repudiating his liberal upbringing, is significant.

---

3 More will be said about these three later in the chapter. Some of the names of the Klan members are aliases, including a couple already mentioned in this chapter.

Hooper not only sang in church choirs (he once toured Europe with a church group, performing in cathedrals) and marched in demonstrations supporting Greenpeace, ecology issues, and the movement to ban nuclear armaments, but he also was raised in a distinctly multi-racial family network. His relatives include Native peoples, and his aunt was married to an eminent black medical practitioner (Hooper used to spend time in this man's home). His brother's wife was partially Jewish, as was one of Hooper's girl-friends. According to Hooper's mother, he was a gentle, sensitive child who could not bear to see an animal hurt, and until he was eleven or twelve was a perfectly normal individual.

What, then, went wrong? A person who knew his family intimately traced his radical transformation back to his family setting. Hooper had been exceptionally close to his older brother, so much so that there were worries that neither of them would have outside friends. When Hooper was about twelve, his brother did make another friend. The younger sibling was devastated. For about a year, he remained inside the house reading. When he emerged from that reclusive stage, he flipped over to the other extreme. He began to run with a gang, and increasingly demonstrated the need to be the centre of attention, with a constant coterie of admirers around him. As a rebellious teenager, he became exceptionally difficult to control. He was brought up, one informant explained, at a time when schools were extremely permissive; not forced to study, he did nothing. He was constantly in trouble with school authorities, and spent five months in the Salvation Army's House. For a brief period he attended a private school – a place for rich kids, he remarked. But his friends ridiculed him and tore his clothes, and for his own sake his mother removed him from that institution. He also went to an 'alternative' school where I was told he smoked marijuana with his teachers – all of whom were Marxists, said Hooper. He managed to complete grade eight, but went no farther.

Coinciding with his turbulent school years was an equally upsetting home life. His mother was definitely liberal in orientation. A professional social worker, she was even a member in the 1980s of the British Columbia Organization to Fight Racism (BCOFR), the major liberal umbrella group in that province opposed to the Ku Klux Klan. His father, an independent businessman, while far from a supporter of the Klan – indeed, I was told that he was constantly in anguish because of his son's involvement, and lived in fear that something horrendous would happen to him – was decidedly conservative in orientation. Hooper was close to his father, and when his parents separated, it was with him that he decided to live. That was in South

Vancouver, an area which Hooper referred to as 'Little India.' There were many street battles between white and East Indian youths, and Hooper himself was beaten up several times. By then he was running with a pack of whites, and he began to question his entire liberal upbringing. The conclusion that he arrived at was that the left-wing and liberal perspectives could not handle the reality that was part of his daily experience – that the different races could not get along together. When exactly he became a committed white supremacist and a member of the Ku Klux Klan I am not certain, but it was quite probably during the period when he began to hang around with a motorcycle gang, which included some members of the Klan.

If Hooper had always sought fame of some sort, he certainly had achieved it by 1982, when he emerged as one of the leading lights in McQuirter's Canadian Knights of the Ku Klux Klan. Then about twenty-five years old, with long blond hair, blue eyes, and a slight paunch, but tall and rangy with a pleasant, almost engaging manner, he had all the pat right-wing answers about the world scene: blacks are genetically inferior, the Anne Frank diary is a hoax, and Jews are spearheading a conspiracy to enslave the white man. What really annoyed him, however, were East Indians and communists. The former he described as the most despicable race on earth. They never, he said, give up their customs, dress, or language, and always smell of curry. He contended that East Indians were taking jobs from whites, and complained that one's landlord in Vancouver rarely was white (another Klansman whom I once met with Hooper had a French-Canadian landlady, which he resented equally strongly). Blacks, Hooper said, weren't very numerous in Vancouver, but were vocally visible and pushy far out of proportion to their numbers. Hooper was very positive about Native persons, but was perplexed that they always sided with East Indians against the Klan in demonstrations.

Hooper told me his own personal goal was to drive communists such as the Communist Party of Canada (Marxist-Leninist) (CPC-ML) out of British Columbia. He stated that he had once infiltrated that organization, but had been exposed because he could not look the leader in the eye, such was his hatred of communism. In 1982 he was found guilty of assault on a member of CPC-ML. He was fined $100, placed on probation, and ordered not to have any further contact with the man he had attacked and to keep off the block where the CPC-ML bookstore was located. While it was clear that Hooper's antipathy towards East Indians and communists was deep-rooted, my impression was that his opposition to Jews was much more shallow. As a member of the Duke-influenced Klan, he was expected to regard Jews as the white man's greatest enemy, and at times he did spout that line. Nevertheless, Jews, he once remarked, were not nearly as visible or dangerous in his part of the country as were East Indians.

As a result of his turn to the politics of racism, Hooper became alienated from his family. He virtually never saw his brother or sister, and had minimal contact with his mother. He was very close to his grandmother, and apparently continued to visit her with a gift on Mother's Day. Occasionally he worked as a labourer and gained some remuneration from a mail-order business for right-wing materials, but generally he was unemployed. On one occasion when I was interviewing a close observer of the far-right scene, he ventured the opinion that a few years down the road neither McQuirter nor Hooper would be part of the movement. Both, he thought, were salvageable. While I am sceptical in McQuirter's case, it is possible that he will be proved correct with regard to Hooper. Hooper once commented that he wondered if the only reason that he had become involved in the Klan was to rebel against his liberal upbringing. There was, in my estimation, an essential difference between McQuirter and Hooper. McQuirter was a single-minded, purposeful individual. Life did not unfold around him accidentally. There was a clear goal to be obtained, and all his thoughts and actions were consciously pointed in its direction. Hooper, in contrast, lumbered through life casually, as surprised as anyone else at the events that unfolded daily. The Klan had brought him the admirers and fame that he had long sought, but one's impression was that his involvement with the men and women in white sheets had always been something of an accident. An individual who knew Hooper intimately observed that although he had sought fame before, he had failed at everything he had attempted, not because he lacked capacity, but because he could never sustain interest in anything very long. This person's fervid hope was that Hooper would ultimately lose interest (and thus fail) in the Klan as well.

MEMBERSHIP

The membership of the Canadian Knights of the Ku Klux Klan was divided into full or active members and associate or secret members. The first were organized into dens, small groups (comparable to cells) ranging from three to twenty people. The second (estimated by one infiltrator to constitute 90 per cent of the membership) consisted of people who subscribed to Klan literature and paid membership fees ($30 annually, plus a $15 initiation fee – less for prisoners and adolescents). Klan leaders claimed there were dens in places such as Kitchener, Hamilton, Walkerton, Hanover, Windsor, and

Barrie; the last, McQuirter stated (*Windsor Star*, 30 September 1981), was particularly suitable, since in 1926 that small city hosted one of the largest Klan gatherings in Canada, supposedly attracting about 2,000 people. McQuirter was called the National Director or Grand Wizard; there also was a Grand Chaplain in both Toronto and Vancouver, and other members had the usual bizarre Klan titles such as Klaliff (second in command in a den), Nighthawk (sergeant-at-arms), and Grand Kleagle (chief organizer).

The policy of refusing to divulge the number of members in organizations such as the Ku Klux Klan served more than one purpose. It was a means to avoid paying income tax on membership fees, and it made possible the gross exaggerations of membership figures. For example, at one point the Klan claimed to have 7,500 members across Canada (*Vancouver Province*, 9 March 1981). The more usual figure given was about 500 members and a further 2,000 supporters and sympathizers who subscribed to Klan literature (*Ottawa Citizen*, 8 July 1980). Droege (*Globe and Mail*, 27 June 1980) claimed a nation-wide membership of several hundred people, while Attorney General McMurtry said there were only about 30 members in Ontario (*Globe and Mail*, 17 October 1980). Neil Louttit, the reporter who infiltrated the Klan for a few months, put the figure at about 200 for that province, adding that the KKK newsletter had a press run of 300 in Toronto. A man with inside information said there were approximately 200 Klan members in Toronto in 1981, and that perhaps 25 to 30 of them were infiltrators or informers (including himself). There also were about 30 Klansmen in Hamilton, about 20 in Kitchener, and a handful in Niagara Falls.

A police officer involved with Klan surveillance said the estimated number of members in British Columbia was about 100. From another source within the organization, the figure given to me for Vancouver was about 75 Klansmen, only 15 to 25 of them hard-core. Another individual within the right wing said the Klan in 1980-1 had about 300 members on paper across Canada, adding that many of them were infiltrators and curiosity seekers, and perhaps only about 20 of them were totally active and committed to the cause. A different person with inside information estimated about 50 hard-core members in Toronto, and 200 in the rest of the country. A British Columbia Klan spokesman claimed (*Vancouver Province*, 15 February 1982) more than 200 members in that province alone. My own data include information on 221 members of the Ku Klux Klan (3 of them were members of fringe-right organizations, but covertly belonged to the Klan); 149 of these lived in Ontario, 62 in British Columbia, 3 in Alberta, and 7 in other provinces or the Yukon.

Most of the Klansmen lived in cities, and according to some commentators were primarily working class or lower-middle class. As Louttit stated (Cerar 1982: 7): 'We are looking typically at a young man in his early twenties, who isn't very bright academically, who finds it difficult to hold down a steady job, and who is looking for some kind of identity or meaning in his life.' Louttit had Ontario in mind, but a similar portrait for British Columbia was drawn by Droege (*Vancouver Sun*, 2 April 1980): 'The typical Ku Klux Klan member in B.C. is a young, blue-collar worker living in Surrey.' McQuirter undoubtedly was successful in attracting several young members without much formal schooling, who were willing to carry out acts such as defacing property. For example, in 1981, five KKK members were charged with spraying racial slogans on construction hoardings (*Globe and Mail*, 16 February 1981). Two were seventeen years old, and the others in their twenties. Three of them received the maximum prison sentence of six months. Significantly, while on numerous occasions in the past, court officials have refused to consider the racist element in such acts, the judge in that particular case said he imposed the maximum sentence *because* the acts were of a racist nature. In Toronto there were regular recruitment meetings each Thursday evening. Usually between six and eighteen people attended. Talks were given by men like McQuirter, Droege, and Prins, or a tape by David Duke was played. McQuirter and other leading Klansmen wore their white robes while initiating new members. Normally only a couple of people would join each week. Some would return several times before committing themselves, and others were turned off at their first meeting by the Nazi line.

While I agree that the Klan probably had attracted more young, relatively uneducated people than had most other radical-right organizations in the country, it would be a mistake to conclude that it did not have its share of highly educated, middle-class members. As one student (she will remain anonymous) who interviewed Klan members in Toronto stated in her essay: 'The Klansmen I spoke to surprised me. They are not stupid people. In fact, they seem more intellectual than most people I come in contact with.' I can state for a fact that the very top ranks of the Klan included four university graduates, with several others among the associate membership. McQuirter sometimes boasted that he was on good terms with a member of Canada's Senate. While I am unable to verify that claim, I can confirm that the senator and McQuirter had a mutual acquaintance in Ottawa who was well known for his anti-Semitism.

There was a difference between the Ontario and BC membership. The latter included some employees of a trucking company, plus several members of a motorcycle gang. One prominent Klan member in Vancouver said that the bikers were a dubious asset, for they gave the Klan a bad image; he added, however, that they came in handy at rallies and confrontations. This man revealed that when the bikers first joined the Klan, there had been a plan to put them all into a single den in order to contain them. But that did not work out, with the result that the bikers began to define the Klan in general.

BELIEFS

A great deal of the arguments of the white supremacists consisted of a blatant confusion between environment and heredity. For example, in one Klan publication (*Spokesman*, vol. 1, no. 3) blacks are portrayed as biologically interior to whites. The proof? There are no important black golfers, hardly any good black tennis players, and in basketball, where blacks predominate, there are few black coaches who succeed against teams with white coaches. Usually, however, the 'modern-thinking' racist's message was more sophisticated. Thus, in Duke's *NAAWP News* (no. 1) it is asked: 'Do you believe in discriminating against a better qualified and harder-working individual on account of race?' In most non-racist publications, the writer would be referring to blacks, but the punch line in this case is that it is white people who are the victims; affirmative action is described as 'a mask for the most massive and intensive program of discrimination in American history.' McQuirter, modelling himself after Duke (including the anti-Semitic emphasis: *Mein Kampf* was his bible, and on the wall of his office was a portrait of Hitler and a large Nazi flag), claimed he did not hate blacks, and was only standing up for whites; if black is beautiful, he stated, why can't whites say that white is wonderful? McQuirter, who preferred the term 'white nationalists' to 'the radical right,' said in an inverview taped by an infiltrator: 'I don't agree with an apartheid system where blacks live on one side and the whites live on another side because there's always going to be animosity. The Negroes will always look to the white side and say, gee I wish I could do that or I wish I could drive in that and I think that's wrong to do that, it's chauvinistic. Allow the Negroes their own life, their own cultures, in their own countries where they're happy. The negro race is best suited to a tropical climate, our race is best suited to the European climate.' McQuirter's plan was to repatriate Canadian blacks to Africa, or to American states set aside for blacks.

Whites, McQuirter remarked, aren't necessarily the smartest in everything. He stated that Japanese and Chinese perform better in mathematics and purely abstract logic. Yet that, in his view, just showed that the races are in fact different, and that whites 'don't sit around and look at numbers all day.' Instead, they are explorers, given to creative acts. As regards IQ tests, McQuirter said one must always make it clear in interviews that one is dealing with averages; thus, an occasional black man's score will be substantially higher than the average white man's score. When critics remark that IQ tests are culturally biased, he said one should say of course they are, for they are testing if a person can 'live, reason and work in the North American environment.' Blacks, he continued, have been in North America for several generations, and still haven't come up to white standards. Rather than pointing his finger at the massive discrimination that has contained them, he concluded that it is a matter of genetics.

McQuirter promoted 'positive' racism, pride in the white race, and said he was opposed to 'negative' racism, the view that non-whites are inferior. He claimed that any fanatics who contacted his organization and said they hated 'niggers' were shown the door immediately. The sophistication of McQuirter's Klan, at least in the public domain, was reflected in a 'notice' that appeared in each issue of the organization's publication, *The Spokesman*:

The Spokesman does not willfully promote hate against any identifiable group. This paper, although it believes in racial differences, opposes racial hatred. All those who oppose multiracialism should attack the politicians who promote it, not the immigrants who are merely its victims. This newspaper is not anti-Semitic, but anti-Zionist. Zionists are not members of an identifiable group, i.e., not a section of the public distinguished by colour, race, religion or ethnic origin. All Zionists are not Jews, and not all Jews are Zionists. The Spokesman believes all statements made in its pages to be true with respect to any that would be prosecutable under Section 281.2 of the Criminal Code.

McQuirter once stated in an interview that the Talmud 'is the most sick and perverted and disgusting book I have probably ever read.' Anti-Semitism dominated *The Spokesman*. In one article in that publication (vol. 1, no. 1) entitled 'Can Zionists Be Trusted?' there is a photograph of former Israeli prime minister Menachem Begin, who is referred to as a terrorist. In the next issue there is another photograph of him, presented in the form of a 'wanted' poster, below which is stated: 'It is believed that this man may attempt to pass himself off as a statesman and a moderate. Do not be fooled. Menachem Begin is in fact one of the most notorious *War Criminals* still alive and at liberty in the world.' Somewhat less prominent in *The Spokesman* was the white supremacist's pernicious view of blacks. In one issue (vol. 1, no. 5) there are drawings of Caucasoid, Negroid, and gorilla skulls; the latter two are portrayed as similar. The same message was conveyed in drawings of white, Negro, and chimpanzee teeth. Despite these attitudes, McQuirter's view was that the greater the amount of Third World immigration to Canada (and the more unemployment and inflation), the happier he will be, because that will help turn whites into genuine racists. The Klan was particularly pleased with the results of a Gallup poll released by former multi-culturalism director Jim Fleming that showed 31.3 per cent of Canadians would support groups working for an all-white Canada.

ACTIONS

The Ku Klux Klan's ultimate goal was 'to assume control of the municipal, provincial and federal governments.'[4] Four distinct stages on the route to eventual power were envisaged: 1 / propaganda; getting media coverage, and putting messages across to whites; 2 / building the hard core of Klan structure: primarily a stage of internal organization, self-examination, and leadership assessment; 3 / the period to go public and show the Klan's strength: this was the time to attract mass support and to gain political offices by contesting elections; it was not a propaganda stage; it consisted of working within the existing political system; 4 / seizing power from the 'liberal left.'

McQuirter, ever the flexible racist, deliberately set out to employ 'left-wing' tactics. In the Klan's *Handbook*, advice is given on how to wrestle power away from rival political candidates: 'All little peculiarities should be made public, such as sexual deviations, personal handicaps, etc. Exaggerate (if needed) any incompetence, and always stress wasteful spending to the taxpayer or consumer. Economics affects everybody and motivates people to act.' One should also, the *Handbook* continues, try to disrupt and divide the enemy by emphasizing its different segments and by infiltrating it and becoming an *agent provocateur*. McQuirter believed that the Klan would come to power in one of two ways: either democratically, through the election process; or violently, in the wake of a gigantic race war. In one interview he declared: 'If the Ku Klux Klan or an organization like the Klan cannot achieve power in Canada legally, then there will be non-whites hanging from lamp-posts in this country.' In addition to *The Spokesman*, there was a publication called the *KKK Canada Action Report*. For a six-week period

---

4 The source for this statement, and others that immediately follow, is the *Canadian Knights of the Ku Klux Klan Handbook* (1981).

in 1981, a copy of this publication was posted in a factory in Toronto where a union organizing campaign led mainly by non-white employees was in process. The union organizers accused the company of intimidation, but company officials claimed employees themselves had put up the poster (*Globe and Mail*, 12 March 1981). The case finally ended up at the Ontario Human Rights Commission.

Following the pattern of earlier organizations such as the Edmund Burke Society and the Western Guard, the Klan sought to recruit members in various secondary schools. Klan spokesmen showed up at Monarch Park Secondary School and D.A. Morrison Junior High School in Toronto, and Klan cards were distributed at other schools. McQuirter spoke to a grade-twelve class at Don Mills Collegiate; following the public outcry, he asked how forty minutes out of 365 days could change the lives of the students. The Klan's access to schools was eventually blocked. As a result, the KKK Canada–White Youth Corps was established and given the task of distributing Klan material in schools. With much fanfare, a Yonge Street office was opened, but the word spread that it belonged to the Klan, and the Jewish landlords kicked the organization out. Cross-burnings took place, including a widely publicized one at the home of Martin Weiche, attended by about forty people (another held in Richmond Hill was ignored by the media, to the chagrin of the Klan). McQuirter announced plans to organize training camps for young people in the use of firearms and explosives. He justified such measures by referring to a prediction made by a prominent member of the Ontario Human Rights Commission that within a few years there would be race wars in Canada.

The Klan also claimed that it had been successful in infiltrating anti-racist organizations, such as the Committee for Racial Equality in Toronto. The man responsible for this line of work was Lau Richardson, the head of the Klan's intelligence section. Richardson's background prepared him well for the task. Born in Brazil, but raised in the United States where he attended the Catholic University in Washington, he had previously been employed by the CIA and the U.S. Army (in its Intelligence Service). He claims he had 'a professional relationship' with the RCMP, and was involved in the early 1970s in monitoring the Toronto Anti-Draft Program (he passed himself off as an American draft-dodger). Licensed as a private investigator, he was employed by a company called Centurion to disrupt left-wing radicals, and to collect information on Chilean exiles in Toronto sympathetic to late President Allende. At one point, he infiltrated the Communist Party of Canada, and later the Riverdale Action Committee against Racism (RACAR). As he stated then (*Globe and Mail*, 1 July 1981): 'As a Roman

Catholic don't I have a right to hate the Klan?' This apparently complex man – a lone wolf, anti-authoritarian, a rebel against conventional society – was the subject of widely varying opinions. A union group described him as 'one of the most dangerous, murderous men in Canada.' Many of his fellow Klansmen, however, suspected that he was an undercover police agent, employed by the RCMP or the OPP. Whatever the case, his public image as a despicable member of a radical right was somewhat blurred by his private life: he was at one time an apparently effective foster parent to severely disturbed teenagers for the Toronto Catholic Children's Aid.

The first chapter of the Canadian Knights of the Ku Klux Klan was established in British Columbia in November 1980. As in Ontario, BC schools were targeted by the Klan. Klan cards were handed out in various secondary schools, and Klan literature was distributed at the BC Institute of Technology. A member of the BC Organization to Fight Racism (BCOFR) claimed that a Klan meeting was held in a church basement in one town. In January 1981, there was a Klan picnic, which also was an occasion for firearms training and a cross-burning. At another cross-burning, a Klan spokesman said (*Ottawa Citizen*, 2 June 1981): 'Let us offer a prayer of thanks to God for creating us in His image, for giving us a white skin and superior intellect.' Yet another cross-burning was dedicated in praise of the assassination of Egyptian president Anwar Sadat, described as a friend of Jews and a traitor to the white race (*Toronto Star*, 19 January 1981). Labour minister Jack Heinrich, it was reported (*Vancouver Province*, 3 June 1981), said he knew of nine cross-burnings in the province. Klan leaders in British Columbia claimed that their followers were more prepared to be open members than members were in Ontario, where most followers were associate or secret members. According to my sources, the BC Klan also was linked to prostitution, pornography, and drug-peddling, constituting a sort of mini-mafia.

The propaganda stage was consciously regarded by the Klan as a crucial but limited step. Its purpose was to wake white people up, to thrust the organization into the public eye. McQuirter told me frankly not only that the Klan was a 'publicity gimmick,' but also that within a year or so it had become a spent force. Without it, one would have been ignored. But to gain power, one had to move beyond the Klan, especially after it had ceased to be a hot news item. The next step, in McQuirter's view, was to establish a political party. In 1982, he announced (*Spokesman*, vol. 1, no. 5) that he was retiring (not resigning) from the Ku Klux Klan. That the was the signal that the stage to contest public office had been reached. Back as far as the summer of 1980, shortly after the Klan's presence in Canada was publicly announced, McQuirter had toyed with the idea of establishing a branch of Duke's NAAWP in Canada, connected to which would be the National Advancement Party (NAP). By 1982, he had changed his mind. Duke's NAAWP, he said, had been a failure. It was just another fraternal organization, and did not even have the explosive connotation of the KKK. McQuirter added that it would have fared worse in Canada, for few Canadians had even heard of the NAACP.

McQuirter said that one possibility was for the Klan to take over the Social Credit party. But what he finally turned to was a new organization to be known as the United Front. Candidates under that banner were to contest municipal elections in Toronto and Vancouver in the fall of 1982. That plan, however, disintegrated when McQuirter was arrested. The Klan was thrown into disarray, but the fact was that it had begun to decline even before McQuirter's arrest. The membership had dropped off, prompting the usual reaction among such organizations that a few totally committed members were better than a great number of lukewarm followers.

It will be recalled that stage two in the Klan *Handbook* consisted of consolidating the Klan's internal organization. A document produced by the National Socialist Party of America defined phase one as the 'publicity at any price' stage, but warned that unless the movement has been well-organized at the grass-roots level, the publicity has no purpose. If there was one consistent criticism of McQuirter within the movement, it was that he was an excellent PR man but weak at organization (a similar comment was often made about Duke). Stage two, that of organization, seems to have been bypassed by McQuirter, who was eager to move on to the level of contesting public office. Some Klan members, including McQuirter himself, explained that they had been caught off guard. They had fully expected that the media would gradually wake up, realize they were being manipulated, and cut off the Klan's coverage. But they did not anticipate that it would be done so quickly. Thus, they were not fully prepared for the post-propaganda stage. And there was, of course, another factor. McQuirter was a young man in a hurry. With the media stage terminated, and with the membership falling, it appears that he decided that desperate measures were called for. More to the point, he realized that he wasn't going to go very far unless he had a sizeable bankroll. As far back as 1977 he had completed a course in 'Basic Security Services.' However, while he was working as a security guard, he was convicted of stealing stationery and a typewriter, and sentenced to a brief jail term (served, apparently, on weekends). For a while he also worked at the hospital where several other radical-right members were employed. Occasionally, the media reported that he was part owner in a landscape business; he was involved in a mail-forwarding venture known variably as 'Arcon' or 'The Privacy People,' and he had begun to follow Andrews's example of purchasing houses with a low down payment and becoming a landlord. But the fact is that after leaving the hospital, he had never held a regular job. He was a full-time organizer for the Klan, although he insisted that the position was an unpaid one, and that his living came from his business ventures. One of his female admirers said that she thought he *should* have had a job, if only for appearances. It is probably true that overt racists, like ex-convicts, often have a difficult time landing a job. Yet my impression was that McQuirter, the man in a hurry, decided to short-cut the process, and tried to get rich overnight. It was then that he embarked on a counterfeiting operation, and became involved in the Dominica caper, which he and his fellow conspirators saw as a potential gold-mine.

ALBERTA

It was not the Canadian Knights of the Ku Klux Klan but instead the Confederate Klan of Alberta that made the headlines in that province. This organization was incorporated in 1972, several years before McQuirter arrived on the scene. It died out in the mid-1970s, but was reincorporated in 1980. The founder, who called himself Tearlach Mac a' Phearsoin, was born as Ivan Ross Macpherson in Prince Edward Island in 1948. Brought up by adopted parents, who renamed him Barry Dunsford, he moved to Calgary in 1965. Mac a' Phearsoin claimed (*Calgary Sun*, 16 July and 12 August 1980) to have seventy Klan members in Calgary and two hundred elsewhere in the province, including twenty-six in Red Deer. The Alberta Klan made history when it admitted a forty-year-old black construction worker, Louis Proctor (*Globe and Mail*, 15 August 1981). Proctor, who grew up in Calgary, said he was honoured to join the Klan, and added (*Calgary Sun*, 14 August 1981): 'I figure if we can get all the Jews and blacks to join the Klan, we can put a stop to the racial trouble in Canada.' (His Ohio-born father, who also lived in Alberta, told me that 'even the name Ku Klux Klan turns my stomach.') By the next month, however (*Calgary Sun*, 19 March 1982), Proctor had been arrested after making a deal with undercover police to sell them cocaine (which apparently turned out to be chicken sauce). Mac a' Phearsoin himself had had his own difficulties with the law after shooting to death a young Mexican companion who lived in his home (*Calgary Sun*, 13 September 1974 and *Alberta Report*, 19 September 1980). He was convicted of criminal negligence and fined $2,000.

When McQuirter's CKKK emerged in 1980, Mac a' Phearsoin described it as a Nazi organization. McQuirter and his followers, in turn, dismissed Mac a' Phearsoin as a nut who shot his male Mexican lover, accepted a black man into the Klan, and even was in favour of Jewish members. Mac a' Phearsoin, they concluded, was actually a member of the Zionist Occupation Government (ZOG).

Over the years this man had been a Free Methodist minister, a spiritualist, a vegetarian, and a participant in seances. By the early 1980s he had become the president and 'officiating priest' of the National Spiritual Church of Alberta. He claimed to be able to cure cancer and other severe illnesses by calling on the spirit of his dead Mexican friend.

OTHER PROVINCES

The white supremacists always claimed that the greater the contact between different races, the greater the racial hatred. Sometimes they pointed to Nova Scotia as a case in point, contending that black and white in that province lived completely separate lives, kept in place by a mutual hatred that had developed over the centuries. The Ku Klux Klan was certainly not an unknown entity in Nova Scotia. In recent years, KKK symbols were painted on a road near Preston, on a junior high school, and on the Coloured Children's Home in Cherrybrook.[5] Yet when the Ku Klux Klan announced its intention to establish a chapter and open an office in Halifax (*Toronto Star*, 26 November 1980), the opposing response was massive. A high-school teacher formed the Coalition Organizing to Oppose the Klan; the African United Baptist Church urged Nova Scotians to be on the alert; the Black United Front declared it was prepared to take preventative action if the Klan went ahead with its plans; Dartmouth City Council passed a resolution calling for new legislation in the Criminal Code against organizations like the Klan; Nova Scotia war veterans voted unanimously to oppose the entry of the Klan; and the Nova Scotia Federation of Labour voiced its strong opposition.

In new Brunswick, the home province of a young man well-known in right-wing circles for his publications condemning Jews, liberal-left clergymen, and abortion, a Klan organizer was appointed. Manitoba was the scene of cross-burnings on lawns of East Indian families. While the two youths who were charged in court apparently had no formal connection to the Klan, one of the East Indian families received a telephone call from a

5 See 'Background on Ku Klux Klan,' Nova Scotia Human Rights Commission.

man who associated himself with the Klan. The Ku Klux Klan claimed (*Globe and Mail*, 17 April 1984) to have members in Manitoba Grassroots, a group opposed to bilingualism in that province. While that may have been no more than a typical Klan boast, it was a fact that some members of the Aryan Nations, a Klan-linked organization, lived in Manitoba. In Saskatchewan, the Ku Klux Klan distributed literature and solicited membership in areas of Regina with a high concentration of Native peoples. On one occasion there was a confrontation in a Regina bar between the latter and a Klan recruiter. One response (*Calgary Sun*, 12 January 1981) was the founding in 1980 of the Native Rights Coalition. According to a report (*In Struggle*, 25 November–2 December 1980), there were actually two different organizations in Saskatchewan: McQuirter's CKKK and a branch of Mac a' Phearsoin's organization. I am a little dubious about the latter, because the Alberta leader could hardly sustain a viable group in his own province.

THE YUKON

White hoods in Whitehorse. It sounds like the title of a bad movie, but in fact one of the more bizarre Klan episodes took place in that northern city. In 1981, two young men, whose first names were Kerry and Terry, opened a Klan office in Whitehorse, a city with no synagogue, about twenty Jews, a half-dozen or so blacks, and a handful of 'boat' people.[6] They said the Ku Klux Klan was needed because of the rampant increase in Chinese, East Indian, and Vietnamese residents. Posters appeared around the city with the message 'I want YOU for the Ku Klux Klan.' Kerry announced he had signed up about thirty-five members (ten of them women), with another thirty or forty imminent members; yet he confided to one of my informants that he had only about twenty members – again probably a gross exaggeration.

The Klan's presence hit the Whitehorse airwaves and the local newspapers, prompting a demand from a staff member of the Skookum Jim Friendship Centre that the media ignore the organization (*Whitehorse Star*, 20 November 1981). Kerry, a diamond driller and blaster who had lived in Whitehorse since about 1978, claimed that an attempt had been made to get Native persons to form their own Klan, but they weren't interested (*Edmon-*

---

6 According to the 1981 Census, the total population of the Yukon was 23,075, of which 10,055 were British in origin. Most residents were Protestant (12,315) or Catholic (5,595), and only 20 were Jews. The Whitehorse Archives had no subject index for racism, Jews, or anti-Semites (note: the *Yukon Economic Review*, 1984, indicated a total population of 23,153).

ton Journal, 23 November 1981). I had heard that a similar invitation had been extended to Native peoples in British Columbia. In response to the Klan's presence, an effort was made to establish the Yukon Human Rights Commission, but apparently it petered out. The Yukon justice minister (*Whitehorse Star*, 20 November 1981) apparently parroted the line that politicians across the country had delivered, stating that the Klan 'has as much right to be in this territory as any other organization ... We can't do anything until they break the law.' He was very much mistaken. A 490-pound Yukon government employee decided the Klan should pack up and leave. An anti-Klan demonstration that he organized drew more than a hundred supporters. High-school students threw rocks and eggs at Kerry's house. A man kicked the door open, pointed a shot-gun at him, and said he was prepared to shoot. The 490-pound government employee cautioned his followers that they should explore the legal route first, rather than taking the law into their own hands, but he personally paid a visit to the Klansman's home wearing a pistol, and persuaded the Klan organizers to sign a statement that they were shutting down the operation. Shortly after, Kerry, his common-law wife, and two-month–old baby were taken off a bus leaving Whitehorse, and charged with fraud and passing bad cheques. He also eventually was charged with violating probation and possession of stolen property, and Terry was charged with fraud. Both men ended up in prison in Whitehorse, although Terry only served two days.

How did they get involved in the Klan in the first place? Terry, born in 1965, and one year younger than his sidekick, apparently simply tagged along with the other man. Brought up in Montreal and Toronto with an older brother and a younger sister, he moved with his parents (a cook and a nursing assistant) to Whitehorse in 1981. There was a problem with alcohol in his family, and this young man, who only went as far as grade eight, seemed destined to a rough life ahead. He had one prior offence (wilful damage) and the prison authorities I talked to were not confident about his future.

Kerry was quite a different case. He had originally joined the Klan a couple of years earlier in Toronto. The reason, he said, was that he was fed up being refused jobs by Orientals, East Indians, Jews, and blacks. Apparently on one occasion he had applied for a job in a Chinese restaurant in Toronto, but was turned down because he was white. Later in Vancouver, where he also was active in the Klan, he had a similar experience, and concluded that one had to be black or yellow to land a job. Kerry grew up in a large family (four sisters and three brothers), and as in Terry's case alcoholism was a problem. For a while he lived in a foster home. He had one fight while in jail, but it apparently had not been racially motivated, and prison authorities were reasonably confident that there was hope for him in the future. Prison usually is considered a breeding ground for racism by white supremacists. Yet while serving his sentence, Kerry came under the influence of a fellow prisoner, anything but a hardened criminal, who enlightened him about racial issues. Kerry also used his time in prison to complete grade ten. He said he had never been opposed to Jews. In fact, his stepfather (his mother had remarried) was Jewish, and had been very good to him. Kerry's plans were to enter a community college after serving his sentence, supported financially by his stepfather. This young man's change of heart was summed up in a letter that he wrote to the editor of the local newspaper (*Whitehorse Star*, 4 February 1982): 'I want to apologize to the residents of the Yukon for any hard feelings I may have caused due to may attempt to start a local chapter of the Ku Klux Klan. At the time, I didn't know what I was getting myself into. I also want to apologize to the minority groups which I have discriminated against. I am sure you must have enough troubles settling here as it is. I regret having anything to do with the Ku Klux Klan.'[7]

DOMINICA AND PRISON

The prospect of ending up in prison was never very far from the thoughts of the white supremacists. In most cases, however, charges against them rarely concerned racial matters or Canada's anti-hate laws (the Zundel and Keegstra cases have been the main exceptions). Instead, the charges involved various illegalities such as theft and assault that were often by-products of their racist orientations. White supremacists viewed themselves as political prisoners, the victims of a legal order (the 'jewdicial' system) weighted against them. Yet they sometimes regarded (or rationalized) imprisonment in a positive light. Andrews claimed that his prison sentence in 1978 was a blessing in disguise; had he not been put in prison, he said, he still would be locked into a dull job as a health inspector, and living in suburbia. Whereas prison often is regarded as a levelling mechanism which undermines the social class and racial basis for advantage that prevails in the outside world, the racists claimed otherwise. Andrews contended that he was a hero in

---

7 From one source while I was in Whitehorse, I was told that a new leader replaced him after he quit, but I was not able to confirm this information. There also was a rumour in Klan circles that a chapter or den would be opened in the Northwest Territories in the summer of 1982, but as far as I know it never materialized.

prison because of his white-supremacist reputation, and that blacks were at the bottom of the totem pole. Another man who spent several months in jail in the Caribbean said that he had got along well with Rastafarians, who, racists themselves, respected his pride in being a white man. An article in the *Nationalist Report* (issue 39) applauded a white prisoner in the United States for shooting four black prisoners, commenting that such action was precisely what was needed to bring about segregated prisons. McQuirter told me that his main worry about going to prison was that it would curtail his effectiveness as the mover and shaker behind the white-nationalist movement. He added that prison was a real breeding ground for racists, people who would not hesitate to use violence on release, and therefore the authorities would be very hesitant to assign him that fate; as he once said in *The Spokesman* (vol. 1, no. 1): 'If I'm in prison, I'll recruit an army.' Nevertheless, by 1983, it was in prison that McQuirter did end up. He was sentenced to two years for his part in the planned overthrow of the government of Dominica, to eight years for conspiring to commit murder, and to five years for conspiring to forge cheques, passports, driver's licences, and birth certificates. The last sentence was to run concurrently with the second, to start after he had served the two-year sentence (*Toronto Star*, 9 February 1983).

If the Dominica escapade had been the plot of a novel, it might well have been rejected by publishers as totally implausible. It all began when an American with a history of right-wing activity hit on the idea of establishing a base for white supremacists in the Caribbean. Mike Perdue was put in touch with Canadian racists, notably Andrews, by David Duke. Andrews, of course, had previously pointed out the importance of controlling a territory which would serve as a refuge and haven for the movement. The original target was Grenada, where the Marxist government led by Maurice Bishop had overthrown Sir Eric Gairy. The plan was to re-establish Gairy as head of state, in return for financial and other gains, but it fell through when he refused to accompany the invading landing party of white supremacists. Andrews had stressed to Perdue that any mercenary operation launched from Canada or the United States was bound to fail, because of the sophistication of the police and the great number of informers around the movement (*Nationalist Report*, issue 37). It was also critical, he argued, if the reaction of the American government was to be avoided, that the target should be a left-wing government. Andrews's idea was to launch the invasion on Grenada from the nearby country of Dominica. When Perdue selected Dominica as the new target, Andrews withdrew from the picture.

Dominica at the time had an interim government, which had replaced Prime Minister Patrick John, who had been involved in a scandal to get rich by leasing part of the island to some Americans. On a visit to Dominica, Andrews learned of a scheme by the leaders of the interim government to sell passports to wealthy Iranians after the fall of the shah. He divulged the information to Opposition leader Eugenia Charles (a former student of Bora Laskin at the University of Toronto), who used it to help her subsequent successful campaign for prime minister. Word later leaked out to her that former prime minister Patrick John, with the aid of white mercenaries, was planning a coup d'état. He and several of his followers were arrested for treason. Even that did not deter Perdue, McQuirter, and their fellow revolutionaries. Marion McGuire, a woman who had joined the Western Guard some years earlier, was persuaded to travel to Dominica as a pre-invasion scout. As incredible as it sounds, a Toronto radio station, CFTR, had been taken into the confidence of the Klan, and provided with a running account of the invasion plans. McGuire's report from Dominica was sent to a CFTR news reporter, who passed it on to the Klan. From that point onwards, things went from bad to worse for the mercenaries. The reporter had told an OPP friend about the planned invasion. The OPP investigated, verified that a plot did exist, and relayed the information to U.S. authorities. The second leak was even more damaging. Perdue had arranged to rent a boat in New Orleans. He confided in the captain that he was leading an attack on Dominica. The captain, as it materialized, was working for the U.S. Bureau of Alcohol, Tobacco, and Firearms. When Perdue and his comrades gathered in New Orleans, they were promptly apprehended.

The arrests took place without a ripple, but the shock waves in the radical right were huge. The ten people placed under lock and key, all of whom had Ku Klux Klan or neo-Nazi connections, included two Canadians. One was Wolfgang Droege, born near Nuremberg in West Germany, and the principal Canadian Klansman after McQuirter (some radical-right people claimed he was McQuirter's intellectual superior). He had told a CFTR reporter before the attempted coup (*Globe and Mail*, 15 May 1981): 'I consider myself a little bit of a rebel in society. And, like, I'm not content to have a 9-to-5 job. I want to live a real life. You know, I want excitement and adventure in my life.' Droege also said he hoped to become financially secure from the Dominica venture, but all that he ended up with was a prison sentence in the United States. The other Canadian was a man called Jacklin from Elmira, Ontario, who had previously established a Klan den in the Kitchener area. This man, who sometimes used an alias, was referred to in *The Spokesman* (vol. 1, no. 5) as Grand Chaplain. According to one report (*Vancouver Province*, 12 May 1982), he was beaten and stabbed by blacks while serving his sentence in a U.S. prison.

The invasion attempt cost an estimated $75,000. While some of the funds apparently came from three American supporters, Perdue testified that Andrews and Weiche had also bankrolled him (both denied the accusation). Another backer supposedly was a Toronto crime figure, Charles Yanover, who shortly after was charged in a plot to assassinate the president of South Korea (*Globe and Mail*, 27 June 1981). Although police authorities took a close, hard look at the radio station, CFTR, which claimed it had fully intended to reveal the existence of the plot before the mercenaries actually landed on the shores of Dominica, apparently nothing concrete was done. One of the most bizarre consequences concerned the attempt to rescue Marion McGuire, who had been sentenced to three years in a Dominica prison for her part in the affair (some reports stated she was the only female prisoner in that country, while others said she was one of three women behind bars there). McGuire, of Irish origin and with past involvement in the IRA, had a history of alcoholism. Her estranged husband, whom she had met while undergoing treatment at Lakeshore Psychiatric Hospital in Toronto, announced his plan to fly to Dominica to see her. Siksna, McQuirter's sidekick, talked about going to the island to rescue McGuire, but he was beaten to it by a man of British origin who used the alias 'Harry Wood.' He was eventually arrested by Dominican authorities, and spent four months in prison on the island. McGuire, in the mean time, was starting to have second thoughts about the right wing. She said (*Toronto Star*, 17 May 1981) that McQuirter had set her up as the fall guy in case anything went wrong with the attempted invasion. There also was a rumour, apparently unfounded, that she had become pregnant by a black person while in Dominica. Following her release after serving one year of the three-year sentence, she said (*Globe and Mail*, 13 April 1982): 'I'm not just a recovered alcoholic but a rehabilitated racist and a born-again Christian.' Remarking on her prison sentence, she added: 'it was the best thing that ever happened to me. I think every alcoholic should have to spend a year in jail.' McGuire, who had been employed as a clerk with the federal Manpower and Immigration department in Toronto, hoped to become a nurse. When she returned to Toronto, she attended a church, with the intention of building a new life. But that was not to be. She withdrew from the church when a guest speaker introduced politics into the pulpit. She also had ended up in one of Andrews's rooming-houses, which certainly was not the environment to sustain her new-found stance against racism. A few months later she apparently was back on the bottle again.

There were others who felt the effects of the Dominica affair. Arnie Polli – the butterfly of the Canadian radical right – came under close scrutiny. Although generally regarded as a genuine believer in the cause, Polli had a reputation of being able to locate sufficient funds to allow him to indulge his penchant for leisure and pleasure. It was rumoured that one sizeable sum of money given to him to purchase a boat for the Dominican attack was exhausted after he had wintered in the sunshine of Florida. And when he was questioned by the RCMP (*Globe and Mail*, 30 May 1981), he said that it was 'only coincidental that his expenses for two trips to Dominica were paid by Michael Perdue.' For whatever reasons – perhaps he was only regarded as a bit player – Polli slid out of the Dominica débâcle on the skin of his teeth, but McQuirter was not so fortunate. For some peculiar reason – maybe he saw the episode as another opportunity to promote the Klan's name, or maybe it was no more than the arrogance of the true believer, who thought he was too clever to be caught – McQuirter openly boasted (*Globe and Mail*, 13 May 1981) about his participation. When he later was charged under a relatively new Canadian law that made it illegal to conspire in Canada to overthrow another country, he complained that he had 'never heard about this crazy law.'

Compared to McQuirter's other legal problems, however, Dominica was only a mild irritation. Within a few months he had been charged on various accounts of forgery and on conspiracy to murder his security chief, Gary MacFarlane. The two charges were not unconnected. MacFarlane, who had killed a man in 1972, but was found not guilty on the grounds of insanity (he was confined until 1979 at the maximum-security mental-health centre at Penetanguishene), had become increasingly disillusioned with the Klan leader. No doubt that was partly because the latter had won over his common-law wife, Jean MacGarry (the three lived in the same house). Several months before the murder plot, it became widely known in the movement that MacFarlane had slit the throats of two dogs that McQuirter doted on, leaving their decomposed carcasses in the bathroom. According to McQuirter, MacFarlane had threatened to kill both the Klan leader and MacGarry.[8] McQuirter was particularly worried that MacFarlane, who used

8 Although I did not pay much attention to it at the time, Zundel and Andrews several months earlier remarked that they expected MacFarlane would soon try to kill McQuirter, which makes the latter's story more plausible.

alcohol and drugs excessively, had become a security risk, and might expose the counterfeiting racket to the police. Yet the latter concern is puzzling. McQuirter must have strongly suspected that his organization had been infiltrated, and that the police already were aware of what was taking place. Indeed, in one of my interviews with him, he stated flatly that his membership included police agents. But that, he said, didn't worry him, because the Klan was not involved in any illegal activities. One of his prominent followers told me they were certain that the police had tapped their telephone. Several months before the forgery schemes were revealed by the media, I had heard all about them from more than one source. For example, a leading figure in another right-wing organization said that McQuirter was determined to get rich quickly, but the RCMP and other agencies were hot on his tail. I would venture the guess that almost anyone who was monitoring the radical right closely was perfectly aware of the forgery business long before it became public knowledge.[9] The only answer that I can offer for McQuirter's action, in the face of the probable knowledge possessed by the police, again concerns the right winger's arrogance, the belief that one is a superhuman, standing above the trials and tribulations of the ignorant masses. A similar lack of concern governed his conduct leading to his arrest for the murder conspiracy. Undercover agents pursuing the forgery racket accidentally stumbled on the murder plot when McQuirter asked one of them if he knew someone who could do a 'hit.' In the unfolding drama that indirectly involved the United States and countries abroad, a wealthy supporter of the right wing inadvertently introduced McQuirter to a man who activated the chain of contacts leading to McQuirter's arrest. I interviewed this well-heeled supporter both before and after the arrest. On the latter occasion, he was still stunned by the effectiveness of the police operation, and had a peculiar feeling that somehow or other he had been an unwitting participant.

The aftermath of McQuirter's arrest was both bizarre and dramatic. With Klan members scurrying for cover, Andrews claimed many of them came over to his organization (some, in fact, did so). During a celebration of Hitler's birthday, light relief was provided by one Klansman who announced with pleasure that Hitler's spirit had entered his body. Mac-

---

9 In the early months of this project, I was always puzzled why the police did not arrest white supremacists who obviously were involved in illegal schemes. Of course, from the radical left's point of view, the explanation was simple: the police were part of the right-wing conspiracy. Yet as I eventually appreciated, it is one thing to have information about illegal acts, but quite another to have the type of evidence that would stand up in court and result in convictions.

Farland, the murder target, was himself charged the following year (*Globe and Mail*, 30 March 1983) with the first-degree murder of a Richmond Hill man who was found savagely beaten in a parking lot in Thornhill, Ontario. Siksna, who was born in Latvia, and brought up in Australia and Canada, became implicated in the plot to kill MacFarlane. Siksna had been acquitted on three earlier occasions for charges of defacing property, stealing a type-writer, and violating anti-hate laws (he was convicted for the fraudulent use of a credit card, receiving an eighteen-month suspended sentence). This man had previously demonstrated his complete loyalty to his leader. McQuirter (*Calgary Herald*, 27 September and 17 December 1981) had once been charged with possession of an unregistered and restricted weapon, with possession of cocaine for the purpose of trafficking, and driving while his licence was suspended (the drug charge was eventually dropped). Siksna told police that the gun was his. In the wake of McQuirter's arrest, Siksna went to the police and confessed that he had put up the money for the 'hit.' He also said that he would have been prepared to take care of MacFarlane himself, thus saving the Klan the expense of hiring a professional assassin. Siksna, a former University of Toronto student and computer programmer, and erstwhile member of the Conservative party, who was a dishwasher at the time of his arrest, was sentenced to six years in prison.

Yet another university graduate, Jean MacGarry, the woman caught between the Klan leader and his security chief, became implicated. This unfortunate woman was the Klan's equivalent of the Nationalist Party's Bob Smith. She told me that she had never been political, not even while attending university. She described her life as an endless line of crises, and wondered if she had become involved in the Klan simply because it constituted for her the equivalent of a religious sect, or whether it was the charismatic personality of McQuirter that had won her over. Like Siksna, MacGarry proved herself a loyal subaltern. Police investigators had provided her with an opportunity to step away from the murder case, but she had refused. She pleaded guilty (*Globe and Mail*, 17 May 1983) to conspiring to murder her common-law husband. Mostly because she suffered from several severe health problems (including cardiac arrest, manfunctioning kidneys, and lupus), she received a suspended sentence and was placed in custody of the Clarke Psychiatric Institute. MacGarry represented a peculiar (and poignant) phenomenon in the radical right – women who were prepared to do evil for no greater reason than to please the men they admired or loved. Among these were two women who risked their careers by pilfering sensitive documents for white-supremacist leaders, and another who was given the task of tapping information in the Jewish community.

On the west coast, McQuirter's various legal problems threw the Klan into turmoil. David Cook, the Klan's main organizer, described the attempted coup d'état as a 'dumb stunt' (*Vancouver Sun*, 29 April 1981), and said the Klan is dead: 'I guess I'll just fold it here ... It's just folded as of now as far as I'm concerned. I've had it.' His comments didn't please McQuirter, and before long he was expelled from the Klan. Yet as one Klansman told me, there had long been plans to shunt this man aside, but they were apprehensive about doing so, because Cook had the Klan membership lists. His vocal negative reaction to the Dominica affair provided the excuse they had been looking for. McQuirter told me that the main problem was that Cook would not take orders from him. Cook confimed this, observing that his problem with McQuirter was merely a manifestation of the East-West split that conditions Canadian politics in general. Who, Cook asked me, appointed McQuirter leader in the first place? Cook thought that McQuirter was too pro-Nazi, and that he was in the Klan just to make money. This man, a fisherman by trade, who had joined the Klan about 1977, commented that Duke had been wise to get out of the Klan when he did. He mused that he might start up an NAAWP branch himself, but said that if he did so nobody would know. Cook told me that he still is a member of the Ku Klux Klan. When he left McQuirter's organization, he took several people with him who formed the nucleus of his own small low-profile group. About the only formal meetings he attended were those of another organization, the Canadian League of Rights. Gostick's people, he said, knew who he was, but left him alone.

Another man, who apparently also attended League of Rights meetings, left McQuirter's organization about the same time as Cook. According to a high-ranking female member, this other man was even more of a troublemaker, basically because he was paranoid. For a while he was involved with a Western separatist group,[10] but they too found him intolerable, which led him to establish his own small separatist organization. He also had his own church group. As we shall see later, there exists in the radical right a Christian religious movement known as 'Identity,' a spiritual blueprint for the white racist. It had several adherents in British Columbia. Closely associated with Identity was an Idaho-based organization called 'the Aryan Nations'; the reputedly neurotic ex-CKKK man started up a branch of that organization in Vancouver.

---

10 Droege earlier said (*Vancouver Sun*, 2 April 1980) that the Klan might have some members in the Western separatist movement.

When Cook was kicked out of the Klan, he was temporarily replaced by a twenty-six–year–old tradesman who had the title of Grand Titan. Eventually, however, Hooper emerged as the main BC Klan organizer and spokesman. For several months plans had been made to move the Klan headquarters from Toronto to Vancouver. After McQuirter's arrest, that plan was shelved. Hooper said he had a half-dozen people ready to run as United Front candidates in upcoming elections, but decided not to go ahead with the idea. He remarked that the Klan was no longer recruiting new members, and would concentrate on small-arms and survival training in the BC interior (he had access to a 'hide-out'). Adding to the Klan's problems was a split between the armchair intellectuals and the activists (including the motorcycle-gang members). The person who emerged as McQuirter's replacement as the Klan's national director was a university graduate, born in 1946, whose alias was 'Ann Farmer'; she formerly had been the Grand Chaplain and secretary general for British Columbia. Blonde, petite, and attractive, but with a hard core characteristic of many of the women and men who aspired to leadership positions in the organization, Farmer had been brought up in South Africa. Like numerous other white supremacists, she had travelled widely, but the experience solidified rather than softened her racial attitudes (her conversation was laced with terms like 'Paki' and 'nigger'). She told me that she had always been a racist, and was delighted to discover the Klan organization in Vancouver. An only child, Farmer considered herself an intellectual (her university professors, which included a fellow South African, apparently did not know about her Klan connection, but should have twigged when she submitted a racist thesis on South African literature). She said she didn't respect many people who did not have a university degree; McQuirter was an exception. She herself was not universally respected in the movement. More than one person remarked to me that Farmer was scatter-brained or simply stupid (despite her claim that her IQ was 140), a judgment no doubt conditioned partly because she was a woman. When she emerged as national director, not everyone was willing to accept her. A splinter group called 'the Imperial Knights of the Ku Klux Klan' broke away from the CKKK, led by the man who had departed from McQuirter's organization at the same time as Cook.

This new organization was just one of several different Klan, or Klan-linked groups, in British Columbia during the past few years. The ones that I was told about included McQuirter's CKKK, the Imperial Knights, a branch of Wilkinson's Klan, a Klan group in Nanaimo, another Klan group in Victoria, Cook's group (possibly linked with NAAWP), the Aryan

Nations, an underground Nazi group in Vancouver (possibly another reference to the Aryan Nations), and a small White People's organization in Victoria.

The reaction to Farmer was similar in Ontario. Some Klansmen there refused to accept her as leader, again because she was a woman. A splinter group, the National Knights of the Ku Klux Klan, was established by one of McQuirter's former lieutenants, who was a commercial diver and truck driver (see Sher 1983: 183). As the Klan's fortunes sunk ever deeper, this man and a few others, including a Detroit-based Klansman, were rumoured to be talking about 'direct action' i.e., violence. McQuirter had always said that that option would become increasingly attractive if he was put in prison. One of the biggest surprises was that Beattie's star began to rise in the wake of McQuirter's arrest. For several years Beattie and Andrews had been on bad terms. Yet an article written by Beattie appeared in Andrews's *Nationalist Report* (issue 43). In the article Beattie revealed that discussions were underway to resuscitate the right wing by establishing an umbrella organization to be known as 'the White Canada Council.' It was to include the British Canada Party, the Nationalist Party, and the Western Guard (Taylor too saw the downfall of McQuirter as an opportunity to climb back into the radical-right limelight).

And what about McQuirter, the man who said he would recruit an army if he was put in jail? His incarceration had brought him few sympathizers within the right-wing movement. The general reaction was that he had acted opportunistically, motivated by thoughts of fame and glory, and that he had ended up with exactly what he deserved. In a letter printed in the *Nationalist Report* (issue 42), written by McQuirter from jail, he dismissed these criticisms as rubbish. All his acts, he declared, were political. The real crime, he said, was not to rip off funds from the Zionists or to use the Zionist-controlled media to promote the Aryan's cause. In McQuirter's words: 'We are at war! Do you know this? Do you think that this is a boy scout meeting? This is total war!' From various sources, I learned that McQuirter had changed his tune somewhat regarding the right-wing potential of the prison population. As he discovered, most prisoners were more interested in 'Hockey Night in Canada' than in the future of the white man. Nevertheless, he had not lost faith in the cause, and as some people like Farmer remarked, he would emerge from prison as an even more capable white supremacist, since he would have had time to read and write, to increase his knowledge in general (he was, apparently, enrolled in computer courses). The general drift of messages that came my way was that

McQuirter was determined when released to pick up where he had left, to lead the troops with even greater vigour.

In case he failed to do so, there was a McQuirter clone waiting in the background. This young man, still in high school when I met him, already had a sound grasp of the right-wing literature. Formerly a member of the Young Conservatives, which he had quit in disgust, his first meeting as a Klansman coincided with a celebration of Hitler's birthday. Heavy-set, close to six feet tall, of British and German ancestry, this young man, who once had been a sea scout, already was firmly set in his ideas. Like McQuirter, it was rumoured that he had some sort of sexual hang-up, although it may have amounted to no more than acute shyness in the company of women. His brother and sister were a decade older than he was, and his parents were divorced. In the majority of cases, the families of the members of the radical right strongly oppose their offsprings' racist beliefs, and that was true of this man's family. His father had once taken him to a psychiatrist. After the latter concluded that he was rather peculiar but nevertheless sane, his father kicked him out of the house; his mother, with whom he went to live, also was opposed to his Fascist activity, but he claimed her main worry was that it would get him into trouble and hinder his future political ambitions. This youthful Hitler enthusiast did not have McQuirter's looks or charm, but he was intelligent, articulate, single-minded, and already totally committed to the racist cause. Should McQuirter fail to regain the leadership reins, or prove inadequate for the job, he was ready to step into the traces.

7

Others on the Radical Right

While the Western Guard, the Nationalist Party, and the Ku Klux Klan, plus the short-lived Canadian Nazi Party in the mid-1960s, have been the most prominent neo-Fascist organizations in Canada since the Second World War, others such as the Concerned Parents of German Descent and the Canadian National Socialist Party also have made their presence known. If the fortunes of the former organizations were highly dependent on key figures, such as Taylor, Andrews, and McQuirter, that has been even more true of the latter organizations, whose memberships in comparison have been negligible. The purpose of this chapter is to round out the picture of the far right in Canada by describing some of the less-prominent groups. Here too I shall look more closely at the type of people who embrace a Fascist orientation, but prefer to remain behind the scenes, or have little formal connection to the organized radical right.

CONCERNED PARENTS OF GERMAN DESCENT

In March 1981, West German police carried out a massive door-to-door raid in an effort to clamp down on the distribution of neo-Nazi literature in that country. What was significant for Canada was that a good deal of the literature had been produced by a Canadian resident, Ernst Christof Friedrich Zundel. A commercial artist, photo retoucher, and owner of an advertising agency, Zundel was for several years a relatively obscure figure, his neo-Nazi sideline being of interest to his comrades-in-arms (like Andrews and Taylor), his principal target (Jews), and the police. By the mid-1980s, however, he had been catapulted into the limelight by a celebrated public trial that relived the horrors of the Holocaust and the Second World War, and for some people uncovered the spectre of Nazism on the rise again.

Zundel was born in 1939 in the Black Forest region of West Germany, where his father and mother, described in his sixty-four page autobiography, *An Mein Volk* (To My People), as a woodcutter and peasant, respectively, raised him on an ancient family farm under the watchful eye of the French occupation troops. His sister apparently became a missionary in Africa, and his brother a lawyer in the United States. Zundel himself attended a trade school in Germany, receiving a diploma as a photo retoucher. In 1958, at the age of eighteen, he emigrated to Canada, settling first in Toronto, then in Montreal for several years, and finally returning to Toronto. He attended Sir George Williams University (now Concordia) in Montreal, but did not graduate, stating that he only had wanted to prove to himself that he was capable of doing university-level studies. His marriage, producing two sons, ended in a separation after nine years – brought about, he said, because of the strain associated with his right-wing activity.

Zundel claims that his own parents were apolitical, and that when he came to Canada he had no strong anti-Zionist or anti-Semitic views. At that time he still believed all the 'propaganda' that the occupation forces had promoted against Hitler and Nazism. A self-described pacifist, he chose Canada as his new home because it did not have peacetime conscription. What, then, caused him to change? Zundel claims that it was the massive stereotyping of Germans as ogres and villains, reflected, for example, in lurid stories in men's magazines, that prodded him into action. In an article published in Andrews's *Nationalist Report* (no. 28), he complained about hate propaganda in Canada against citizens of German origin. He appeared before the Pitman Committee to argue the existence of widespread discrimination against German Canadians, and at one point provided me with information about two high-school girls in Scarborough of German descent who were handed a document warning all 'krauts' to leave the country. He also distributed reprints of an article that appeared in *Maclean's* (6 October 1980) by Russel Doern, a former teacher and member of the Manitoba legislature, who lamented that thirty-five years after the Second World War Germans were still being subjected to vicious discrimination and stereotyping. Zundel, who sometimes refers to himself as a 'human rights activist,' has claimed that he isn't an anti-Semite, racist, or Nazi (*Globe and Mail*, 6 December 1983), and would never join a Nazi party (Toronto *Sun*, 25 March 1981). Certainly, if his views were no different from Doern's, who explicitly rejected the extremism of the political right and expressed his repugnance for the Nazi regime, there would be no reason to include him in this study. The fact is, however, that he soon drifted away from a mere concern about German-Canadian stereotypes to a full-blooded neo-Nazi line.

The transformation appears to have occurred in Montreal, where he came in contact with Arcand. As Zundel stated in his autobiography, Arcand brought order to his confused mind: 'In distant Canada he made a German out of me.' Until he met Arcand, he said, he actually believed the horror stories about the Nazis.

The word must have spread in Canadian Fascist circles that a promising new recruit was around, for it was not long before John Ross Taylor visited Zundel in Montreal. No doubt helping to make Zundel's name known was his decision to run for the Liberal leadership during 1968, contending that Trudeau was a communist. That experience, he told me, was the most humiliating of his life. Countless people, he claimed, called him a dirty German and Nazi, which confirmed his judgment that anti-German prejudice was widespread. After a seven-month trip around the world, he returned to Canada to make a living and begin the business of setting the record straight about Germans and Jews. Zundel said that his real love is pure art (he paints), and that like Hitler he used to be keen about architecture. He established himself as a successful businessman, and on the side sold Nazi art posters, wrote about UFOs from a right-wing perspective, and according to a Toronto journalist (Toronto *Sun*, 19 April 1978) wrote a book entitled *The Hitler We Loved and Why*. Zundel has denied that he is the author of that book (*Globe and Mail*, 22 February 1985), and I suppose the attributed author's name, Christof Friedrich, Zundel's two middle names, might have been a mere coincidence. Zundel's major efforts were devoted to proving that the Holocaust was a hoax. The Holocaust, in his view, consitutes hate propaganda against Germans. He said that he mails his anti-Holocaust literature to thousands of people around the world, including every member of parliament in Bonn. He takes credit for making the world question the Holocaust, which, he claims, virtually nobody accepts as fact today. His contention is that the present government in West Germany is illegitimate – indeed, an occupation government – and his long-range plans are to overturn the Nuremberg trials and achieve the unification of East and West Germany.

Zundel told me that non-Aryans are not creative (at one point he said the same about Anglo-Saxons). As evidence, he pointed to the motif on Oriental and Arabic rugs, which almost never changes. Race, he said, has been the key to history, and only Hitler had the necessary vision to create a happy, sound society. He talked about the 'missing dimension' of racism, which he thinks all writers have failed to identify. He called it the 'imponderable' of race, and said perhaps the closest to what he meant was Jung's racial archetypes. Zundel's belief is that all people have a sort of racial memory or racial soul, something that imperceptibly but fundamentally guides their actions and thoughts. In this context he referred to whites in Australia who have never seen a European landscape and yet paint pictures of them. Despite his belief in Aryan superiority, Zundel, I observed, was on friendly terms with the Chinese waitress in a restaurant where we had lunch, and had non-whites working for him. As he pointed out, one's intellectual orientation to race and one's everyday life are two different things.

Zundel's right-wing activity was channelled into the following organizations: the Concerned Parents of German Descent, Samisdat Publishing, and the German-Jewish Historical Commission (he also was a member of the federal Liberal party and the Hollow Earth Society, and had a telephone-recorded 'News Hotline' which people could dial to get 'the German view-point' on world news and current events). Under the banner of the Concerned Parents of German Descent, Zundel went to bat for a German Canadian who had been expelled from a course on the Holocaust offered by the History department at the University of Toronto, after his repeated protests that the course constituted hate propaganda against Germans. The expressed purpose of the German-Jewish Historical Commission, according to a press release, was 'the airing of non-Zionist, neutral findings in respect to the Holocaust.' Under his Samisdat Publications ('samizdat' is a Russian word meaning self-publishing, i.e., illegal or underground publishing in the Soviet Union), he said he mailed anti-Holocaust and other materials to 45,000 people in forty-five countries and in fourteen languages (Toronto Sun, 23 November 1981). His estimated mailing costs in 1981 were $35,000. In April of that year he applied to the Canadian Jewish Congress for the advertised position of director for the National Holocaust Project. In a letter listing his qualifications, he referred to his vast knowledge about and sensitivity to the Holocaust issue, and stated that he would 'bring a very definite attitude of dedication' to the job. Of course, Zundel was simply playing a game, as was revealed towards the end of his letter: 'I hope that my German birthplace will not be viewed as a handicap in my selection for this position, as we are all aware that the use of public funds prohibits any discrimination of this nature, and the Holocaust Documentation Bank is, as such, a publicly-funded project.'

Although in terms of his racist and Fascist orientation Zundel was little different from men like Andrews and Taylor, his tactics were far from the same. He said he wanted nothing to do with wild people, those who scream racist slogans and prowl the streets for likely victims. Zundel believed in the power of the printed word. Most of his efforts were devoted to writing and distributing his right-wing materials. These were carefully prepared with an eye to local legislation, whether in Canada or abroad, in order to avoid arrest. Zundel also attempted to establish amicable relationships with Jews. He once put a paid notice in a Toronto newspaper saying hello to all his Jewish friends. In an open letter addressed 'To the Rabbis and Leaders of the Jewish Community of Canada,' he said he had done all he could to establish a dialogue with the Jewish community in order to break down stereotypes detrimental to both Jews and Germans.

Zundel's tactics earned him few kudos among his fellow Fascists. While virtually nobody doubted the sincerity of his neo-Nazi beliefs, he was known in the movement as a loner. Some condemned him for not running a regular right-wing organization with membership cards, slogans, banners, demonstrations, and formal meetings. Others complained that Zundel, financially secure as a result of his legitimate business ventures, rarely made available his printing equipment to other organizations, or helped them in any way. In an article in *The Nationalist Report* (nos. 37 and 38), Zundel was mocked because of his efforts to appear respectable and nice, as simply a man concerned to reduce unfair anti-German stereotypes. The general opinion in the radical right was that Zundel's attempt to maintain a dialogue with the Jewish community did not fool anybody – especially Jews – about his real motives and beliefs. This was borne out on 21 May 1981, when a large demonstration against Zundel was held outside his house. Zundel showed me a videotape that he had made of the demonstration (plus photographs of Prins, Andrews, and McQuirter stuffing envelopes), pointing out people whom he referred to as members of the Jewish Defence League plus some of his own followers dispersed surreptitiously throughout the crowd.

The May 1981 demonstration was a prelude of things to come. Although Zundel told me he had done everything he could to avoid legal prosecution, the post office's Board of Review, prompted by a complaint lodged by the Canadian Holocaust Remembrance Association, issued an interim prohibitory order against Samisdat Publishers Ltd in November 1981. On behalf of the Jewish organization, a specialist in communications did a content analysis on two of Zundel's publications, 'The West, War and Islam' and 'Backlash,' in which he revealed their consistent anti-Semitic messages. The Board of Review, however, was not very impressed. It observed that the specialist was affiliated with the Canadian Holocaust Remembrance Association and remarked that an 'independent' witness would have been more helpful. I agree that the specialist's analysis, which basically consisted of picking out key words and phrases and indicating their underlying slur on Jews, was superficial and unsophisticated. But the board's decision to find Zundel not guilty and to restore his mail privileges (*Globe and Mail*, 11

December 1982) on the basis that the whole matter was essentially an ethnic quarrel between Germans and Jews is more difficult to understand. Perhaps the board was influenced by the Canadian Civil Liberties Association whose representatives defended Zundel on the grounds that postal services should not be denied to anyone not convicted of a crime; or maybe it was merely the good impression made by Zundel, who voluntarily supplied the board with documents. At any rate, it appears that the board failed to understand the essential aims and motivations of Zundel, and the nature of his materials, which went far beyond the mere defence of the image of German-origin peoples.[1]

Shortly after his postal privileges were restored, Zundel also was found innocent by a West German court of disseminating hate propaganda in connection with the materials uncovered by the 1981 police raid. No doubt Zundel was at that time feeling pretty cocky regarding his carefully selected tactics – in fact, he tried (unsuccessfully) to have a paid advertisement put in *The Canadian Jewish News* to inform his Jewish clients about the good news of his innocence – yet some people in the Jewish community, especially the Canadian Holocaust Remembrance Association, were not ready to call it quits. Latching on to an obscure and little-used law, they managed to have Zundel charged in court with two counts of knowingly publishing false news that caused or was likely to cause damage to social or racial tolerance. The two articles subject to the charges were again 'The West, War and Islam' plus 'Did Six Million Really Die?' The former postulated an alliance involving international Zionism, international secret societies like Freemasonry, and international banking and communism. The latter portrayed the Holocaust as a gigantic hoax.

From the outset there was a farcical, almost incredulous, air to the trial. A senior vice-president of the Royal Bank of Canada soberly testified that his bank was not involved in any way with international communism. The presiding judge rejected the defence's request that Jews and Freemasons be excluded as jurors. To a great extent it seemed that the Jewish people and the Holocaust – not Zundel – were on trial. As the prosecuting attorney, Griffiths, put it, the trial 'put the Jewish community through the type of ordeal rape victims used to endure' (*Globe and Mail*, 26 March 1985).

The trial also dramatized the essential incompatibility between the roles of the academic and of a witness in the court of law. The former's business is to carefully qualify every claim, and to be receptive to opposing view-

---

1 In a letter to the editor of the *Ottawa Citizen* (7 January 1983), Ben Kayfetz, a spokesman for the Canadian Jewish Congress, justifiably criticized the board for dismissing the case as a private ethnic quarrel.

points. But the latter must stick to his or her guns at all costs. It was not surprising, then, that an academic expert on the Holocaust from the United States who testified for the Crown was not too effective. Somewhat more successful was a Canadian academic, a Czech Jew who had escaped from Auschwitz. Rather than relying on textbook knowledge, he testified that he *saw* mass gassing of Jews. In the ensuing acrimonious exchange with Christie, the defence attorney accused him of lying in order to perpetrate the 'hoax' of the Holocaust. Perhaps the most effective Crown witness of all was a mild-mannered man who also testified about the gas chambers at Auschwitz, and remarked sadly: 'I'm just wondering why in the devil I have to relate this after 42 years' (*Globe and Mail*, 29 January 1985).

Four of the defence's witnesses were on the editorial advisory board of the Institute of Historical Review (IHR) in California, an organization which publishes *The Journal of Historical Review*, devoted mainly to historical revisionism, a euphemism for the denial of the Holocaust; these were a former French academic, Dr Faurisson, Ditlieb Felderer from Sweden, and William Lindsay and Charles Weber from the United States. Dr Faurisson, who had previously been successfully prosecuted in France, contended that the Holocaust was a hoax which benefits Israel in the form of reparation payments. Not a single gas chamber, Faurisson argued, existed in Nazi concentration camps. Other defence witnesses included Keegstra and one of Zundel's sons; the latter described how his family had been harassed over the years as a result of his father's efforts to revise the public's conception of the Holocaust. A well-known west-coast broadcaster and journalist, Doug Collins, testifying for Zundel, remarked that discussing Santa Claus is technically spreading false news, and that the weatherman is always giving false news. He added that 'Did Six Million Really Die?' did not contain a single abusive reference to Jews, and should be freely available to Canadians (*Globe and Mail*, 19 February 1985).

Most of the defence's witnesses stayed at Zundel's home, and each day following the trial about twenty or twenty-five of the 'Zundelites,' as they were known, returned there to review the day's events. A videotape of all television coverage of the case that day was played, and a collage of newspaper clippings was displayed. Zundel then would review the events of the day, summing up the degree of success or failure, and apparently his lawyer, Christie, would sometimes deliver 'a mission-accomplished statement.' In September 1984, a pipe bomb had damaged Zundel's car, and threats had been made on his life. Zundel's house, in which hung a West German flag and a Canadian flag, plus a portrait of Hitler in the dining-room, had been turned into a virtual fortress. There were television monitors and barbed wire at the back, and super-sensitive microphones.

During the trial, the Simon Wiesenthal Center in Los Angeles gave a news release indicating that the long-sought Nazi, Josef Mengele, may have briefly lived in Canada. The reaction in the Zundel camp was that the news release had been conveniently timed to influence public opinion about the trial. Nevertheless, there was a bouyant air among the Zundelites. Their feeling was that they were headed for victory, partly because they thought the crown attorney was weak. Yet their hopes were dashed when Zundel himself entered the witness box. Zundel acknowledged involvement with tracts extolling the virtues of Aryans and denigrating non-whites and Jews, and declared the Holocaust was a hoax and that the media were controlled by Zionists. In short, under cross-examination it became clear that the man was a firm believer in Aryan superiority and a die-hard anti-Semite. As Griffiths later remarked, the turning-point in the trial was Zundel's own testimony, during which he 'convicted himself' (*Globe and Mail*, 1 March 1985). Zundel was again acquitted regarding 'The West, War and Islam,' but found guilty in connection with 'Did Six Million Really Die?' After the jury's decision, Zundel remarked (*Globe and Mail*, 1 March 1985): 'I keep my pain to myself. We consider it manly and, may I say, Aryan.' During the trial, it transpired that Zundel was not a Canadian citizen. He said that he considered himself to be living in exile, and that he had been judged in enemy territory.[2] There were immediate calls for his deportation to West Germany. Zundel retorted (*Globe and Mail*, 2 March 1985) that such a fate would be like being sentenced to paradise, but he had no reason to anticipate a warm welcome, for in 1982 the West German government had refused to renew his passport. Shortly after, Zundel was, in fact, ordered to be deported by an immigration commission adjudicator, but that was a regular formality in such cases, and no action could be taken until his criminal appeal was heard.

Although the court case concluded with the successful prosecution of Zundel, there had been strong opposition to the trial in the first place by many prominent Canadians and organizations. Rabbi Gunther Plaut (*Globe and Mail*, 28 February 1985) said the trial only served to provide Zundel with a platform, and to render his views semi-legitimate. Alan Borovoy, on behalf of the Canadian Civil Liberties Association, remarked that the court case 'represents a serious – perhaps even unconstitutional – misuse of Canadian law on false news' (*Globe and Mail*, 26 March 1985). Civil libertarians are often considered by the far left to be part of the orga-

---

2 Zundel had once told me that he considered himself a better Canadian than most others because he had chosen to live in Canada, while he could have settled in the United States, South Africa, or Australia, all of which he thought were superior to Canada.

nized right wing, and in this respect one civil libertarian's comment to me was interesting; he, too, opposed the trial, but not because it was potentially unconstitutional, or a slap in the face to the country's freedom of speech – instead he remarked that the trial was in essence 'a terrorist attack' on Jews. There also was a wide split within the organized Jewish community. The Canadian Jewish Congress was opposed to the legal prosecution of Zundel, fearing that it would only serve to broadcast his views, and concerned that legislation was worded in such a way that the outcome of a trial was far from certain, regardless of the depth of a defendant's anti-Semitism. The Canadian Holocaust Remembrance Association, which was one of the parties that brought the case against Zundel, was formerly associated with the Canadian Jewish Congress, but withdrew because of the latter's reluctance to openly and aggressively tackle people like Zundel. Which of these parties was correct? That question is exceedingly difficult to answer. After the trial, Zundel crowed that he had gotten a million dollars' worth of free publicity and, despite the sentence of fifteen months and the prohibition against discussing the Holocaust in public, declared he was the victor. Yet, at the same time, it was no longer business as usual for him. [3]

Quite apart from the possibility that a public trial would simply provide Zundel with a forum to broadcast his message, there also was the massive loophole in the legislation governing anti-hate laws. The jury had not only to determine whether Zundel's published statements were false and would cause mischief, but also whether he truly believed what he published – if he did, then the jury would have to acquit him. Did Zundel genuinely believe what he wrote, published, and distributed? There is no doubt in my mind that the answer is yes. However, this observation must be qualified as regards the Holocaust. For numerous anti-Semites, including Zundel, the Holocaust is to some degree a convenient instrument for striking out at Jews. It was not the conclusion that the Holocaust is a hoax that caused them to become anti-Semites. It was their anti-Semitism that led them to attack the Holocaust. If the Holocaust had never occurred, Zundel and his crew would have found some other focus for their anti-Semitism. Put otherwise, Zundel's opposition to the Holocaust was partly instrumental and manipulative, and in this sense only can it be said that his beliefs were not absolutely genuine. Yet this qualification is to a large extent spurious, for the motive to attack the Holocaust is consistent with the underlying philos-

3 The last part of this statement must be qualified. Just before the final draft of this study was submitted for publication, Zundel won his court appeal to have a new trial (*Globe and Mail*, 27 January 1987). For more information on the Zundel case and its wider impact, see Weimann and Winn (1986).

ophy of the Aryan prince and the Jewish devil. In my opinion, then, justice was served in the Zundel trial, but that was despite the laws of the land. In other words, the jury, recognizing the type of person it was dealing with, soared ahead of the existing legislation.[4]

Finally, there was again the issue of freedom of speech. The presiding judge (*Globe and Mail*, 10 January 1985) remarked that freedom of expression is not absolute, and pointedly instructed the jury (*Globe and Mail*, 28 February 1985) that it was not an issue in the trial. Zundel's lawyer, in contrast, who reportedly argued that there never were any gas chambers to exterminate Jews, or a German government policy of genocide, claimed that the real issue in the trial was freedom of speech (*Globe and Mail*, 5 February 1985). On Zundel's return to court to hear the judge's sentence, he arrived with a large cross labelled 'Freedom of Speech.' Others such as Paul Fromm declared (*Globe and Mail*, 28 March 1985) that all Canadians concerned about freedom of speech should be upset by the conviction of Zundel. An English professor from Alberta testified on Zundel's behalf because of the freedom-of-speech issue. This man remarked (*Globe and Mail*, 16 February 1985) that the only restriction acceptable to him would be on material which urges people to commit violence against others. He did not deny that Zundel was in the business of peddling hate, but questioned whether he should be denied the right to do so. Of course, radical-right members like Zundel are perfectly aware of the benefits that accrue from transforming their cases into a freedom-of-speech issue. Moreover, the irony is that they themselves do not espose unlimited freedom of speech. Zundel, for example, in a document in my possession dated 28 March 1978, argued that all reading material, especially for children in schools, containing 'excessive stereotyping and slander' against the German people should be removed from circulation and burned, and that all television programs and audio-visual materials for schools and universities should be similarly dealt with.

CANADIAN NATIONAL SOCIALIST PARTY

In 1972, following the headlines in the Toronto *Sun* that the Ku Klux Klan was in the city, the newspaper *Contrast* received a letter declaring there were

---

4 Of course, some people would state that Zundel had to be found guilty to protect Canada's international reputation; and racists themselves would contend that in the face of massive Jewish pressure behind the scenes, the trial's outcome was a foregone conclusion.

no Klan members in Canada, simply 'ordinary white folks who don't like niggers.' The author of the letter identified himself as Martin Weiche, the chairman of the National Socialist Party, which had replaced Beattie's Canadian Nazi Party a few years earlier. Weiche was born in the East German town of Lebus in 1921. In 1938 he moved to Berlin with his parents. He became a member of the Hitler Youth Movement, and later a Luftwaffe pilot, ending up as a prisoner of war in a Canadian-run camp in Holland. In 1951 he emigrated to Canada, settling in London, Ontario, near which he now lives on a twelve-acre estate.

Weiche said that his father had been decidedly anti-Semitic, but he himself only found out the truth about Jews through his various business ventures. Jews, he declared, always stick together, and never keep their word with non-Jews. They also, he insisted, have an insatiable thirst for wealth, unlike Aryans who, when they achieve financial security, prefer to move on to more noble pursuits, such as art and music. Weiche, who was himself a wealthy building contractor, rehearsed the conventional radical-right line, declaring that only whites are creative, that mongrelization will destroy the world, and that foreign aid is a Jewish plot to undermine white society; he added that whites, nevertheless, have a moral responsibility to look after non-whites, because the latter lack the capacity to care for themselves. It will be recalled that Weiche denied that he had provided funds to McQuirter and Perdue for the Dominica venture. Yet in 1981 he said he wanted to move to a Caribbean island filled with whites who shared his political and racial views (*London Free Press*, 25 June 1981). He told me a few months later that plans had been drawn up to establish an autonomous island haven for whites.

By the time I interviewed Weiche in 1982, he apparently had gone bankrupt, losing in the process an estimated 270 apartment units in London and another 74 in Sarnia. The bank, he claimed, had foreclosed on his loan because of his Nazi views. One newspaper account (*London Free Press*, 25 June 1981) reported that he had been reduced to living on cashed-in life-insurance policies. Nevertheless, he still had his impressive home, where a large framed portrait of Hitler adorned his living-room. In his gun-lined den, modelled after Hitler's Alpine retreat, there was another picture of Hitler, plus photographs of George Lincoln Rockwell and Queen Elizabeth II, and several German military books. Weiche, a stocky man in his early sixties, still handsome and with an interesting face, was apparently on his third marriage (*London Free Press*, 25 June 1981). He had seven children from his first marriage, including one son who had dropped out of the right-wing movement after a period of intensive involvement. Weiche, who had been barred from his local German-Canadian club, created a ripple of amusement in right-wing circles when word spread that he had advertised for a wife in a Munich newspaper. More than one potential candidate made the trip to Canada, leading to a domestic wrangle that at one point involved the Ontario Human Rights Commission. At the time of our interview he had a three-year-old son whom in my presence he treated with kindness and patience. Yet there was no doubt that he could fly off the handle. After talking to him for nearly four hours, during which the interview was relaxed and matter of fact, out of the blue he exploded that I was probably an RCMP agent sent to pick his brain. For a couple of minutes the tension has high, but then just as suddenly he dropped the subject and returned to his spirited account of the halcyon days of Hitler.

In 1968 Weiche ran for federal political office under the banner of the National Socialist Party; his campaign brochures claimed Trudeau was a communist and homosexual; he received fewer than one hundred votes. Later he was a Social Credit candidate, and in 1976 he ran for mayor of London. It was during the 1968 election campaign that Weiche first met Zundel. Despite their mutual German origins and enthusiasm for Hitler, these two men, to put it mildly, were not close friends. Zundel told me that Weiche, who spoke English with a heavy accent, was not a German at all, but indeed a Jew. Weiche, for his part, thought that Zundel's main interest – discrediting the Holocaust – played right into the hands of the Jews, for in a way Zundel was contributing to their design of keeping the Holocaust in the minds of people. Ironically, whether or not to attack the Holocaust represents for the right wing the same Catch-22 situation that anti-racists confront at the opposite end of the scale: does confrontation aid or hinder the enemy?

The acrimony between Weiche and Zundel was typical of the relationships among members of the different radical-right organizations. Taylor confided that Weiche may not be a genuine member of the movement. The latter apparently had received financial backing from the Central Mortgage and Housing Corporation, which Taylor said was usually denied to his fellow believers. Andrews, who had been present when Zundel told me that Weiche was not a German, later scoffed at the accusation, dismissing it as snobbery on Zundel's part, reflecting class and ethnic differences among German people. Ironically, both Weiche and Zundel referred to Andrews as an 'East-European non-Aryan' whose Balkan origins had bestowed on him a narrow mentality.

THE CANADIAN ANTI-SOVIET ACTION COMMITTEE

The Canadian Anti-Soviet Action Committee (CASAC) was founded by Geza Matrai, the man who in 1971 had been named the Western Guard's man of the month for his attack on Kosygin.[5] Matrai lived in Hungary for the first thirteen years of his life. When the 1956 revolution broke out, his family emigrated to Edmonton, Alberta, where his father continued to work as a veterinarian, and his mother and sister became teachers (one of his grandfathers had been a teacher in Hungary).

Matrai eventually moved to Toronto, where he joined the Edmund Burke Society. Sentenced to three months for his attack on Kosygin (he served only two months), soon after his release he again was in trouble with the police. He was charged with spraying mace during a gay rally in 1972 at the St Lawrence Hall in Toronto. He fled to Miami, Florida, where he sought political asylum. While in Miami, he became active with Alpha 66, an anti-Castro group, and again ended up in jail, where John Ross Taylor apparently visited him. His next move was to Spain, where he said he came in contact with the extensive international radical-right network; he also lived briefly in England. In addition to his membership in CASAC, the Edmund Burke Society, and Alpha 66, over the years he also has been a member of the Canadian Friends of Biafra, the Hungarian Freedom Fighters Federation, the Social Credit party (his membership was suspended by the national executive in 1972), the Progressive Conservative party, and possibly the Anti-Bolshevik Youth League. In 1978 (*Toronto Star*, 26 September 1978), Matrai won a court ruling against Canadian customs, allowing him to import a guerilla-war handbook, which he said he would draw from to write his own guidebook for revolutionaries. In the early 1980s, he and another man attempted to hold up a banner supporting Solidarity at a performance at the O'Keefe Centre by a Polish dance group. He was found guilty in court, but not fined – his first conviction, he told me, in ten years.

In order to understand Matrai's political orientation, a sharp distinction must be made between his beliefs and his tactics, especially during recent years; his beliefs belong to the radical right, his tactics to the fringe right. Matrai told me that one of his best friends in Hungary had been a Jew, and that his family had been on good terms with its Jewish neighbours. His Fascist orientation, he said, took root at the time of the Hungarian Revolution, when several of his friends were killed. Yet he claimed that it was not until he moved to Canada that he became truly anti-Semitic. For several

5 After the attack, his Hungarian citizenship was withdrawn.

years he worked as a hairdresser, and it was in that capacity that the stark differences between Jews and Christians became apparent to him. Most of his clientele in Toronto were Hungarian Jews. Matrai claims they were extremely friendly until they found out he was a Catholic; then they treated him, he said, 'as a piece of dirt.' His attitude towards blacks took shape when he was in jail in Miami. Blacks, he observed, behaved like animals, and out of the blue would attack whites who had been friendly towards them.

Matrai remarked that for many people there is something very satisfying about coming out publicly as a Fascist, joining a Nazi party, and singing Nazi songs. Even the demonstrations and the fights, he said, can be great fun for a young man. Nevertheless, he gradually came to believe that organizations such as the Nationalist Party had no chance of changing the political scene of Canada.[6] In his opinion, Paul Fromm was the most successful right-wing figure in the country, and he thought anything more extreme than Fromm's style was doomed to failure. This point of view has had direct consequences for Matrai's tactics. He has been careful not to join organizations such as the Western Guard, the Nationalist Party, and the Ku Klux Klan, although he said that people like Andrews and Taylor know he is one of them in spirit. The only path to success, Matrai thought, was through the established political system. His hope was to get elected first as a school trustee, and then to become a candidate for one of the established parties. Although he was a member of the Conservative party, he considered running for the Liberals, assuming that as an ethnic candidate he might do better there (shortly before I interviewed him, he helped a Liberal candidate in an election); or if he returned to Western Canada, he thought the Social Credit party might be a better bet. He did not even rule out the possibility of running for office under the NDP banner, a party which he almost joined as a young man in Edmonton. In Matrai's opinion, it was irrelevant which party he ran for; all that was important was to get elected, for only then could one begin to influence the political scene. Trudeau, he claimed,

6 Matrai estimated that there were about 1,000 radical-right people across the country. Only about 25 of these, he thought, were members of the Klan, and among them there probably was one RCMP agent, one OPP agent, a Marxist, and one or two Jews posing as members. Perhaps another 25 to 40 belonged to the Nationalist Party, mostly lackeys, he said, for Andrews (whom he seemed to admire personally, although he thought the organization was going nowhere) wanted people around him who idolized him. Despite the few members in these organizations, Matrai said the police have to monitor them closely, for there always were one or two individuals ready to set off a bomb or kill someone.

would have run for office under any of the banners of the three major parties, as long as there was a probability of winning office.

CASAC was a perfect example of the differences between Matrai's personal beliefs and his chosen tactics. With about two hundred members, including some professors at the University of Toronto where it was formally registered as a student organization, CASAC was founded to serve as an umbrella group for all those opposed to the Soviet Union. One flyer indicated that it grew out of discussions between militantly anti-Soviet Muslims, Afghans, East Europeans, and other Canadians. Attending its meetings were representatives from the Moonies, the Nationalist Party, and the Ku Klux Klan. Matrai, who said he did not exclude Jews (although he personally felt they never could be completely trusted) or homosexuals, made it clear that one of his biggest tasks was to persuade the various individuals to subordinate their personal philosophies for the common cause of attacking communism. On one CASAC flyer was the old Edmund Burke Society adage: 'The only thing necessary for the triumph of evil is for good people to do nothing.' On another, it was contended that the Soviets have been supported by the most powerful capitalists; Matrai himself was in favour of some socialist measures such as medical and dental care and wage guaranties for 'the little man.' Another flyer proclaimed that pacifism is insane, a cancer, and that the only road to peace is through military strength. A CASAC bumper sticker stated: 'Support Slavery: Buy Lada.' As Taylor correctly pointed out, CASAC was aggressively anti-communist, but not racist.

In 1980 a member of CASAC, Nikola Sahounov, a thirty-three–year–old Toronto resident who reportedly (Toronto *Sun*, 2 November 1980) had been forced as an eleven-year-old boy in Bulgaria to watch KGB troops behead his grandfather with an axe, went to Afghanistan to do battle against the Soviets. Apparently CASAC had hopes of being rewarded with a base for its movement there, comparable to the Dominica plan, but it never worked out that way. As Matrai told me, a white man can't have a viable position in such a country.

By 1982 Matrai was enrolled as a part-time student at the University of Toronto, partly with the idea that a university degree would provide him with further legitimacy. Few members of the radical right, however, gave him much of a chance to make any headway in establishment politics. My impression was that Matrai, who was another victim of historical circumstances only slightly less tragic than those that had shaped Andrews, would not easily relinquish his anti-communist views, but might eventually take a more moderate stance regarding racism and anti-Semitism; in other words, if he continued to contend that only the fringe right could open the doors to success, he eventually might begin to believe it.

ARYAN NATIONS

It would seem to require quite a stretch of the imagination to describe the Ku Klux Klan as a conservative, non-radical organization, but that is precisely how it is regarded by some white-supremacist groups. In the *National Vanguard* (no. 94, April 1983), for example, that U.S.-based publication complained that the Klan only wants to keep blacks in their place, rather than separating them geographically from whites, and is suspicious of foreigners such as 'Germans, Poles, Irishmen, Yankees.' The Ku Klux Klan, it stated, remains 'the most conservative of the racially conscious White groupings.' Prominent among the extremist organizations that have replaced the Klan, or in some cases drawn it towards an even more radical position, is the Aryan Nations, with its headquarters at Hayden Lake, Idaho.[7] The organization was founded by Richard Butler, born about 1920, and described in party literature as formerly having been a flight instructor for the U.S. Air Force, the owner of a machine plant, a marketing analyst, and a senior manufacturing engineer for Lockheed Aircraft Company in California. The Aryan Nations represents a continuation of the Church of Jesus Christ Christian established by Dr Wesley Swift in California, who had a major influence on Butler.

At the front gate of the Aryan Nations headquarters is a sign 'Whites Only.' Swastikas decorate the desks in the organization's school, and on its membership form are the words: 'Declaration: I am of the White Aryan Race. I understand ... and agree with the Aryan Nations exclusion of Jews, Negroes, Mexicans, Orientals, and Mongrels.' In one of the organization's publications (*Aryan Nations*, no. 39) it is written: 'We are not the majority in America. The majority of Americans would mate with a chimpanzee if the federal tax laws gave them a 50% reduction for doing so.' The article continues by saying it is time to give up the attempt to reach the majority; instead an Aryan state within the United States must be created. In another article in the *Aryan Nations* (no. 42), Pastor Robert Miles, the Ku Klux Klan leader from Michigan who attended a Western Guard banquet in Toronto in 1972, contends that Christianity has been a principal force in destroying the white man. Christianity, he argues, has degenerated into hundreds of denominations, mostly opposed to 'race,' encouraged in its decline by Jews and race-traitors. Miles, who uses the term 'mud peoples' to

---

7 Actually, it makes more sense to describe the Aryan Nations as the Ku Klux Klan under a different name. Moreover, this organization acts as an umbrella for several white-supremacist groups, including Klan groups that have embraced the 'new look': uncompromisingly and militantly racist.

describe non-Aryans, concluded his article by declaring that since traitors are in power it is nothing short of treason to obey the laws of the land. The Aryan Nations is intrinsically linked to the radical-right religious movement known as 'Identity,' and believes that only the white race is descended from Adam, and that there are literal children of Satan descended from Cain.

The Aryan Nations claims it has representatives in all fifty states and in Canada (Anti-Defamation League of B'nai B'rith, 1982).[8] In 1984, a copy of 'Did Six Million Really Die?' was mailed by the organization to a resident in Guelph, Ontario, but most of its clout was in Western Canada. In October 1981, a joint conference of the Aryan Nations and the BC branch of McQuirter's Canadian Knights of the Ku Klux Klan was held at Hayden Lake, Idaho. Another conference there in 1984 attracted about eighty people, fully one-quarter of whom were Canadians.[9] Among these were a former Alberta elementary-school teacher and a former national vice-president of the Social Credit party; the latter, Tom Erhart, who lived in Calgary, said (*Winnipeg Sun*, 3 September 1984): 'I'm an Aryan. I'm not ashamed of it.' Another Albertan who attended the conference said he had been a founder of the Western Canada Concept Party (*Winnipeg Sun*, 6 September 1984). In the September 3 issue, it was reported that the Canadian leader of the Aryan Nations was Lester Morris, a former shipping clerk who lived in Fort Langley, BC.

By 1984, Alberta had its own Aryan Nations leader. This was a man named Terry Long. In an Aryan Nations press release, Long is referred to as the founding president of the Christian Defence League (established to provide aid to Keegstra), and as a political organizer and candidate for the Western Canada Concept Party (Long told me that the links between the Aryan Nations and radical right in general with the WCCP were virtually non-existent). In the press release, Long stated his intention of revealing 'the Jewish nature of Communism and the genocidal intent on the part of the Jew-Communists to destroy the white race.' A letter to Long from Aryan Nations leader Butler (dated 14 November 1984), which opended with 'Greetings Aryan Warrior Priest,' acknowledged Long as the Alberta boss.

Tall, bearded, raw-boned, with a surprisingly pleasant smile when the topic of discussion was light, and about thirty-six years old when I interviewed him in 1984, Long had been brought up in California from the age

---

8 In France in January 1986 I was not a little surprised to see a television news brief on the Aryan Nations.

9 See the excellent coverage in *The Winnipeg Sun* (2–7 September 1984), prepared by two Winnipeg men (one a journalist) who attended the conference incognito.

of six to twenty. It was there, remarked one of his relatives, that his extreme right-wing orientation took root. Long returned to Canada to attend the University of Alberta, graduating in 1972 in electrical engineering. When I met him he was living with his wife and children a few miles from Eckville, Keegstra's hometown, where he ran a sawmill; his right-wing views, he said, had cost him many potential jobs in his profession, and also were responsible for harsh mortgage terms on his farm.

Long, who commented that he had only become truly committed during the previous three or four years, claimed that there recently have been significant changes in the radical right. First, the movement was more intellectually oriented than before, having attracted a new cohort of highly educated people (the Aryan Nations had its own computer network). There also, he remarked, was a positive feeling throughout the movement, a sense that real progress had been made and that victory was in sight. Another difference, according to Long, was that members were now *truly* radical, ready to lay down their lives, to be violent if the circumstances demanded it. The word 'radical' in the radical right, he declared, meant just that – full-blown violent action, people prepared to fight in the streets when the Jew-communists launch the battle. Several times Long commented that some people were ready to put a bullet in the enemy's head; each time, he carefully added that he himself was not necessarily condoning such violence.

PROFILES

My emphasis so far in this study has been on the active members of the various far-right organizations, people who openly proclaim they are Fascists and racists. But what about the even more plentiful true believers who for one reason or another remain in the background, out of the public eye, or have little formal contact with the organized radical right? The ten examples that follow give us some idea of the nature and variety of individuals who fall into this category. Eight of the ten were men; five lived in Toronto and the other five in or near Ottawa; two were reputed to be millionaires; five were university or college graduates; three were born in Eastern Europe, and the remaining seven were either born in Britain or had British roots; three of the ten people claimed that they had previously been left-wing–oriented until they had seen 'the light.'

We begin with one of our millionaires. In the early 1980s I began to hear stories about a formerly high-ranking civil servant, a diplomat, who was not just a friend and financial backer of the far right, but was himself supposedly involved in activities with foreign governments, including a computer bank on selected Canadians, that bordered on sedition. The man's beliefs and activities were no secret to the police. Indeed, under the pressure of their constant surveillance, he was, I was told, on the verge of a nervous breakdown. When I first interviewed him in Ottawa, I found a furtive-eyed man who was keenly aware of and concerned about the interest the police had taken in him. Nevertheless, he did not strike me as a person on the verge of cracking. He still had a basic confidence and defiance, and hung on to the belief that he could outwit the opposition.

Slim, with thin greying hair, and a lineless almost young-looking face, he was born in 1925 in Ottawa (his parents were from Nova Scotia). He was a graduate in economics from a Canadian university and was married, with four grown children. In the mid-1960s, he was the number-two man in the Canadian Embassay in Lebanon. In charge of the trade section, he attempted to increase business with Arab countries, but his recommendations were ignored in Ottawa. He had had a similar experience when stationed in Sri Lanka from about 1959 to 1961, where he had come to the conclusion that foreign aid in the form of outright donations was detrimental to the welfare of a country. He told me that he came up with an ingenious self-help plan for Sri Lanka's fishing industry that would simultaneously benefit the Canadian economy. On different occasions he even had discussed his novel ideas for foreign aid with Lester Pearson and Paul Martin, but to no avail. Trade, he was told in no uncertain terms, was political.

In Lebanon, he was informed that if he didn't change his tune, which meant dropping his apparent anti-Semitism, his career would be ruined; but if he co-operated he would reach dizzying heights in the diplomatic corps. As the man explained to me, he had always been stubborn, and refused to compromise his principles. The direct result was that he was returned to Canada before completing his tenure in Lebanon, and in essence fired. What happened was that he was made non-rotational. That meant that he could not be transferred to any other job or take up a post abroad. The Department of Trade and Commerce concluded that his usefulness was finished; he was released, and then rehired in a junior post where he has been stuck ever since. The man told me that he is treated with contempt in the section of the government where he now works, with no chance of promotion. The department's personal file on him, he said, contains the statement that he 'lacks judgment.'[10]

---

10 On one occasion when I interviewed him, he said he had initiated a court case against the government, contending that he had been wrongfully demoted, and claiming back wages at his former diplomatic rank.

This man contended that prior to his forced removal from Lebanon, which put an end to his promising career (had he not been demoted, he told me, he would certainly have been an ambassador today), he had not been anti-Semitic. Like to many other committed racists, he also claimed that he previously had numerous Jewish friends, such as his room-mate at university. Over the years, however, experience taught him that Jews were untrustworthy. In the early 1960s, before he was removed from Lebanon, he had a small dental-equipment business on the side. His two partners, however, both Jews, plotted together to force him out, leaving him with nothing. He remarked that that experience taught him a lesson about how Jews conduct business. Despite the man's description of his formerly benign attitude towards Jews, it is clear that his anti-Semitism and racist views in general pre-dated his experiences with his business dealings and in Lebanon. He told me that while in Germany a few years after the Second World War, he decided to visit a high-ranking official who had served under Hitler, to get his side of the story; he also at that time advocated that the Canadian government sell airplanes to the Luftwaffe. When he was stationed as a trade representative in Detroit in the early 1960s, he was requested to write a report about the American Civil Rights Movement. The document he eventually produced drew from Coon's contention that blacks are 200,000 years behind whites in evolutionary terms, repeated the claim that Lincoln was really a racist, and promoted white supremacism. Not surprisingly, it received a very cool reception in the Department of Trade and Commerce.

With his diplomatic career on the rocks, and his income decreased, the man began to dicker in real estate. He now owns several buildings in Ottawa, including one previously occupied by a foreign embassy; he also was part-owner of at least one restaurant. His opulent, book-lined home was decorated with the hides of game animals, racks of spears from Third World societies, and collector's guns (much of it amassed by his father-in-law). The man's political stance was boldly announced at the entrance of his home, where a rubber mask of Hitler hung on a hat rack. Elsewhere there was a photograph of Mackenzie King, whom he greatly admires, and small swastikas – 'conversation pieces' for the interested – rested here and there on the bookshelves. He told me he also had an autographed photograph of Hitler. This man had met McQuirter several times, and said they thought very much alike about racial issues. Like McQuirter, he not only was an anti-Semite but also a white supremacist, believing that whites were on the verge of extinction. The major threat to Canada and the world, he contended, was Israeli subversion. That country, he said, has the best secret police in the world, for all Jews everywhere are spies for Israel. As far as

Arab nations are concerned, and especially the PLO, he remarked that they deserved Canada's support for two reasons; one was that their cause was just; the other was that to do so was in Canada's self-interest, although that fact was concealed by Jewish lobbying and propaganda. This man, who once ordered a subscription to Gostick's *Canadian Intelligence Service* for the Department of Trade and Commerce, denied that he was a member of the Ku Klux Klan. He said that while he does not belong to any formally organized group in Ottawa, except for his Thursday-evening musical session, there are a number of like-minded people who get together regularly; they did not organize themselves formally, fearing that such a step would only lead to police infiltration and to jeopardizing their careers.

Although this man would have it that he has been much-maligned by the government (even his passport apparently had been taken from him) and harassed unwarrantedly by the police and Jews, it is a fact that his links with the radical right are extensive. Members of the latter on visits to Ottawa were often put up in one of his properties. Moreover, according to my sources within the police, there was documentary evidence that he was, indeed, a member of the Klan. Finally, it was this man who unwittingly started into motion the series of contacts among individuals that led to the videotaping and arrest of McQuirter for conspiring to murder his former security chief.

Our second millionaire was a very different figure. An immigrant from Czechoslovakia, where he was born in 1922, with a grade-five education, he was anything but the urbane and sophisticated racist. Instead, except for his wealth, gained mostly in real estate, he came close to the media and public stereotype of the rough and ready, wild-eyed white supremacist. I had arranged to meet the man at his house, but when I showed up, he closed the door in my face, remarking that for all he knew I might be an RCMP agent, and demanding that we shift the venue immediately to a nearby restaurant. There, despite his wealth, he virtually ordered me to buy his meal, and twice asked the waitress if coffee was included. For the next couple of hours, he expounded on his right-wing beliefs, spreading his racist literature across the table, and talking excitedly about Hitler, Jews, blacks, and women. He swore constantly and used terms like 'nigger,' drawing the curiosity of those at nearby tables. Hitler, he claimed, was a hundred years ahead of his time in his attempt to cull out the Jews. He contended that Jews control Canada today, but despite his opposition to them, expressed admiration for their intelligence. There is nothing novel, as far as the radical right goes, about these views. But this man went a step farther. Hitler, he insisted, was himself a Jew, and thus knew firsthand the danger to society that they posed. The man added that he himself probably had

Jewish blood, for the English interpretation of his name was 'foreskin.' (The man had a good sense of humour and may have been pulling my leg here.) He thought blacks were stupid, but was of the opinon that Sikhs were very intelligent; of course, they were, he said, Aryans. According to this man, women were intellectually inferior, 'natural,' and the weakest link in the Aryan's chain. By 'natural' he meant that they exist for one reason – procreation – and that they will have intercourse with anyone at any time, regardless of race. The flip side of the coin here was his concern about homosexuality. Unmarried himself, he dwelled repeatedly on homosexuality, referring often to one politician whom he described as 'a socialist homosexual frog.' Christ, he claimed, was a homosexual. Although he himself was a Catholic, he detested the Jesuits, stating they were part of the conspiracy.

This man, who in the past has run for public office, claimed he was not 'one of those wild racists.' He said he was simply against socialism, homosexuality, and parasites on society. His belief was that the majority of people, regardless of race, are stupid; even among Germans and English, only about 7 to 10 per cent are intelligent, he estimated; all others are inferior parasites, which is why they want socialism. At one point he declared that he couldn't hurt a flea, but at the same time he remarked that anyone over thirty-five years old who still is a socialist should be shot; he himself was a socialist as a young man. He added that homosexuals and parasites – people who don't pull their own weight – also should be slaughtered. He anticipated that the right wing in the United States would kill off all its blacks, socialists, and homosexuals. The only hope for the future in Canada, he thought, was if Reagan would send in the marines to take over the country.

Part of the explanation for this man's right-wing orientation seems to be related to his status as a self-made businessman. He declared that what angers him is that he has worked so hard for what he has achieved, and now the government is taking it all from him and giving handouts to the parasites. He claimed that a few years ago he was friends with high-ranking politicians in Ontario; if he had a problem with tenants or tax assessment, he would simply contact someone in the political party and it would be taken care of. But it doesn't work that way anymore, he complained. He said that whenever tenants refused to pay the rent or to evacuate his properties, he tried to fight them physically; but he added that in recent years he can only get away with it if the tenants are white; if they are black, the courts will jump on him. He contended that the vote should be taken away from all people who don't own property, all women, and all those who work for the government; moreover, only 5 per cent of government employees should be lawyers.

This man, who called himself a conservative nationalist, had little admiration for existing radical-right organizations like the Nationalist Party and the Ku Klux Klan; all of these, he remarked, are out of date, and none has an effectual leader. He described himself as an extremely intelligent man, so much so that most people are unable to converse with him. Members of the radical right, who themselves make a distinction between those in the movement who are sane and useful and those who are crazy and a liability, had their own strong views about this man. He was, according to many of the Fascists, the perfect example of the 'nut-cases' the movement attracts. One prominent Fascist, whose own reputation for sanity was often questioned, told me about the time the gentleman in question, pursued by the police, jumped on to the subway tracks in Toronto to make his escape. The man was in the habit of joining and resigning repeatedly from organizations like the Nationalist Party and the Klan, and one leading figure once remarked to me that the man's membership fee was not worth the price of having to put up with his rantings at meetings. This same person described the man as 'an insignificant idiot – just plain stupid.' In my opinion, that was unfair. The man in question was far from being stupid. But he certainly was highly individualistic, with his mind located somewhere on the far side of idiosyncrasy.

Our next two examples are women. The first was brought up in Poland, where her parents still live. She came to Canada in 1973 (a brother followed her later) after running into trouble with Polish authorities for her covert political activity. In 1977 she graduated with a BA from a Canadian university, and at the time of our interview was enrolled in graduate studies. Slim, dark, possibly thirty years old, with an ascetically attractive face, this intelligent woman, who spoke four languages, was very definitely a confirmed racist and anti-Semitic. She stated that she absolutely hated blacks (plus East Indians), could not stand their smell, and in their company became physically ill. She often wondered if blacks were animals rather than human beings. Even if there was only one seat left on a bus, she always made a point of refusing to sit next to a black person. On one such occasion, an individual pushed her. She made a scene, the police were summoned, and she ended up in court, accused by the black man of racism. The case, however, was dismissed, because, the woman explained, the judge like herself was a racist. She did, nevertheless, have a police record – the result of a spitting incident involving an RCMP officer; whe was put on probation for six months.

Whereas she thought blacks were stupid, she regarded Jews as clever, and thus all the more dangerous. Jews, she said, controlled the world's finances (her landlord was a Jew). In her view it was ridiculous to argue that the Holocaust never occurred, but said maybe three million rather than six million died. Hitler, she added, had been absolutely right in his plan to kill off Jews, but she could not go along with him completely because of his negative attitude towards Slavs. At one point she was teaching Russian and Polish. One of her students was a Jew, and she purposefully introduced literature such as *Mein Kampf* in order to embarass him. Adamantly anticommunist, and brought up as a Catholic (but now an agnostic), she was of the opinion that all mentally retarded and physically handicapped people should be killed.

My impression was that this young woman, another classic victim of environmental influences, was exceptionally unhappy. She had been previously married in Poland, with one son. In Canada she remarried. Her husband, a Scottish Presbyterian, was at first opposed to her racism; but as she commented, it was easy to convert him, because after all he was British. At the time of our interview, she had a five-month-old daughter who bored her. The baby cried constantly during the interview, but was ignored by its mother. It was natural, the woman said, for Poles to hate Jews; anti-Semitism is ingrained in them. Her parents detested both blacks and Jews. Her father was in the military in Poland, and she related an incident involving a visiting Cuban delegation; when one of them kissed her mother's hand, the latter wiped it off immediately to remove 'the stink.' This young woman was no longer involved formally in the right wing, although around 1978 she had been a member of an organization. Nevertheless, she was a true believer in every sense of the word. She even, as she told me, had trained her dog to bark at Jews.

The second woman had been, in her own words, a perfect teenager, without an ounce of rebellion in her. She had been brought up in Nova Scotia, moving to Ontario in 1967, where she studied marketing and accounting at a community college. Her mother had three sons by a previous marriage. This young woman, about twenty-six years old when I met her, had belonged to the United Church, and one of her past ambitions was to become a minister; by the time I met her, she had no formal church connections, but said she believed in a form of reincarnation.

Her radical-right orientation took shape after seeing McQuirter on television. She was attracted physically to him, and later met him in Ottawa and Toronto. Her mother warned her to stay away from the Klan leader, but as her daughter remarked, she no longer was the compliant offspring, and her mother's warning simply increased her interest. She added that while her mother had not been conscious of being a racist, she nevertheless had prepared her daughter for her new-found belief system. She apparently always had warned her daughter to stay away from 'Nigger Hill' in the town in Nova Scotia where they had lived; she also refused to allow her daughter to bring black girl-friends from school to their home, and cautioned the daughter about shopping in stores owned by Jews. At first, this young woman claimed, she couldn't accept the literature provided by McQuirter that denied the Holocaust. But she said she had been taught that there are two sides to every story, and when she failed to locate right-wing, pro-KKK literature in the public library, she began to think that a conspiracy does exist to suppress the truth. At the time of our interview, she was reading Rockwell's *White Power*. Many of her friends were aware of her new racist orientation, and often she was asked to leave parties. She thought it was all so hypocritical because in her view most of those same people were closet racists.

Compared to other women in the movement whom I met, such as Ladas of the Nationalist Party, and even Farmer of the Ku Klux Klan, this woman, although she remained behind the scenes, was exceptionally devious, arrogant, and ambitious. She had a fetish about security. Although she subscribed to the Klan's journal, *The Spokesman*, she had not signed a membership form, for fear that the information would end up in the hands of the enemy. She used an alias when she wrote to McQuirter, which he used when replying, sending his letters to a third party, who in turn passed them on to her. She believed that she could outwit the slow-thinking opposition. If the police ever did come after her, she said, she would protest that she is just an innocent girl who met the Klan leader at a disco, or pretend she is stupid – an easy and credible front for a woman, she added. She had coined her own term, 'UEG' (Undesirable Ethnic Group), which she and her friends could playfully quip when they found non-whites present in restaurants and similar establishments. She spoke very harshly and coldly about her mother, even though the latter had only recently died. At one point she related her comical experiences with a boy-friend. When she realized that he was Jewish, she showed him her collection of white-supremacist and Nazi literature, and said she enjoyed watching him squirm.

This woman, who said she formerly was left wing, wanted to become known in the movement. She had plans to travel in the United States and in Europe to meet Fascist leaders (she called it 'networking'). She professed a hope that a blood-bath could be avoided, but did not rule out the necessity of violence. Her goal, she said, was simply to get Canada back to the way it was, with good old values and without Jews and blacks. She lamented that there was not an organization in Ottawa that espoused her views, and indicated her plan to establish her own group. What she had in mind, she said, was an organization with the public image of Fromm's groups, but with the covert beliefs and goals of the Klan. Her strong opinion was that an organization, to be successful, had to be publicly respectable, at least at the beginning, with a middle-class membership; that was why she was opposed to promoting the Klan. She admired the Aryan Nations' approach of combining a religious front with a racist orientation. Perhaps, she said, she would set up an equivalent to the Aryan Nations in Canada.

The remaining six men were all committed racists, but none to my knowledge was at the time of my research formally associated with a specific organization. They constitute the type of individuals who under the proper circumstances can be seduced into organizations like the Klan and the Nationalist Party. At the same time, if anti-racists are to succeed in eradicating racism, these several individuals are precisely the type who must be reached with a countervailing message. The first person, a boyish-looking man born about 1936 or 1937, and a meteorologist by profession, was raised in the Ottawa Valley, having previously lived in a small town outside Toronto and in Toronto itself. He had met both Andrews and McQuirter, but was disturbed by the roughnecks in their organizations. He was enthusiastic about everything British, and equally negative about blacks. Whereas he was prepared to state that Asians in general, and especially Japanese, are intelligent, he thought blacks were stupid; in this respect, he alluded, as others did, to Coon's thesis that blacks had evolved into homo sapiens 200,000 years after whites had done so – a thesis, incidentally, that has virtually no support among professional anthropologists. His main concern was immigration. Blacks, he declared, breed like flies, and would soon take over Canada; the only solution was to send them all back to Africa. Not only well-educated, this man had also travelled fairly widely, an experience, he said, which only confirmed his belief in white superiority. At the time when I met him, he was living with a woman whom he described as a left-wing university professor. Apparently she argued that all of his beliefs were based on hatred. He agreed.

Our next figure was born in England in 1948. He had a working-class background, but blessed with superior intelligence, he found his way to university. He too told me he had been a committed socialist when he was younger. However, he came to the conclusion that the left wing was too ideological and narrow. The right wing, he discovered, was much more intellectually oriented, which translated probably means it was more compatible with his prejudices. He joined the National Front in England, where he knew one of its former leaders very well; that was Martin Webster.

In 1969, this young man arrived in Canada to undertake graduate work in the sciences (he now has an M SC). A fan of Reagan (a form letter from the president adorned the man's living-room wall, thanking him for his support in his election campaign), he said he has not joined any right-wing organization in Canada. Nevertheless, he added that most of his friends are right wing, and they periodically got together for parties. His former girlfriend had served in Africa with a well-known Canadian organization for the idealistic; she had to conceal her right-wing sympathies from her fellow volunteers. This woman did graduate studies in sociology, which itself is significant, because the general attitude within the right wing is that sociology is socialistic, Marxist. The man told me about a sociology professor who also was right-wing–oriented, and I learned in other interviews about additional members of the right wing who had taken their degrees in sociology. One was a woman associated with the Nationalist Party. Another had completed an MA in sociology by the time he became active in the Western Guard.

In conclusion, this young man, who had a delightful sense of humour, gave the impression that his right-wing activity was sort of a lark. Right wing he was, but that, he seemd to be saying, did not mean he was an indiscriminate racist or madman. When he was sixteen, he had visited Israel. He also had been on holiday twice to the Soviet Union. It was ridiculous, he stated, to hate all blacks. He also was opposed to blanket anti-Semitism. What was important in his opinion was nationalism, what was good for a country. Thus, if Jews are loyal to Canada, fine; but if their allegiance is to Israel, they can be justifiably condemned. None of this sounds like the normal line spouted by committed racists, and perhaps I have been wrong to include him in that category. Nevertheless, the individuals who first told me about him, and attested that his racist credentials were impeccable, were themselves devoted anti-Semites. And one thing is certain; this young man, had he wished to do so, was certainly sufficiently bright and subtle to string me any number of lines.

The remaining four individuals, all teenagers, were secondary-school students in Toronto. They began to attend classes dressed in battle fatigues, distributing Fascist literature, and speaking out against blacks, Jews, and homosexuals. The thirteen-member school staff included a Chinese and a black teacher, and blacks and Jews were well-represented in the student body. Consequently, the budding Fascists were firmly opposed, and for a while were suspended from the school. All four students had been in the militia, and it was there, one of their secondary-school teachers thought, that they had been converted to Fascism (McQuirter, it will be recalled, had also been in the militia). Yet the teacher added that several other students from the school also belonged to the militia, and they had shown no signs of having picked up Fascist baggage. To my knowledge, none of the four students went on to join the Nationalist Party or any other Fascist organization – on the contrary, it seemed that their racist orientation had slowly petered out – but they were precisely the type on which Andrews and McQuirter rested their hopes for the future.

CONCLUSION

The radical right in Canada has been only one expression of the increasingly bold Fascist thrust in several Western nations, and the links between Canadian organizations and those abroad have been extensive. Canadian publications were regularly exchanged for their counterparts in the United States, Britain, France, Australia, and South Africa. Outsiders often displayed a keen interest in the Canadian scene. As we earlier saw, Rockwell was in contact with Beattie (he may have visited Vancouver around 1960), and Duke made more than one trip north of the border. David McCalden, a National Front member in Britain, visited the Western Guard in Toronto in 1974 (Fielding 1981: 65), observing that the latter was more extreme than his own organization. An article by the National Front's Martin Webster was printed in *Straight Talk*, (vol. 6, no. 5, n.d.). In 1974, as well, J.B. Stoner, chairman of the National States Rights Party, was hosted at a Western Guard banquet; his planned appearances at Trent University and Brock University were cancelled as a result of vigorous protests. That same year brought another visitor to Toronto from below the border – Matt Koehl, a long-time leader of the American radical right. In the present decade, other prominent U.S. Klansmen like Karl Hand and Dale Reusch have been repeated visitors.

Canadian Fascists, in turn, have travelled frequently abroad to participate in white-supremacist functions. Taylor was often in the United States (his postal box was located in Buffalo); Prins had visited local Nazis in Mexico, and had represented the Western Guard on trips to Europe. Members of the Canadian Knights of the Ku Klux Klan participated in the Aryan Nations' conference in Idaho. In late 1982 two Klansmen from British Columbia and two from Ontario attended a Klan rally in Georgia. Earlier, in 1975, the Western Guard had been an active participant in the White Confederacy held in Cleveland. I could easily add to this material, but the point, I believe, has been made: there are extensive links between Canadian white-supremacist organizations and those in other countries. As Matrai stated, an international radical-right network very definitely exists. That does not mean, however, that the radical right is poised to take over the world. Despite repeated efforts, all attempts to unite the far right under one umbrella organization have failed. The lack of unity is even more pronounced when one gets closer to the ground and examines the state of affairs within a specific country. In Canada, for example, the radical right was characterized by constant internal squabbling, suspicion, and schism. Unlike a comparable state of affairs on the far left, this was not because of disagreements about theory or tactics (as they related to Marxism); instead, it was mostly due to the aspirations of men and women each of whom wanted to be führer. Sometimes people simply got on one another's nerves, especially with the pressure of the police in the background, and as the prospects of organizations flowered and withered, members circulated from one group to another.

As far as recruitment and socialization went, most people who joined the radical right did so through accidental contact with an existing member; or they came across an organization's literature, or saw a representative like McQuirter on television. Most new recruits were one-issue men and women. They did not like Pakistanis, or they were strongly opposed to communism. Whatever their initial motivation, they all went through a general process of socialization. Their existing prejudices were expanded into a broader racial perspective of the world, and they were then taught that behind communism and racism lurked the key to the world's problems: the Jewish conspiracy.

The membership of the far right in Canada no doubt contained its share of undercover agents, infiltrators, and informers. Although I cannot claim to have learned the identities of more than a small proportion of these, I did come up with information on twenty-six candidates. Five of them were undercover police agents; six were other types of infiltrators – including a private investigator, a journalist, and four men connected to Jewish organizations; four of the informers were themselves radical-right members, including two who had held leadership positions; a further seven quite possibly were undercover agents and informers, but I was not able to confirm their status from more than one source; three others were strongly suspected by right-wing members to be infiltrators or informers, and one man, himself a prominent right-wing figure, told me that the police had tried to recruit him as an informer on several occasions (whether or not he accepted the invitation I am not sure). Once again, we are confronted with the problem of the purpose and effect of informers. In general, my impression was that regardless of whether they were police agents, other types of infiltrators such as reporters, or members who made a few dollars on the side, their combined efforts helped to undermine organized racism in the country. Nevertheless, the possible role of the police in establishing the Edmund

Burke Society must be remembered. One might also wonder about the motives that led the RCMP to recruit William Hart (*Globe and Mail*, 30 April 1980) to infiltrate black groups in Canada in the early 1970s.

Finally, there is the important question of finances. McQuirter once remarked that the era of Henry Ford was marvellous for the right wing, with numerous financial backers, but said that in recent years most donations go to the left wing, provided by wealthy capitalists who feel guilty. McQuirter denied that he received financial backing from U.S. Klans, but said that donations sent to the United States from Canadians were forwarded to his Canadian organization. Zundel claimed that unlike the far left, whose luminaries included Mao and Che Guevera, the radical right has no heroes, and thus fails to attract millionaire backers; he did state, however, that he gets about $60,000 annually from various contributors. The major sources of funds for the extreme right were membership fees and individual donations. Over the course of the project, I learned the identities of twelve people who regularly gave funds to organizations such as the Klan and the Nationalist Party. Usually the amount was between $200 and $300. Most of the backers were men who remained behind the scenes, including a lawyer, an inventor, and real estate agents. On the occasion of an election campaign, contested by one Toronto organization, a wealthy backer provided $200 for every comparable donation. Another man, I was told, gave $1,000 to help pay for the rent of the Klan's office on Yonge Street in Toronto. The largest donation from an individual (as opposed to an organization) that I heard about was $10,000. Precautionary steps usually were taken to protect the identity of the donors. For example, one potential contributor to the Western Guard was given a code identity consisting of the last three letters of his name reversed.

Before the Second World War, Arcand, according to Betcherman (1975), had received funds from foreign sources, and the same holds true for current organizations like the Ku Klux Klan, the Nationalist Party, and the Western Guard. Two of these organizations, according to one informant, were provided funds from a foreign government in exchange for mounting propaganda in Canada against Israel; the amounts on two occasions were $800 and $1,200. Taylor, it was rumoured, had travelled to Texas in 1979 to solicit funds from wealthy individuals. On a similar trip in 1980, a Canadian Klansman apparently raised about $10,000. In a letter in my possession, a wealthy American wrote to the Nationalist Party, requesting further information on the organization's activities and goals, on which basis he would decide whether to make a donation. Other sources of funds ranged from the mundane, such as the various 'straight' jobs held by members of the movement, to illegal scams, such as McQuirter's counterfeiting scheme; quite a number of the racists also were reputed to be involved in selling drugs. One man apparently lived off an inheritance, another struck it rich on a German lottery, and McQuirter's car was a gift from a female admirer. Perhaps most bizarre of all was a contribution of $500 supposedly made to one white-supremacist organization on the condition that none of its members opposed him as a candidate in an upcoming election. This politician, whose unsavoury reputation in a different matter had been reported by the press, lost the election anyway.

As far as the fringe right was concerned, there was not the same effort to solicit donations from all and sundry, nor do we find the phenomenon, common to the radical right, of the individual who simply doesn't want to work for a living. Virtually all of the prominent members of the fringe right held down regular jobs (Gostick, who appeared to live off membership fees and donations to his organizations, plus the sales of right-wing literature, was the glaring exception). I suppose part of the explanation why the fringe right could be more blasé about finances was its potentially greater backing from well-heeled individuals and even large corporations. However, I only learned of three people who had contributed sizeable amounts to fringe-right organizations. The one man apparently left an inheritance of several thousand dollars to different right-wing individuals. In addition, a large corporation provided funds, as did a nationalist organization which hoped the recipients could influence the Canadian government to recognize its claim to be the legitimate government of a country under communist control.

The most sensational source of funds I have left for the last. On one occasion, while talking with a prominent Jewish spokesman in Canada, he mentioned the Odessa Fund, supposedly an enormous sum of money put aside after the Second World War to carry on Hitler's plan to conquer the world and eradicate the Jews. When I pointed out that his belief in the existence of such a fund, plus the organization that would have to be behind it, was merely another variation on the conspiracy theme, he readily concurred, but said he had a gut feeling that it was real. Curiously, a prominent Canadian Klansman remarked that McQuirter's planned United Front was to have been supported from the same source that had backed previous experiments of this sort since the failure of 'the final solution' – the Odessa Fund.[11]

11 I do not mean to imply that the Odessa Fund therefore exists; indeed, if the information about it was all as superficial as what I have provided, we could happily write it off as far-fetched and ridiculous.

PART THREE / THE FRINGE RIGHT

8

Fromm and Gostick

In part 2 we dealt with members of society who openly admitted to or boasted about being white supremacists and Fascists. In part 3 we shift the focus to the fringe of the radical right: people who would object to being labelled racists, but at the same time are strongly critical of what they often refer to as 'pink' conservatives. Because they eschew violence and explicit white supremacism and anti-Semitism, they do not belong in the radical-right category. Yet, let me make it clear that they are quite distinct from the wider citizenry. They are much more prepared than most other people, including elected members of parliament, to speak out publicly against a range of issues such as foreign aid, immigration, communism, homosexuality, and the country's eroding freedoms. They also at times express what might be termed borderline racism – veiled statements about the dangers posed to Western civilization by blacks and Jews, but racist by innuendo nevertheless.[1]

This chapter revolves around two of the key figures, and their various organizations, in the fringe right: Paul Fromm and Ron Gostick. I shall begin with Fromm, whose story already has figured prominently in this study, picking it up again at the juncture where the Edmund Burke Society split in two, with part of the membership following Andrews ever deeper into the racist's camp, and the rest opting to straddle the gap between the far right and establishment politics.

---

1 As we shift out focus to the fringe right, it is appropriate to emphasize what was stated in chapter 1: if the radical right did not exist, and was not the implicit measuring rod, the fringe right would look a great deal nastier. One left-wing interpretation, indeed, is that the radical right is created or encouraged by the power élite in order to render the fringe right's political program relatively more acceptable to the wider population.

PAUL FROMM

Organizations and Publications

Fromm's resignation from the Western Guard in 1972 did not bring an end to his right-wing activity. Over the years he has been a central figure in several organizations, the major ones of which are described below.

Countdown

Almost immediately after cutting his ties with Andrews and the Western Guard, Fromm became editor of a new publication called *Countdown*, published four times a year as a magazine and several times as a bulletin. Its first issue (vol. 1, no. 1, June 1972) stated: '*Countdown* is being launched to serve the growing anti-communist movement in Ontario and to report on matters of interest to those concerned with preserving our Western Christian Civilization.' The symbolism of the magazine was apparent: 'It is our belief that we are living in dire days; that truly a countdown is in progress. Time is running out for our civilization.'

Campus Alternative

By November 1973, Fromm also had established a new organization, Campus Alternative. In a letter published in *The Varsity* (30 November 1973), he stated that Campus Alternative provided an opportunity for conservative students to exchange views, and an alternative to the usual left-wing politics at the University of Toronto. By 1975, the organization had affiliated groups at York University and the University of Waterloo. *Countdown* (said to have had a circulation of about 1,000) and Campus Alternative were in essence a continuation of *Straight Talk* and the Edmund Burke Society. For example, the slogan on the front page of *Countdown* in 1972 was almost identical with that carried on the front page of *Straight Talk* in 1971, stressing the values of 'Western Christian Civilization' and opposing communism, socialism, and welfare-state liberalism. Even some of the people in Fromm's new organization had been with him in the Edmund Burke Society. Jeff Goodall, for example, had resigned from the Burkers in 1970 to found his own organization, the New Right, and his own publication, *The Challenge*, which merged with *Countdown* in 1972.[2]

---

2 At least two other people who resigned at that time from the Western Guard founded new organizations. One was the Western Socialist Workers' Party; it was anti-communist, but called for 'civilized socialism.' The other was the Canadian Liberty League, founded by a man who sometimes had been referred to as Fromm's bodyguard; this

With the founding of the Campus Alternative, a new bright star appeared in the fringe-right galaxy – James Hull, who eventually replaced Fromm as the president of the organization. Born in Montreal in 1954, Hull graduated from the University of Toronto with a B SC in computer science in 1977 and an MA in the history of technology in 1980; by 1982 he apparently was enrolled as a PH D candidate in economic history at a Canadian university. In addition to his connection to Campus Alternative, he eventually was a co-founder and president of C-FAR, the meetings director for Alternative Forum, and on the executive committee of CAFE (these organizations are described below).

Alternative Forum
While the basic thrust of *Countdown* and Campus Alternative did not match the belligerence and viciousness that were eventually to dominate the Western Guard, it nevertheless was not much different than the Edmund Burke Society had been, emphasizing anti-communism and containing its share of what might be regarded as implicit racism and anti-Semitism. As the 1970s drew to an end, however, Fromm's message had become more subtle. That change was clearly reflected in the new organizations with which he became associated, notably Alternative Forum, C-FAR, and the Cornerstone Alliance.

By 1982, when I met Fromm for the first time, Alternative Forum had entered its eighth series (each series consisted of several forums). In 1981 (*Globe and Mail*, 6 May 1981), Fromm was listed as secretary of the organization. The president then was Greg Robinson, a Toronto man who, as we shall see in chapter 10, has been the force behind Young Americans for Freedom (YAF) in Toronto. In 1983 Alternative Forum had been established in Ottawa (Fromm was one of the initial speakers). In that same year the organization sponsored meetings in Orillia, Barrie, St Catharines, and Belleville. One document states that Alternative Forum was supported by organizations such as the Alliance for the Preservation of English in Canada, C-FAR, and the Canadian League of Rights. Most of the forums featured people and topics in the news at the time. For example, Forum 1 in the eighth series hosted Dan McKenzie, an MP whose public support for the white regime of South Africa after visiting that country became a media issue in Canada. Forum 4 in the same series was addressed by Bruce Knapp,

man said he resigned from the Western Guard because of its irresponsible, radical turn. Of course, there were others associated with these organizations, and by 1980 at least a couple of them had begun to interact with members of the radical right.

referred to in a pamphlet as Ontario's best-known tax rebel. Other forums had speakers such as Kim Abbott, former director of Canadian Immigration Services under both Pearson and Trudeau, who apparently opposed the switch from European to Third World immigration; the president of Victims of Violence, featuring a man whose daughter had been murdered; John Gamble, MP, who provided a behind-the-scenes look at Ottawa, revealing the rip-offs and hand-outs that 'incredibly, had the support of all three political parties.' Foreign aid, compulsory metrication, and the decline of freedom in Canada also were prominent themes at Alternative Forum. To my knowledge, the thrust of the forums, while representing a perspective clearly to the right of centre of the political spectrum, was not openly racist or anti-Semitic.

Citizens for Foreign Aid Reform (C-FAR)
If Fromm has made a name for himself in anything over the past decade, it has been in connection with his relentless critique of foreign aid – a critique which often found a receptive audience among Canadians who were themselves feeling the effects of inflation and unemployment, and were sceptical about government spending sprees. C-FAR was the major unbrella organization for the attack on foreign aid. Its principal publication was the *C-FAR Newsletter*, published twenty times per year. According to Fromm, the newsletter had subscribers in every province in the country. In a questionnaire issued by the organization to its readers, it was found that 35 per cent of them lived in Metro Toronto, 28 per cent elsewhere in Ontario, and the remainder in other provinces; 48 per cent of the readers passed the newsletter on to others after finishing with it, thus increasing the range of the message; 32 per cent drew from the content of the newsletter to write letters to MPs; and 27 per cent reported they used it in preparing letters to editors of newspapers. Fromm and Hull also published a book-length critique of foreign aid – *Down the Drain?* – and there was a C-FAR Canadian Issues Series – several booklets dealing with themes such as over-population, immigration, church-sponsored terrorism, CUSO's Marxist orientation, and even the implications of sociobiology for the survival of the Western world.

Cornerstone Alliance
Cornerstone Alliance, founded by a former policeman, is described in one of its leaflets as a 'non-partisan group of concerned Canadians with traditional values that put principle before party.' Their beliefs include a God-centred moral order, law and order, individualism, the fundamental importance of the family, limited government, a free (as opposed to a planned)

society, and a relentless opposition to communism. This organization's advisory council contained former MP John Gamble, who was quoted as saying: 'There is a systematic attempt being made to destroy our country.'' Burke's dictum, 'The only thing required for evil to prevail is for good men to do nothing,' appears on one of the organization's leaflets, which stated: 'By taking a stand to oppose the forces that would destroy our country, we risk confrontation and attack. This can be so cunningly devised that you can find yourself questioning your own actions. It is most important for you to maintain a rock-hard belief in our principals – The Cornerstone Alliance can provide the strength needed to resist outside pressure.' Except possibly for the above statement, the general message of Cornerstone Alliance was quite mild, and certainly not explicitly racist. Among its members were Paul Fromm (he sat on the advisory committee) and Paul Hartman, a follower of the Norse god Odin, and in 1974 treasurer of the Western Guard.

Catholics (or Christians) against Terrorism and Church Watch
In an interview in 1982, Fromm expressed the opinion that C-FAR had been so successful because of its narrow, specific focus. Over the years, he has been involved with several other one-issue organizations, such as Catholics against Terrorism, Christians against Terrorism, and *Church Watch*. Fromm himself was a Catholic, and these organizations essentially expressed a Catholic point of view. That does not mean, however, that only the Protestant churches were singled out for criticism. Christians against Terrorism once launched a major campaign against the Canadian Catholic Organization for Development and Peace (an organization involved in Third World development issues). In addition, Fromm and his associates (*Globe and Mail*, 30 March 1974) apparently had hoped of persuading Protestant churches to join them in their campaign against socialist clergymen. Christians against Terrorism was endorsed by *Countdown*, by Campus Alternative, and by the Friends of Rhodesia Association. *Church Watch*, published by C-FAR, came out in 1979 as an eight-page tabloid devoted to exposing the involvement of church groups with leftist-Marxist politics, particularly in the Third World.

Canadian Association for Free Expression (CAFE)
and the Committee to Stop Bill 7
The Canadian Association for Free Expression (CAFE) was founded in 1980. Its focus, as its name suggests, was on free-speech issues across the country. Both Fromm and Hull were on the CAFE committee. The president in 1983 was a man named Harry F. Barrett, who also was on the advisory council of

Cornerstone Alliance. In a letter that I received from Fromm, he wrote: 'CAFE came into existence because of the very real efforts by both establishment and far-leftist forces to stifle conservative discussion especially of race and immigration.'

Connected to CAFE was a regular two-page publication, CAFE Quarterly, which apparently was distributed in Quebec, Ontario, and the four western provinces. Its first issue (vol. 1, no. 1, Winter 1981) contained an article entitled 'Toronto Board of Education Gags Free Speech.' The reference was to the board's stated intention to withdraw books and other school materials containing racial or ethnic biases. The CAFE Quarterly writer concluded: 'The resulting texts will be nothing but self-serving minority propaganda. Honest history will disappear. Texts will have to suppress the barbarity of the Indian caste system, or the wretched backwardness of many African nations.' In subsequent issues of the publication there were articles declaring that the Toronto Star's description of the Ku Klux Klan as a terrorist racist group may be libellous; linking the Liberal government's immigration policy to increased racial tensions; and contending that Zundel's mailing privileges should be restored. Occasionally CAFE gave out Freedom Awards. Two recipients in 1982 were well-known metric critics, including Neil Fraser who was fired from the civil service because of his vocal opposition to metrication. Fraser, who received a cheque from CAFE's legal fund, was quoted as saying (CAFE Quarterly, vol. 2, no. 4, August 1982): 'Prime Minister Trudeau is more of a threat to parliamentary democracy than Hitler was to the Freedom of Europe.'

Fromm also was involved with the Committee to Stop Bill 7. The latter consisted of proposed legislation by the Ontario government to revise and strengthen the province's Human Rights code. A leaflet sent by Fromm in 1981 to members of the Ontario legislature declared that Bill 7 promotes 'the unfair and discriminatory practice of "affirmative action." '

Early Beliefs
The basic beliefs and goals shared by *Countdown* and Campus Alternative were essentially those embraced by the organization they had just replaced – the Edmund Burke Society. Articles appeared supporting capital punishment and opposing abortion, one-world government, gun legislation, and the 'insane immigration policies of the Trudeau government.' The Ontario Human Rights Commission was portrayed as a coercive body that promotes the welfare of immigrants at the expense of native-born Canadians. Individual freedom, limited government, and free enterprise were singled out as the corner-stones of Western civilization. In *Countdown*'s first issue, Presi-

dent Chiang Kai-shek was saluted, Governor George Wallace was applauded, and President Nixon's policies were described as 'far to the left of any democrat.' In the second issue of *Countdown*, the emphasis on equality was strongly opposed, and the Canadian government was accused of underminig the nation's morality by promoting pornography, homosexuality, and abortion. Elsewhere there were references to 'mass murderer abortionist Henry Morgenthaler,' to OXFAM's support of revolution in the Third World, and to Red Tories such as Joe Clark who voted against capital punishment. Bumper stickers were sold with messages such as: 'Trudeau, Canada's Biggest Mistake'; 'Abortion Is Murder'; 'To Hell with Socialism'; 'Register Communists, not Firearms'; and 'Crush Castro, not Rhodesia.'

Anti-communism was a regular theme in *Countdown*. In an article entitled 'The Marxist Mafia at Our Universities,' Fromm (*Countdown*, vol. 1, no. 1, June 1972) argued that one has to be a Marxist to survive as a student or faculty member. As evidence, he pointed to the shoddy treatment on campuses given to Shockley (a former Nobel Prize scientist and in later years a promoter of the view that blacks are intellectually inferior to whites) and Ezra Pound (Mussolini's backer and a social-credit advocate), while the Marxist revolutionary Herbert Marcuse was embraced with open arms. In another article, Nixon was described as 'a man who speaks like a conservative and acts like a socialist,' and socialism was said to have been 'planned, pushed and underwritten by so-called "capitalist" international financiers' (*Countdown*, vol. 1, no. 2, July 1972). The decision of the Chase Manhattan Bank to open a branch in Moscow was seen as evidence of the conspiracy between socialists and capitalists. Red China was accused of flooding the West with opium, and Fromm expressed horror that Canada 'broke diplomatic relations with Taiwan in order to recognize the rebel regime of mass butcher Mao.'

The same type of borderline racist statements that had begun to appear in *Straight Talk* around 1970 were repeated in *Countdown*. An article entitled 'Guess Who's Coming to Canada' (*Countdown*, vol. 1, no. 4, September 1972) stated that during the last couple of decades non-white immigration had increased from 6 per cent to 33 per cent. The writer asked: 'Is Canada a White nation with a European cultural heritage and backbone, or are we to smother our uniqueness in the universal causes of ultraliberalism?' Elsewhere, reference was made to unassimilable Ugandan Asians who 'will add to our welfare roles and/or take jobs from Canadian citizens' (*Countdown*, vol. 1, no. 5, October-November 1972), and it was stated that 'Ugandan Asians and certain other groups' should not be admitted to Canada because whites and coloured people can't live peacefully together (*Countdown*, vol. 1, no. 4, September 1972). A letter from Robert Andras, minister of manpower and immigration, was printed in *Countdown*, in which he rejected the accusation that Canada's open-door policy has led to racial problems in the country. Fromm and his friends were not convinced. One school in Toronto, they reported, had been polarized along racial lines, caused by Negro resentment of white students who out-perform them. School standards themselves had dropped, it was claimed, because of the influx of black immigrants. The rape of two women by a black person was seen as justification for the right wing's opposition to Third World immigration. There also were references to a race riot in Montreal and to attacks on innocent subway commuters in Toronto. Although on the surface these attacks were condemned, underneath there seemed to be a hint of satisfaction that clashes between white and black were indeed on the increase.

One writer (*Countdown*, vol. 1, no. 8, February 1973) complained that it is always the white man who is accused of racism, while the racism of non-whites is ignored or excused. Support was expressed for Alberta Klan leader Mac a' Phearsoin's policy of marrying within one's racial colour or religious faith.' Finally, in a brief submitted by *Countdown* to the Special Joint Committee on Immigration Policy, it was stated: 'This magazine believes that Canada should remain a basically European country,' and 'We owe the Third World nothing.' Any doubt about the intended racist innuendo here evaporates under the light of a further comment in the brief: 'cockroaches seem to be camp followers of certain Third World Immigrants.'

As far as anti-Semitism was concerned, there was little in *Countdown* that matched the scurrilous attacks by the Ku Klux Klan or the Aryan Nations, but Israel was certainly not high in the estimation of Fromm and his Campus Alternative associates. It was denied that Jews are singled out for special persecution in Russia. Indeed, in one article (*Countdown*, vol. 2, no. 1) it was claimed that 'you have to be a Jew to have justice much in the same way that you have to be a Jew to be able to leave the Soviet Union today.' In the next issue, Fromm rejected the Israeli cause as just, and added that Israeli terrorism has equalled or surpassed Arab terrorism. In the following issue, former prime minister Menachem Begin was referred to as the past commander of a terrorist organization (the Irgun); the writer observed: 'Begin ... smells very much like a war criminal deserving "Nuremberg" trial.' Under Fromm's editorship (*Countdown*, vol. 1, no. 9, March 1973), there was an article condemning Israel, and arguing that all trade between that country and Canada should be cut off. The writer concluded: 'We cannot retain normal relations with butchers.' Anti-

Semitism itself was dismissed as a ploy on the part of Jews themselves. The argument was that it was Jews who distributed anti-Semitic literature, or provided media exposure to people like Arcand and Rockwell, thus creating a favourable climate for passing anti-hate legislation. There was an angry report about the banning of Christian prayer in the North York Council, stating that it was the work of the borough's numerous Jews and atheists, and Father Gregory Baum was referred to as 'a leftist German Jew, who claims to have converted to Catholicism.'

Espousing, as they did, the same sort of causes as the Edmund Burke Society and *Straight Talk* before them, Campus Alternative and *Countdown*, not surprisingly, generated opposition from similar quarters. In a letter in *The Varsity* (23 November 1973), one writer who signed off 'Heil Fromm!' stated: 'Hitler fans don't fret. There's a new fan club at the U. of T. – the Campus Alternative.' Fromm's response (*Varsity*, 30 November 1973) was to claim that many of the stories in the campus newspaper could have appeared in the Canadian Communist Party's organ. Fromm's new right-wing organizations locked horns with the radical left. Fromm had complained that Canada's immigration laws were so lax that even Hardial Bains, an immigrant from India, and the head of the Communist Party of Canada (Marxist-Leninist), had been admitted. A member of that organization was eventually convicted of assault on Fromm and sentenced to a year in jail. Another left-wing organization, the Revolutionary Marxist Group at the University of Toronto, also tore into Fromm. In one of its leaflets, entitled 'Fascism – What It Is and How to Fight It,' it is stated: 'here at U. of T., Paul Fromm has crawled out of the sewer to form the Campus Alternative. Fromm ... is now editor of *Countdown*, an anti-semitic, sexist, racist and anti-working class rag.' In another leaflet, Fromm is described as 'a well-known fascist,' and James Hull as a supporter of racism and apartheid in South Africa. Whereas the usual reaction is to dismiss alleged racists and Fascists as mentally unbalanced idiots, yet another leaflet produced by the Revolutionary Marxist Group warns the reader: 'These people are not ordinary "crackpots," they know what they are doing.'

Fromm and his friends did not fare much better within the right wing itself. Despite his acrimonious departure from the Western Guard, he had made a determined effort to avoid infighting among the various segments of the right wing. This was clearly reflected in *Countdown*'s slogan: 'No Enemy on the Right.' It was also *Countdown*'s policy to report positively on the activities of other groups like the John Birch Society, and to offer moral support to fellow right wingers. Thus, warm wishes were extended to

Armand Siksna in his attempt to become elected as a school trustee; John Ross Taylor, also contesting public office, was described in *Countdown* (vol. 1, no. 9, March 1973) as a man of 'courage, forthrightness and integrity.' Nevertheless, a major source of opposition to Fromm and his new organizations came from the Western Guard itself. Some of its members apparently threatened to smash a meeting attended by Fromm, and to break his arms and legs if the police were contacted (*Countdown*, vol. 1, no. 2, July 1972). Later in that year, several signs put up in Toronto by *Countdown* were pasted over by Western Guard posters.

Later Beliefs

The Western Guard, the Edmund Burke Society, Campus Alternative, and most of the other organizations that we have examined so far embraced the entire gamut of issues that excited the right wing. Towards the end of the 1970s, a new sophistication could be detected in the organizations with which Fromm was associated. Many of these, such as C-FAR, CAFE, and Catholics against Terrorism, had a narrow focus. Moreover, the topics they dealt with were those that often seemed to agitate ordinary citizens – wasteful aid to Third World countries, the church's involvement with revolutionary groups, the fundamental importance of freedom of expression, and the menace of communism. Anti-Semitism all but disappeared in the written materials produced by these organizations, and racism in general was rarely a topic of direct discussion. No doubt Fromm and the people surrounding him by the late 1970s and early 1980s had become more polished, more professional, and nowhere was this more evident than in relation to the treatment of foreign aid.

If C-FAR had been restricted to exposing foreign-aid scandals, or to a critical analysis of aid programs in terms of their long-term impact, there would be nothing out of the ordinary about its message. But C-FAR goes a great deal further. The Third World is portrayed as primitive, saturated in superstition. One article in the *Newsletter* (no. 66, 1 January 1981) deals with torture and mistreatment of dogs in the Philippines 'where dog meat is considered a delicacy.' In an earlier issue (no. 54, 1 May 1981), it is stated: 'Religious taboos prevent many Third World peoples from utilizing the resources they have ... A good case in point is the refusal by Indian authorities to control wild monkeys that destroy huge quantities of food and injure people.' Elsewhere, there is an account of slavery in Mauritania, and Uganda is said to have slid deeper into primitivism since the British pulled out; by primitivism, C-FAR appears to mean instability and economic collapse, brought about by the country's socialism. In *Down the Drain?*

Fromm and Hull write (1981: 23): 'All cultures are not equal. A culture that condemns its womenfolk to the degradation and agony of sexual mutilation is not just backward, it is inhuman!' Here also they point out that religious taboo often means rats can't be killed in countries like India, nor can sacred cattle be eaten. Disease, poverty, and hunger, they claim, are not the real problems of Third World countries, but instead bad sexual practices like clitoridectomy, superstition, attitudes towards work, over-population, mismanagement, primitive methods of agriculture, and debilitating socialism (1981: 52, 56).

Socialism was the brunt of repeated criticism, to the extent that foreign aid only appears as a convenient vehicle with which to approach it. Numerous negative remarks were directed at Red Tories who support foreign aid. Doug Roche, Flora MacDonald, Walter McLean, Ron Atkey, and David MacDonald were identified as culprits (C-FAR Newsletter, nos. 77 and 81); people like Don Monro, Ron Stewart, John Gamble, and Sinclair Stevens were said to exemplify a growing Conservative viewpoint that is exactly the opposite of that espoused by the Red Tories.

Fromm remarked to me that immigration is a more volatile issue to raise with MPs than foreign aid. Nevertheless, it is clear that C-FAR saw foreign aid and immigration as two sides of the same coin. It was contended (Newsletter, no. 62, 1 November 1981) 'that massive Third World immigration is a form of foreign aid, as it tends to benefit others, rather than Canada.' W. Harding Le Riche (1983: 5), described as a medical practitioner who was born and educated in South Africa, wrote in *Over-Population and Third World Immigration* that most Third World immigrants 'multiply more rapidly than do Canadians.' He observed that some people think the government has deliberately set about to turn Canada into a Third World country, and asks rhetorically if Canadian Jews are pleased about the large influx of Muslims. Le Riche, let it be said, was not apparently opposed to all coloured immigration: 'Some hardly visible minorities such as the Chinese, Koreans, and Japanese are perfectly well accepted.'

One might wonder why C-FAR, supposedly concerned with foreign aid, would report in one of its newsletters that in Toronto during recent years there has been a 200 per cent increase in leprosy. Another article (*Newsletter*, no. 66, 1 January 1981) states that Canada has been invaded by the Third World; specific reference is made to Haitian immigrants and their belief in voodoo and human sacrifice. All this suggests that behind the attack on foreign aid lies a world-view that was struggling to get out. In fact, C-FAR's analysis tells us more about the right-wing perspective than about Third World poverty itself. While not a little of the material in C-FAR appeared to be mildly racist by implication, it was not the same variety as found in the Western Guard and the Ku Klux Klan. It usually took the form of commentary about the cultures of the Third World peoples, rather than extolling the virtues of white superiority, and was presented more subtly.[3] For example, one article in the newsletter was entitled 'Canadians: An Endangered Species,' whereas in the Western Guard's *Straight Talk* it would have been 'Whites: An Endangered Species.'

As it has been pointed out in previous chapters, science has often been called upon to support the beliefs of committed racists. In the 1970s, the Canadian fringe right discovered a body of scholarly writing that seemed tailor-made for its particular perspective: sociobiology. As far back as the days of *Countdown* and Campus Alternative, an interest was shown in socio-biology, but it was with the later organizations like C-FAR that is took on a central focus. In *Sociobiology: Blueprint for Survival*, Fromm and Varey (1983: 3) interpret this theoretical orientation to demonstrate that man is 'a hierarchical, territorial, aggressive, xenophobic being also charac- terized by gender inequality and leanings toward more or less permanent, monogamous sexual relationships.'[4] After emphasizing territoriality as an innate instinct, they state (1983: 6): 'Systems that attempt to deprive man of his property (communism) or excessively restrict his use of it (socialism) or those that seek to induce him to abandon his preference for his country in favour of a one-world government (World Federalism) are doomed to crash on the rocks of human nature. Patriotism, the love of one's territory or group land and one's people, is not some outmoded virtue, but essential to survival.' Xenophobia, the rejection of the stranger, is said (1983: 7) to account for the 'widespread public anger at Canada's open-door immigra- tion policy.' In fact, it is claimed that hostility among Canadians towards Third World immigrants is rooted in their genes.

The same arguments occur in other C-FAR publications such as the *Newsletter* and *The Canadian Lifeboat* (Hull 1982). The general viewpoint is that socio-biology constitutes scientific proof that liberalism is unnatural. As Fromm and Varey marvel (1983: 11–12):

---

3 According to the Western Guard's 17 June 1976 recorded telephone message (Crysdale and Durham 1978: xvic), Fromm held a seminar in a Toronto hotel on the anthropolog- ical differences between the white and black races.

4 Varey, who died in 1983, had been a founding director of C-FAR. For several weeks in 1974 he ran a regular Saturday-afternoon session on sociobiology and ethology. He also had been one of the organizers for Campus Alternative symposia, several of which featured sociobiology.

In Sociobiology, conservatives have an extraordinary blueprint and assurance. It points to a national policy that seeks to stem Third World immigration and protect the ethnic balance; that promotes a property-owning, free enterprise economy; that reduces regulations and curbs institutions, like human rights commissions, that restrict the use of private property; that abolishes artificial programmes to enforce equality, such as affirmative action schemes; and that protects the family unit. These have traditionally been planks in a conservative ... platform. Sociobiology gives these planks added strength. They are not the mere outcomes of whim or preference; they are scientifically correct because they are in tune with our human nature.

Sociobiology, at least as interpreted by right wingers, may well be a blueprint for its world-view. But with its glorification of xenophobia and trumpeting of the genetic basis for racial discord and mankind's incapacity to surmount its lower instincts, it also is a perfect example of what I have earlier argued: the right wing capitalizes on mankind's weaknesses; it attempts to build a philosophy out of the flaws in the human condition.

In view of the perspective of C-FAR, it is not surprising that CIDA and CUSO came under constant attack. CIDA was not only criticized for its massive waste, but also for its politics. Canadian aid, stated one writer (*Newsletter*, no. 71, 14 March 1982), goes 'promiscuously' to both allies and enemies. The Canadian government is condemned for its opposition to South Africa's apartheid system, and for its support of Marxist regimes and terrorist organizations. Two books in particular, *Down the Drain?* (Fromm and Hull 1981) and *CUSO and Radicalism* (Lapajne 1983), mount a massive attack on CIDA and CUSO. In the latter book, CUSO is described as part of the terrorist-support network, as an organization with a radical socialist bias. Its activities in countries like Cuba, Angola, and Zimbabwe are condemned, as is its support for independence movements in Namibia and South Africa.[5] After *Down the Drain?* was published, C-FAR attempted to engage CIDA in a television debate, but CIDA officials would have none of it (*Newsletter*, no. 58, 1 September 1981). The reaction of CUSO to Lapajne's book was quite different. The organization's executive director, Chris Bryant, not only decided to respond to Lapajne's criticisms, frankly admitting that development was a complex issue, with few success stories, and emphasizing that it was intrinsically linked to power (*CUSO Forum*, vol. 2,

5 In recent years, CUSO, and perhaps especially SUCO (the independent Quebec equivalent), have demonstrated a willingness to be politically forthright. However, when I was a member of CUSO in Nigeria in the 1960s, the usual reaction of militant Africans was to regard CUSO volunteers as insufficiently political. They dismissed organizations like CUSO and the American Peace Corps as neo-colonial appendages of their governments.

no. 1, January 1984), but also invited C-FAR to write a column in *CUSO Forum* on the subject of aid. James P. Hull, then president of C-FAR, quickly wrote to Bryant (17 January 1984), accepting the offer and expressing appreciation for the opportunity to engage in 'constructive dialogue.' Shortly after in *CUSO Forum* (vol. 2, no. 3, May 1984), Hull's formal reply was printed. He had been invited to write on the subject of aid, and on C-FAR's world-view, but that was not what *CUSO Forum* got. Instead, Hull opened with some nice words about the Canadian men and women of high ideals who have filled the ranks of CUSO, and went on to produce an innocuous reply that leaned over backwards to placate the organization, again expressing gratitude for the generous offer of dialogue. His prose gave virtually no hint of the content of C-FAR's *Newsletter* and its related publications.

In a more lengthy reaction by CUSO's executive director, 'Additional Notes on C-FAR' (unpublished but available in mimeo), Bryant stated that he had been tempted to follow the advice of some people to ignore *CUSO and Radicalism*, rather than dignifying it with a reply. That, of course, would have appeared to be the height of irrationality. Dialogue, after all, is perceived as a value only slightly less hallowed than motherhood. Nevertheless, I have come to the conclusion that CUSO was wrong to address C-FAR's charges, and especially to invite a response from that organization. In my opinion, C-FAR did not want a dialogue; it was not interested in debating development issues, with the possibility of influencing CUSO or in turn modifying its own viewpoint. Instead, what C-FAR sought was legitimacy. Hull's innocuous reply would seem to confirm what I am saying. By engaging in dialogue with C-FAR, CUSO conferred on that organization and its viewpoints a momentary degree of respectability that had not previously existed.

Foreign aid is a shooting duck. There can be few targets easier to hit, and credit must be given to Fromm and his associates for having had the wisdom to select it as the focus of their attack. Virtually everyone has some scepticism about foreign aid. The hard-pressed taxpayer, generally uninformed or misinformed about the Third World, wonders what happens to all that money donated to Tanzania or India, and why those countries can't look after themselves. Marxists dismiss aid as an aspirin (or a soporific), when what is needed is an operation – indeed, aid is thought to sustain the relationship of inequality between poor and rich nations, a relationship created by capitalism in the first place. For some academics, let us admit it, foreign-aid projects are little more than an opportunity to see the world at double their regular salaries. Even the sincere among them must have qualms about the long-range impact of their contributions in the face of the Third World's encapsulation by the international market. Yet there is a world of difference between criticisms that question the value of particular kinds of aid and those that use the aid issue to mask prejudices about Third World cultures, political ideology, and opposition to non-European immigration. One might say that just as anti-Semites would have found another focus for their attack if the Holocaust had not occurred, Fromm and his associates would have come up with an alternative bogeyman if foreign aid had not been so readily available. In both cases the target was only the detonator. The dynamite was the message behind it.

Actions

In the years following his resignation from the Western Guard, Fromm continued to speak at high schools, to attend meetings such as a World Anti-Communist League Conference in Mexico, and to participate in East European functions such as an Independence Day reception organized by the Estonian Central Council. Obviously an intelligent man, he also had immense energy. While a student at the University of Toronto, he had managed to take an active part in right-wing politics, while at the same time performing well enough to earn both a BA and an MA. After he graduated, he became an English teacher in a Mississauga secondary school, and still found time to participate in a whole range of organizations, including some that I have not mentioned, such as YAF (see chapter 10).

Unlike members of the far right such as Taylor and Andrews, Fromm did not display much interest in running for public office. This does not mean that he has been politically inactive, of course, since his public appearances, writings, and efforts in a range of organizations all have been directly political. Moreover, over the years he had held formal office in the Social Credit party (to be elaborated on in chapter 10), has been a Metro Separate School Board trustee (from 1976 to 1978), and has served as chairman of the political action committee of District 10 of the Ontario Secondary School Teachers Federation. Undoubtedly, however, his greatest success, especially since it involved establishment politics, was his election in 1981 to the position of treasurer of PC-Metro, an umbrella organization linking thirty-one federal ridings in the Metro Toronto region. In a newspaper interview (*Globe and Mail*, 28 April 1981), Fromm was reported as saying that his election showed 'a definite trend to the right' within the Progressive Conservative party, which he stated had previously been dominated by the Red Tories. But during the interview his past association with the Edmund Burke Society was brought up, and it was reported that he 'believes in restricted immigration, thinks the boat people should have been sent to inhabit desert islands and expresses the belief that a supreme race of intelligent people "is a good idea." '

The outcry across the country was not long coming. Joe Clark, prime minister at the time, and a man whom Fromm considered to be one of the Red Tories, said Fromm's views do not represent party policy (*Globe and Mail*, 29 April 1981). Peter Blaikie, the Conservative party's national association president, asked for Fromm's resignation. Fromm eventually bowed out under all the pressure, but that was not before he had remarked (*Globe and Mail*, 28 April 1981) that Premier William Davis was not a real conservative, complained that he hadn't done anything to require him to resign, and denied being anti-Semitic. Fromm formally resigned on 30 April 1981; a week later several letters to the editor appeared in the *Toronto Star* (6 May 1981), contending that he had been a victim of a media smear job, and that his views on immigration had considerable merit. A few days after that, the Toronto *Sun* (15 May 1981) printed an article entitled 'Tory Called "a Hitler" for Fromm Ouster.' The Tory in question was Peter Blaikie, vilified in front of the Albany Club where he was giving a speech. Later in the summer, *CAFE Quarterly* (vol. 1, no. 3, Summer 1981) lamented that PC leaders had followed the suit of the media, rather than condemning the unfair attack on Fromm.

Referring to his forced departure from PC-Metro, Fromm remarked to me that leftists are virtually never scrutinized by the media and the public, but right wingers seem to be fair game for all and sundry. There exists, he said, a clash between Europeans and Third World peoples, and his worry was that the former had lost the will to defend themselves. His belief was that cultures are simply different, and can't be mixed. In this context, he referred approvingly to Mackenzie King's contention that Canada should remain a 'European' country. What appeared to frustrate Fromm was his perception that so many Canadians privately agreed with him, but publicly denounced him. He did, however, claim that many of the back-benchers in the Conservative party to whom he talks are sympathetic to his views, and opposed to the party leadership. And in the summer following his ousting from PC-Metro, there was a meeting of nearly three hundred people (including Fromm) in Toronto from across Ontario; referred to as the New Right Coalition, its program was nothing less than to move the Conservative party and the country farther to the right.

RON GOSTICK

'God bless you,' said the man, then in his early sixties, still handsome and vigorous, with a definite presence that bespoke of authority and assurance. This was Ron Gostick, whom I had just interviewed, a man probably even more reviled in liberal and left-wing circles than Paul Fromm. In terms of longevity, Gostick was the John Ross Taylor of the fringe right, having begun his political career shortly after he had been discharged from the armed services in the late 1940s. Gostick had come by his right-wing stance honestly. Raised in the Gadsby district of Alberta, where his parents had been farmers, his mother had served as an MLA from 1935 to 1940 in William Aberhart's Social Credit government. Around 1950 Gostick moved to the small village of Flesherton, Ontario, where he and his family have lived ever since (his wife is a school principal, and two of his children are teachers). Over the years, Gostick has built a reputation as perhaps the major supplier of right-wing literature in the country, and as the man behind the Canadian League of Rights, a grass-roots organization bent on exposing communism, opposing totalitarianism, and building a new society resting on a mixture of Christian principles, social-credit economic policies, small government, and light-skinned citizens.[6]

Organizations and Publications
Gostick is the owner of Canadian Intelligence Publications, described as 'a private firm engaged in research and education in the defence of freedom and Christian values.' Two of its major organs are the *Canadian Intelligence Service* and *On Target*.[7] The first, founded about 1950 and published monthly, concentrates on world problems. Appearing on each issue are again the words of Edmund Burke about good and evil men. The second, established in 1967 and published weekly, concentrates on Canadian topics. On each issue of *On Target* appear the words: 'Ye shall know the truth, and the truth shall make you free.' A great deal of both the *Canadian Intelligence Service* and *On Target* consists of reprinted newspaper articles, and sometimes stories in one appear again in the other. In addition to these two publications, Gostick runs a vast mail-order business for right-wing literature – materials as he has said (*Canadian Intelligence Service*, vol. 31, no. 6, July 1981) that are 'not readily available through the usual channels' (Gostick adds here that the views expressed in these materials do not necessarily reflect his own).

6 As was stressed in chapter 1, the division of the right wing into the radical and fringe categories is crude, and this is especially true with regard to Gostick. In many respects, Gostick and his organizations seem to belong somewhere between the fringe right and the radical right, although to have created a category solely for his case would have been awkward in terms of the organization of the study.
7 The Minutemen, a prominent right-wing organization in the United States in the 1960s, also had a publication called *On Target* (Albares 1968: 38).

In 1968, Gostick established the Canadian League of Rights. It grew out of his earlier organization called the Christian Action Movement. The Canadian League of Rights was founded, apparently, in response to his readership who felt that to be informed was not enough; in addition, they felt, there had to be a vehicle for action. The Canadian League of Rights, according to one leaflet, was designed 'to assist people to get involved in public affairs and political life of our nation, but outside and beyond the narrow bounds of *party* politics.' By the early 1980s, it was reported (*Edmonton Journal*, 6 May 1983) that the organization had about 10,000 followers, 4,000 of them in Alberta. Certainly it was in the Western provinces that the Canadian League of Rights had its greatest impact. There were specific directors of the organization in Manitoba (John Bellows), Saskatchewan (Art Boehme), Alberta (Eric Boswell), and British Columbia (Phillip Butler). Butler, the son of a right-wing activist in Australia who led a comparable organization, was one of two young men being groomed to replace Gostick and Pat Walsh (his main lieutenant); the other was still a student at a university in southern Ontario when I met Gostick in 1982.

Walsh, an Irishman raised in Quebec, was himself reaching retirement age. In addition to his affiliation with Gostick, he was the general secretary of the Freedom Council of Canada, which is the Canadian chapter of the World Anti-Communist League; his business card in 1982 also listed him as a member of the executive board of the latter organization, and as chairman of the Canadian Friends of Free China Association. Walsh, virtually always identified by people in the movement as a former RCMP undercover agent, did not have the austere, even dignified bearing of Gostick, but he seemed to be much more popular in the movement, and enjoyed the reputation of contributing freely of his time to other groups. For a supposedly former RCMP agent, he also was a remarkably compliant subject to interview.

Beliefs

In a leaflet entitled 'Introducing the Canadian League of Rights,' the organization's goals are set out as follows: to promote loyalty to God, family, and country; to defend the constitutional monarchy and Christian heritage; to encourage personal responsibility and individual initiative; to oppose centralized power and bureaucracy; to uphold sovereignty and ties of Common-wealth; and 'to oppose and expose every form of totalitarianism – be it "Nazism," "Communism," or any other "ism." ' In numerous articles in *On Target* and the *Canadian Intelligence Service*, it is argued that the World Council of Churches supports terrorism in Africa. At one point Gostick stated (*Canadian Intelligence Service*, Supplementary Issue, September

1976): 'The World Council of Churches today has become little more than the ecclesiastic arm of the international Communist Conspiracy.' An article by Peter Worthington in the Toronto *Sun* dealing with the World Council of Churches' aid to terrorists is reprinted, and the United Church is referred to as the United 'Communism' Church of Canada. Western civilization, states Gostick (*Canadian Intelligence Service*, vol. 21, no. 5, May 1971, Supplementary Section), has been correctly described as Christian civilization. One article links Christianity to the monarchy, and Canadian League of Rights meetings usually opened with a prayer. There were other articles on foreign aid – repeating Fromm's criticisms and viewpoints – on sexual permissiveness in schools, on abortion, on gun control, and on fluoridation. Even in some of these, the Christian theme pervaded. For example, one article on foreign aid (*Canadian Intelligence Service*, vol. 13, no. 4, April 1963, Supplementary Section) declared that such aid 'is in fact a direct violation of God's first and greatest Commandment.' Another (*Canadian Intelligence Service*, vol. 14, no. 2, February 1974, Supplementary Section) contended that fluoridation, forced upon people, violates the basic Christian concept of personal freedom and responsibility, and contributes to totalitarianism.

Totalitarianism itself was one of the central themes in Gostick's materials. The *Canadian Intelligence Service*, he states, was published to combat the deadly threat posed by totalitarianism, which was fostered by communism, centralization of power, and inflation. The existence of separatist movements in Quebec and Western Canada is explained as a consequence of excessive centralization of power; Gostick himself advocated strong provincial and municipal government. While the communist variety of totalitarianism was the brunt of his attack, he made it clear that he was opposed to the phenomenom everywhere. The political left and right, he contended (*Canadian Intelligence Service*, vol. 25, no. 3, March 1975, Supplementary Section), are actually identical in one sense: both propose the centralization of power. In my interview with him he drew a circle, stating that the right and the left come together at the open ends. Gostick took pains to deny that he was a radical-right fanatic. He said he was not sure what the right wing is, but if it existed, claimed he was not part of it – again because both the far right and far left are totalitarian.

Gostick argued that one can't just organize a political party and create a revolution; instead, the latter must come from the grass-roots, and that was where he had directed his message and activities. He was opposed to people contesting elections; the only thing that achieved, in his view, was to put people's names in the press. He also was opposed to the formation of new political parties. It was not the latter that were needed, he said, but instead a grass-roots, non-party movement, exemplified by the Canadian League of Rights. Only if established political parties did not rise to the occasion in the wake of a revolution would there be a legitimate need for new parties. In Gostick's view, neither Reagan nor Thatcher had the answers to the world's problems. They saw only two alternatives – inflation and high interest rates. Yet there is another alternative, said Gostick, a more scientific route: social credit. While he was in favour of the social-credit monetary approach and general philosophy, he was opposed to any party calling itself Social Credit, such as in Alberta in the past and in British Columbia today. Instead, social-credit principles should be incorporated into existing parties. His point was that once a party calling itself Social Credit was established, the economic philosophy of the movement was bound to be contaminated. Establishing such a party, he said, would be similar to creating a Christian Party. People being what they are, it would not be long before it was no more 'Christian' than any other party.

We now turn to the topic of racism. Gostick told me that while racism is not one of his major concerns, he could understand in the face of massive Third World immigration and unemployment how people become attracted to organizations such as the Ku Klux Klan. Yet he argued that such organizations were futile; throwing bricks through windows, shouting racist slogans, and attacking minority members served no purpose, except possibly to strengthen the hands of those who were out to further restrict the country's freedoms. There were, nevertheless, numerous references to racial matters in Gostick's publications. For example, an article on Rhodesia defended white rule in that country (*Canadian Intelligence Service*, vol. 15, no. 11, November 1965). Canada's immigration law was described as a laughing-stock (*Canadian Intelligence Service*, vol. 24, no. 7, July 1974); multicultural society can be enriching, states one article, but multi-racial society 'infers a deliberate race-mixing which usually brings tension, violence, race problems, and ultimately mongrelization' (*On Target*, no. 613, 15 October 1979). In another article on immigration, Gostick asks (*Canadian Intelligence Service*, vol. 24, no. 11, November 1974): 'Do we want our country to become another India, a Brazil, a Jamaica? Do we want our great-grandchildren to be cross-breeds of every colour? Tut tut! Restrain those bleeding heart screams of "racism" and "bigotry". After all, this is our country.'

Elsewhere (*On Target*, no. 638, 21 April 1980) there is a report on Kim Abbott's address at an Alternative Forum meeting, in which the former director of Canadian Immigration Services reportedly expressed his strong opposition to the switch from European to Third World immigration, and remarked that each of the 60,000 boat people sponsors up to 15 others, meaning an eventual influx of 900,000 people. Abbott's apparent contention that Canada is a lost country unless a grass-roots movement emerges to oppose the government's insane immigration policies was heartily endorsed by *On Target*. Although the United Church usually was seen as part of the socialist thrust, *On Target* (no. 612, 8 October 1979) was enthusiastic about former moderator Robert McClure's recommendations that the boat people be settled in tropical countries like Borneo, on the grounds that the costs would be reduced (and thus more families could be accommodated), and that the climate in Canada would be unbearable for them. Gostick's views about immigration were, according to Gordon (*Contrast*, 19 March 1982), stated pretty plainly during an open-line radio program in 1978. Gordon quotes Gostick as saying: 'I would like to see Canada develop at the present time as a White Country. Primarily a white country yes.' When it was suggested that he must therefore be a racist, Gostick apparently replied: 'A racist in that sense, yes.' He continued weakly by claiming that he was not opposed to black people or anybody else, but simply wanted to retain the God-given individual identities of the different races.

In an interview in 1983 (*Globe and Mail*, 15 June 1983), Gostick stated: 'There's no truth to the charge that we're anti-semitic, but we're strongly opposed to political Zionism.' Elsewhere, Gostick expressed his opposition to Nazism on the grounds that it was merely another form of totalitarianism. Despite these qualifications, Gostick was certainly not very favourably disposed towards Jews. There is no evidence, one article states (*Canadian Intelligence Service*, vol. 31, no. 12, December 1981), that Jews are prosecuted in the Soviet Union; in fact, only Jews are allowed to emigrate from that country – Christians must risk their lives by squirming under barbed-wire fences. Several years ago (*Toronto Daily Star*, 8 December 1960), Gostick apparently portrayed the Supreme Court's integration order in the United States as a Jewish plot, and pointed out (*Canadian Intelligence Service*, vol. 13, no. 5, May 1963) the extensive influence of pro-communist Jews in America, including their control over the NAACP. The Anti-Defamation League, according to a pamphlet distributed by Gostick entitled 'The Bigots behind the Swastika Spree,' does little to encourage tolerance and goodwill. Instead it 'promotes hate, fosters racial and religious prejudice, and deliberately fans the flames of anti-semitism.' The Anti-Defamation League, the pamphlet continues, 'is controlled and directed by pro-communists, professional hate-mongers, *and* fanatic bigots, who victimize Jew and gentile alike.' In one article, Arthur Koestler's hypothesis that most Jews originate from Asia, and are Khazars rather than Jews, is discussed, pointing out that if Koestler is correct the Zionists have no claim at all to Jerusalem. Anne Frank's diary is referred to as a fraud and propaganda hoax (*Canadian Intelligence Service*, vol. 10, no. 2, February 1960), and an article attributed to a former Liberal MP is reprinted (*Canadian Intelligence Service*, vol. 27, no. 7, July 1977, Supplementary Section no. 1) in which it is stated that former Israeli prime minister Menachem Begin was a terrorist in charge of the Irgun. Finally, included on the *Canadian Intelligence Service*'s reading list were materials such as *The Hoax of the Twentieth Century*, *Anne Frank's Diary: A Hoax*, and 'Did Six Million Really Die?' Ages (1981: 390) claims that Gostick also was peddling the 'Protocols of the Elders of Zion,' which he describes as 'probably the most scurrilous piece of literature ever directed against Jews.' In one document in my possession, it is contended that on display at Gostick's speaking engagements was a publication, 'Waters Flowing Eastward' – the 'Protocols,' under a different title.

Gostick has his own peculiar interpretations of anti-Semitic incidents. Behind the periodic apparent increases in anti-Semitism are the communists and the Jews themselves (which in his view seemed to be linked). Anti-Semitism is a scare tactic that enhances the passing of restrictive legislation, and thus brings us a step closer to one-world domination. Gostick not only claims that outbreaks of anti-Semitism seem to occur conveniently just prior to an Israeli bond drive, but also retails a pamphlet that contends that the Anti-Defamation League in conjunction with the American Jewish Congress 'actually supports financially Nazi, fascist and anti-Semitic groups to keep them in operation.' Closer to home, David Stanley and John Ross Taylor are described as Nazi twins promoted by the CBC in order to shock Canadians, and thus assure the passage of anti-hate laws used to silence anti-communists. In Gostick's view, McQuirter's Ku Klux Klan served an identical function. Ironically, then, Gostick and his far-left foes share a similar perspective about the radical right: it is little more than an instrument of the state. However, whereas Gostick believes that organizations like the Klan merely play into the hands of the communists bent on world domination, the far left's interpretation is that such organizations are employed by the capitalist state to divide the working class and disguise the real locus of economic and social oppression.

Actions

While probably best known for his mail-order business, and weekly and monthly publications, Gostick did not confine himself to the armchair. He told me that he and Walsh had founded the Friends of Rhodesia Association, and Walsh said, whether true or not, that the two of them had driven the first oil tanker from South Africa to Rhodesia after the Unilateral Declaration of Independence. The major activities, in addition to the various publications, were the frequent speaking engagements in connection with the Canadian League of Rights. For example, in 1974 Gostick toured the Western provinces, during which he participated in twelve radio and television programs. In 1979 Walsh travelled to the Maritimes, apparently giving one talk at St Mary's University. In 1980 there were Canadian League of Rights meetings in Ottawa, Toronto, Belleville, St Catharines, Montreal, Quebec City, and Fredericton; and Walsh toured the Prairies, speaking in community halls, schools, hotels, a senior citizen's centre, the Royal Canadian Legion, libraries, service clubs, and at Olds College in Alberta. In 1982, meetings took place in London, Bobcageon, Burlington, and Flesherton; the Burlington meeting was held at the home of one of the organization's members, and the Flesherton meeting at the Royal Canadian Legion.

Sometimes larger conferences were organized. At one of them at the Georgia Hotel in Vancouver, 21–22 March 1969, about 120 people attended. There apparently was no overt anti-Semitism, although a visitor from Australia, Eric Butler (the father of Phillip Butler, the Canadian League of Rights' man in BC), complained about the West's policy of treating Israel as a sacred cow. Gostick's speech stressed the importance of a letter-writing campaign, and Walsh talked about subversion on university campuses. A much more recent Canadian League of Rights conference, held in Calgary, 28–29 October 1983, attracted about four hundred supporters.[8] Most of these were from Alberta and British Columbia, although handfuls had come from the United States, Mexico, Britain, Australia, and New Zealand.[9] The daughter of Major C.H. Douglas, the original architect of social credit, sent her best wishes, with the hope that the conference would encourage 'the many staunch supporters of my father's farsighted and enlightened ideas.' Perhaps the most outspoken guest was Colonel Jack Mohr. Referred to as the highest decorated soldier in the Korean War, and a former speaker for the John Birch Society, Mohr lectured the audience on 'White Christian Civilization.' After stating that virtually all moral, spiritual, and physical progress in the world was the fruit of the white race, he declared: 'If this truth makes me a "racist," then so be it!'

---

8 See the report on the conference in the *Canadian Intelligence Service*, vol. 34, no. 1, January 1984.

9 The links between the League of Rights in Canada and similar organizations in Australia and New Zealand will be dealt with in more detail in chapter 12.

Walsh, who was in charge of security, apparently had his hands full. The CBC, according to members of the Canadian League of Rights, tried to barge into the conference, and at least one individual, a woman, was threatened at the hotel by intruders. I had heard various tales of planned attempts to infiltrate the conference by opponents of Gostick's organizations, who hoped to record the proceedings on tape (the hotel, I was told, was owned by Jews). Ironically, the Canadian League of Rights made its own tape of part of the show available at a price to all those who were interested.

CONCLUSION

Fromm and Gostick penetrated the right-wing spectrum at much the same angle, and I suppose that accounts for their mutual admiration. Fromm once remarked that years ago Gostick was considered crazy for claiming Trudeau was a socialist, but now virtually everyone realizes he was correct. Gostick, on his part, advertised Alternative Forum and printed numerous articles by Fromm in *On Target* and the *Canadian Intelligence Service*. The differences that existed in their ideologies and tactics were minor. In recent years, Fromm has focused on single-issue themes such as foreign aid, whereas the Canadian League of Rights was set up to tackle totalitarianism from every conceivable direction. Gostick's message was presented more consistently in Christian language (although Fromm, it must be remembered, was closely associated with organizations like Catholics against Terrorism), and he was much more enthusiastic about social credit; indeed, Fromm once said to me that social-credit principles bore him. Gostick also was more in favour of a grass-roots movement rather than attempting, as Fromm did, to influence establishment politics or work within a particular party.

One document (Levy, n.d.) suggests that Fromm, like numerous other right wingers, formerly was attracted to the left and was an admirer of Fidel Castro. Certainly that was not his public image. As a newspaper account (*Toronto Star*, 6 July 1980) put it: 'Paul Fromm, private citizen, sounds a little like Archie Bunker and a little like flinty economist Milton Friedman – all in the same sentence.' His reputation as a right-wing activist was reflected in the media outcry, no doubt spurred on by interested anti-racist organizations, that followed his appointment as treasurer of PC-Metro. In earlier chapters I indicated the acrimony that existed between Fromm and the extreme right. While his forced resignation from PC-Metro was publicly condemned by members of the far right, privately they were amused, their views confirmed that Fromm could never progress through establishment channels. At the height of the PC-Metro case, Fromm remarked (*Toronto Star*, 1 May 1981) that he had joined the Edmund Burke Society when he was seventeen, an impressionable age (he was born in 1949). He regretted that he had been a member and claimed his beliefs have changed since then. When I interviewed him, he said that during the Edmund Burke Society days he and his associates knew nothing about organization or publicity, but now they have the know-how and the facilities to effectively put across their political views. There is no doubt that over the last decade Fromm has become more polished and sophisticated. Yet what has impressed me has been the relentless consistency of his beliefs, no matter how obfuscated, since his student years at the University of Toronto.

Gostick's public image was, if anything, even more negative than Fromm's. Ages (1981: 390), as I mentioned earlier, stated bluntly that Gostick was selling crude anti-Semitic literature, and a couple of decades ago Epstein and Forster (1967: 136) referred to him as the 'publisher of the anti-Semitic *Canadian Intelligence Service.*' It is true that whereas on C-FAR reading lists we find conventional academic books such as Wilson's *On Human Nature* and Tiger and Fox's *The Imperial Animal*, Gostick's recommended reading includes various works holding the Holocaust up to ridicule. Yet, as in Fromm's case, members of the far right saw Gostick as a lightweight, even as part of the liberal-left enemy camp. Many of them regarded him as a has-been, a man who no longer understood the Canadian political scene and what was required to achieve victory. Andrews remarked that Gostick had a great line at the end of the Second World War, but now was anachronistic. One Nazi sympathizer said that Gostick is not pro-Nazi, but only pro–Anglo Saxon. This man related an incident that he claimed occurred several years ago. Suspicious of Gostick's right-wing credentials, he arranged to meet him in order to ask point blank if he was opposed to Jews. According to the man, Gostick was non-committal, and the other went away with the opinion that Gostick's organization in reality was a RCMP front. During an interview with Taylor, he remarked that Gostick was strong on anti-communism but weak on the Jewish question. In Taylor's view, too, Gostick was an RCMP agent or informer. Terry Long, the Alberta leader of the Aryan Nations, thought likewise (he also said Tearlach Mac a' Phearsoin's KKK was a Jew-Communist front). And Martin Weiche remarked to me that it had been so long since he had heard anything about Gostick that he thought the man was dead.

In recent years, Gostick's image, like Fromm's, appears to have improved somewhat. Gostick told me that when he first settled in the small village of Flesherton after the Second World War, people thought he was anything from a nut to a communist to a Nazi. Yet during the past few years there has been a real change. Flesherton residents, he claimed, now are rallying to his side, appreciating at last the wisdom of his words. For example, at a meeting held in the village in 1981 he expected a turn-out of about twenty people, but said almost eighty appeared. Gostick also told me about his experiences on a radio show in Vancouver in 1981. At one point, the host turned to him and exclaimed in so many words: 'My God, Gostick, but you have mellowed. You used to be a right-wing fanatic.' But as Gostick pointed out, it was not himself who had changed, but the radio host, and indeed the entire country. Canadians, he declared, were finally waking up. Actually, his claim that the tide had turned went back almost a decade earlier. Again in response to the remark that he had mellowed politically, Gostick retorted (*Canadian Intelligence Service*, vol. 24, no. 7, July 1974) that it was the media and the country that had shifted to the right, and concluded wryly: 'As I observed on several occasions, if this shift continues any further I shall be finding myself on future Western visits in the embarassing position of being considered somewhat of a "left winger"!'

9

Keegstra

What makes good men and women countenance racism? Can one be a good father, a respectable member of the community, a man of high principles, and a racist simultaneously? Can a devout individual, a Christian who happens also to be an anti-Semite, be called a good man? Time after time in my interviews with the residents of Eckville and surrounding communities, James Keegstra, the former school teacher and mayor whose racist orientation cost him both jobs, was defended as a man of exemplary conduct and pristine morality. Many of those who opposed him, of course, held a different opinion. They saw him as a madman, a monster, a peculiarly evil individual. Often outsiders regarded Eckville in the same light: a strange, ignorant little community (its population in 1983 was 842) which somehow had drifted away from the main current.

This chapter will be guided by two themes. The first concerns the paradox of the good man who also embraces a racist world-view. The single most important factor, I shall argue, that makes Keegstra tick in his orientation to religion. It is from his particular interpretation of Christianity that the two most noteworthy facets of his being stem: his apparent goodness and his inclination to racism. The second theme concerns the wider significance of the Keegstra case. Those who contend that Keegstra is some kind of exceptional ogre, and that Eckville is a peculiarly malignant community populated by nuts and bigots, have failed to understand the case. Such a viewpoint distorts and trivializes the Keegstra phenomenon. To argue otherwise is to ignore the degree to which prejudice and discrimination can be embraced by ordinary people across the country.[1] The only extraordinary

1 Indeed, I would suggest that the most effective way to study the Keegstra affair would be to do it elsewhere, in a community of similar sociological properties selected at random. Should the results display a comparable degree of racism and anti-Semitism, the study would be that much more powerful.

features of the Keegstra case were the prominent positions that the man held: teacher and mayor. Even these elements are not without precedent in the country; other teachers and other mayors, as I have learned, while less celebrated than Keegstra, have embraced similar views regarding blacks and Jews.

The media coverage of the Keegstra affair has been extensive, and the inevitable production line of books has already begun (see, for example, Bercuson and Wertheimer 1985 and Mertl and Ward 1985). If there is anything special about my own treatment, it rests on the numerous original interviews that I conducted with Keegstra and those closely associated with the case. I shall begin with an overview of the various school board and legal proceedings that centred around the man. This will be followed by a three-part scheme intended to take the reader behind the scenes and make sense of the case. The first part will focus on Keegstra's opponents, all of whom thought he was unsuited for the position of teacher, but not all of whom regarded him as a totally evil man. The second part will examine his supporters, who uniformly viewed him as a virtuous man, a model citizen, an innocent victim of an atheistic society. The third part will focus on Keegstra himself and what he professes to believe. By allowing Keegstra to present his own case, so to speak, I hope to provide the basis from which the reader can draw clear conclusions about the character, motivations, and beliefs of the man. As it will become apparent, just as Zundel convicted himself by his own testimony, much the same can be said for Keegstra.[2]

BACKGROUND

The beginning of the end of Jim Keegstra's teaching career occurred in December 1981, when R.K. David, superintendent of schools for the County of Lacombe, Alberta, received complaints about a man in Eckville who supposedly was lecturing his students on a Jewish conspiracy to take over the world. That was not the first time that Keegstra's class room conduct had been challenged. As far back as 1973, and again in 1976 and 1977, there had been complaints about his anti-Catholic comments. A former principal of Eckville Jr-Sr High School during the period 1970 to 1975 testified (*Globe and Mail*, 24 May 1985) that he had tried then to have Keegstra removed from teaching grade-twelve social studies because of his tirade against Russians. Yet one wonders if anything more than a half-

---

2 In order to protect the identities of those connected to the Keegstra case, I shall omit much of the biographical material.

hearted effort had been made, because when that same man received a complaint from a student of 'professed Jewish ancestry' regarding Keegstra's anti-Semitic comments, his reported advice to the student was simple: since the course was not compulsory, she should just drop it (*Alberta Report*, 2 May 1983). What is perfectly clear is that nothing concrete came of these early complaints. One popular explanation was that the superintendent of schools at that time, who apparently had been satisfied that Keegstra had modified his course content (*Alberta Report*, 2 May 1983),was himself a Catholic. He did not want to reprimand Keegstra for fear that such action would appear self-serving. Another factor was that the nature of Keegstra's message changed over the years. Whereas anti-Catholicism originally informed his teaching, he eventually began to introduce negative views about blacks, and finally became an overt anti-Semite. At the same time, he grew more and more bold about voicing his peculiar interpretation of the world scene.

It was not until David became superintendent in September 1979 that the various complaints against Keegstra were given serious attention. David's involvement with the case actually began in September 1981, when the editor of Eckville's local newspaper asked him to attend a meeting of parents who were concerned about the content of Keegstra's teaching. However, when the superintendent went to Eckville, he found that the meeting had been cancelled. Keegstra and the Eckville school principal, Ed Olsen, told him the meeting was of no consequence, and denied they knew why it had been called. On 15 December 1981, David was contacted by Eckville school trustee Kevin McKentee, who relayed a number of parental complaints against Keegstra. David also received a telephone call from the first of two Eckville women who were to play key roles in the Keegstra affair: Marg Andrew. A Catholic herself, she had been one of those to protest several years earlier about Keegstra's anti-Catholic sentiments, specifically his accusation that the Irish Republican Army (IRA) was a Marxist organization. In Andrew's opinion, Keegstra definitely was teaching hatred towards blacks and Jews. She told me about one student who wouldn't see the film *On Golden Pond* because Keegstra had said the Fondas are Jews, and the student didn't want any of his money to go even indirectly to a Jew. One of her daughters once wrote an essay for Keegstra, praising Hitler; her grade was 95 per cent. Andrew confirmed what I had often heard previously: that boys seemed to be much more receptive than girls to Keegstra's message. The explanation that many Eckville people offered was first that Keegstra taught subjects such as mechanics that boys liked, and helped them fix their cars; and second, that he was the complete male chauvinist, who saw women in negative terms, as part of the conspiracy, and purposefully aimed his message at the male students. One of the Eckville teachers, for example, herself a Keegstra fan, told me that Keegstra had criticized her for not remaining in her home to look after her husband and children.

Andrew sent David student notes that had been dictated by Keegstra, and made a presentation to the Lacombe school board about the matter. She also wrote a letter to the minister of education, David King, who replied (12 October 1982) that because the local school board was addressing the problem, it would be inappropriate for the government to intervene. At a later hearing in Edmonton the next year, a woman approached Andrew, saying she was from Europe, and declared that she knew from her own experience that Keegstra was right about Jews. Andrew was variably described to me by Keegstra's supporters as a gossip, a communist, and an IRA member herself. Yet she impressed me as strong, quietly confident, level-headed, and just. She said she didn't know Keegstra well personally, and was only concerned about one thing: the impact of his teaching on the students.

On 18 December 1981, David again went to Eckville, where he talked to Keegstra and the principal, examined class notes, and interviewed some of Keegstra's students. From this, David arrived at two important conclusions: first, Keegstra was indeed teaching a brand of anti-Semitism; second, the students believed him. The superintendent immediately wrote Keegstra a very forceful letter, accusing him of teaching the Jewish conspiracy as fact, directing him to eradicate his biased presentation, and stating that failure to do so would result in severe disciplinary action. A month later (19 January 1982), he again sent a letter to Keegstra, stating that the Lacombe school board would be considering the possible termination of his contract at its meeting on 9 February and inviting Keegstra to attend and present his case before the board made its decision. In a letter (25 January 1982) confirming his attention to appear before the board, Keegstra remarked that he was shocked that it was considering firing him without having first given him an opportunity to defend himself.

The school board's complaints against Keegstra were threefold: his failure to comply with the Alberta social-studies curriculum; his teaching of biased, discriminatory theories as fact; and his failure to modify sufficiently the content and approach of his teaching materials. At the board hearing on 9 February Keegstra proceeded to deliver a lesson in history, confirming in the process his belief in the Jewish conspiracy, of which the Holocaust hoax was a part, and arguing that his perspective merely offset the socialist line of other, uninformed teachers, and thus enhanced the students' overall educational development. On 9 March 1982, David wrote to Keegstra, stating that his presentation at the board reinforced David's earlier impression that he taught his particular version of history as documented fact. As David pointed out: 'The issue under review at the hearing was not your competence as a teacher or your ability to teach the subject matter. Nor was the issue the esteem or regard that is held for you by your colleagues in Eckville or by the Town Council of Eckville, but simply, the content, approach and emphasis placed in your Social Studies program on questionable and controversial theories of history.' Nevertheless, the board decided not to terminate Keegstra's contract. It obviously had been impressed by the persuasive teacher, and no doubt influenced by the support provided him by the Alberta Teachers' Association (ATA), and by numerous letters attesting to his character and competence. A man who attended that meeting told me the board had been both shocked and impressed – shocked by the interpretation of history that Keegstra presented, and impressed by the man's oratorical skills. Indeed, one of the considerations that later led to Keegstra's dismissal was the board's perception that the man was such a good communicator – one who could easily sway his pupils in any direction he chose.

There also was another factor involved. Not all of the members of the Lacombe school board were surprised or upset by Keegstra's historical interpretations. The board consisted of sixteen members, only fourteen of whom voted at any one time, seven of them school trustees and seven of them county-council members. At least four of the board members were reputedly sympathetic to Keegstra's historical interpretations. The two whom I met were thoroughly acquainted with the right-wing literature, and one of them was, if anything, even more overtly racist than Keegstra himself.

Although the board decided not to terminate Keegstra's contract, David made it clear that his presentation in the class-room of the Jewish conspiracy as historical fact was unacceptable, and concluded that unless he complied with the board's directives it might again consider dismissing him. Keegstra was anything but contrite. On 18 March 1982, he wrote to David stating that he had always taught within the curriculum guide-lines, and would continue to do so. That was not the response that the board had hoped for, and the superintendent conveyed its lack of satisfaction in yet another letter (7 April 1982). Nevertheless, I suppose a sort of stalemate had been reached at that point, and the whole matter might have died, except that a few months later the school superintendent received another complaint against Keegstra. One of the board's obstacles up until then was that while there had been numerous complaints, nobody had been willing to put their charges in writing. But in October 1982, an Eckville parent, Susan Maddox, did just that. She was the last important Eckville figure to become involved in the Keegstra case, but her role was critical, because she forced the issue to crystallize at the very point when it was beginning to fall apart.

In Maddox's formal complaint, a two-page letter dated 11 October 1982, she stated that in a grade-nine class attended by her son, Keegstra spent most of his time on creationism and evolutionism; contended that anyone who believes in evolution is a communist, that the metric system is a communist conspiracy, that all judges are corrupt, and that bankers are crooks; focused at length on Oliver Cromwell and presented him as an admirable figure; taught anti-Semitism; and omitted more mainstream but essential themes in history. She concluded by observing that in her opinion the course was 90 per cent indoctrination and 10 per cent fact, and requested that Keegstra be dismissed as a teacher. Her letter was well-argued, coherent, and consistent with her son's class notes, which she also submitted to the school superintendent. A little over a week later (19 October 1982), she wrote again to David, stating that she had met with Keegstra and the Eckville principal. On that occasion Keegstra had given her three tracts representing his interpretation of history: these, along with her son's notebook, she sent to the superintendent. Maddox later made a presentation to the Lacombe school board, attempting to refute Keegstra's interpretation of history. Her presentation apparently had a dramatic effect on the board.

Maddox's courageous confrontation of Keegstra (and to some extent the school system) led to her being named by *Chatelaine* magazine as one of Canada's top twelve women. But as in the case of Andrew, her willingness to stand up against what she considered wrong brought slurs on her reputation. She was painted as a forceful, spiteful, insensitive woman, whose overbearing ways were responsible for the ill health of one of her family members. One of the Eckville teachers who sided with Keegstra said that Maddox was aggressive and dogmatic, and that if you are in her way she will just bowl you over. Even a man who admired her immensely for her actions involving the Keegstra affair described her as a particularly strong-willed, determined individual. He compared her to Keegstra in this respect, and made the comment not only that in one dimension were they much alike, but also that perhaps it took a single-minded individual such as Maddox to get rid of the equally single-minded Keegstra. Maddox herself denied (Kotash 1984) that she had a reputation as a trouble-maker, and in my opinion what was surprising is that the gossip about both her and Andrew was so mild. Given the degree of resentment and anger towards them in the Keegstra camp, we can pretty well conclude that they both were solid citizens, otherwise the world would have been promptly told about their foibles.

Maddox's formal letter of complaint set off another investigation into Keegstra's teaching content, which David found had changed little since 1981. On 7 December 1982, the Lacombe school board met again, and this time Keegstra was fired; the dismissal took place on 8 January 1983, following a paid suspension of thirty days. At that meeting the ATA continued to defend Keegstra, arguing that although the board had a written complaint, it could be construed as harassment by a parent out to get the man. The ATA also argued that freedom of speech was involved, and that there was not enough evidence against Keegstra to justify releasing him. Keegstra, with the support of the ATA, appealed, leading to a board of reference hearing in Edmonton in March 1983. He lost the appeal.

Following his dismissal, there was an extensive RCMP investigation involving interviews over a four-month period with about two hundred people (*Calgary Sun*, 13 January 1984). On 11 January 1984, Keegstra was served a warrant charging him under section 281 of the Criminal Code of Canada of unlawfully and wilfully promoting hatred against the Jewish people. The preliminary hearing at Red Deer in June 1984, found sufficient evidence to take the case to trial. In October of that year, a pre-trial motion was heard in which Keegstra's lawyer, Christie, the same man who had defended Zundel, contended that the charge against Keegstra violated guarantees of freedom of expression under the new Charter of Rights and Freedoms. The presiding judge rejected the argument, and on 9 April 1985 the trial, which would last seventy-one days, finally began. Keegstra eventually was found guilty and sentenced to a fine of $5,000 or imprisonment for six months (*Red Deer Advocate*, 22 July 1985).

There were many similarities between the Keegstra and the Zundel court cases, in addition to the fact that both defendants had the same lawyer. As in the Zundel case, the defence attempted to turn the trial into an examination of the freedom-of-speech issue. Christie said the case was the most important test of freedom of speech ever to occur in the country. Keegstra showed up at the opening of the trial in April 1985 wearing a 'Freedom of Speech' button. Keegstra, like Zundel, had to be found not guilty if in the jury's view he genuinely believed what he said (in my judgment, both Zundel and Keegstra were true believers). Finally, Keegstra, too, basically convicted himself. It is correct that at the preliminary hearing in 1983 he argued that he had only presented the Jewish conspiracy as theory, not fact; and at the trial in 1985 he said only about 7 per cent of Jews were part of the conspiracy, not all Jews. Yet from his first appearance in front of the Lacombe school board until his final court conviction in 1985, he made little effort to deny his alleged interpretation of history. Instead, he attempted to persuade the various audiences that his views were valid. In that sense, he was much less disingenuous than Zundel.

OPPONENTS

By 1983 the Keegstra affair had become a national – even an international – story, attested to by an article on the case in *The New York Times* (26 May 1983). However, the opposition against Keegstra had actually begun slowly, and only as the months went by did Eckville people realize that they were in a fish-bowl, examined by outsiders as if they were an exotic species, bombarded by media coverage, and subjected to the criticisms of a range of organizations including, belatedly, the government of Alberta and the church. I shall begin by discussing the opposition within Eckville itself, and then turn to that which grew outside the community.

Keegstra and his supporters categorized their opposition within Eckville as follows: newcomers, parents without children in the school, 'the hockey jock group,' and the hospital conspirators. It was true that some of the key opponents were newcomers to the community, such as the two local doctors, the minister of the Presbyterian church, and the assistant administrator of the hospital. However, they were balanced by others such as the president of the Chamber of Commerce (he was also on the local council) and a member of the Canadian Legion whose family roots were in Eckville; moreover, others such as Maddox had spouses who were natives of the area (this woman herself, by the time she lodged her complaint against Keegstra, had lived in the Eckville area for about fifteen years). It was also correct that some of Keegstra's opponents were childless, or their children were not yet old enough to attend secondary school; yet for others among the opposition this was not the case: the children of people like Andrew and Maddox had been taught by Keegstra. By the hockey jock group, Keegstra meant those people who were active in the minor-hockey program or in figure skating. According to Keegstra, this group, bored and restless, set around complaining about their lot in a little town, and passed the time of day dissecting and criticizing the teachers. At least two of his most effective opponents were included in this group: Kevin McEntee, who was a school trustee, a member of the Chamber of Commerce, and active as a coach in minor-league hockey; and Susan Maddox, who was on the executive of the figure-skating club.

As far as the hospital was concerned, it was a fact that several of the most articulate spokesmen had some kind of connection to it. I have already referred to the two local doctors; McEntee was the assistant administrator of the hospital, and his superior, George Schmidt, also was a consistent opponent. Maddox was a nurse in the hospital, and I learned about at least one other nurse who considered Keegstra to be unsuitable for the position of teacher. This woman's sister was a strong supporter of Keegstra, which brings us to an important point: sometimes members of the same family found themselves in different camps over the Keegstra affair. This often was the case among those students who believed Keegstra implicitly, much to the chagrin of their parents and it was occasionally the case among adults as well. For example, one of the men to whom I have just referred found himself in the uncomfortable position of not only putting his business at risk as a result of his opposition to Keegstra, but also jeopardizing his relationship with his father who defended Keegstra to the hilt. One man said to me that the opposition to Keegstra came mostly from the educated residents of Eckville. In general, that observation was correct, but as I shall soon point out, there was one extremely important exception – Keegstra's fellow teachers in the Eckville sceondary school.

A distinction must be made between those who openly opposed Keegstra, and those who did so covertly. Almost all the people mentioned so far belonged in the first category. The hidden opponents consisted of individuals who were not prepared to risk their jobs or businesses by coming out clearly against Keegstra. For example, one middle-aged businessman told me how he went to elaborate steps to avoid being interviewed by reporters. Nevertheless, he was quite active behind the scenes in opposing Keegstra, whom he regarded as a confirmed neo-Nazi. Another covert opponent had an equally sensitive position in the community. The Keegstra affair had been very traumatic for this woman and her family. Her son was a complete convert to Keegstra's ideas. He used to drive his parents crazy with his racist and anti-Semitic arguments, picked up in Keegstra's classes. The daughter, in contrast, was absolutely horrified at what she had been taught by the man. The parents, both of whom grew up in the Eckville area, told me that their daughter had a most difficult time in his classes, and finally, in order to pass, just wrote what he wanted. I read one of her essays – a tirade against Jews – for which she received a mark of 75 per cent. The mother of this girl said that Keegstra once remarked that a family in the area that bought a Russian tractor was for that reason communist. Her father stated that Keegstra was an excellent teacher in drafting and mechanics, but even in those subjects his historical interpretations crept in. He also remarked that there are lots of twenty-five–year–olds walking around in Eckville today who believe there never were any German concentration camps. Both parents were deeply concerned about their son's future.

Apparently since the school board hearings and other legal venues, he had been 'neutral' as regards the validity of Keegstra's historical interpretations. But Keegstra, his parents said, was dangerously persuasive, and they were not confident that their son would be able to shake off his influence entirely.

Part of the opposition within Eckville took the form of petitions. The first, initiated by Marg Andrew in 1981, called for the removal of Keegstra from the school; sixty people signed it. A later petition was spearheaded by a loosely organized group, about fifteen strong, called the Concerned Citizens. It was directed solely at Keegstra's position as mayor, and actually consisted of two separate petitions – one for those calling for his resignation, the other for those who continued to support him. Of those who signed 247 (79.9 per cent) agreed that Keegstra should step down, and 62 (20.1 per cent) thought he should not – about sixty people refused to sign either of the petitions. While the majority of Eckville people were thus clearly opposed to Keegstra, at least in his capacity as mayor, two things must be pointed out. First, both the pro and the con petitions were taken around the town by members of the Concerned Citizens group – a built-in bias that would be inadmissible in any social-science endeavour. Second, Eckville residents appeared to be as concerned about the reputation of their town as they were about the racist beliefs embraced by Keegstra, and were sick and tired of having reporters and other outsiders around; these factors, rather than any deep dissatisfaction with their mayor, may have been responsible for at least part of the negative response to him.

THE MEDIA

I now move on to consider the type of opposition that emerged beyond Eckville, specifically among the media, the churches, the government, and the Jewish community.

After Keegstra lost his appeal at the board of reference in Edmonton, he remarked to a reporter: 'Maybe you guys can help me find a job since you had a hand in this' (*Toronto Star*, 24 April 1983). That remark summed up precisely the attitude of Keegstra and his supporters towards the media. At least three Eckville people told me that reporters had to submit their stories to the Jewish Defence League (JDL) for inspection. Keegstra himself stated that one reporter told him: 'Jim, I am controlled by my editor.' Keegstra also claimed that another reporter who tended to sympathize with him was for that reason fired (I asked a couple of local reporters about this, but they never heard of the case). Sometimes a Keegstra supporter would point his finger at a specific reporter, who had moved on to greater things after the

Keegstra affair, and remark bitterly that he had got his reward for crucifying Keegstra. One prominent spokesman for the Jewish community asked me how Keegstra and his supporters regarded him. I told him they thought he was a member of the JDL, and related how they claimed they saw him manipulating the media at the Edmonton hearing. As the man explained to me, during the Keegstra case he had got to know many reporters, several of whom were his own age, with a similar educational background. Most of them were green, especially on the topic of anti-Semitism, and some of them used to telephone *him* for information and interpretations. At the Edmonton hearings, he said, he was merely associating with some reporters who had become his friends, and not trying to shape or dictate what they wrote.

It must not be thought that it was only the Keegstra camp which was antagonistic towards the media. That reaction had become general throughout the community, largely because of the perception that the media had made Eckville people look evil and silly. A member of the Eckville Chamber of Commerce talked about the naivety of some people. As the TV cameras rolled, they would open up and unrestrainedly give their views about Keegstra and racist issues. That was how the media ruined the town's reputation, he said. Ironically, this man, intelligent, reasonably articulate, and a thoroughly responsible member of the community, had himself given a couple of interviews in front of his store, coming out clearly against Keegstra. Many of his customers were peeved and stopped shopping at the store, which eventually closed down. Another businessman told me that Eckville people were sick of journalists. They just wanted to forget about the Keegstra mess, but the media wouldn't let them, and neither would Keegstra, who in this man's opinion revelled in the media attention.

By the time I had travelled to Eckville in the fall of 1984, it seemed to me that the media coverage of the Keegstra case had gone through three distinct stages: first, disinterest; second, an aggressive attack on Keegstra; third, a more neutral commentary. Several people close to the Keegstra case gave me their opinions about the hypothetical three stages. All of them agreed that the initial reaction was general lack of interest: the case was for the most part ignored. They also concurred that there was then a massive critical reaction to Keegstra, but they disagreed about what caused it. One man said that reporters were simply shocked when they began to appreciate what Keegstra believed and taught, and their stories reflected their astonishment. Another person's interpretation for the second phase was that reporters finally realized that the story was a gold-mine; may of them, he remarked, made their reputations from the case. There also was agreement that a third stage eventually emerged, in which the attack on Keegstra was toned down, but again there were differences in interpretation about its significance. Keegstra himself claimed that eventually a more balanced coverage – even a sympathetic coverage – had emerged. As he explained to me, at first reporters expected to find an unruly monster, a wild man in jackboots, but in fact they discovered that he was always courteous and reasonable, which led them to change their tune. A prominent member of the Alberta Jewish community concurred that the three phases were accurate, but the third, he contended, was not one in which the picture had become more balanced; instead, it simply reflected the increased maturity of both the Jewish community and reporters. Virtually all of them, he remarked, were inexperienced novices as far as anti-Semitism was concerned; some of the reporters were young, and many of the province's Jews had never gone through the Holocaust experience or the establishment of Israel. When both Jews and reporters realized the significance of the Keegstra case, they were dumbfounded, and they overreacted. It took several months before they were able to cope with the case more wisely, and put it into perspective.

A final interpretation for the toning down of the attack on Keegstra was simply that after the story had been around for a while, interest waned, and reporters dropped it.[3] In other words, the coverage had gone full circle, back to the initial stage. This was the firm conviction of another spokesman in the Jewish community, and from other sources it seemed to ring true. One reporter told me that Eckville people were sick and tired of reading about Keegstra, and her editor was opposed to further coverage on the case. This reporter, incidentally, shared the general view of her associates that Keegstra's historical interpretations were inaccurate and distasteful. However, she said she admired Keegstra for having the courage to stand up for his beliefs, and commented that the only unacceptable thing about the man is that 'he pushes where he should not': that is, he expresses his personal views in public places, notably in the class-room and in the council chambers. Indeed, most of Keegstra's opponents whom I met remarked that if the man wants to spout his pet theories on the street corner, who cares?

THE CHURCH

A representative of the Calgary Jewish community expressed anger that churches and other community organizations hadn't clearly and loudly con-

---

3 There was, of course, an additional factor, not mentioned by those whom I interviewed. Keegstra's court case was, in 1984, just a few months down the road, and reporters no doubt were inhibited in what they could write about the case.

demned Keegstra's anti-Semitism (*Edmonton Journal*, 6 May 1983). His complaint appears to have been justified. For example, none of eight churches contacted by a journalist (*Calgary Herald*, 30 April 1983) had bothered to formulate an official response to the Keegstra affair. On another occasion, two out of seven Edmonton ministers reportedly expressed doubts about the extent of the Holocaust (*Edmonton Journal*, 5 May 1983). It was not until 12 May 1983 that a joint statement by Christian and Jewish leaders was finally issued condemning all forms of bigotry and racism, and describing anti-Semitism as blasphemy (*Jewish Star*, Calgary Edition, vol. III, no. 16, 13–26 May 1983).

Within Eckville itself, the story, with one notable exception, was little different. The approximately thirty to forty members of the Diamond Valley Full Gospel Church, where Keegstra's son was pastor, supported Keegstra implicitly. The handful of Jehovah's Witnesses apparently remained neutral. The reaction within the Presbyterian church was more complex. The minister, Kenneth MacLeod, was one of Keegstra's most determined opponents. Yet his parishioners were certainly not behind him 100 per cent. One man, himself a member of the Presbyterian church, and a consistent opponent of Keegstra, expressed his surprise at the extent of racism within the church itself. Another member of the Presbyterian church, but a fan of Keegstra's, observed that most of MacLeod's parishioners were of the opinion that because of his public position he should have remained absolutely neutral regarding the Keegstra case. This woman complained that the minister, a newcomer to the town, had jumped into the affair without having any idea what it was all about. She also sniffed that he was always off in Edmonton at the University of Alberta taking 'some kind of course.'

By the time I had arrived in Eckville, MacLeod had returned to Nova Scotia. Several Eckville people told me that his parishioners had forced him to leave. More sympathetic observers remarked that the man had simply found the entire Keegstra affair, with its blatant racism and anti-Semitism, hard to take. One person told me that MacLeod, who was particularly upset because Keegstra's rantings seemed not to bother most Eckville people, decided he had to get his family away from the town.

THE GOVERNMENT

Premier Lougheed was criticized for not speaking out promptly or loudly enough against Keegstra, and for not expelling an MLA (Stiles) from the Conservative caucus after he had expressed doubt that there had been a Holocaust. When Lougheed did finally address the issue (*Globe and Mail*,

Edmonton Journal, 13 May 1983), he reportedly said he was deeply disturbed by Keegstra's anti-Semitic teaching, but did not think there was any notable increase in anti-Semitism in the province. One prominent Jewish spokesman told me that some people thought Lougheed had to respond slowly and carefully in order not to arouse the extreme right wing of his own party. This same man remarked that while at first the government did nothing, it eventually realized that political profit could be made from the affair, which led to the Ghitter Commission.

On the national level, Eric Neilsen, in his capacity as Conservative Opposition leader, spoke out clearly against Keegstra (*Edmonton Journal*, 17 May 1983), referring directly to his own personal experience when as an Allied military man he entered Belsen at the end of the Second World War. This brings us to the reaction of the local branch of the Royal Canadian Legion. An Eckville resident once remarked to me: 'If the Keegstra affair can happen today, what are we in for down the road when all the W.W. II veterans are dead?' Before visiting Eckville, I had had mixed reports about the Legion's reaction, some of which suggested that it had turned a blind eye. Yet Eckville people for the most part insisted that that had not been the case, and the facts tend to confirm what they said. For example, one of the earliest complaints against Keegstra, in the form of letters to editors, was made by a member of the Eckville Legion. In addition, a motion was passed in the Legion to issue a formal statement condemning Keegstra; about fifty members voted for it, with only a couple opposed. The Legion also sent a letter condemning Keegstra to the Alberta government, and was one of the parties that presented a brief opposing Keegstra to the Ghitter Commission. Curiously, the Legion man who seemed to spearhead the opposition to Keegstra not only was the uncle of one of the most dedicated right-wing members in Alberta, but was himself considered to be somewhat of a character, especially as a result of his vocal opposition to seat-belt legislation and the metric system. The lesson is salutary: extreme individualism, the inclination to go off the beaten track, is not itself lamentable, nor is it informed by a unidimensional world-view.

THE JEWISH COMMUNITY

The Keegstra affair was, in a way, a test for society. What is one's responsibility when confronted with blatant racism and anti-Semitism? As we have seen, the churches and the government did not pass the test with flying colours. But it must not be thought that all was straightforward for the Jewish community. Of course, the very term 'the Jewish community,' despite its vaunted organization, is something of a myth, for it too has its internal divisions. A reprersentative of B'nai B'rith in Calgary told me that his group had to bear the brunt of the load in the confrontation with Keegstra, because that city's branch of the Canadian Jewish Congress was simply unprepared to deal with it. Just as Eckville residents resented outsiders poking into the town's affairs, much the same attitude prevailed among some Alberta Jews. I once telephoned a representative of the Canadian Jewish Congress in Calgary, who made it clear that outsiders like myself were a nuisance. There was a similar, almost comical reaction to Mel Lastman, mayor of North York in Ontario. He had received material on the Keegstra case from the Lacombe school board, and at one point announced his intention of travelling to Eckville to help put things in order. However, the director of the Jewish Federation of Alberta bristled that he didn't want Lastman around, describing him as a very flashy guy who likes publicity. Another spokesman declared that should Lastman fly to Alberta, he would meet him at the airport and put him on the next return flight to Toronto. Even a Jewish organization in Toronto, according to one of my documents, worked behind the scenes to dissuade Lastman from becoming involved in the affair.

The depth of feelings about the Keegstra case among Jews was reflected in the huge turn-out at a meeting held in Edmonton: fully one thousand people, one-quarter of that city's Jewish population. One of the most difficult tasks faced by Jewish leaders was simply to calm people down. This was especially true regarding older people who had lived through the Holocaust years. Indeed, it appeared to me that it was the younger people who were more mentally equipped to deal with Keegstra, at least after they had woken up to the reality of the case. One man related to me what had transpired in a meeting with Lougheed. He was astounded, even sickened, to observe that all the powerful Jews at that meeting were so obsequious. It reminded him of how Jews apparently had acted during the Second World War. As a young, new-generation Jew, he thought such weakness was despicable; he wanted nothing less than direct confrontation, with no apologies to those sitting on the fence.

SUPPORTERS

Who would line up behind a man accused of being anti-Catholic, anti-black, and anti-Semitic? Could such a man count on any supporters at all? Well, as it turned out, quite a number of people rallied to Keegstra's side, and the majority of them must be considered normal, average citizens in almost every respect; if there was something distinctive about them, it was their devout Christian orientation and their inclination to be highly individualistic – self-made people, throw-backs to the days of the pioneers.

On one occasion as I sat on an Eckville resident's porch, he gave me a running commentary about those who passed by, pointing out which of them were Keegstra supporters. For example, as one elderly lady walked by, he said one can't say anything negative about Keegstra in her company. This man thought that Keegstra could count on about sixty supporters in the town, and stressed that many of them were members of the Presbyterian church. Keegstra himself told me that most of his supporters were local, rural-based, older people who had lived in the area all of their lives. Younger people, he commented, could not be blamed for turning against him because they had been brainwashed by the educational system. Those who did rally behind him, he contended, did so because they resented the interference of outsiders in the town's private affairs – especially big-city people – and thought that he was a helpless creature who had been unfairly and severely punished by secular society and atheistic outsiders and believed that he had done nothing wrong in the first place.

It was Keegstra's role as a teacher that initially landed him in hot water, but it would be a grave error to assume that he had been persona non grata in the school system. A week after he was fired on 7 December 1982, 94 of Eckville's 116 senior-high-school students signed a petition in protest. A close inspection of their names reveals that some of them were the offspring of those who had been among Keegstra's most determined opponents. Another petition opposing Keegstra's dismissal was circulated among parents and former students, drawing 128 signatures.

As far as Keegstra's fellow teachers in the Eckville school are concerned, there was, at least publicly, virtually unanimous support for him. However, that had not always been the case. At least two of the teachers were against Keegstra at the beginning. As time passed, and the screw was turned tighter tighter on the man, they switched to the side of his supporters. Keegstra told me that without exception all of the teachers backed him when the crunch came. That, too, however, was not quite true. First, the strongest support came from the older teachers; the exception apparently was a young woman who had been taught by Keegstra. In addition, at least two teachers continued to oppose him, but kept their views a secret, believing that had they done so their own jobs would have been in jeopardy. The almost universal support among the Eckville teachers did not necessarily reflect agreement with the man's beliefs. A great deal of it would have to be labelled union support – fellow employees closing ranks – complemented by the perception that Keegstra was an underdog, with no chance to emerge victorious in view of the forces massed against him. In addition, most of the teachers were asking the question: who next? Some of them thought that Keegstra had been the victim of only one or two parents with an axe to grind. One of the teachers told me about a former member of the staff who advocated premarital sex, pornography, and drugs. In her judgment, that teacher, and not Keegstra, posed a danger to the students, and yet it was Keegstra who was fired. Another teacher told me about overhearing a colleague criticizing Trudeau in the school library. Shouldn't that mean, the teacher said, that the other person should be dismissed?

A frequent comment was that a former social-studies teacher in the school had been left wing; Keegstra, thus, was simply balancing out the long-range picture. Much was made of the famous clash of ideas between Keegstra and another man who supposedly was inclined towards socialism. Students apparently would leave Keegstra's class and make a bee-line for this other teacher, to see if he could refute Keegstra's interpretations of history. It might be supposed that this man would have been the one member of staff to stand up against Keegstra. From what I have been told, he certainly had the intellect to do so. Yet, in the end, he too capitulated. Perhaps that again was an expression of union solidarity, and the perception that Keegstra, the underdog, had suffered enough. Yet what finally came out was that the so-called radical thinker of the Eckville school was not as socialistic as usually was portrayed. When asked at the board of reference hearing in Edmonton to define his political position, this man replied that he was a 'liberal,' which to him and his fellow employees apparently put him far out on the left.

While none of the Eckville teachers may have been true believers in the same sense as Keegstra, at the same time few of them appeared to find his social philosophy and view of history objectionable. Keegstra told me that the principal, Olsen, had been especially pleased when his son, under Keegstra's influence, began for the first time to take an interest in world events. Olsen had been aware that Keegstra was teaching anti-Jewish material, but apparently wasn't upset because it seemed to inspire student interest. According to a member of the Lacombe school board, Olsen once stated that since he himself was not a Jew, Keegstra's anti-Semitic thrust wasn't his business. In Olsen's view, Keegstra was a God-fearing person who had no intention of indoctrinating the students. He said he would hate to see Keegstra turned out of the school system completely, and would be happy to see him reinstated in Eckville. Eckville's vice-principal also sent a letter of testimony on Keegstra's behalf, and one of the teachers in the school wrote: 'Jim is an asset to our school staff and is highly respected by most students and teachers. His total contribution to the education of our students is immense. He is a man whose morals are beyond doubt ... a most respected member of his community, in and out of school. The Eckville school is fortunate to have Jim Keegstra as a member of its teaching staff.'

Many of the Eckville teachers wondered why Keegstra had not simply been transferred to another school or removed from the social-studies and science courses, and reassigned classes like mechanics and drafting. The Lacombe school board actually had considered the latter option, but decided against it on the fear that somewhere down the road the man might again find himself teaching social studies. When Keegstra finally was fired in December 1982, Eckville teachers were shocked and angry. One of them told me that Keegstra had all along given the impression that everything was working out fine. Such a comment must be taken with a grain of salt, in view of the massive opposition to Keegstra, but it is always possible that in true-believer fashion he thought he was untouchable by the system. David, the superintendent of schools, aware of the degree of hostility towards him, nevertheless personally went to the Eckville school on 8 December 1982, to formally deliver Keegstra's resignation. When I met this sensitive man two years later, it was clear that he had been extremely upset by the animosity of the Eckville staff. But as he pointed out, things could have been worse for the teachers, and especially for the principal. Several people were calling for Olsen's blood too. The view was that he was a nice man, but had failed to rise to the occasion in the Keegstra affair. He had avoided the knife, I was told, partly because all of the teachers were already going around the bend, asking who was to be the next victim, and partly because of the perception that he was weak and defenceless. With regard to the latter, however, it must be pointed out that from the first rumblings against Keegstra in 1981 to the eventual court case in 1985, Olsen determinably defended Keegstra, when others, who saw the handwriting on the wall, backed down.

This brings us to the Alberta Teachers' Association. From the outset, the ATA supported Keegstra. It provided him with legal representation at the Lacombe school board hearings and at the board of reference in Edmonton; the Alberta School Trustees' Association (ASTA) provided the school board with its own lawyer. The ATA's position was that insufficient direction had been given to Keegstra with regard to modifying his teaching content, and specifying the parameters of the social-studies curriculum. Moreover, the school board, it insisted, had moved too hastily to have Keegstra removed. Keegstra himself spoke warmly about the ATA's support, observing that the organization was perfectly aware that he had done nothing wrong. In an interview on the CBC's 'Journal,' an ATA executive officer rationalized his support for Keegstra by saying that as a tolerant person he thought Keegstra should be allowed to hold his own views.[4] The ATA's backing of Keegstra brought it considerable criticism. The general complaint was that the organization was completely self-serving. Its only concern was for the welfare of its members, not for that of the wider public. One Eckville man remarked to me that the organization should be called the Alberta Teachers' Union. Nevertheless, the Ghitter *Report* (1984) was fairly sympathetic to the ATA, pointing out that part of the problem was simply 'the convoluted and ambiguous procedures' in dealing with a teacher's conduct. The ATA's response to criticism was that it had no other choice than to defend Keegstra; he had to be presumed innocent until proven guilty. But as a columnist in the *Edmonton Journal* (24 April 1983) acutely observed, that would have been appropriate if Keegstra had been accused of anti-Semitism but *denied* the charge, instead of openly acknowledging his belief in a Jewish conspiracy and the non-existence of the Holocaust.

In October 1983, the ATA revoked Keegstra's teaching certificate, an act which to many people was too late to be meaningful. Keegstra claimed that what had happened was that the JDL and B'nai B'rith visited the ATA and 'put the fear and the terror into them, and of course I had to go.'

Earlier I alluded to the government's slow reaction in making a formal statement about the Keegstra case, possibly because Lougheed was wary of arousing the right wing within his own party. Two of these gentlemen did in fact make noises that could be interpreted as support for Keegstra. One was Stephen Stiles, the other Bowden 'Bud' Zip, both MLAs in the Conservative party. Stiles had remarked to a reporter: 'Well, what was the Holocaust? I mean, the Holocaust is the name of a movie.' While he did not think there was any Jewish conspiracy (*Edmonton Journal*, 21 April 1983), he did state: 'I haven't seen anything in terms of documentary evidence to prove to me that they were necessarily prosecuted.' To be fair to Stiles, a close reading of the reporter's transcript suggests that he had been led rather forcibly (but cleverly) into a position where he made his injudicious statements, and he did eventually apologize for his comments in the Alberta legislature. Furthermore, in a later interview with the same reporter (*Edmonton Journal*, 5 May 1983), he said he wasn't very happy being lumped together with

---

4 McIntyre's documentary (I viewed both the original, uncut version, and the aired version) was one of the most effective journalistic pieces on the Keegstra affair. What made it successful was that rather than simply allowing Keegstra to deliver his pet theories, McIntyre continuously challenged what Keegstra said.

people such as Keegstra, and expressed his concern about the number of anti-Semites who had contacted him after his public comments. Yet at the same time he stated that he supported Gostick's Canadian League of Rights, was adamantly opposed to all forms of totalitarianism, and worried about the erosions of our freedoms. Among the reactions to Stiles's new-found fame, at least one was light-hearted: he was granted a membership in the Flat Earth Society (*Edmonton Journal*, 28 April 1983).

The Zip case, occurring after that of Stiles, was somewhat of a rerun, and the public reaction was quick but brief. Keegstra told me that B'nai B'rith 'soon zipped up Zip's mouth.' Another man, a Keegstra enthusiast, said that Zip got all his right-wing material from his church and the Ukrainian community, remarking that the latter knows all about Jews.

Stiles and Zip were not the only well-positioned outsiders to line up behind Keegstra. For example, a retired university professor, who had been recommended to me as a long-time Social Credit member, declared that the entire affair could be blamed on 'that stupid man King,' the Alberta minister of education, whose 'ignorant and precipitous action' had created a problem out of nothing. The former professor had once spent a few weeks in Africa under the auspices of the Canadian government, with the purpose of setting up new secondary schools. His recommendation to Ottawa was not to bother; as he told me, the country in question and its leader were totally evil, corrupt, and incapable. That, incidentally, was only one of several examples that I had learned about over the years in which educational and economic programs in developing countries had been sabotaged by racially oriented foreign experts. A second man, also a college professor, had become the darling of the right wing as a result of his public protest against the RCMP seizure of Butz's *The Hoax of the Twentieth Century*. In his case, however, he rejected the right-wing label, claiming that his only interest was the defence of free speech, plus a curiosity about the right-wing phenomenon itself.

PROFILES

In order to illustrate more concretely the kinds of people who supported Keegstra, I shall focus on a handful of individuals, beginning with two Eckville residents. Our first example is a man who was on the Eckville town council during the Keegstra affair. In his opinion, it was the newcomers in the town who had ganged up on Keegstra. He named the Presbyterian min-ister and a new doctor as major culprits, and contended that after the minister had publicly expressed his horror at Keegstra's teaching content, people stopped attending church, and eventually forced him to leave town. People in 'positions,' he declared, had a duty to be neutral in the Keegstra case. He claimed that the amount of support for Keegstra actually would have been greater except that some of those who represented outside companies were pressured to remain neutral so as not to jeopardize business. If that was true, however, the opposite was as well: people who considered Keegstra to be wrong and evil, but had to keep quiet or risk losing their jobs. This man also resented the intrusion of outsiders, concerned about anti-Semitism, into the town's private affairs. 'What,' he asked, 'has Hitler to do with Eckville?' The media in particular came under his scathing criticism; the newspapers, he contended, had completely misrepresented Keegstra, and initially he refused to see me until I suggested it was important that he set the record straight.

This man, it must be made clear, did not support Keegstra because of the latter's racist and anti-Semitic pronouncements. In fact, he distanced himself from such views. Moreover, he did not believe that Keegstra embraced them either. Keegstra's enemies, he insisted, were not really against what he taught, but instead the man as a person, especially because he had the guts to stand up against them. The basic issue in the case, he declared, was freedom of speech, and that was why Keegstra had to be supported. Nevertheless, it was apparent that the man was himself 'soft' in the area of Keegstra's beliefs. Finance, he remarked, rules the world, and because finance is at the root of Keegstra's message, such as his opposition to usury, his enemies were legion. Nobody, he continued, had proved Keegstra wrong yet. He argued that all history is reinterpreted with the passage of time, and that was all that Keegstra was involved in. This man also glaringly contradicted himself at times. 'What is a Jew?' he asked me. On television he had seen blond, black, and yellow Jews; Jews are not a race, but instead a religion, stated the man. Yet he then remarked that Jews basically look like Turks. At one point he stressed that contrary to the media image, the Eckville area is a multinational community composed of dozens of ethnic groups. The implication was that in such an environment racism could not flourish. But in the next breath he remarked that there had been a backlash in favour of Keegstra among people from Europe who remembered how nasty Jews had been during the Second World War. Although this man had little formal education, he was thoughtful, and to the extent of his abilities tried to reason matters out and to judge issues carefully and fairly. He definitely could not be described as an evil man; on the contrary, one might regard him as 'the salt of the earth.' Yet to some degree he was susceptible to the same racist stance adopted by Keegstra. His support for Keegstra was no secret in Eckville, and on several occasions he had been called a bigot and a redneck. As he remarked to me, he didn't even know what a redneck was, and couldn't find it in the dictionary.

Our second example, a university graduate, was a much more sophisticated Keegstra fan. When the Keegstra affair broke out into the open, she asked her son, who was in one of Keegstra's classes, what was going on. Her son became angry, declaring that Keegstra would never have said any of the evil things attributed to him. On inspecting her son's notebooks, she could detect nothing alluding to the Jewish conspiracy, or resembling anti-Semitism in any form. She knew Keegstra fairly well, and in her experience had not found him a prejudiced man. From her sources in the school, she concluded that Keegstra never brought up his alleged racist opinions in the staff room, nor did he relate them to his students. She went on to say that what happened, in her opinion, was that when the rumours began that Keegstra was being questioned about his historical interpretations, some of the students, out of sheer mischief, began to pepper their notes with anti-Semitic comments, pretending they came from Keegstra. In other words, she believed that the whole anti-Semitic line had been fabricated by the students.

Later this woman stated that Keegstra was only against 'darkness.' What she meant was that he was opposed to all shady and unethical practices, and did not hesitate to bring them out into the open. That, she said, may explain why so many people were determined to destroy him. The woman added that the Catholics, especially the IRA, were behind the attempt to ruin Keegstra's career. She herself was a devout Presbyterian, and she described her own unfortunate experiences with Catholics. On one occasion she had attended mass, but was not allowed to take communion since she was not a Catholic. She also related some of her experiences with Jews in the wake of the Keegstra affair. In her opinion, Eckville people had learned nothing from Jews who had visited the town, nor from their travels to Jewish centres, because they already were well-informed – taught by none other than Keegstra himself. As this woman talked to me about what a fine man Keegstra was, about his opposition to only a small portion of Jews, and about Nazism and the Holocaust (including her doubts that Jews were ever persecuted during the Second World War), it became clear that she harbored a large range of prejudices. Her case is important, first because it indicates why it was so difficult and took so long to remove Keegstra from his teaching position, and second because she was visibly a good person, a perfect lady, gracious, pure, sensitive, and devout. The racism that she did unconsciously express was done as one might expect: daintily.

I now move on to three of Keegstra's supporters who lived outside Eckville. The first man, who was a university graduate and local business-man, told me over and over again that Keegstra was a good man, a sincere man, who had been greatly maligned by the media. Keegstra, the man said, is not anti-Semitic, but only anti-Zionist. He doesn't deny that Jews were killed in concentration camps, but only questions the numbers – perhaps seven hundred thousand or so rather than six million. This man insisted that Keegstra's undoing came about because of his Christian orientation. As he pointed out, Keegstra had been reprimanded for always referring to the Bible in class in order to legitimate his arguments. This man dismissed the members of the school board who had opposed Keegstra as simply ignorant and misinformed. At one point he remarked that if Keegstra is found guilty in court, that will be the end of Canada.

In order to understand this individual's rock-hard support for Keegstra, we must appreciate his own position regarding the same issues. Hitler, he said, was psychotic, but also had some interesting ideas and was good for Germany. The man was very defensive about the world's unfair treatment of Germans, and remarked that if we can't say anything bad about Jews, we should not be able to say anything negative about Hitler and the Nazis. He described Zionists as agnostic or atheistic, people who are not constrained by moral codes. He strongly supported Keegstra's views about the evil of central banking, controlled by Jews, and demonstrated a familiarity with right-wing literature and historical revisionism. He also had attended meetings of the Canadian League of Rights. At one point he expressed the opinion that universities were not examining the critical issues and getting at the real truth – by which he meant the truth from a right-wing perspective. Intelligent, articulate, well-educated, a solid member of society, this man supported Keegstra not simply because he regarded the latter as a superb teacher and a high-principled individual; more significantly, he shared many of the same right-wing beliefs. Little wonder that some observers were concerned that Keegstra was just the tip of the iceberg.

'Keegstra turned out more Christian students than did the majority of actual Christian Bible schools.' These words were spoken by another strong supporter of Eckville's best-known citizen. Originally from Holland, about sixty years old, he had known Keegstra for several years. He declared that everything that Keegstra had said about Jews was absolutely correct. He told me how Edmonton Jews had instructed the media what to write about the Keegstra case, talked about secret internment camps in Alberta, remarked that blacks (backed by communists) had made a mess out of Africa, and that South Africa – which he and his wife planned to visit – was one of the world's most admirable nations. At one point, there was a report that he had helped round up Jews in Holland during the Second World War for transportation to concentration camps. He formerly belonged to the Social Credit party, but told me he had started to question some of its monetary policies. Tall, raw-boned, outspoken, forceful, hard-working, law-abiding, highly individualistic, and a devout member of the Christian Reformed Church, this person was another classical example of the good man who also was soft on racism, a mixture informed principally by his Christian orientation. He was not nearly as smooth or subtle as our previous example, and indeed he appeared to be more blatantly bigoted than Keegstra himself, a fact that was not lost on some sectors of the far right. For example, an Aryan Nations member, who considered Keegstra to be a 'kosher conservative' – not nearly far enough to the right – referred to this other man as 'all right,' meaning he was a genuine member of the club.

My final example also was a highly individualistic farmer and a devout Christian, having been raised as a Mennonite, but eventually joining the United church. He remarked to me: 'It is absolutely essential if democracy is to survive that there are alternatives to the public education system.' Like the previous man, he once had been involved with Keegstra in establishing a Christian college in Edmonton. Several factors, he explained, led to Keegstra's down fall: 1 / Keegstra had once slapped a student for smoking on school property and for swearing, and was charged in court with assault; Eckville people have never forgiven him for his actions. 2 / Andrew's family are members of the IRA, which Keegstra accused of being communists; thus she had a personal reason to destroy Keegstra; this man also said that Maddox is Irish-Catholic, although Keegstra told me he had never been able to find out what religion she belonged to, if any. 3 / Keegstra taught creationism, not evolutionism, and atheistic schools can't tolerate that. 4 / Keegstra was known to be anti-communist. 5 / He was opposed to usury, which made the students' parents angry. 6 / He argued that monetary reform is necessary, which threatened the power and privilege of big business and finance. 7 / Judaism and Christianity are intrinsically opposed, and Keegstra's teaching, fully informed by Christianity, ran up against Jewish interests. 8 / Keegstra was simply an extraordinarily competent teacher, and he threatened other members of his profession.

In some respects this man came across as a typical member of the right wing. He agreed with Keegstra that monetary reform was necessary, and argued that there is no record that Hitler ordered Jews to be destroyed. Communism, in his view, was a constant threat, and homosexuality was an abomination. He described himself as old-fashioned, against what he referred to as the Elvis Presley syndrome, and in favour of the policies of President Reagan. He referred to modern education as contemporary man's forbidden fruit: one becomes educated, thinks there is nothing more to learn, and thus doesn't need God.[5]

There were, nevertheless, significant differences between the beliefs of this man and those of the two previous individuals and Keegstra himself. First, he said he would not support Keegstra if he thought the latter was a white supremacist. Second, he said he has never agreed with Keegstra about the Jewish conspiracy; Jews, he remarked, are simply paranoid! There were, in his opinion, several important reasons to support Keegstra: his Christan orientation, the freedom-of-speech issue, his record as an excellent teacher, and the fact that he had been wrongly accused (in the man's opinion) of being a racist. He thought that had Keegstra dwelled more on the positive than the negative, he might have been treated more favourably by the press and the public. So many organizations, he pointed out, are consumed by negativity. For example, he used to belong to the Canadian League of Rights, but no longer does, because that organization always is anti-this and anti-that. Too much such concentration, he remarked, can destroy one, and he went on to say that Satan employs whatever means he can to undermine the human spirit, and pehaps he might even be using supposedly Christian organizations like the Canadian League of Rights.

Of all the Keegstra supporters whom I interviewed, this man, about fifty years old and born in Canada, with his roots in Germany, the Ukraine, and Holland, was the most impressive. Like most of the others, he was a devout Christian and a responsible member of the community. But he was more intelligent, more thoughtful, less rigid and dogmatic. Although he only had a grade twelve education, he continued to enjoy the play of ideas. However, his intellect, lacking the salutary influence of a critical sounding-board, had grown inwards, rendering him all-too-certain about how the world should be constituted.

5 This man told me about one of his neighbours who was absolutely demonic about Keegstra. If his neighbour didn't have a conscience, he said, he would shoot Keegstra. He traced the source of his neighbour's hostility back to the Second World War, and remarked that it was not Hitler's atrocities that inflamed the other man; instead, he claimed, the neighbour, an exceptionally arrogant Englishman, could not forgive Hitler for assuming Germany was superior to Britain.

A Calgary police officer told me about another man who had approached the police to ask what their reaction would be if he knocked off Keegstra. When I later interviewed this man, he said he had decided not to kill Keegstra because in the end that would not have achieved much. Instead, he said he did what he could to undermine Keegstra's dignity and economic security.

OTHER SUPPORTERS

What stands out about the various Keegstra supporters that have been described so far is that virtually without exception they were solid, God-fearing, law-abiding citizens – the backbone, one would think, of healthy, vibrant communities. Yet not all of his fans fell into this mould. Numerous individuals with long histories of dedicated Aryan superiority emerged to applaud Keegstra, no doubt hoping to get mileage for their own goals out of his respectable social position. John Ross Taylor, for example, wrote Keegstra, offering him funds, and in the fall of 1984 travelled to Alberta to meet him. Taylor, incidentally (*Calgary Sun*, 18 January 1984), reportedly said that the Western Guard would punish all the RCMP officers involved in the prosecution of Keegstra. Zundel also made a pilgrimage to Alberta, parading in front of the court in which Keegatra's case was being heard with a sign proclaiming 'Freedom of Speech.' Keegstra was publicly supported by Wally Klinck, the owner of the C.H. Douglas Social Credit Supplies in Sheridan Park near Edmonton. Klinck, born about 1935 and an industrial laboratory technician, thought that Herb Katz, one of the most articulate Jewish spokesmen against Keegstra, might be an *agent provocateur*, trying to stir up trouble between Jews and Gentiles. Another fan was Tom Erhart, one of those who had attended an Aryan Nations conference in Idaho. Erhart declared that Keegstra was absolutely correct about Jews, and dismissed the Holocaust as a hoax.

Finally, Keegstra had the support of organizations like the Canadian League of Rights, the federal branch of the Social Credit party in Alberta, and the Christian Defence League.[6] The last had been founded specifically for the aid of Keegstra. Associated with this organization were people like Erhart as well as a Red Deer man who sold vacuum cleaners, a retired Red Deer resident, and Jim Green and Terry Long. Long, the Alberta head of the Aryan Nations, actually had been president of the Christian Defence League, but was shunted aside by those who thought he was too radical. Green replaced him as president, and Keegstra himself became vice-president of the organization established on his behalf.[7]

---

6 An organization with an identical name has existed in the United States for several years, but to my knowledge there was no formal (or even informal) connection between them. The Canadian organization was much less radical in orientation.

7 More will be said about Green in the next chapter in relation to the Social Credit movement.

LETTERS

As Keegstra's fame began to spread, letters to editors of newspapers and to the Lacombe school board trickled in from across the country. An Ontario teacher wrote to say that he was disgusted to have Keegstra in the same profession. A Nova Scotia man insisted that the principal and vice-principal of the Eckville school should also be fired. A war veteran in Saskatchewan, who observed that the only person in the school system worthy of bouquets was David, went a step farther: the entire Eckville teaching staff ought to be dismissed. Perhaps the most poignant letter of all appeared in the *The Lacombe Globe* (11 May 1983), in which a Dutch woman related her personal experiences of Nazi atrocities against Jews during the Second World War.

Not everyone, however, was opposed to Keegstra. In fact, the opposite was true, at least as regards those who contacted newspapers and the Lacombe school board. For example, an editorial in the *Edmonton Sun* (18 May 1983) revealed that an alarming number of letters and calls had been received from Albertans who shared Keegstra's views. The number of calls to the *Calgary Sun* (13 May 1983) supporting Keegstra outnumbered those against him. A letter printed in a local newspaper concluded: 'Support him and cherish him – for courageous and honest men are a rarity.' One writer accused Jews of practising human sacrifice. Another described Susan Maddox as 'a haughty person – anti-social – a loner.' Several additional letters were written by Keegstra's former students. One of these students, a college graduate, wrote: 'I have learnt in his class the only thing close to explaining what goes on in this world.' Another stated: 'his presentation of little known but well-documented facts combined with the "accepted" ones stimulated my thinking and expanded my world view much more than any teacher before or since.' A third student remarked that all that Keegstra was attempting to achieve was to get his pupils to think for themselves. An RCMP constable, who had been taught by Keegstra, commended him as an excellent teacher with an exceptionally high moral standard. Another student stated: 'In this day and age where evolution seems to be taught as fact rather than theory, I am glad that Mr. Keegstra is teaching some Christianity! I hope that he will still be teaching when my daughter attends high school.' Finally, yet another former student wrote that there must be some truth in the conspiracy theory or else Keegstra wouldn't have been fired. Of course, Keegstra himself often said the same thing. For example, after the board of reference rejected his appeal, he remarked that that just proved that a Jewish conspiracy does exist.

After Keegstra lost his job as a teacher, the entire matter might have died out except that in front of television cameras at a council meeting he stated that the council should ask MacLeod, the Presbyterian minister, to leave town. That had been after MacLeod had been accused of running down the reputation of the town in a story reported in a Calgary newspaper. Keegstra declared that he did not mind it if MacLeod attacked him personally, but he wouldn't accept his slurs on the town's reputation.

Up until that point, people opposed to Keegstra had tried to keep separate the man's roles as teacher and mayor. However, his affront to the Presbyterian minister was interpreted as evidence that his private views had clearly entered the council's chambers, and the immediate result was the attempt to force him to step down as mayor. It was then that the petitions for and against Keegstra were circulated among Eckville's residents. At a council meeting on 2 May 1983, a motion asking for Keegstra's resignation was introduced. Immediately before that particular meeting, Keegstra received a telephone call, he claimed, from a high-ranking government official who encouraged him to remain mayor, pointing out that in three short years he had brought the town out of debt. Another telephone call, Keegstra told me, warned him: 'Don't you dare go down there because this will be the last meeting you'll be at.' One councillor, himself a Keegstra supporter, declared that Keegstra was the best mayor in Eckville's history, always well-organized and courteous, and especially adroit with visiting businessmen. Even Keegstra's opponents confirmed that he had done an excellent job as mayor.

At the council meeting, three different delegations gave briefs. One was from the Chamber of Commerce, which asked Keegstra either to resign or to call for an early election. A second was from the Royal Canadian Legion, which said it could not condone Keegstra's views. A third was from the Concerned Citizens group, which declared that Keegstra had far exceeded his authority in asking the Presbyterian minister to pack up his bags. One councillor, Schmidt, read excerpts from various newspapers which depicted Eckville in a bad light, and suggested that if Keegstra had any compassion for the town he would resign. When Keegstra refused, Schmidt called for a vote. Two councillors voted in favour of his resignation, and four against it; the latter included Keegstra himself; another councillor (there were six altogether) was absent. Keegstra, thus, came out on top on that occasion, but in a sense the vote was not of great moment because he declared that regardless of the outcome he would not step down as mayor.

Keegstra's victory was to be short-lived, for eventually an election had to be held. His opponents were extremely worried that nobody would step forward to run against him. Keegstra, of course, never had been elected to public office in the first place. In 1974 he had become a councillor by acclamation. Harold Leach, elected mayor in 1977, fell ill, and Keegstra, then the deputy mayor, took over in 1978; two years later he won the office by acclamation. One man whom I talked to had refused to run against Keegstra, even though he was a prominent member of the Concerned Citizens group. Finally, Leach, the former mayor, agreed to contest the election, although he apparently said it would be fine with him if Keegstra was re-elected (*Red Deer Advocate*, 20 September 1983). Fully 92 per cent of the eligible voters turned out at the polls, and Leach won with about 70 per cent of the vote (Leach got 278 votes, Keegstra 123); Marg Andrew, too, was elected, becoming the first female councillor in Eckville's history. In Leach's victory speech, he said he hoped the media would now finally get off Eckville's back. No doubt the election results reflected numerous complicating factors. Some people obviously voted for Keegstra because they thought that he had become a much-maligned underdog. Yet Leach's comment reflected the greater impulse: people who were determined to put the town back on a normal course, beyond the media's eye, regardless of what they personally thought about the Keegstra case. Keegstra himself told me that a vicious hate campaign had been mounted against him, orchestrated by the media. In his words: 'You see, the media was such an ugly bunch. I mean, any provocation and they were here shoving a microphone and a camera, a microphone down their throat and a camera into their eyeballs, and I think basically that the main reason why I was voted out was that so they won't get this attention.'

THE MAN AND HIS BELIEFS

In 1928, on the eve of the Depression, Keegstra's parents immigrated to Canada form the north of Holland. They settled in Vulcan, Alberta, where Keegstra, the youngest of seven children, was born. His father became a farm worker. Both his parents belonged to the Dutch Reformed Church, and eventually were attracted to the Social Credit party. Jim Keegstra entered the working world as a mechanic, but later enrolled at the University of Calgary to pursue a Bachelor of Education in Industrial Arts. After two years of part-time and a further two of full-time studies, he graduated in 1967. Before moving to Eckville in 1968, he had taught at Cremona from 1961 to 1963, at Red Deer from 1963 to 1966, and at

Hillcrest Christian College in Medicine Hat from 1966 to 1968. Married, and with four children, one of whom was a teacher (Keegstra's sister also taught under the Lacombe school board), over the years he has been active in several churches: Christian Reformed, Evangelical Free, the United Brethren, the Nazarene, and the Baptist. Although he had never been a minister, he filled in several times in that capacity. He also had taught Sunday School and adult Bible classes. When I interviewed him in 1984, he remarked that it was too dangerous to belong formally to a church, because then the hierarchy wants to dictate what you think. At that time he worshipped regularly at his son's church near Eckville, the Full Gospel church. There, Keegstra said, one doesn't sign a membership card; one becomes a member by attending, and by supporting the church. Keegstra explained that he became interested in 'unofficial' history in the early 1960s. He got literature from acquaintances and from the Canadian League of Rights, an organization to which he belonged. By the time he had graduated from university, he had read most of Douglas's writings on social credit. Twice in the 1970s, and again in 1984, he ran for public office under the Social Credit banner. Referring to his political activity, as well as his role as mayor, Keegstra said he is 'a bit of a Calvinist,' indicating that one's spiritual and mundane realms can't be separated, and that as a Christian he felt obligated to participate in public affairs. His attitude, of course, flew in the face of all those supporters who condemned people in 'positions' such as the Presbyterian minister for failing to remain neutral when confronted with a moral issue. Unlike many of the right-wing members in Canada, Keegstra had not travelled widely; indeed until his testimony for Zundel in Toronto, he had never been east of Winnipeg. Despite his prominent positions as teacher and mayor, and his political activity with the Social Credit party, he said he is anything but a social butterfly. He neither drinks nor smokes, and has no hobbies; when he wants to relax he works. He described himself as 'a bit of a loner,' and said he has few contacts with people outside a small circle of friends and his church.

Although he was about fifty years old when I met him, he still retained a boyish look, with a pleasant smile and a courteous, affable manner. To a somewhat lesser degree than in McQuirter's case, he was conscious of the good impression conveyed by his appearance. Several times he remarked that those people who had taken the trouble to come to talk to him were always surprised that he was not an ogre or monster. Most of the bad press, he claimed, was written by journalists who never bothered to interview him.

Keegstra reviewed for me the series of events and incidents that led to his eventual removal as teacher and mayor. When he first began to teach in

Eckville, the school, he claimed, had had a terrible reputation. The students were uncontrollable, and teachers were simply driven out. For this reason, he had to be stern – even rough – at the beginning. The students were in the habit of smoking cigarettes on school property, but he put an end to it. He told me about one crisis in 1971 that landed him on the bad side of the local policeman, who already had been concerned about Keegstra's physical punishments of students. According to Keegstra, one of his pupils was tripping girls as they passed by his desk. Then he refused to take down lecture notes. Keegstra gave him 'three good lashes across the back.' The student proceeded to record his notes, but in gibberish. Keegstra lashed him again. After school was finished that day, some students rushed to tell the policeman what had occurred. The officer had the wounds on the student's back photographed, and took him to the local doctor. The case ended up in court. Keegstra was found not guilty, and as a direct result, the teacher claimed, the policeman left town. Keegstra said that the case had been very important in Central Alberta at the time, because student misbehaviour was extremely widespread. Had he lost the case, he commented, some schools would have been uncontrollable.

In view of his obvious capacity to handle unruly students, Keegstra was assigned classes that nobody else could teach, at least effectively, such as social studies. Keegstra told me that he still had to give a couple of students 'pretty good lickings.' He also, he said, 'gave them some points of view they never heard before, about equality, about civil rights, and all these things.' The principal, he claimed, was delighted, for at last there was an instructor who could make the subject-matter interesting. Reflecting on his capacity to stir the interests of his students, Keegstra remarked to me: 'Before it was just boring, because these guys [the other teachers] would use a lousy textbook, and can you think of anything more boring? I just ... I wouldn't even go into, I always prepared my lesson and when I went into the class-room, boy, I seldom used notes, because to me when somebody reads notes, I could have just almost spit in their face.'

Successful as he apparently was in the eyes of the principal and the students, not everyone was enthralled. The initial opposition, he stated, came from his fellow teachers, not parents, and the issue involved was his avowed creationist stance. Keegstra said many of the teachers were teaching the students evolutionism. At one point he suggested: 'Let me teach them creation, and you guys teach them evolution. Now, I said, they're getting two points of view, which a lot of other schools don't give.' Keegstra contended that the opposition that eventually emerged from parents was minuscule, involving, indeed, only two of them: 'But you see, I got crossed up on two parents. Now the one parent I got crossed up on was IRA [Irish Republican Army]. Now we have to deal with that in the curriculum and I showed them how that they were Marxist-backed, and Marxist-oriented, and everybody knows that, but this lady because she is IRA, she got so mad at me. She said, I am going to get you if it is the last thing I do, even if I have to kill.' The woman in question, of course, was Andrew. She has not denied that her father, who emigrated from Ireland to Canada in 1923, had been involved in the IRA (*Alberta Report*, 2 May 1983), but took strong objection to the claim that he had been a communist. As far as the supposed threat of violence towards Keegstra, what struck me about Andrew was the respectful manner in which she referred to him, and her level-headed attitude towards the affair, despite her opposition to what he had taught her children.

Keegstra said that he ran into a real battle in 1978 when Lacombe County got a Roman Catholic superintendent. Yet after the latter examined Keegstra's notes, he said, according to Keegstra, that he couldn't see any evidence of anti-Catholicism, and wouldn't even bother writing Keegstra a formal letter about the affair. The whole matter, Keegstra ruminated, would have died out, but then a second woman – Maddox – appeared on the scene, concerned about what he was teaching her son in a grade-nine class. By then, there was a new superintendent of schools, David. As Keegstra put it: 'he came out and he just gave the attitude, hey look, I'm the boss and boy you guys better heel.' As we saw earlier, David and the school board accused Keegstra of not sticking to the curriculum. Keegstra told me heatedly: 'That's the biggest lie there is.'

Keegstra went on to talk about others who had opposed him. Most of them, he insisted, were newcomers or parents without children in the school. He talked bitterly about the hockey jock and figure-skating group, dismissing them as gossips who had nothing better to do than to sit around all day and pick the teachers apart. Referring to the 'hospital conspiracy,' he remarked jocularly that if he fell ill, he wouldn't dare show up there. While in his view the attack against him had originated in the tainted minds of two parents, within a year or so it had spread like wildfire. By then, he said, the Jews had recognized his case as a windfall, a golden opportunity to promote their plans to destroy Christianity and take over the world. The subsequent hearings and trials, Keegstra told me, were just a joke. Justice was impossible. As he remarked to me: 'I told the students ... look I'm teaching you stuff that others have been crucified for, smeared beyond imagining, so if it happens to me one day, it won't surprise me.'

Keegstra stated that Christianity is the basis of everything he thinks. He said it would be impossible for him to teach outside the parameters of the

Christian faith, and remarked that he wondered if the entire mess that he was involved in was anything more than a massive Jewish attack on his Christian principles. When I asked him what Jews could hope to gain from opposing him, he replied that he constituted a test case for them, to see how far they could go. If there was not too much anti-Semitism, they could move faster to take over the world. He said in addition that Jews needed a scapegoat in order to get control over the education system, which they had achieved with the Ghitter Commission, Ghitter himself being a Jew.

One teacher told me that in the staff room Keegstra had once compared blacks to mules and horses. He also, stated another person, had declared that no black person had ever been an important leader. When asked about Martin Luther King, he apparently retorted that the late civil-rights leader had merely been a puppet set up by Jews. Nevertheless, Keegstra rejected the accusation that he was anti-black, although it angered him that whites are always blamed for the world's problems, such as starvation in Africa. Never, he claimed, did he judge a person on the basis of skin colour. Several years ago he had a black student who complained that her low mark in his course was a result of her skin colour. Keegstra's response was that the student herself was a racist, brandishing her pigmentation as an excuse for her poor performance.

Keegstra went on to give his views about equality. Nobody, he believed, is equal to anyone else. Everyone is unique and different. When I asked him about his views on white superiority, he said that he did argue in class that white society has been superior in terms of cultural and technological advancement, but explained it all in terms of religion, not race. As he stated:

I say that whites are where they are and have a better standard of living, have a better, and have more freedom and all these things and therefore are in that sense blessed – and that's the term I want to use – they have been blessed by God because they, in their culture and that, they do follow Christian principles and institutions and this kind of thing. Now, I'm saying that the blessings which we have ... is simply because of ... the Christian factor. I'm not saying that we are superior. I'm saying that we are receiving blessings which I'm beginning to think now that we don't deserve, because – but you see how I would explain it; rather than on a race basis, I'm saying no, it's religious basis.

Keegstra talked about the financial support that he had received from all around the world, as his case became internationally known. Some of the supporters were themselves white supremacists. Keegstra said that he wrote back politely, thanking them for their contributions, stating that he respected their right to believe what they wished, but adding that he could only accept money on a no-strings-attached basis, because he can't interpret the Scriptures and Christianity the way they do. In his words: 'when they start equating Christianity with racism, I can't go along with that.' He specifically referred to both the Western Guard and the Aryan Nations in this context, saying: 'To me, they – to me, they're just Judaism tipped upside down.' What he meant was that they were in their own way as racist as he perceived Jews to be – people who considered themselves superior to all others. Keegstra remarked that after receiving money from John Ross Taylor, he told him he would never join the Western Guard because of its belief in white supremacy. He also once met four members of the Aryan Nations, and claims he dismissed their views about white supremacy as ridiculous. From all this, can one conclude that Keegstra has been unfairly accused of believing in (and teaching a form of) white superiority? It would appear not. What he had just articulated was a white-supremacist viewpoint based on religion rather than biology. As supposedly well-versed in history as he was, he should have known that before the biological basis of racism took hold, religion once served the same purpose; his particular interpretation of white superiority may thus have been anachronistic, but it was thoroughly racist nevertheless. Even his even-handed reaction to overtly racist organizations contained a flaw. He once remarked to me that being broad-minded is dangerous. His argument was that it was wrong to assume that all beliefs and values are equal and valid. To think so, he said, is to fall into the trap of moral relativity or situational ethics. However, by not condemning people like Taylor, in spite of his view that their beliefs were insupportable, he seemed to fall into the trap himself. The only way he could avoid the contradiction, I suppose, would be to activate another important value – freedom of expression.

We now come directly to anti-Semitism, the issue that more than anything else landed Keegstra in hot water. Keegstra told me that he does not hate anyone – indeed, most of the hatred, he claimed, came from the other side: parents out to get him, and Jews gleefully backing them up. He also rejected the accusation that he was anti-Jewish, pointing out that he always said that only a small portion of Jews was dangerous to mankind. Nevertheless, Keegstra's views about Jews were essentially the same as those embraced by the radical right. Jesus, he claimed, was not a Jew; 90 per cent of Jews are Mongol-Turks (or Khazars), rather than Semites. Israel, he remarked to me, is the world's least admirable nation. That is because of its intolerance towards Christians, its treatment of black Jews as third-class citizens, and its status as a military state. Elsewhere (*Red Deer Advocate*, 2

April 1983), he apparently said that Jews hate Christians, and that the latter shouldn't fraternize with them. In one of his student's essays, we find: 'Everywhere that Jews have been involved we have had nothing but problems and chaos. They are sneaky, wise people who manipulate and deceive others to achieve what they want.' Another essay begins: 'The two things that are most opposed in our world are Judaism and Christianity. These two religions have totally different beliefs. Judaism is the religion of hatred and deception.' It was reported that one of his students also revealed that Keegstra taught that during the French Revolution a Jewish-controlled group committed ritual human sacrifice involving cannibalism (*Globe and Mail*, 7 June 1984). His teaching also included the message that the Illuminati, a secret society formed in 1782 and run by Jews, exists to gain world control; Jews, he claimed, were the forces behind the First World War and the Russian Revolution. Referring to Jews during one of my interviews, he said: 'they are extremely powerful; apparently they control Peter Lougheed and his group completely.' Describing Lougheed as an 'atheist if anything,' Keegstra declared: 'Peter's a terrible man as far as I'm concerned, as far as freedom and truth, you know, and this type of thing; he's very dangerous.' Trudeau, for his part, was, according to Keegstra, completely controlled by Jews. He pointed out that Trudeau's home riding was at least 80 per cent Jewish, and that Trudeau had been part of a group who had put together Canada's first 'hate' bill – an instrument for Jews to ensconce their control over the country. The red rose in Trudeau's lapel, he remarked, gave only one message: that he was a socialist.

Evidence of the insidious power of Jews, in Keegstra's view, was everywhere. The very mess he was in, he claimed, was a Jewish onslaught against Christianity. The media, he believed, were completely controlled by Jews, thus accounting for the negative image that he had. It was Jewish pressure, according to Keegstra, that led to the volte-face of the ATA; and referring to the board of reference in Edmonton, he said: 'we won that hearing completely but she [the judge] ruled against me because at our hearing the B'nai B'rith, and you know who they are – the Jewish organization, secret, or pressure-group – controlled by Israel – they were there all the time. They surrounded all the press; did you know that the press could not release anything without them reading it first?' Keegstra added that the JDL were there too, checking everything that reporters wrote. He said that he was told that Herb Katz, a businessman who was in the forefront of the opposition against Keegstra, was a member of the JDL, and that David, the Lacombe school superintendent, may have himself been a Jew. On another occasion, referring again to the board of reference, he said: 'the judge, she had no choice. It was either me or her because if she would have found me not guilty, she would have lost her job.'

Other examples of the conviction of Keegstra and his friends that Jewish manipulation was everywhere are not hard to find. Gostick, who once spoke to one of Keegstra's classes in Eckville, wrote (*Canadian Intelligence Service*, vol. 33, no. 7, July 1983) that a representative from the Israeli government was present when Stiles made his apology in the legislature. Premier Lougheed (*Edmonton Journal*, 12 May 1983) had received a telex from Nazi hunter Simon Wiesenthal, urging him to speak out against Keegstra and to launch an educational program on the Holocaust. On learning of the telex, Keegstra remarked that Wiesenthal might be part of the international conspiracy bent on world domination.

Keegstra defined Zionism as atheism, arguing that Zionists don't believe in a supreme being. They do believe in a Messiah, he added, but the Messiah is the Jewish people collectively. Thus, any attack on a particular Zionist is tantamount to attacking what they mean by God. Because they are atheists, claimed Keegstra, Zionists are not constrained morally in their pursuit of world control. Keegstra contended that the Holocaust as popularly perceived never took place. He defined 'holocaust' as massive death by fire. A holocaust in that sense, he said, did occur in Germany during the Second World War, but it consisted of the Allied bombing of Dresden. According to Keegstra, it is now official that no gas chambers in Germany were used for human beings. He also believed personally that nowhere did gas chambers, in the hands of Germans, exist for the purpose of killing human beings, nor was there an official German policy to kill Jews; the 'final solution,' instead, consisted of deportation and emigration. The camps in Poland were inaccessible behind the Soviet Iron Curtain for ten years following the war, he pointed out, and thus any kind of fabrication would have been possible. Like others I interviewed, Keegstra claimed that Jews were far safer in concentration camps than outside them, where partisans and undisciplined soldiers could attack them.

I asked Keegstra what kind of evidence he would accept as proof of the Holocaust. His reply: 'It has to be logical. It has to be, uh, verifiable. It has to be distinctive. It can't be by the so-called Holocaust survivors – not *one* of them saw first-hand anything. They just saw a relative led away, and they didn't *know* that relative went to gas, uh, chambers. Now what kind of, uh, evidence is that?' Keegstra believes that Hitler has been greatly smeared, that he actually had been a positive force in Germany and Europe as a whole. Keegstra added that over the entire gamut of the school-board and court hearings, nobody had attempted to disprove his theories; he said he only wished that those who accused Hitler of atrocities would produce some hard evidence. When I pressed him farther on the nature of evidence that would change his mind about the Holocaust, and the gas chambers specifically, he admitted that virtually nothing would do the trick, repeating his observation that even what might look like proof for the gas chambers could easily have been constructed after the war itself. That was why, he added, he had declined an offer to visit the European concentration camps.

Just as Keegstra did not see himself as a white supremacist, he also distanced himself from beliefs of Aryan superiority over Jews. At one point, he elaborated on the arguments of a well-known right winger, Colonel Mohr: 'the Jews are claiming, and I'm talking about the Rabbis and the leaders, I'm not so sure about the rank and file, I'm talking about the leadership, and the leadership claims that they are the only human beings. Nobody becomes a man until he goes through the Bar Mitzvah and this type of thing and everybody else are beasts. Okay, then comes along Colonel Mohr and he brings all this out ... and he says, hey, the white race is superior, the white race is chosen; everybody that isn't white is a beast; well, now what kind of nonsense is this? And I had to disagree with him there.'

The implication is clear: in Keegstra's own mind, he was definitely not a proponent of Aryan superiority. Some of his supporters, indeed, claimed that quite contrary to his public image, he actually was a warm and generous friend of minority-group members. Several people told me about the time he had opened his home to a destitute Jew. That poor man, Keegstra confirmed, had actually stayed with him on two different occasions. Through his wife's charitable work in a prison, Indians and Eskimos, down on their luck, also had benefited from his hospitality. After pointing all this out, Keegstra asked me how people can accuse him of being a racist. These charitable activities, regardless how paternalistic, certainly fly in the face of the man's public reputation. However, some of his opponents provided a different interpretation: Keegstra's philanthropic work, they claimed, was all belatedly fabricated and exaggerated in order to show what a fine man he really was. In view of the situation in which Keegstra found himself, such efforts after the fact to repair his image would not be unexpected, but I lack the data to confirm whether that indeed was what had transpired. What I can do, however, is to draw the obvious conclusions about the man's beliefs and motivations. There is little doubt that Keegstra is a genuinely devout Christian, or that he believes precisely what he states about the danger of Jews. However, no matter how he dresses up these beliefs, rationalizes them away from outright bigotry, or presents them as the manifestation of the clash between Christianity and Judaism, they inevitabley fall into the category of racism and anti-Semitism. That is the bottom line in the Keegstra case. It does not mean that in so many apparent ways he is not a good man. But it does mean that this good man also is a racist.

AFTERMATH

Had a mass murderer been on the loose in Eckville, or had the town been hit by a hurricane – rather than merely by the notoriety of the Keegstra case – the consequences would not have been the same, for people would have joined in a common front to overcome their problems. The Keegstra affair, in contrast, left the town divided down the middle, sometimes even within families. What was particularly frustrating, one man told me, was that it was so difficult to predict who would be for and who would be against Keegstra. Referring to the same problem, an elderly couple explained that they just stopped talking to their neighbours about the case, in order to avoid disagreements. One of the Eckville teachers remarked that by 1983 there was a general air of distrust among Eckville residents; people were inordinately polite to each other, but maintained superficial relationships. Yet by 1984, claimed one man, who had been a vocal supporter of Keegstra, things were starting to return to normal, reflected in the fact that he had begun to do business with both factions. Some individuals also commented that the affair had had a depressing impact on the town's economy. One man, himself a prominent businessman, said several businesses had folded, and a few families had left the town. Another resident described the town, previously vibrant and friendly, as dull and sullen, and remarked that people in the surrounding area no longer came to Eckville to shop. Keegstra rejected all this, claiming that even if it was true that nearby farmers had decided to avoid Eckville, it was to protest the manner in which he had been treated. [8] There also were problems for Eckville residents farther afield. Two of the town's ambulance drivers, I was told, were once requested to vacate a restaurant in Calgary simply because they were from Eckville. Apparently, as well, some people ceased wearing jackets identifying them as Eckville residents.

The effect on the Eckville students was much more nebulous. Despite Keegstra's consistent legal losses, many of them apparently still believed what he had taught them, as witnessed by various letters of support by former students. At the June 1984 graduation ceremonies at the Eckville

8 By 1984, according to a local reporter, three new businesses had been established in the town.

high school, somebody (students, I was told) had painted 'Keegstra for Prime Minister' on the outside wall of the school, plus a comment about Jews. While such graffiti might normally be ignored for weeks, this time it was painted over by school authorities the next day.

Quite another question concerns the impact of the various legal hearings on the students. One woman claimed that some of the students who testified against Keegstra loved the experience; she said they were show-offs, and were unconcerned that a man's dignity and livelihood rested in the balance. Yet her remarks were exceptional, and probably malicious. For quite a number of the students, the court experience was a terrible ordeal. Some of them cracked under the pressure, bursting into tears, and the mother of one of them related how her daughter, for the first time in her life, suffered from severe chest and stomach pains, brought on by the trauma of the courts. The mother of another witness for the prosecution remarked that one of her real concerns was that the court experience has been so traumatic for her own child and for others that they might in future, if faced by a comparable moral dilemma, decide it was not worth the anguish to become involved.

With Keegstra gone from the Eckville school, a replacement had to be found. Although the young man who stepped into the lion's den was relatively inexperienced, the fact alone that he survived attested to his personal strengths, for as David stressed, he was given a very rocky welcome by both the teaching staff and the students. This young man was a member of the Christian Reformed church, and I had wanted to contact him not only because he had been Keegstra's temporary replacement (by the end of the 1983 school year he had moved to a diffent institution), but also because several individuals had insisted that the Christian (sometimes 'Dutch') Reformed church had increasingly become prone to a racist ideology. This young instructor revealed (personal communication) that on his very first day in the school one of the teachers asked him if he was David's spy. During the trial in 1985, an Eckville student stated (*Globe and Mail*, 13 April 1985) that he suspected the new teacher was a spy working on behalf of the international Jewish conspiracy. Although this man apparently had tried to maintain a neutral image at the school, after he appeared at the board of reference hearing in Edmonton in 1983, it became public knowledge that his views were the polar opposite of Keegstra's, and from that point on at least two Eckville staff members avoided him. By coincidence, his parents, who also had emigrated from Holland, had been friends of Keegstra's own parents, although he himself did not personally know his celebrated predecessor.

In response to my questions about the Christian Reformed church, the replacement teacher sent me an issue of that church's publication, *The Banner* (1 October 1984), which contained an article on racism. In the article it is stated: 'Racists are not only wicked; they are also stupid.' That would seem to be a pretty clear repudiation of any racist tendency. Yet ironically the same issue contained another article on 'Modern Jews and Jesus.' Although the article sensitively dealt with the antagonism of Jews towards efforts of Christians to convert them, it ended up declaring: 'Without faith in Jesus Christ there is no salvation for either Jews or Gentiles.'

In the wake of the Keegstra affair, a number of steps were taken to remove his influence from the Eckville school and the province in general. In addition to the Ghitter Commission, a public-education program with a budget of $540,000 was unveiled by the chairman of the Alberta Human Rights Commission and the government's minister of labour (*Red Deer Advocate*, 5 October 1983). The program consisted of a multi-media advertising campaign, a resource centre on racism, and materials profiling ethno-cultural communities. In Eckville itself, Principal Olsen wrote to Superintendent David in May 1983, indicating the several activities planned to give students in his school 'a more complete view of history and a more positive attitude toward a variety of groups of people.' These plans included using the recommended texts containing the 'traditional view of history,' and taking students to Red Deer to see the film *Gandhi*.

Some of the efforts to counter Keegstra's influence did not seem to be very successful. For example, three Holocaust survivors who visited the Eckville School apparently drew a small audience. One Eckville man commented caustically: 'Now who would bother taking a look at a Calgary Jew?' On one occasion, six grade-twelve students were hosted in Vancouver by B'nai B'rith. The teacher who accompanied them told me that their hosts were totally amazed about and unprepared for the knowledge and sophistication that the students already possessed about Jews and the Holocaust – knowledge, she said, that had been provided by Keegstra himself.

Much more ambitious was a trip to Germany for Eckville students, the brain-child of a retired army man, Jack Downey. He initiated an essay contest on 'Canada as a Multicultural Nation.' The plan was to send the winners to Europe to observe first-hand the Nazi concentration camps. From the outset there were problems simply finding enough students interested in the trip, and then with the quality of the essays. Finally, two students, a boy, and a girl, both sixteen, were selected as winners; they were accompanied by an Eckville teacher, who happened to be the mother of the boy. Their visit to Dachau, the teacher told me, wasn't very effective. One reason was that they went there immediately after the all-night flight to Germany, and were too tired to appreciate what they saw. Another reason, she said, was that Dachau had been 'cleaned up' and did not reflect the gruesome horrors of a supposed death camp. She said there was a crematorium there, and gas heads on the showers, but they were sparkling clean and looked quite new and unused. From Dachau the two students and the teacher were taken to Breendonck in Belgium. Unlike Dachau, the teacher said, Breendonck had never been cleaned up, and thus had much more of an impact on them. But she added that Jews had never been kept there, but instead Belgian and Dutch nationals. She went on to say that what really created the greatest impression were not the concentration camps, but instead the Canadian cemetery, Adagem, just outside Brussels. The sight of all the graves of dead Canadians made the Second World War a reality.

On return to Canada, one of the students wrote an essay entitled 'Dachau, 1983.' He documented vividly the horror of Dachau, and his revulsion to the immense suffering that had occurred. Yet he did not specify Jews as being especially prominent among the victims, nor did he relate what he saw and felt to the more general question of the Holocaust, which after all had been the purpose of the trip. The teacher herself, who told me she never wrote 'Eckville' on hotel reservation cards, because one never knows who might read them, said that she had learned nothing new about Jews, the Holocaust, the Nazis, or the concentration camps from the trip. She did state that she had been enlightened about the German people. She had been told that Germans were cold and superior, and was surprised and delighted to discover that they were in reality so friendly and co-operative. One interpretation, I suppose, is that this woman and the students, especially her son, were in fact knowledgeable and sophisticated in terms of the Holocaust before the voyage itself.

From the viewpoint of the people of Eckville, with Keegstra gone as teacher and mayor the affair was finally finished. But that was not to be. On the near horizon loomed Keegstra's stiffest and potentially most far-reaching test yet: the trial in court, where he was charged with wilfully promoting hatred against an identifiable group. Significantly, I never met a single individual in Eckville and the surrounding area, including his opponents, who was in favour of the further legal prosecution of the man. The general attitude was that what had to be done was done – removing him from his prominent positions – and any further steps against him were unnecessary and bound to turn him into a martyr. Leading figures such as

Andrew and David both thought the trial was a mistake. Maddox said much the same (*Red Deer Advocate*, 14 January 1984), commenting that the RCMP investigation and eventual legal charge were just a political manoeuvre on the part of the Alberta government to demonstrate (after the fact) its concern about the Keegstra affair. The superintendent of the Medicine Hat Catholic Board of Education, it was reported, urged (*Red Deer Advocate*, 18 January 1984) charity towards Keegstra, remarking that he had already been punished enough. Even Leach, the man who replaced Keegstra as mayor, expressed his unhappiness with the continuing legal procedures (*Calgary Sun*, 13 January 1984): 'if Jim Keegstra had murdered someone,' he wryly observed, 'it would have appeared once and been forgotten about by now.' Farther afield, Alan Borovoy (*Toronto Star*, 29 July 1985), general counsel of the Canadian Civil Liberties Association, spoke out strongly against Keegstra's eventual conviction, as he had done in regard to Zundel's case. His argument was that the law under which Keegstra had been charged was extremely vague, a serious threat to freedom of speech, and moreover that the trial had only served to provide Keegstra with another platform.

Why, then did the case go to court? The answer, as far as I can understand, is that at least three interest groups would not let it die. One was Keegstra himself. Whether motivated by a latent martyr complex, or simply by the firm belief that he was right, he made no effort to withdraw from the fray, and demonstrated little aversion to the limelight. The media, to some extent, also had a stake in the case, solely because of its sensationalism. Finally, just as various neo-Nazis tried to use Keegstra to promote their own causes, Keegstra also had become somewhat of an instrument for anti-racist organizations. For example, in a document compiled by the Joint Community Relations Committee, Canadian Jewish Congress, reference is made to the reluctance of attorneys general to prosecute under the anti-hate laws because of the chance of losing as a result of the defence that the accused genuinely believes what he says. The document goes on to state that the Keegstra case would seem to be ideal for testing the law, for even if Keegstra won, that in itself might help to demonstrate the necessity of amending the law. Elsewhere, Alan Shefman, national director of the League for Human Rights of B'nai B'rith, Canada, remarked that the Keegstra case had broken the log-jam (personal communication, September 1984). What he meant was that with the legal charges against Keegstra as precedent, the courts will no longer be unprepared to prosecute under the anti-hate laws. Strange as it may seem, in one respect racists and anti-racists sustain each other. They constitute a bizarre social relationship, the one providing the other with a platform and confirming beliefs in an insidious conspiracy, the other constituting the proof positive that racism is on the increase and that an all-out attack must be launched.

CONCLUSION

On one occasion while in the Eckville area I asked a reporter if there was anything negative that could be said about Keegstra if his racist views were forgotten for the moment. The answer was crystal clear: not a single thing. Keegstra, the reporter declared, was an excellent teacher, a responsible member of the community, a good family man, devout, honest, and just. This brings us back to our opening question: can one be a racist and a good man simultaneously? In his classical study of anti-Semitism, Sartre wrote (1948: 8): 'A man may be a good father and a good husband, a conscientious citizen, highly cultivated, philanthropic, *and* in addition an anti-Semite. He may like fishing and the pleasures of love, may be tolerant in matters of religion, full of generous notions on the conditions of the natives in Central Africa, *and* in addition detest the Jews.' But Sartre did not believe this. In the strongest terms he contended that a man can't be an anti-Semite and a good man at the same time, for even his generosity and kindness will be conditioned by his racist orientation. From a similar perspective, the editor of *The Jewish Star* (vol. III, no. 18, 10 June–14 July, 1983, Calgary Edition) took exception to a journalist's suggestion that Keegstra was neither a looney nor a latent Nazi ogre. The journalist had talked about the normality of the Keegstra phenomenon, stating that he was not much different from the ordinary man on the street. That, of course, was precisely how Hannah Arendt, the philosopher, had described Eichmann at the Nuremberg trials. But in the editor's opinion, both Eichmann and Keegstra were atypical ogres, madmen, evil incarnate.

In my experience, the editor's viewpoint accurately represented that of the wider Jewish community. One man, a university professor, when asked to comment on the concern among many of Keegstra's opponents that in the end he could not lose, for even if he was found guilty in court that would only reinforce his belief in the conspiracy, remarked: who cares about that nut's interpretation? Another man's reaction was much the same. He had become heavily involved in the public exposure of Keegstra, although he had never previously been very active in the Jewish community, and did not go out of his way to associate with Jews; he said he himself had never experienced anti-Semitism, and indeed he used to think it was Jews who were prejudiced. Two things woke him up: Abella and Troper's book on

Jewish refugees during the Second World War, and the Keegstra case. Three or four times he remarked that he felt like punching Keegstra and his supporters. His reaction in the circumstances was not extra-ordinary, but it did underline what I found to be a widespread phenomenon among Jews in Alberta. Rarely did I talk to anyone who tried to come to grips with the paradox of the apparently good man who also harbours racism. In a sense, of course, understanding is a scholarly luxury, something to engage in after the fire has been doused. Most Jews whom I met were frantically manning the buckets, rather than attempting to comprehend Keegstra's personality, or the background conditions that produced him. By depicting Keegstra as a totoally evil monster trying to pass as a human being, their task may have been rendered less difficult, especially since it disguised the uncomfortable notion that he might just be the tip of the iceberg. Yet in the long run such obfuscation can only elongate, not abbreviate, racism and anti-Semitism.

An exception among prominent Canadian Jews was Alan Shefman. Not only did he stress that the Keegstra case could have occurred anywhere in Canada, and thus there was nothing unique about Eckville, but he also stated (*Red Deer Advocate*, 2 April 1985): 'A person who is a bigot and a racist doesn't have to be an ogre. We can't blind ourselves and say these people are all red-necked, uneducated jerks because it's not true.' Keegstra undoubtedly was a high-principled, devout individual. To deny this is to overlook part of the reality. In the end, however, one must weigh his apparent goodness against his racist orientation. In my judgment, the latter overwhelms the former, rendering him a flawed individual in the eyes of humanity and the very God he worshipped.

Keegstra was not only defended by his supporters as a man of exemplary conduct, but also as a brilliant, revolutionary thinker. One right-wing member from British Columbia, after meeting Keegstra, described him as the most intelligent person he had ever encountered. An Eckville woman who took Keegstra's side remarked that he definitely considers himself superior to women, but added maybe – with good reason – he also thinks he is much more gifted than most men. A reporter told me that she always was intimidated by Keegstra when she interviewed him, because he was so extremely intelligent and well-read. Others contended that Keegstra was the equivalent of earlier revolutionary thinkers like Galileo – people whose profound insights challenged conventional wisdom. Some of them remarked that if only Keegstra had taught at the university level, all would have been well, because his brilliance would have been applauded rather than condemned. In my judgment, however, Keegstra was not a particularly intelligent man, nor was he unusually well-read and innovative. He was, it is true, fond of employing pseudo-scientific language, and urging his students, and even his opponents, to evaluate the logical and empirical validity of his historical interpretations by employing the resource material in his own library. However, that library only contained works supporting his interpretations, because, he said, he had not been able to locate any to the contrary. As far as the comparison of Keegstra to creative giants such as Galileo, Newton, or Freud is concerned, the case is clear-cut. The ideas that Keegstra promoted were not new, something never before heard. In all my interviews and reading in relation to the Keegstra case, I never came across a single idea – even a small one – which Keegstra could claim to have originated. At the very most, he can be labelled a spokesman, an apologist, for an interpretation of history that has long lingered at the borders of some men's minds.

Not everyone would accept the analytic distinction I have drawn between the radical right and the fringe right, and in one sense Keegstra, whom I have placed in the latter category, would seem to repudiate the division. Whereas many members of the fringe right would be prepared to state that they are anti-Zionist, those among them who are anti-Semitic usually conceal that fact. Keegstra, in contrast, openly claimed that the Holocaust never occurred, and that a minority of Jews are conspiring to take over the world. These pronouncements, in view of his formerly influential positions of teacher and mayor, may have been even more despicable than comparable messages emanating from organizations such as the Western Guard.

Nevertheless, Keegstra distanced himself from the goals of white supremacism, and especially the plan to create an Aryan stronghold by violent means; in a sense, indeed, he was less of a right-wing activist than the majority of those in the fringe right. For many of the latter, the political arena was where the action was; the fringe-right position itself was often a calculated one – deemed the most effective vantage-point from which to promote their programs. That was not the case with Keegstra and most of his supporters. They were guided by a world-view dictated largely by fundamentalist religious principles, meshed with a pre-urban and pre-industrial model of society. Certainly, their racist inclinations flowed from that world-view and at times intersected with the political arena. Such consequences, however, were secondary to the beliefs themselves.

Keegstra and his like-minded fans were to some extent political innocents, anachronisms in a changed social environment. In this respect, they have much in common with similar figures in recent history, such as Billy James Hargis, a prominent Christian right-wing activist in the United

States several decades ago. Redekop (1965) has referred to Hargis's position as Christian authoritarianism, and has contrasted it with the liberal democracy which has superseded it. What is interesting, Redekop argues, is that rather than being deviant, Hargis's Christian authoritarianism meshes nicely with the early American value system. It is that value system itself which has changed, thus making individuals like Hargis appear to be deviants. In a great many respects, the same could be said about Keegstra. He too represents a bygone era of Christian authoritarianism, and one might well argue that in earlier times he would have been held up as a paragon among citizens. The fact that just the opposite is true today underlines both the degree to which society has secularized and the progress made in snuffing out intolerance, especially the religious variety. As Redekop (1965: 18) wrote: 'It is only when the majority has fallen away from the faith that the true believers, the exponents of the traditional status quo, take on the aura of reactionism.' The implication is clear: Keegstra, from his point of view and that of his supporters, was born a century too late.

Few communities have been put through the hoops to the same extent that Eckville has. With that in mind, perhaps it is not out of step to let its citizens have the last word. In the wake of the Keegstra affair, many Eckville people were proudly saying that what makes the town unique is not the existence of a man like Keegstra and the latent anti-Semitism, for they can be found in almost any community. Instead, in their words, it is the fact that 'we did something about it.'

10

Others on the Fringe Right

A frequent complaint among people in the fringe right was the tendency of their critics to equate strong conservatism with a racist orientation. Are the two necessarily linked? To the extent that conservatism implies the shoring up of power and privilege, it has by definition a potential vulnerability towards racism, which is one of several mechanisms that sustain differential social advantage. However, to some degree that holds true for any power structure, including, in the opinion of some Marxists, the revisionist government of the Soviet Union. Most of the organizations in this chapter, while vocally opposed to communism, homosexuality, moral laxness, and the erosion of the nation's freedoms, eschewed any display of racism. The exception was the social-credit movement. As Ages (1981: 388–9) has remarked, it has been the one mainstream political party in Canada that has come closest to having anti-Semitic overtones.

SOCIAL CREDIT

My own interest in the social-credit movement concerns its links to the right wing at two different periods. One was around 1971–2, when the Edmund Burke Society attempted to gain control over the movement in Ontario. The other was in connection with the Keegstra affair. From the outset it must be made clear that there have been many different expressions of social credit in the country, ranging from a Christian-oriented, borderline anti-Semitic form to what for all intents and purposes has been conventional conservatism by another name. The distinctions between the national or federal Social Credit party, with its provincial organizations, and the autonomous provincial organizations must also be appreciated. In Ontario in the early 1970s it was the independent provincial organization that was most extreme, with the federal entity trying to suppress it; but in Alberta in the early 1980s, the situation was reversed: the 'radicals' like Keegstra belonged to the federal organization.

The social-credit movement, founded by Major C.H. Douglas, a British engineer, incorporates both an economic program and a philosophy of society. One of its fundamental principles (Holter 1934) is that the root of economic problems is 'not inability to produce, but inability to consume.' That is, the consumer lacks purchasing power, which thus holds up production. The simple solution is to give the consumer money; in social credit's jargon, this is called the 'national dividend,' a sum of money that is provided to all consumers, whether employed or not. The social-credit approach, its proponents argue, would greatly reduce or even eliminate taxation. Some idea of its unconventional economic notions is reflected in the attitude towards exports and imports. Whereas it is normally assumed that the former must exceed the latter in a healthy economy, social creditors believe exactly the opposite; exports, in their view, deplete a nation's natural wealth, rather than building up foreign exchange. Social credit is based on 'the Christian way of life.' It promotes the sanctity of the family and the home, individual freedom and initiative, and private enterprise (Holter 1934), and 'is irreconcilably opposed to Communism, Fascism, and all forms of totalitarian government which make the individual citizen subservient to the State' (Kirk 1962).[1] As one writer summed the movement up (Toronto *Telegram*, 4 September 1962): 'Social Credit stands four-square for God, the monarchy and lots of spending money for everybody.'

The first social-credit government in the world, led by William (Bible Bill) Aberhart, was established in Alberta in 1935, with its promise of a dividend of $25 per month. Palmer (1982: 152) points out that while anti-Semitism was at that time relatively weak in Alberta, it was somewhat more pronounced within social-credit circles. Within a few weeks of coming to power, Aberhart travelled to the United States to discuss economic programs with Father Charles Coughlin and Henry Ford, both well-known anti-Semites. According to Palmer, Aberhart was himself prone to anti-Semitism, but not nearly to the degree espoused by Major Douglas. The latter, who visited Alberta in 1934, turned increasingly in that direction as it became apparent that the world was not going to switch to social credit overnight. It was the Jewish conspiracy, he thought, that was holding up the works. Aberhart publicly repudiated anti-Semitism in his party, as did his

---

1 On the first page of Kirk's work is again the conservative's clarion call: 'The only thing that is necessary for the triumph of evil is that good men do nothing.'

successor and former student, Ernest Manning.[2] Manning actually expelled Earl Ansley, a former minister of education in the province, because of his promotion of the international conspiracy theory, although Ansley's home riding continued to elect him as an independent MLA (*Alberta Report*, 16 May 1983).

In Quebec in 1936, Louis Even, a journalist, founded the League of Social Credit. Eventually Réal Caouette emerged to lead that province's social-credit forces, described by Stein (1973, 1975) as a right-wing political protest movement. In British Columbia yet another form of social credit took root. Whereas both Aberhart and Manning intermingled religion and politics, Premier Bennett was decidedly opposed to such a package. On one occasion he apparently quipped: 'Social Credit is conservative policy without the nuisance of democracy.'[3] That, ironically, comes close to some of the comments directed at a more recent BC Social Credit government after a bill was introduced to slash bureaucracy, increase taxes, remove job security for public-sector employees, and disband the British Columbia Human Rights Commission (*Globe and Mail*, 8 August 1983). Some critics, indeed, compared the Socred administration to Nazi Germany (*Globe and Mail*, 9 August 1983).

Although apologists like Holter and Kirk contend that social credit has nothing to do with Facist policies, that point seems to have been lost on members of the right wing. Rockwell, the former leader of the American Nazi Party (Toronto*Telegram*, 13 March 1963), once expressed his admiration for Canada's social crediters, although he observed that they were more moderate than his own people, especially concerning Jews. It was at that time that Carmichael, the Toronto coin and stamp dealer and social-credit candidate, was getting newspaper headlines for his pro-Hitler, anti-Semitic pronouncements. A vice-president of the Ontario Social Credit Party referred to Carmichael as 'a leftover from an era we would sooner forget about' (*Globe and Mail*, 12 March 1963). After being expelled, Carmichael founded the Social Credit Action Party, and eventually the Credit Jubilee Party. At that time there also was an organization called the Young Social Crediters (aged ten to sixteen), members of which were supposed to recruit fellow public-school students.

Prominent right wingers such as Beattie, Weiche, Andrews, Taylor, Prins, Matrai, and Fromm all were associated at one time with the social-

2 See the series of articles by William Stevenson in *The Globe and Mail* (30 April–4 May 1962) on Social Credit in Alberta, as well as the more recent appraisal by Elliott (1985) regarding the Keegstra affair.
3 Quoted in Stevenson, above.

credit movement in Ontario. In London, Ontario, in 1973 a blatantly racist recorded telephone message existed in the name of the Social Credit Party of Canada. It was around then that a struggle for control of the movement took place in Ontario, involving the Edmund Burke Society. As Fromm stated (*Straight Talk*, vol. 10, no. 6, March 1972): 'At the present time, the Social Credit Party of Canada looks like a good vehicle for a strong anticommunist, pro-Western patriotic movement.' The two main social-credit organizations in Ontario were the autonomous Social Credit Association of Ontario and the provincial branch of the national Social Credit party. In 1971, Fromm was elected president of the former, and Matrai became one of its vice-presidents; altogether about thirty members of the Edmund Burke Society belonged to the Social Credit Association. Some of them also held membership in the provincial branch of the national organization. With Fromm leading the way, an attempt was made to gain control over it as well. At a party convention in Barrie, Fromm seized the podium from the latter's president, a Collingwood medical practitioner, who had been determined to get rid of the Edmund Burke Society element. With the meeting in an uproar, it was forced by the hotel management to reconvene elsewhere (actually in a local school), where Fromm-dominated supporters held elections for office. The Collingwood surgeon was nominated in absentia, but lost his presidency. Fromm was elected as vice-president. In other words, not only did Fromm and his supporters control the Social Credit Association of Ontario, but also the Ontario branch of the national Social Credit Party of Canada. That, however, did not last long. The Social Credit national president placed the entire Ontario branch under his personal trusteeship. His prompt action, of course, did not affect the autonomous Social Credit Association of Ontario. On 4 October 1973, Fromm resigned as the association's president, partly, he said, because some members were unwilling to accept the results of elections – a rather ironical statement in light of the manner in which the president of the national branch had been pushed aside.

In 1973, fourteen members who refused to remain in Fromm's Social Credit Association of Ontario formed a new group called the Social Credit League of Ontario. In the following year, Weiche announced (*Globe and Mail*, 27 February 1974) the merger of Social Credit and the National Socialist Party of Canada; the new group was to be called the National Social Party, and its charter called for an emphasis on 'white racial aspects of Canadian political life together with the fight against international bankers.' This new organization, which existed virtually in name only, was denounced by the national Social Credit party, which pointed out that there had been no accredited Socred organization in Ontario since 1972. In 1977 (Toronto *Sun*, 2 October 1977) there was a report that the Social Credit Party of Ontario had been renamed the Canadian Party of Ontario, in order to avoid the illusion that it was socialistic. A proposal was to be introduced at a national Social Credit meeting in Winnipeg the next year to change the Social Credit Party of Canada's name to the Canadian Party, but that did not materialize. By the 1980s social credit was no longer at the heart of right-wing activity in Ontario. McQuirter once ruminated that social credit might be a useful vehicle with which to contest elections, but took no steps in that direction. Taylor told me that social credit and the Western Guard are one and the same thing. He also claimed that the Western Guard still held the charter for the Social Credit Association of Ontario. During the 1980s, there were occasional rumours about resuscitating the Social Credit Association, but the only persistent ones that came my way involved employing it as a front to manipulate and politicize discontentment among Ontario farmers faced with low prices and unmanageable mortgages.

If the 1970s belonged to the Ontario right-wing element of the social-credit movement, the 1980s belonged to the Alberta equivalent. One of the sideline consequences of the Keegstra affair was the dismissal (*Alberta Report*, 16 May 1983) of Keegstra (a vice-president), Tom Erhart (also a vice-president), and James Green (referred to as a regional director) from the Social Credit Party of Alberta, the national organization's provincial branch. Not all Socred members were pleased. Another vice-president (*Edmonton Journal*, 8 May 1983) complained that three fine Christian gentlemen had been let down. About a dozen Socred members signed a letter protesting Keegstra's dismissal; one of them later changed her tune when it became evident to her that Keegstra was indeed preaching an anti-Semitic line. The Social Credit party's president, Martin Hattersley, made clear his intention of asking for the resignation of all those who supported Keegstra's views, regardless of the consequences for the party's membership (*Edmonton Journal*, 4 May 1983). In the end, however, Keegstra, Green, and Erhart were reinstated as members, and as a direct result Hattersley resigned.

Since adequate attention has been paid to Keegstra in previous chapters, and Erhart is a peripheral figure, here I shall only elaborate on Green's story. Green was born in Brooks, Alberta, in 1921, where he was raised on a farm. From 1941 to 1946 he served in the RCAF. During his lifetime he has been a farmer, a storekeeper, and a garageman. Married, with seven children, by the time I met him in 1984 he was retired and living in the small village of Bentley, not far from Eckville.

Green was baptized as an Anglican, but over the years joined and withdrew from several denominations: United church, Mennonite, United church again, Evangelical Free; by 1984 he was a Seventh-Day Adventist. When a member of the United church several years ago, he used to teach Sunday School, but quit when he came to the conclusion that its teachings went against the Scriptures. In former days he also accepted the teaching that Jews are God's chosen people, but eventually changed his mind. Like his friend Keegstra, Green sees Christianity as being at the centre of the universe. His home is decorated with spiritual signs: verses on walls, Bibles on coffee tables and book shelves. In Green's view, the Social Credit party, which he joined in 1962 (he also was a member of the Canadian League of Rights and the Christian Defence League), is based entirely on Christianity. Politics and religion, he argued, cannot be separated. In 1972, 1974, 1980, and 1984 he ran for public office under the Social Credit banner. His campaign literature in the 1984 election stated: 'I have no desire for position or power as such. I do know that not only Canada but this world is going down the drain, unless it smartens up, returns to God, and obeys his commandments.'

Green, who expressed the opinion that the Holocaust has been blown all out of proportion and that Anne Frank's diary is a hoax, observed that the only difference between the Conservatives and the Liberals is that one is in power and the other isn't. He complained that they both push bilingualism, metrication, human rights, world peace, higher freight rates, abortion on demand, and secular humanism. Neither, he added, has ever been on the side of labour and small businessmen and farmers; instead, they both obey the 'power boys' of international finance. Green was equally unflattering about 'false' social-credit versions. He dismissed the British Columbia Social Credit Party as just another conservative party completely controlled by financiers. As far as Alberta was concerned, he contended that Manning had destroyed the 'real' Social Credit party. His most scathing comments, however, were reserved for the autonomous provincial Social Credit party, to which I now turn.

It will be recalled that in Ontario in the early 1970s it was the independent provincial organization that harboured right-wing members, with the national-linked organization trying to get rid of them. In Alberta, the process was reversed. When Hattersley resigned as president of the provincial branch, he joined the autonomous Alberta organization. Born in England in 1932, married, with three children, Hattersley was a lawyer, an honorary assistant Anglican priest, and a member of the Confederation of Church and Business People. He talked about the severe anti-Semitic problem in the Alberta Social Credit Party in the 1940s, which was effectively suppressed by Manning. He stated that he himself had found it necessary to bring things to a head, to polarize Social Credit members with regard to Keegstra and anti-Semitism. As a result of his actions, he apparently was courted by the Conservatives, but went over to the autonomous Social Credit Party of Alberta, because, as he commented, social credit was in his blood. His parents had first met at a social-credit function in England, and following Aberhart's electoral success, moved to Alberta. Hattersley, too, remarked that the Socreds in British Columbia were basically no different from conservatives, because they lacked Douglas's monetary-reform policies. He defined conservatism as the art of maintaining the status quo, and social credit as the art of changing it. Social credit, he said, advocates an economic floor of security, a basic guaranteed living income for everyone. It constitutes, he added, a political system that realizes socialist objectives by free-enterprise means. Suave, subtle, and smart, Hattersley was one person who emerged from the Keegstra affair with his reputation intact.[4]

In the wake of the Eckville crisis, and its links to social credit, the autonomous provincial social-credit organization faced an uphill climb, especially since not all Albertans appreciated the difference between that organization and the provincial branch of the national Social Credit party. The man who seemed to take on the responsibility was Ray Neilson, interim leader of the Alberta organization. Middle-aged, a small businessman and salesman, Neilson, like Hattersley, was born in Britain, and brought up in the Church of England. Unlike Hattersley, he had adopted social credit tenets only recently. He told me that he joined the party about 1981 after reading that it was withering up and dying. According to Neilson, the Alberta branch of the federal Social Credit party had about sixty members, while his own organization had about nine hundred members; his mailing list was about three thousand.

Neilson ridiculed Green's denial of the Holocaust, and commented that Alberta's cultural mosaic has been enriched by immigrants such as East Indians. Green, he said, thinks people are anti-Christ if they don't interpret

4 Hattersley had been national Social Credit leader Robert Thompson's personal secretary in 1962, the period when Carmichael's anti-Semitism was embarrassing the movement. Thompson wrote a letter (*Globe and Mail*, 19 March 1963) to the Canadian Jewish Congress dissociating his party from Carmichael's views.

the Bible literally, and don't believe every word that Douglas wrote. Neilson, who said he rarely attends church, remarked that religion and faith are healthy inputs to a political party, but asked how one can limit a party to Christianity. What would that mean, he added, if a Moslem or a Buddhist wanted to join? He did not vote for the federal Social Credit party during the 1984 election, because he said that would have been tantamount to voting for Fascism. Neilson contended that several features in society today indirectly exemplify social-credit principles. The entire Chargex system, for example, constitutes a credit line consistent with Douglas's monetary reforms. The same is true, he said, with subsidized medicine, which in effect represents a dividend spread throughout the populace.

Neilson was opposed to both conservatism and socialism, but rejected liberalism as the obvious alternative in the centre. Conservatives, he said, are like rapists: they take without asking; they rape the timber, the land, the oil fields. The problem with socialism, however, is that all human endeavour is reduced to the lowest common denominator. Social credit, he argued, is against monopolies, which both socialism and conservatism favour. Although Neilson found little to praise in conservatism, which he said amounts to the defence of privilege, he described himself as an élitist. But what he meant was that he was in favour of meritocracy, of a stratification system with no built-in obstacles against talent. To illustrate his position, he referred to the Olympics, where the best athletes in the world compete. They constitute the cream of the crop, the élite. To *not* be élitist in this sense, the most gifted runners would have to have weights tied to them to give their opponents a fair chance. Neilson also talked about fair (not free) enterprise. People, he said, should be allowed to make all the money they can, but they must do it fairly, and must have social responsibility. Neilson saw himself as the Social Credit party's guru, as its thinker and innovator, the man who would come up with the ideas for others to put into practice. One of his ideas certainly was novel: to offer the leadership of his party, after it had got its act together, to none other than former prime minister Joe Clark.

Green, who said that in 1983, for the first time in social-credit history, every member of the federal executive was a Christian, was not overly impressed by the interim leader of the autonomous Alberta Social Credit Party. In a letter addressed to party members (18 August 1984), Neilson had alluded to the danger of allowing extremists to gain control. About a month later (15 September 1984), Green sent him a hand-written reply: 'You might think your [*sic*] smart but you should not call yourself Social Credit.' Green went on to describe Neilson's version of social credit as traitorous to Major

Douglas, and concluded by inviting him to join the communists or 'start studying true Social Credit and get on the side of Christ and Christianity.'

RENAISSANCE

It all began around 1974 when Rev. Ken Campbell, president of the Campbell-Reese Evangelistic Association, who has justifiably been described as the man with the Billy Graham smile, launched his protest against secular humanism and immorality in the school system. The issue that triggered Campbell's outrage was homosexuality, specifically the visit of four representatives to the school in Halton County, Ontario, attended by his children. The story of Campbell's battle against moral laxity in the schools and wider governmental bureaucracy is told in his own book, *Tempest in a Teapot* (1975).[5] There Campbell describes Renaissance as 'a non-sectarian, non partisan citizens' group seeking to exert the civilizing influence of parent-power in public education.' With a flair for the catchy phrase, he labelled the current philosophy guiding the educational system as 'sexual fascism' and 'totalitarian secularism.' In Campbell's view, it seemed that just about everyone involved in the educational system was organized except parents and taxpayers. He remarked to me that there was a time in history when people had to be liberated from religion, but now the reverse situation exists: we must be liberated from atheism. Renaissance was in favour of banning its version of immoral and atheistic books, and was successful in having *The Story Makers* removed from Halton County board schools. Campbell advocated that creationism be taught alongside scientific theories of the origin of the universe, and contended that alternatives to the public educational system must be made available to Canadian citizens. He actually withdrew his own children from the public system, and put them in private Christian schools. On one occasion (5 September 1979), he sent a letter to the United Nations formally protesting the Ontario government's failure to provide private-school facilities.[6]

---

5 The title was derived from one of Campbell's critics, who dismissed his elaborate protest as a tempest in a teapot.
6 One of the sub-issues focused on in the Ghitter Report was the nature and role of private, especially religious, schools. In an article entitled 'Evangelical Higher Education' published in *Faith Alive* (vol. 2, no 1, March 1984), the quarterly organ of the Evangelical Fellowship in Canada, a summary of such schools is provided. There were a total of 89 Bible, seminary, and liberal-arts colleges (with a religious orientation) across the country. Of a total of 11,451 students, 7,954 were in Bible colleges, 1,306 in theological seminaries, and 2,191 in liberal-arts colleges. Despite the West's lower popula-

Campbell told me that he did not condemn consenting adult homosexual relations, but was adamantly opposed to the attempt by homosexuals to intrude into into public places, such as schools. On one occasion (3 October 1980) he wrote to the chairman of the Ontario Human Rights Committee to complain about the Toronto Board of Education's motion to ban discrimination in schools based on sexual orientation. Campbell argued that gays (which in the context meant militant, licentious homosexuals) are not typical of the majority of homosexuals who accept the social limitations placed on them, and conform to the criminal code's dictum that homosexuality be limited to consenting adults in private. Some of the articles in *Body Politic*, in his opinion, constituted hate literature; to illustrate the threat of gays to the moral well-being of society, he showed me a copy of a well-known pamphlet entitled 'Homosexuality Fact Sheet.' In one issue of *Liberation*, a periodical founded in 1971 which eventually came under the Renaissance umbrella, there is a reference to remarks made by Stephen Lewis on a radio program about distasteful gay life in California as depicted by a CBS-TV program; the implication in *Encounter* was that Lewis was a Renaissance man at heart. On learning that he had been warmly welcomed into the Renaissance family, Lewis appeared even more disturbed than he had been by the television documentary. He blasted Renaissance (see Information Services, 590-CKEY, 24 October 1980) as 'a twitchy, thin-lipped group ... determined to bring truth, purity, piety, morality, and Christianity to society in general and to the school system in particular,' and described its members as 'narrow, intolerant, mouthy and insufferable.'

To protest against the public-school system, Campbell hit upon a dramatic tactic: he refused to pay the education portion of his property taxes. With the threat of expropriation of his home and property hanging over him, he donated them to Coronation College, which planned to build a new campus on the site. Coronation College originally was known as Richmond College, which opened in 1967. Campbell was the president in 1981 when the change of name occurred. Coronation College assumed responsibility for Campbell's back taxes, and in turn Campbell, his wife, and his mother were permitted to live on the property for the rest of their lives.

Campbell's original organization, the Halton Renaissance Committee, founded in 1974, was a modest affair, confined to the county level. Eventu-

tion, most of the schools and students were located there. These included 42 of the 68 Bible schools, and 69 per cent of the students. One of the interesting observations in the article (p. 13) concerned the turn towards the right in the country: 'In the past we feared higher education because of the threat of liberalism. Today liberalism is functionally dead, at least for now.'

ally Renaissance became a provincial and then a national movement, composed of several different organizations: Renaissance Ontario, Renaissance Canada, Renaissance International, and Renaissance Family Institute. Renaissance Canada was set up as the political-educational arm, and Renaissance International as the charitable-religious arm. It was the latter that published the journal *Liberation*; on each of its issues was the same message that appeared on Gostick's *On Target*: 'You shall know the truth, and the truth shall make you free.' Renaissance also published the periodical *Encounter*, and had a political wing called 'Solidarity.' The Heritage Forum, connected to Renaissance, was established, according to Campbell, to act as 'a voice for the "moderate majority" in Canadian church life providing a sane and sensible alternative to the "leftish" tendencies of establishment church leadership in Canada.' By 1980 (*Globe and Mail*, 25 December 1980) Campbell claimed that Renaissance had about 10,000 members across Canada, and a mailing list of 100,000. Its prominent members included an ex-parliamentarian, a lawyer, a university professor, and a psychologist.

While Renaissance's initial protest was directed towards the educational system, the organization eventually branched out to the wider political arena, and again the main issue was homosexuality and moral degeneracy. In January 1980, a mail survey of the candidates of the three major political parties concerning ten 'urgent and moral issues' was conducted by Renaissance. The majority of the 10 per cent who responded supported the organizations's position regarding the importance of the family, the necessity of curbing drug abuse, and similar issues. In the fall of that year, Campbell, in the face of what he perceived as a mounting gay presence, decided that Renaissance would actively campaign for pro-family candidates in Metro Toronto's municipal and board of education elections. Renaissance placed an advertisement in the Toronto *Sun* (apparently *The Toronto Star* had refused to run it) urging people to vote for Toronto the Good, not for San Franciso North. The latter was a reference to Toronto's homosexual community. In a later report in *Encounter* (vol. 9, no. 4, Fall 1980), it was claimed that Renaisssance's crusade against Mayor Sewell's open support for gays played a major part in his defeat. George Hislop, a homosexual who lost his bid for alderman in the election, referred angrily to Renaissance's advertisement, and demanded: 'I want to know how a political movement masquerading as a religious organization can be registered as a charitable organization and why its contributors are entitled to deduct their donations for tax purposes.' Campbell's reaction was to declare that if the government wouldn't interfere in the religious sphere, religious groups would stay clear of politics. As a direct result of Renaissance's involvement in the Toronto elections (*Globe and Mail*, 25 December 1980), its status as a charitable organization was challenged in court. Renaissance won the case.

How are we to regard Campbell? Is he simply a courageous and honourable clergyman who had the fortitude to stand up for his version of decency and morality? Or is there more to him than that: is he a genuine member of the right-wing club? To answer these questions we need to delve more deeply into the man's background and wider political beliefs. Campbell was born in Hartford, Ontario, in 1934. His father was a Baptist minister, and Campbell himself was 'saved' at the age of eighteen. He attended a Bible college in Tennessee, and became a moderately successful evangelist. As one journalist observed (*Canadian*, 15–16 September 1979): 'Certainly he has all the equipment you'd expect of the evangelist. Neatly groomed, innocuously dressed, with clean-cut white bread good looks, he has a brisk, forceful voice and an exhaustingly joyful manner.' The same writer commented that Campbell was 'decent, serious, earnest and, like most obsessives, something of a drip.' Campbell has preached at Jerry Falwell's church in Virginia, who in turn once spoke at a Renaissance meeting in Canada. Married, with five children (his first wife died tragically in 1960), Campbell was pastor at Emmanuel Baptist Church in Milton, Ontario, by the time I met him in the early 1980s. His evangelical career, he told me, had been ruined as a result of his many years of involvement with Renaissance.

Campbell said that while he had never been accused of being a racist or an anti-Semite, he often had been called a bigot. He resented the label, insisting that he was a moderate, not a radical, and indeed was often attacked by both the far left and the far right. Heritage Forum in one leaflet was described as 'a voice for the moderate majority.' In material that Campbell provided to me, it was written: 'Renaissance is "radical" only in the sense that *we dare to speak forthrightly to the urgent issues*, the views which "the moderate majority" only thinks!'

Campbell, who struck me as the type of person who is uncomfortable with silences when in conversation with others, was not averse to the limelight. He was a frequent participant on radio and television shows, and whenever he addressed a letter of complaint to a school or government official, copies often were sent to the appropriate media. He also impressed me as a man with a martyr complex, or at least with a flair for melodrama. For example, in his book (1975: 13) he pontificates: 'I knew I'd rather lose my property than my family, my social and economic security than the integrity of my Christian conscience, and my life than my Christian liberty.'

Elsewhere, in a letter (31 May 1983) addressed to 'Dear Friend of faith, family and freedom,' in which he strongly objected to a short story in the local high-school curriculum, he sighs: 'although bone-weary and well-nigh wiped out by this decade-long battle to save our children and our families, I am constrained by the love of Christ to continue the battle knowing that "if we die a-fighting, it is no disgrace." '

Campbell remarked that if he had not spoken out as he did, he would have been nothing more than a fraudulent evangelist. He saw his actions as his *duty* as a Christian and parent. And that, presumably, was much the same motivation that inspired Rev. MacLeod to oppose Keegstra. If we applaud the one, on what basis do we condemn the other? The simple solution, I suppose, is to look askance at all spiritual intrusions into world affairs; to follow, for example, the official position of the Catholic church against 'liberation theology': priests, the Pope has made clear, should stick to saving souls, rather than involving themselves in the battle of the poor against the rich. Yet the persistent criticism in Alberta was that the churches had ducked their responsibility to confront an immoral problem in society.

There are a number of other tricky parallels between the Campbell and the Keegstra case. In his role as parent, Campbell can be compared to Andrew and Maddox; all three were horrified with what was being taught to their children and did something about it. Just as numerous Keegstra opponents were condemned as outsiders, Campbell was too; a petition was circulated in the high school attended by his daughters requesting the principal to stop 'outsiders' from interfering in the school's affairs (*Oakville Beaver*, 10 October 1979). Just as Andrew and Maddox were subjected to gossip and condemned as busybodies, Campbell received nasty phone calls, and on one occasion a rock was thrown through the window of his home. Just as the sons of Maddox and Andrew were labelled by Keegstra supporters as stupid, unreliable, weak-charactered show-offs, Campbell's own children were the brunt of insults from their fellow students. Just as Keegstra supporters declared that as a minister, MacLeod should have remained neutral, Campbell's opponents criticized him for allowing his religious views to flow over into the public realm. Just as many of Keegstra's opponents said that he can't preach his racist line in the school, but can spout whatever he wants as a private citizen on the street corner, Campbell stated that homosexuals can be allowed their private lives, but must steer clear of the schools and the political arena. Finally, there is the overlap between Campbell and Keegstra. Both are confirmed theists. In each case, their acts in this world were merely the expression of their Christian principles. To reiterate, if we celebrate the actions of MacLeod, on what basis do we denigrate those of the other two? Does God speak truthfully to one person and deceitfully to another? Is religious motivation amenable to rational judgment at all? The answer may well be no, but most of us in this world are practical men and women, and we don't hesitate to reduce metaphysical issues to a mundane level. I am reminded of a situation that developed several years ago in connection with my research in West Africa when numerous Yoruba prophets, supposedly inspired by God, began to challenge the colonial system. The authorities quickly clamped down on the incipient rebellion, observing that 'God told me to do it' is not a legal defence.

In the end, the reasons why Andrew, Maddox, and MacLeod are applauded and Campbell criticized are rather simple. The Eckville individuals were opposing an almost universally accepted evil: racial indoctrination. But Campbell was reacting against what in essence are changing norms and values in society. Campbell probably was correct in claiming that a substantial portion of the silent majority privately agreed with him. However, a more acute observer of social life would have realized that public values always look cleaner than those expressed in private, and that whenever people are pressed to articulate their views on controversial matters, they are constrained to mutter motherhood statements. By forcing the Keegstra affair onto the public stage, his opponents were virtually assured of victory, regardless of the degree of submerged racism in the setting. By doing likewise with regard to immorality in the schools, Campbell effectively cut his own throat, for what were motherhood statements to him no longer were those embraced by the wider society.

Finally, and most critical of all, there is the issue of Campbell's broader political orientation. If Campbell's opposition to homosexuality and immorality in the school system constituted the sum total of his protest, one might well give him a pat on the back for having the courage and integrity to stand up for what he believes, regardless of what one might personally think about these issues. Yet there is considerably more to his attack. He wants more discipline in school, and a return to the basics. He protests against expressions of anti-Americanism in the schools, and refers positively to Reagan for his preparedness to militarily defend the Christian West, and negatively to Trudeau for his unwillingness to do so. He comes down on the side of the hawks in the debate over nuclear disarmament, and supports the testing of the Cruise missiles over Canadian territory. He applauds Reagan's military invasion of Granada; indeed, he even sent a telegram to the American president commending him on his 'humanitarian response' in Granada, while referring to Trudeau's record of evading military service during the Second World War (*Encounter*, vol. 12, nos. 3 and 4, December 1983). All of this adds up to a consistent picture: that of an undoubtedly decent individual leaning towards the right. Campbell's criticism of immorality in the school system was not something that came out of the blue, and pushed him along the reactionary road; more probably, it was simply a concrete expression of a more general world-view that already had been lodged firmly to the right of centre.[7]

SPEAK-UP

That is precisely what Gil Urbonas, the founder of *Speak-Up*, described on its pages as 'a scrappy little monthly tabloid with the courage to tell it "like it is",' has been doing for several years, especially regarding the threat posed to the Western world by communism. Born in Lithuania in 1921, and a former pilot in Hitler's Luftwaffe, Urbonas came to Canada in 1958, after a brief spell in Argentina.[8] By the time I met him, he had worked as a clerk in a bank in downtown Toronto for twenty-six years. His fellow employees, he said, joke about his underground activity, but treat him well. A pleasant, gentle-appearing man, now divorced, with an almost lineless face, although he suffered from high blood pressure and hypertension, Urbonas has been described as 'the gentlemanly battler.' He formerly had been an active member of the Edmund Burke Society. However, he was not happy with that organization's turn towards militancy and white supremacy, and claims he told Andrews that his radical inclinations would ruin it. He also was opposed to demonstrations of any kind, pointing out that there never are enough people to make them impressive; much more effective, he thought, was the dispersion of the right-wing perspective in various forms of literature. After he resigned from the Edmund Burke Society, he founded *Speak-Up*, which has been the main focus of his life since then.

Despite Urbonas's attitude towards Andrews, *Speak-Up* was supported by the Nationalist Party (*Nationalist Report*, vol. 2, no. 6), and John Ross Taylor claimed that although Urbonas carefully avoids racial remarks and direct attacks on Jews, he in reality is a complete Fascist.[9] In one issue of *Speak-Up* there was an advertisement for a book called *God the Original*

---

7 In chapter 1 I suggested that another category could be inserted between establishment politics and the fringe right: neo-conservatism. I have no objections to readers who may wish to place Renaissance – indeed, all of the organizations in this chapter – into the neo-conservative category, as long as they realize that there still is an important line between it and the political mainstream.

8 Another source places his arrival in Canada in 1956.

9 Members of the far right often found it amusing to publicly announce that well-known conservative-leaning individuals were secretly their Fascist brethren, and thus all such accusations must be taken with a grain of salt.

Segregationist. There also was an article about the Christian Defence League, signed 'T.L.' – obviously Terry Long, who later emerged as a leader of the Aryan Nations. For the most part, however, *Speak-Up* was not much to the right of the Toronto *Sun*, and apparently under a special arrangement it reprinted articles from that newspaper without charge. As the following sampling of articles suggests, the message in *Speak-Up* was similar to that in the various publications associated with Fromm and Gostick: affirmative-action programs and CIDA aid to Guyana are opposed, socialism is said to have ruined Tanzania's economy, and Soviet aggression in Latvia and Estonia is condemned; an entire issue (February 1981) in the form of a comic book was devoted to Trudeau, arguing that he has strong communist sympathies, and has turned Canada into a dictatorship. Several prominent members of the fringe right such as Fromm, Walsh, and Phillip Butler periodically contributed articles to *Speak-Up*, as did Patricia Young, whose column used to appear in *Straight Talk* and *Countdown*. In *Speak-Up*, reference is made to Fromm's Alternative Forum (which Urbonas told me he attended) and Campbell's Heritage Forum, and in one issue there was a full-page advertisement for the National Citizens' Coalition. There also was an article by Malcolm Ross entitled 'Gun Control – Good or Bad?' Elsewhere there was a comment about Ross's book on abortion. *The Real Holocaust*. This man is a relatively important right-wing figure in Canada, and it will be worth while to dwell on his case for a moment.

Born just after the Second World War, married with two children, Ross graduated with a BA from the University of New Brunswick and became a teacher in Monction. His father was a Presbyterian minister. In 1978 Ross published *Web of Deceit*, a book which rehashes almost all the pet targets of the right wing; Ross claims that 'Red Mike' Pearson started Canada on its decline, refers to Anne Frank's diary as a hoax, and states that a conspiracy consisting of international communism, international finance, and international Zionism exists against Western Christian civilization. An article in *Speak-Up* (vol. 10, nos. 11–12, 99–100, November-December 1983), which refers to Ross as 'a gentleman with a delightful sense of humour,' states that following the publication of *Web of Deceit* he was harassed unmercifully, and for a while his teaching post was in jeopardy. Gostick told me that the man's health also failed, and that he had to keep a very low profile in order to retain his job. Walsh, who said that Ross had recuperated his health by 1982, showed me a photograph that the New Brunswick teacher had recently sent him of his new-born child.

By the early 1980s, Ross had once more begun to make his views known to a wider public. In a New Brunswick newspaper, *The Times-Transcript*

(22 March 1983), there is a letter to the editor from him containing what could be interpreted as a mild anti-Semitic message. Much more significant was his new book, *The Real Holocaust – The Attack on Unborn Children and Life Itself*. Ross contends that Christian moral values are under attack, and wraps his lament for the future of white Christian society in the writings of the revisionist perspective on the Holocaust (*The Real Holocaust*, incidentally, was given to me by a Canadian member of the Aryan Nations). Ross also published a thirty-one–page booklet, *Christianity versus Judeo-Christianity* (undated), a rehearsal of several basic anti-Semitic themes: the anti-Christian thrust of The Talmud, the non-Semitic Ashkenazim Jews, the links between Jewry and communism, the Holocaust hoax, plus the support of the World Council of Churches for Marxist terrorism and the evils of secular humanism and the new morality. By 1983 or so, Ross had become the executive director of the Maritime branch of the Christian Defence League. His formal link to Keegstra was appropriate. Not only were they both teachers, but in addition Ross strikes me as a Keegstra-like figure: a devout individual; a good, honourable man crying out in anguish; a tragic victim of changing times that have left him behind, while at the same time a genuine believer in the right-wing cause.

Urbonas said that he normally prints about three thousands copies of *Speak-Up*. Its strongest support, he remarked, was in Western Canada, especially British Columbia and Alberta. As Urbonas, on the verge of retirement from his bank position, surveyed the world around him, he was not happy with what he saw. He especially lamented a change that he had detected among East European immigrants in Canada, commenting that they are no longer disturbed by communism. He also was disappointed that the right wing had failed to unite across the country. As we talked in a bar at Toronto's Union Station, he remarked that sitting around us there might be four or five people who were right-wing–oriented, but nobody knows them and they don't know each other, simply because there is no overall, effective right-wing organization in the country.

CANADIAN INSTITUTE OF GUARDIANSHIP

A few years ago, a professor in a Canadian university suddenly realized that lawyers, nurses, social workers, etc., were trained in universities, but not the police. When he wrote to police authorities to suggest that a special program be established at his own university, the response, he claimed, was enthusiastic. He then attempted to establish a new 'Faculty of Protection,' but the resistance among his colleagues was stiff, and the project failed (he also at one point played around with the idea of founding a new university, but nothing came of it either). In another venture he was more successful: setting up an organization called the Canadian Institute of Guardianship. The term 'guardian' was taken from Plato. As the man said, if we care about what is happening in our country, we are all guardians. One of the main purposes of his organization was to ensure respect and support for the police. He talked about a celebrated case in Toronto in which a black person had been killed by the police. Realizing that the police were being crucified by the media and left-wing radicals, he offered to establish a citizens' group to support them, but to his consternation the police were not interested. Privately, he added, the police applauded his efforts, but publicly they kept their distance.

While this man's central focus was on law and order, a number of other issues concerned him, particularly the country's declining morality, especially as shown by the upsurge in pornography, drug abuse, and homosexuality. His organization, he claimed, working behind the scenes, had been instrumental in preventing the legalization of marijuana in Canada. Communism was another sore spot. He talked animatedly about communist control of the universities, and about the sharp decline in the country's military capability, brought about single handedly by Trudeau, whom he described as a communist. On one occasion he wrote a letter to Trudeau, criticizing the proposed new constitution, but to his anger did not receive a reply.

This man, Scandinavian in background, in his late fifties when I met him, raised in Toronto, marvelled about how safe the city had been when he was a youngster – a time when neighbours would look out for and control one another's children. How and why, he wondered, have we lost that kind of benign society? The Canadian Institute of Guardianship was committed to recapturing that golden age. Among its patrons and supporters, the man said, were several prominent people (whom he named), as well as a senior anthropologist at a large Canadian university.

MOONIES

Where do the Moonies fit into the right-wing picture? The far left tends to classify them into the extreme right. The far right, as we saw in earlier chapters, dismisses them as kosher conservatives, despite their reputation as anti-communists. The general attitude of people like Andrews is that the Moonies are only mildly, almost harmlessly, anti-communist; that they are race-traitors, because they promote interracial marriage; and that the hostility that they do draw from the wider society mostly comes from Jewish organizations, concerned abut the large number of young Jews who have joined the cult; even the Christian Reformed church (*Banner*, 1 October 1984: 13) referred to the 'alarmingly high percentage' of Jewish youth among the Moonies and the former Jim Jones sect.

Only the fringe right wants to claim the Moonies for their own (for example, Urbonas stated that the Moonies – and especially the publication *Our Canada* – constitute a very significant part of the right-wing picture in the country), and that in my estimation is where they belong. *Our Canada*, according to one prominent member of the Moonies in Toronto, represents the 'old time liberal' perspective. One of the publication's chief concerns, he said, was to warn the public of the threat of creeping socialism and the left wing, which in his judgment was much more dangerous than the far right. The Moonies, he pointed out, aren't racists (he himself was engaged to a Jamaican), and that clearly separates them from organizations like the Ku Klux Klan. He also claimed that *Our Canada* was not nearly as radical as *Speak-Up*. An inspection of *Our Canada* reveals that it is certainly right of centre, but not radical or intemperate in comparison with *The Nationalist Report* or *Straight Talk* during the Andrews era. There are articles on 'radicals' such as John Sewell in the city hall; on the unscientific status of Marxism; on Trudeau's disastrous reign; on the funding of terrorist groups in Africa by CIDA, CUSO, and OXFAM; on C-FAR's important watch-dog role regarding foreign-aid abuses; and on the advisability of capital punishment. There also (*Our Canada*, vol. 5, no. 10, 1–15, June 1982) is an article defending Israel on the simple grounds that Moscow opposes it. From the perspective of the Moonies, no further reason for its own support of Israel is required, because anti-communism is the organization's raison d'être.

NATIONAL CITIZENS' COALITION (NCC)

This organization was regarded by the far left, the far right, and the fringe right in much the same manner as the Moonies. The left-wing publication *7-News* (5 June 1981) claimed that the NCC was one of the big-business organizations aiding the Ku Klux Klan. *In Struggle* (September, 1981), another left-wing organ, referred to the NCC as 'perhaps the most influential and credible of the political/economic right wing groups,' and suggested that it 'speaks for those elements of big capital linked to the oil and energy industry.' A member of the Nationalist Party, in contrast, dismissed the NCC as self-interested entrepreneurs little different from the pink conservatives. As in the case of *Our Canada*, it was the people whom I have placed in the fringe-right category who spoke glowingly about the NCC. Urbonas referred to it as an admirable organization, and in Fromm's *Countdown* (vol. 2, no. 7, 29 December 1974) there is a statement that Campus Alternative will promote 'the fiscal sanity and the pamphlets and posters published by Colin Brown's Citizens' Coalition'.

In a brief interview with a high-ranking NCC member, I was told that although the organization has sometimes been labelled right wing and even Fascist, it was simply a political-action group, and had no formal connection to any political party. The non-partisan nature of the organization was stressed in its own literature. For example, in *Consensus* (vol. 9, no. 1, February 1984), one of its organs, it is stated: 'For years, the media have either ignored the Coalition or dismissed us as a "right wing lobby group." We have always been non-partisan.' Nevertheless, the evidence does suggest that the organization embraces a right-wing (but not radical right) orientation. In the same issue of *Consensus* there is an excerpt from a member's letter requesting a regular review of literature 'which articulates the "New Right" point of view.' There also is a reference to a recent debate at the University of Toronto in which the speakers favouring capitalism drew enthusiastic support from the audience. The article points out that only a decade earlier, Dr William Banfield, a noted right-wing thinker, was shouted down, and concludes that there has been a dramatic change in mood. On one NCC leaflet, we again find the right wing's slogan: 'The only thing necessary for the triumph of evil is for good men to do nothing.'

The NCC member to whom I talked referred favourably to *Speak-Up*, to two right-of-centre student newspapers at the University of Toronto and McGill University, and to *Our Canada*, although the last named in her view was flawed by its Moonie connection. She also referred favourably to Fromm, remarking that it was terrible and vicious how he had been forced out of PC-Metro, the victim of a 'hatchet job.' At one point she said she wasn't sure what conservatives meant, and asked rhetorically: 'Are there any real conservatives in the PC Party?' This woman added that she did not agree with all of Fromm's views, and made it clear that the NCC draws the line at the point where people like Gostick enter. Gostick in her view was a despicable anti-Semite and right-wing radical, and had absolutely nothing in common with the NCC.

The National Citizens' Coalition was founded by Colin Brown in 1967 and became a non-profit corporation in 1975. Listed as a member of its advisory council is the Hon. Ernest C. Manning of social-credit fame. Its literature indicates a membership in Canada of 30,000. In addition to *Consensus* (its newsletter) it publishes *Overview*. The emphasis in these organs is on smaller government, a free-enterprise rather than a welfare-state economy, and the defence of the country's eroding freedoms, which includes, for example, siding with individuals who have protested against the metric system, and supporting airline deregulation. Paid advertisements in the media were among its main methods of making known its views about important issues. One of its most brilliant successes was its campaign to overturn Bill C-169, 'designed to stifle freedom of speech and make this election a closed shop for politicians' (*Globe and Mail*, 19 July 1984). The ebullient organization placed a full-page advertisement in *The Globe and Mail* reporting on its success, and in *Consensus* it crowed about the packed press conferences in cities across the country and the talk-show appearances that its protest against Bill C-169 had generated. Also in *Consensus* was a note indicating that an information package was in preparation for members to be used when participating in call-in shows or when writing letters to editors and MPs. All this has a familiar ring. As far back as the days of the much more militant Edmund Burke Society, a similar sensitivity to media exposure and public relations was evident.[10]

JOHN BIRCH SOCIETY (JBS)

The final two organizations to be dealt with were basically American ones that had minor representation north of the border. The John Birch Society was founded in 1958 in Indianapolis, Indiana, by Robert Welch, who had been educated at the University of North Carolina, the U.S. Naval Academy, and Harvard Law School. The organization was named after a fundamentalist Baptist preacher from Georgia who had been killed by Chinese communists during the Second World War. Like many of the groups within the radical right, the JBS was organized into 'Home Chapters' comparable to cells of supporting members who did not wish to be publicly identified (Epstein and Forster 1967: 195). Generally, the JBS is depicted as standing midway between the far right and conservatism (Westin 1964: 242). A report in the Toronto *Telegram* (18 December 1961) remarked that it no longer can be said that the organization consists of crackpots, for numerous solid, respectable citizens and community leaders belong to it. The organization promoted individual responsibility, free enterprise, and small government, and was opposed to communism in any form. Organizers for the JBS claimed that it was not racist, and pointed out that a

10 The National Citizens' Coalition is an organization that clearly falls towards the neo-conservative side of the fringe right, and the same applies to YAF, described below.

large percentage of its members were Catholic and Mormon, with at least two Negro chapters; they also stated that numerous members with racist, especially anti-Semitic, views had been expelled. It would be a mistake, however, to conclude that the JBS was merely the equivalent of the Progressive Conservative party. For example, in the mid-1960s in *American Opinion*, the organization's periodical, there is a report on how the communists took over Canada; Robert Stanfield is labelled a socialist, Pierre Trudeau and Lester Pearson communists, and Tommy Douglas a Marxist (this article also was available as a thirty-two-page pamphlet). A decade or so later there was a report (*Toronto Star*, 25 February 1977) that Trudeau and Nelson Rockefeller were among five people whom a secret, dissident JBS faction intended to assassinate.

Several years ago, in 1962, a Conservative expressed doubt (*Toronto Daily Star*, 12 March 1962) that the JBS would ever take hold in Canada. Yet by 1968 there was a report (*Globe and Mail*, 12 December 1968) that the organization planned to set up a branch on Canadian soil. Peter Worthington observed in 1971 (Toronto *Telegram*, 8 May 1971) that like it or not, the JBS is determined to save us in Canada. In that same year a JBS member from the United States toured Canada to raise funds. The following year saw the organization's first public meeting in Canada, which attracted about a hundred people, despite the fact, as Fromm's *Countdown* stated (vol. 1, no. 4, September 1972), that its entry into Canada was vilified by both the left and the right. The organizer then was an American, William J. Schreck, who was soon replaced by Charles Green. In a 'social report' on a JBS dinner comparable to what might be expected on the Granite Club or the Lion's Club (*Globe and Mail*, 20 January 1975), the organization's Canadian membership was estimated at three hundred with chapters in Toronto, Ottawa, and Montreal (there also was a JBS bookstore in Toronto). Special mention was made of podiatrist Norman Gunn, 'the only non-American on the national council of the JBS in the United States.' The irony of Gunn's connection to the JBS was not lost on everyone. The following day a high-ranking member of the Canadian Jewish Congress wrote a memo pointing out that Gunn had been the 'favourite Gentile' of the N3 group opposed to Beattie in the 1960s. Gunn also apparently had been connected to the Canadian Taxpayers Union several years ago, and had been a guest speaker at an early Edmund Burke Society meeting (*Varsity*, 13 November 1967). In view of his energetic opposition to Beattie's Nazi Party, one might wonder exactly what it was that led him to cavort with the fringe-right oranizations. Whatever the answer may be, by the late 1970s the John Birch Society presence in Canada was virtually a thing of the past.

YOUNG AMERICANS FOR FREEDOM (YAF)

YAF was founded in 1960 by William F. Buckley, Jr. Around 1972, the University of Toronto chapter of YAF was established by Greg Robinson, born about 1950, and apparently a graduate in business from Centennial College and in political science from the University of Toronto. Robinson had been a member of the Edmund Burke Society, but like many others did not follow Andrews down the white-supremacist path; instead, when the Edmund Burke Society blew apart, he established the YAF chapter. Robinson also has been a member of the John Birch Society and C-FAR, a spokesman for the Toronto Alliance of Christian Laymen, secretary of the Friends of Rhodesia Association, press officer of CAFE in 1981, and president of Alternative Forum in the same year. Robinson said that most of his activities in connection with YAF consisted in disseminating literature. He apparently published a small journal called *Hot Line*. Describing himself as a continentalist, Robinson remarked that being a member in Canada of an American organization did not pose a problem for him.

One writer, a libertarian (Rothbard 1969), referred to YAF as dictatorial and Fascist, an apologist for the oppressive policies of the state. An American academic told me that YAF was inclined to racism. When I raised these issues with Robinson, he heatedly insisted that YAF is not racist, pointing out that there are black members in the United States. Just because YAF is a conservative organization, he complained, some 'fools' think it must also be racist. YAF, he explained, is similar to the Young Tories and to organizations like C-FAR and Alternative Forum. It stands for private enterprise, small government, individualism, liberty, and state rights; it opposes all expressions of communism. YAF's political position was reflected in its periodical, *New Guard*. In one issue (Summer 1982), it was reported that YAF members had worked for the Reagan Agenda (Reagan himself apparently had had a long association with the organization), supported Soviet dissidents, and opposed reverse discrimination and SALT II. Various articles in this issue defended freedom to carry hand-guns, supported the pro-life lobby, criticized Billy Graham's visit to the USSR, claimed that pacifism is a growing threat, and argued for capital punishment. Robinson, however, stated that there is no formal YAF position on capital punishment, or on abortion and homosexuality. His apparent personal view was reflected in a short letter to the editor attributed to him (Toronto *Sun*, 30 July 1982) which referred to the murder of three prison guards by convicts, and concluded: 'If prison overcrowding is a problem, let capital punishment relieve it.'

THE RIGHT WING AND HOMOSEXUALITY

At the best of times there existed an uneasy relationship between the radical right and the fringe right, and more often than not they were at each other's throat. There was, nevertheless, one issue on which they agreed: the iniquity of homosexuality. As Petchesky (1981) has pointed out, reproductive, sexual, and family issues have been central to the new right's political program, especially anti-abortion, anti-feminism, and anti-homosexuality. Often homosexuality was portrayed as an abomination in the eyes of God. In one issue of Taylor's *Aryan* (Winter 1977–8, WGU 1), for example, it was written: 'How can anyone advocate homosexuality and still claim to be a Christian?' Several right-wing organizations existed with the sole purpose of combating homsexuality and gay rights. The League against Homosexuals was founded by a Parisian-born former member of the French Foreign Legion, who also has been a mercenary in Africa and Brazil. Two of its flyers state: 'Queers are Against God and the Christian Bible,' and 'Queers do not produce, they seduce!' Positive Parents of Canada was established by a Toronto jeweller, himself a victim of homosexual rape at age five. This man claims that he got 18,000 signatures in a petition against setting up a liaison committee between the Toronto Board of Education and the homosexual community. Another organization, Metro's Moderate Majority, was responsible for compiling the 'Homosexuality Fact Sheet' that Campbell had showed me. A somewhat similar organization existed in British Columbia called Citizens for Safety and Justice; its main purpose was to encourage stronger regulations for known sex offenders.

On the other side were homosexual organizations waging war on the right wing. For example (Gays and Lesbians against Racism Everywhere (GLARE) co-operated with the (Riverdale Action Committee against Racism (RACAR) to oppose McQuirter's Ku Klux Klan in Toronto. GLARE organized the Fight the Right Festival, and another group, Rock against Racism, appeared in 1981; one of its spokesmen stated: 'We can counter Klan propaganda. We believe our music, be it reggae, soul, punk, funk, folk, jazz, or rock, can be important weapon in the fight against racism.' Perhaps that was so, but music per se was not necessarily on the side of the left. One only needs to remember the anti-Semitic composer Wagner, and in more recent times the 'Oi' movement in Britain with its celebration of the white man's cause.

At an early stage in this research project, my working hypothesis was that there was an affinity between the left-wing and gays and the right wing and anti-gays. That is, the left wing would be pro-gay and vice versa, and the opposite would be true of the right wing. Further research, however, revealed that the hypothesis was imprecise in certain respects and simply wrong in others. For example, there *are* homosexual members in right-wing organizations. A former member of Beattie's Canadian Nazi Party, I was told, was a homosexual, and the same was true of a couple of members of the Nationalist Party. One of the latter claimed that numerous homosexuals have begun to join Fascist organizations. The leader of another group told me point-blank that at least two of his followers were homosexuals. Then, of course, there was the small right-wing group in California – queer Nazis, Andrews remarked – consisting entirely of homosexuals. What became apparent was that homosexuality within the right wing added up to a residual sin. That is, it was tolerated until a person defected, or ran amuck in some manner. Perdue, the kingpin in the attempted take-over of Dominica, reportedly was a homosexual, but that was overlooked until the coup exploded in his face. Martin Webster, for years a leading figure in Britain's National Front, turned out to be a homosexual, the bad news only becoming public as the fortunes of that organization plummeted. Even if people were not actually homosexuals, the very fact of acting as a police informer, or defecting, brought on the inevitable accusation. Thus, David Stanley, Beattie's Nazi twin in the 1960s, was, Taylor told me, a homosexual. Others such as McQuirter (plus a Western Guard man), whose reputations as committed Fascists were sometimes suspect, were labelled homosexuals or bisexuals. Clearly, homosexuality was not only a residual sin, a debit entry on the books to be raised when, as one man said, a person 'screwed up,' but it was also a cane, an instrument to lash wayward members and enemies of the movement in general.

The basis of the right wing's oppostion to homsexuality, a gay spokesman explained to me, is entirely a matter of sex and politics, reflecting biological assumptions of racial differences and white superiority. White gays are regarded as race-traitors. They squander their semen and deplete the white genetic pool by not reproducing. Racists ask what will happen to Aryan society if homosexuality becomes pervasive. Although in this man's opinion the right wing was almost totally anti-homosexual, he too referred to the 'Gay Nazis' in California, and remarked that one strand of the right wing, the libertarians, supports gays on the basis of individual rights and privacy.

The equation between the left wing and gays is even more dubious. As my informant in the Toronto gay community pointed out, the left wing does not take part in the gay-baiting that occurs on the right. Moreover, the left doesn't embrace the same views about radical identity and the importance of the gene pool. By definition, he added, the left is receptive to changes in society, including sexual mores (Campbell remarked that it is the left's traditional support for the underdog that puts it on the side of gays). Nevertheless, he insisted that the left is not uniformly supportive of gay rights. Some strands of the left regard homosexuality as part of capitalist decadence, which will disappear with the victory of socialism. Nor is the reverse necessarily true: uniform gay support for the left and opposition to the right. Organizations like *The Body Politic*, it is correct, run 'intelligence' on right-wing groups; for example, in *The Body Politic* (December-January 1980–1: 11) there is an overview of anti-gay, right-wing organizations. And both *The Body Politic* and GLARE threw their weight behind RACAR to confront the Klan. However, my informant, himself closely associated with *The Body Politic*, candidly admitted that they were promoting their own cause as much as they were fighting racism. As one writer in *The Body Politic* (no. 102, April 1984) stated, normal gay is white; coloured gays are regarded in much the same inferior light as is found in heterosexual society. To sum up, it appears that at the organizational level gays usually will support anti-racist groups like RACAR, even if their motivations don't entirely concern racism. But at the individual level, gays are probably no less racist than the average white citizen, and no more likely to be left-wing–oriented. As my informant put it, whether or not a gay is left or right wing has much more to do with his class position than his sexuality.

RACISM AND THE SOCIAL ARENA

Whereas white supremacists conceive of racial classification as the potential harmonizer in a world gone wild, in reality it chews up the social fabric, infecting and polluting all it touches. Racists themselves more often than not stalk one another with daggers at hand, anti-racist organizations squabble over how to confront the white supremacists, and the victims of racism fight among themselves. The radical right, as it has been repeatedly shown, was divided internally to a remarkable degree. My impression was that the fringe right, while far from united, was not characterized by the same amount of infighting. The explanation partly concerns the different degrees of intensity and commitment. Membership in the radical right is a total experience, rendering all else extraneous or secondary. In contrast, fringe-right members can aggressively pursue their concerns with morality in the schools, homosexual rights, and the socialist inclinations of the government while still holding down a job, enjoying hobbies, bringing up a family – in short, while continuing to participate in conventional society.

There is, as I have also indicated, another locus of division within the right wing – that between the radical right and the fringe right. People like Andrews and Weiche regard men like Fromm and Gostick as sell-outs, lacking the courage to go all the way and proclaim the superiority of the white man. Indeed, the fringe right is often considered to be a greater danger to the movement than are wishy-washy liberals. For example, in the Western Guard's *Straight Talk* (vol. 5, no. 10), several reasons for despising 'kosher conservatives' are given:

Firstly, they siphon off badly needed funds for the White Peoples' Cause by luring unsuspecting political novices into their do-nothing sandbox ... The rookie right-wing politico is given the impression that he is really doing something in this enemy-made 'playpen.' Secondly, some people have said that these groups should be allowed to exist because they serve as a 'prep school' for future White Nationalists. In reality, the opposite is true, and the Party leadership, through numerous experiences, can attest to this. These organizations serve as a corral or comfortable political-mind prison by insuring that potential White Nationalists never leave to work in the White People's Cause ... They keep good White Nationalist people idle, and they take money from White Nationlist hands, while all the time spreading invective against the Party.

The fringe right, for its part, regards its more radical brothers as beyond the pale, so far out of the mainstream that nobody takes them seriously. As one man said to me, organizations like the Klan and the Western Guard are simply packaged by the media, placed in a far corner of society, and thus completely controlled, stripped of any potential influence on the political life of the nation.

Just as the radical right saw the fringe right as an even greater enemy than the Liberal party, both the radical and the fringe right seemed to despise the Conservative party, especially former attorney general Roy McMurtry and former premier Bill Davis. Professor Wilson Head, a black civil-rights activist, once singled out McMurtry (*Toronto Star*, 19 November 1977) as the one government leader who had bothered to speak out against racism. That was not news to the white supremacists, but they held quite a different opinion about the man. For example, more than any other official in Ontario, one writer in the *Nationalist Report* (issue 32) stated, McMurtry has harassed and persecuted white nationalists while simultaneously championing the rights of racial minorities. The article concludes: 'Roy McMurtry is clearly the most dangerous man in Ontario to the White Nationalist movement.' In a Western Guard white-power recorded telephone message (9 June 1976), McMurtry is referred to as 'Mr Hypocrite of the Year.' In *Straight Talk* (vol. 7, no. 7, n.d.), an article entitled 'Anatomy of a Race Traitor: Roy McMurtry' accuses him of courting the Jewish and ethnic vote to advance his political career. McMurtry has described himself (*Canadian Jewish News*, 11 June 1981) as a 'Christian Zionist,' profoundly affected by his trips to Israel, and committed to its survival. During one of my interviews with Taylor, he remarked that McMurtry might have Jewish blood.

Davis was regarded by the far right as a partner in crime with McMurtry. As it was stated in the *Nationalist Report* (issues 33 and 34), 'the kosher conservative Davis government ... has surprisingly acted far more pro-minority than both the Ontario NDP and the Liberals combined.' An article in issue 40 declares that 'the government of William Grenville Davis and the Ontario Conservatives is the most dangerous legislative body operating against the interests of White Canada.'

It may be thought that fringe-right members would look more favourably on the Conservatives. It is a fact that if they had any formal association with establishment politics, it usually was with the Conservative party. But that was essentially because there was nowhere else for them to go, and certainly not because they had any admiration for the party, which they thought was dominated by red Conservatives. People like Fromm contended that privately, if not publicly, many Conservative MPs supported the fringe right's programs. From the far left's perspective, the fringe and radical right are merely 'silent' partners in the Conservative party's plan (and the Liberal's as well) to surreptitiously usher in a new era of Fascism. Nevertheless, there has been no formal indication that the Conservatives have had a soft spot for those to its right. Indeed, it was in Conservative-controlled provinces that the trials of Zundel and Keegstra took place. And significantly, McMurtry (*Canadian Jewish News*, 11 June 1981) has expressed concerns about Reagan's attempt to revive old-time rugged individualism and free enterprise, while Davis (*Globe and Mail*, 26 October 1981) has cautioned the right wing of his party against getting caught up in the religious-like ultra-conservatism of Reagan and Thatcher. With the animosity in mind between the radical right and the fringe right, and between both of them and the Conservatives, a generalization seems to be warranted: the closer the political factions, the greater the mutual hostility.

We now turn to another locus of division: that concerning anti-racist organizations, as well as the victims of racism themselves. On different occasions in British Columbia in 1981, rallies organized to combat the Ku Klux Klan turned into pitched battles between the BC Organization to Fight

Racism (BCOFR) and the Communist Party of Canada – Marxist-Leninist (CPC-ML). The first group, an umbrella organization composed of liberal-oriented citizens, sometimes accused CPC-ML of simply being another form of Fascism. Vancouver mayor Mike Harcourt (*Vancouver Province*, 21 October 1981) apparently remarked that the Marxist organization was no different than the Klan itself. Charan Gill, BCOFR's president, accused CPC-ML of focusing on 'class ideology when the problem is race' (*Vancouver Sun*, 12 March 1981). Charles Boylan, a CPC-ML leader, explained (Toronto *Sun*, 18 October 1981) that he was opposed to BCOFR because it was not only unconcerned about the working class, but also wanted to involve the state in the fight against the Klan, which in his view was 'the kiss of death.' As Boylan pointed out to me, it was ironical that while he had never been physically beaten by the Klan, he had been by members of BCOFR.

At the root of the hostility between BCOFR and CPC-ML were different assumptions about the nature and causes of racism, as well as the most effective means to combat it. Is the simple answer to ban the Klan, or is that futile in view of the wider reaches of the capitalist system? Should organizations like the Klan be confronted or should they be ignored with the hope that they will wither away? McMurtry once remarked that the Klan was 'bloody well not welcome' (*Globe and Mail*, 28 June 1981), but he said there was nothing he could do unless it broke the laws. McMurtry was in favour of new legislation to curb the activities of organizations like the Klan, but it was in British Columbia that such legislation was passed. The Civil Rights Protection Act prohibited the promotion of hatred or doctrines of superiority based on race or ethnic origin. Ironically, Ann Farmer, a leading Klan member in Vancouver, claimed that the new legislation would not only fail to curb its cross-burning and recruiting activities, but would in fact be used against those who promoted hatred against the Klan and white people. Even a BC Civil Liberties Association spokesman (*Vancouver Province*, 2 July 1981) stated that the new legislation might actually protect the Klan while entrapping the innocent. Al Hooper, following McQuirter's arrest, thought he would be next. But he insisted that he would welcome that outcome, because it would provide him an opportunity to test the new laws. The latter, he claimed, had worked to the Klan's advantage, because Jews could no longer attack his organization.

Even other types of attacks against the white-supremacist organizations were often regarded in a positive light. The Ontario Federation of Labour's campaign against racism, with the slogan 'Racism Hurts Everyone,' was interpreted by the Nationalist Party as concrete evidence that it had indeed been effective. When the House of Commons formally condemned the Klan, members of the latter were pleased; that only proves, they observed, that they had become a force to be reckoned with, otherwise the government would have ignored them. In similar fashion, McQuirter remarked in an interview: 'the degrees of attacks against us are awards, they show us how effective we are, the powers that be will not attack anyone who is not successful.' These reactions, no doubt, can largely be dismissed as wishful thinking and unjustified boasting. Nevertheless, they do reflect a dimension to racism that not always is appreciated. Just as the media and white supremacists often form a symbiotic bond, so do racist and anti-racist organizations. Opposition itself constitutes a social relationship.

The victims of racial prejudice and discrimination are themselves far from united. Canada's black community is immensely complex (Winks 1971; D'Oyley 1978), made more so in recent years with the increased numbers of Third World immigrants. The National Black Coalition of Canada (NBCC) was established to provide a greater organizational impetus and capacity. It has, however, been less than successful, not only because of the community's complexity, but also possibly because of the social-class differences between its leaders and the bulk of poor blacks in the country.

Canadian Jews have a reputation of being more unified, and in comparison with Canadian blacks that probably is true. Yet they too have their internal problems. The Canadian Jewish Congress appears to be at odds with B'nai B'rith. In 1982, after forty-four years of combined efforts, the Joint Community Relations Committee of the Canadian Jewish Congress and B'nai B'rith formally separated (*Canadian Jewish News*, 11 February 1982). On more than one occasion I was cautioned by representatives of the one organization not to work too closely with the other. There also are significant ethnic, religious, political, and regional splits within the Jewish community: the Ashkenazim versus the Sephardim in Montreal – the first largely English-speaking from Europe, the second largely French-speaking from North Africa (Lasry 1981); Orthodox versus Conservative versus Reform Jews; the Chassidim, ultra-religious Jews, about three-thousand-strong in Montreal, next to whom Orthodox Jewry appears secular (Shaffir 1981); the Jewish Defence League; left-wing organizations led by or connected to Jews versus the increasingly conservative wider Jewish community; Eastern Canadian Jews versus Western Canadian Jews, to some extent a reproduction of the regional strain that conditions the country at large. Finally, not all Jews, as I learned, support Israel in reflex fashion. Indeed, during the Lebanese crisis in the early 1980s, some young Jews whom I met were beginning to re-examine their previous assumptions about the exalted morality of the Israeli government – and under the list of clubs in the University of Toronto Student Directory (1981–2) was the Alliance of non-Zionist Jews.

Not only are there complex and sharp divisions within both the black and the Jewish communities, but as in the United States (Clark 1971; Gordis 1971) the relationships between blacks and Jews in Canada are no longer harmonious. A few years ago, Winks (1969: 7) observed that the predominately Jewish-led Canadian Labour Congress had done more for black civil rights in Canada than had any other organization. Yet by 1984, Rabbi Gunther Plaut was moved to exclaim: 'now that Jews have largely made it, many of them have forgotten how it was once for them, and are no longer ready to battle for the rights and privileges of all' (*Currents*, vol. 2, no. 2, Summer 1984: 8). The writer Rick Salutin (1982: 30) remarked on the growing parochialism among Jews, which Alan Borovoy apparently described as 'a willingness to screw the general interest for the Jewish interest.' In an article Charles Roach (n.d.), a prominent black civil-rights lawyer in Toronto, traced the roots of antagonism between blacks and Jews in North America, and underlined the (unfortunate) potential anti-Semitism that could emerge among Canadian blacks. Two other prominent blacks said to me that in their judgment Jews were opposed to black aspirations, and therefore part of the enemy. One of them referred to Jews as 'the moneyed people.' The other remarked that Jews used to be sympathetic to blacks, but now are part of the power structure. A third prominent black insisted that several well-known Jewish politicians, whom he named, were racist.

Several years ago a rabbi in the United States (*Varsity*, 5 February 1969) apparently remarked that Jewish-Negro conflict was insoluble. The rabbi, director at the time of the B'nai B'rith Hillel Foundation at the University of Pittsburgh, lamented the increasing militancy of the black movement. He also was reported to have said: 'The Negro today gets preferential treatment, and can get into university regardless of ability.' Jews, the rabbi observed, have to look out for themselves, for nobody else is going to. History, certainly, gives credence to his latter statement, but the path that he would have Jews follow was interesting to say the least: 'The best position for the Jew in America is right wing and conservative.' Goodwill towards one's fellow men is not a one-way street. As an editorial in the black newspaper *Contrast* (10 October 1980) asked, why did so few blacks show up at a well-advertised anti-Klan march in Toronto? The answer, I suspect, has a lot to do with the perception among blacks that the Klan has become the Jewish community's problem. McQuirter once told me that he hoped to organize a joint Klan-black rally against Toronto Jews. That plan never materialized – indeed, the very idea was far-fetched – but it reflected an appreciation for the crack in the armour among the Klan's principal targets.

Finally, we come to a rather intriguing phenomenon: the contrasting and sometimes overlapping atitudes of individuals, organizations, and interest groups towards the issue of racism. The NDP's Bob Rae has charged (Toronto *Sun*, 3 November 1981) that Canada 'is still a racist society because those with real power are reluctant to share it with those who have little.' Jim Fleming, a former Liberal multiculturalism minister, sounded the alarm against growing racism in the country. His Conservative successor, Jack Murta, remarked (*Globe and Mail*, 9 May 1985) that racism, anti-Semitism, and anti-Catholicism seem to be on the rise again. The perspective of these men, however, was very decidedly exceptional. The usual reaction among politicians was to downplay or deny racial strain in the country. In 1977, for example, an American television network aired a program that labelled Toronto a racial time-bomb (*Toronto Star*, 1 January 1977). The official reaction was quick to come. Immigration minister Bud Cullen condemned the program as 'blatant distortion.' Toronto mayor David Crombie dismissed the program as irresponsible journalism. Metro chairman Paul Godfrey at a later date was quoted as saying (Toronto *Sun*, 15 June 1980) that while there is some racism in Toronto, it is not a serious problem. Lining up behind these politicians are most ordinary, liberal-oriented white Canadians, who continue to regard Canada as a remarkably tolerant country. Joining them, too, are some Marxists – those who contend that racism doesn't really exist, that the 'people' aren't racist, that instead racism is a smoke-screen thrown up by the power élite to conceal the real locus of strain: the class system.

If establishment politicians, conventional Canadians, and Marxian radicals make for strange bedfellows, the same is true for the opposite camp: the disparate types of individuals and interest groups who exclaim that racism has a throttle-hold on the nation. White supremacists like Taylor, Andrews, and McQuirter contend that racism has become exceptionally widespread. Some Marxists would concur, especially those who see beyond economic determinism, as would many anti-racist organizations. To this list we would have to add the names of people like Doug Collins, the Vancouver-based journalist who wrote *Immigration: The Destruction of English Canada* (1979). In Collins's judgment, it is ridiculous to claim that racism in Canada is limited to the lunatic fringe like the Western Guard. An immigrant himself from Britian, Collins apparently is another case of a man who once was 'left of centre politically' (Toronto *Sun*, 19 July 1979)[11] or a 'left-leaning liberal' (*Saturday Night*, January-February 1979: 6) who moved over to the right. Gostick recommended that I meet Collins, as did Fromm, who described him as a 'remarkable man.' As one academic observed (McAlpine 1981: Appendix 1): 'one could ... argue that there is little in the Klan literature that was not written in the Vancouver Sun by Doug Collins in 1979 and 1978.' A former director of the Human Rights Commission in Vancouver reportedly accused Collins (*Vancouver Province*, 23 October 1978) of being a racist. Collins denied the charge, stating that he doesn't believe his own race is superior. He said he was indeed formerly a liberal, but changed his tune when he began to appreciate the effects of the immigration laws introduced in 1967.

What are we to make of these strange alliances? To understand them, we must consider two critical factors: the level of analysis and the perspective of the actor. Individuals of widely contradictory political persuasions can agree at one level, but disagree at others. For example, Collins, McQuirter, and active anti-racists would concur that racism is widespread. At another level, however, differences would emerge; Collins and anti-racists, I assume, would regard racism as ubiquitous but bad, while the Klan would regard it as ubiquitous but good. At an even deeper level, there would be further disagreement. Collins would argue that to resolve racial problems, Third World immigration must be stopped; anti-racists would argue that racism, not immigration must be smothered. The implication is clear: only at the most superficial level of analysis – that of identifying the problem in the first place – is there agreement among these otherwise polar-opposite interest groups.

As far as the actor's perspective is concerned, the key factor is whether or not one is a target of racist organizations. Generally speaking, the propensity to both recognize the degree of racism that exists and fight against it depends on this dimension. Those who are not the victims can indulge in abstract discussions of the relative importance of free speech versus the suppression of racism. The targets are not so fortunate. As one person wrote about the Holocaust in a letter to the editor (Toronto *Sun*, 22 October 1980): 'It's easy for people on the sidelines not touched by those terrible happenings to play it cool. I can't play it cool ... I am the only leftover of a family of more than 150 people, all of them killed by the Nazis.'

---

11 This newspaper article, a review of Collins's book written by Peter Worthington, was reprinted in Gostick's *Canadian Intelligence Service* (vol. 29, no. 8, August 1979).

In this context, the reactions of some academics to my study are not a little interesting. As indicated in chapter 1, before embarking on this project I spent considerable time consulting specialists about whether the study should be done, or whether it would merely provide the racists with free advertising. Virtually without exception, prominent black and Jewish spokesmen, plus active anti-racist academics, urged me to go ahead with it. It was, therefore, much to my surprise that I began to come across academics who expressed hostility towards the study. One asked if I had joined the Klan yet. Another remarked that by undertaking the study, I had defined myself outside the boundaries of anthropology. How can this be explained? Well, as Moodley (1981: 14) has stated: 'The extent of Canadian racialism remains very much an academic taboo.' In addition, some of the academics may have genuinely believed that to focus on racists is to legitimize them, and no doubt a few of them were influenced by the antagonism towards Zionism in some left-wing circles. Yet there is another factor. As the months went by, and the same negative reaction continued from some academics, I began to take systematic notes about them. What was significant was that while they came from all political colours, from highly conservative individuals to Marxists,[12] they all had one thing in common: they were white. Not once in the course of the project did a black person or a Jew exhibit anything but support for the project. Perhaps those who were opposed to the study, not being victims themselves, merely had a blind spot about the anguish experienced by the targets of racism. Yet the fact that they were uniformly white suggests that their reaction was in some vague manner informed by racism itself.

---

12 At the risk of alienating some of my colleagues in academia even further, a qualifying note is warranted. Contrary to popular opinion, not all Marxists are radical. Some of them, especially in the university setting, embrace Marxism as an intellectual tool, and lead otherwise conventional middle-class lives, which rarely cross with the activities of committed Marxists on the firing line engaged in overturning capitalist society. In this context, we can speak of conservative Marxists. It was this type that was inclined to make disparaging remarkes about the present study. Not only, then, were the critics all white, but in a sense they also were mostly conservatives.

PART FOUR / EXPLANATIONS AND PUZZLES

11

Institutional Racism

How can so many radical- and fringe-right organizations exist in Canada, a country that has enjoyed an enviable reputation for tolerance? Are they atypical manifestations of the wider society, or are they implicated in it? In order to answer these questions, we shall have to consider the historical and structural setting of right-wing expression – and especially racism – in the country. This chapter, it must be emphasized, is different from any of the others in the study. Its focus is not on the organized right wing. Instead it focuses on the institutional framework alongside which the right wing has flourished, and it raises intriguing questions about the links of racism and anti-Semitism to power and privilege.

SOME INCIDENTS

Not all the evidence of racism in Canada has been buried in academic tomes, inaccessible to lay people. In order to illustrate this point, I shall begin with several recent incidents, selected at random, which were duly reported by the media.[1] In 1976 a forty-nine–year–old immigrant from Tanzania found himself sprawled on the rails of the Toronto subway, both legs badly broken. Two of the young white men who had attacked him eventually were sentenced to prison terms of two and a half and years and twenty-one months, respectively. The attack, so clearly vicious and unprovoked, generated a ground swell of sympathy for the unfortunate man, who spent more than four months in hospital. Metro Toronto citizens collected

---

1 For the same reason I shall occasionally draw from media reports later in this chapter. Let it be clear, however, that had I chosen to do so, it would have been easy to restrict the references in this chapter entirely to scholarly works.

$5,560 for him, and the Ontario Criminal Injuries Compensation Board awarded him $15,000 (*Toronto Star*, 16 March 1977). The attack obviously was racially motivated, but the presiding judge declared that was irrelevant to the case (*Globe and Mail*, 2 December 1976). The attorney general Roy McMurtry, disagreed, and on his appeal the sentences were extended (*Toronto Star*, 23 April, 17 May 1977). That turn of events was particularly significant because some people today believe that when a crime is racially motivated, an additional sentence should be levied.[2]

In 1981 in British Columbia a lighted five-gallon container of gasoline was tossed through a window of a house owned by an East Indian family. A month later, and only about a mile away, another East Indian family was awakened by the sound of molotov cocktails smashing through a window (McAlpine 1981: 17). An Asian student on a Canadian Commonwealth Scholarship was only in Canada about six months when she was kicked and insulted on the street; ironically, she had had a choice of studying in Canada or England, but chose Canada because she was told it was free from discrimination (*Vancouver Sun*, 27 October 1978).[3] In 1984 in a small city near Toronto, swastikas were painted on the windows and front door of a synagogue, and posters of Hitler were taped to utility poles. The local newspaper wrote an editorial condemning the defacement of the synagogue. Two teenagers were eventually apprehended after brandishing the editorial around school, boasting that they had been responsible. The whole thing, they said, had been a prank. One of them had been enrolled in a German class. When he realized Hitler's birthday was approaching, he and the other teenager, who was in a different school, photocopied a picture of Hitler from a textbook and bought paint to draw swastikas. There was no evidence that the two young men, both of whom were Protestant, had any contact with Fascist organizations in nearby Toronto; nor did their anti-Semitic actions seem to reflect deeply held convictions about Jews, although the leader of the two, who had previously been convicted for theft and shoplifting, apparently displayed little remorse for defacing the synagogue. Eventually they were found guilty of public mischief and sentenced to thirty days in jail, plus two years' probation.

The sceptical reader might dismiss all of the cases so far as the weird antics of a handful of irresponsible thugs, motivated no more than by a

---

2 From a contact associated with the institution in which the two young men were placed, I learned that they were treated as heroes by some of the other inmates because of their racial attack.

3 For an overview of the recent foreign-student experience in Canada, see Groberman (1980).

desire to raise hell. But what about an incident in 1980 involving a Manitoba 4-H Club that cancelled an exchange with the same organization in Ontario because the latter group included Native persons? According to a reporter, one of the mothers asked: 'Would you send your child to sleep with Indians?' Another apparently said all Indians are the same: they drink and fight, and pose a danger to children. Both women denied they were prejudiced (Toronto *Sun*, 15 June 1980) and a columnist in the same issue of the newspaper opined that the remarks of the women in question were so insulting to Indians that they shouldn't have been reported by the press. In similar fashion, a principal of a newly integrated school in Nova Scotia said it was his policy not to raise any questions about racial conflict. Both the journalist and educator were manifesting the 'avoidance syndrome' (Hill 1977: 41), assuming that by ignoring problems, or refusing to confront them, all would be well.

From respectable mothers we go to a respectable television station. In 1979 CTV aired a 'W5' program called 'The Campus Giveaway,' claiming that well-qualified Canadians were being denied access to university because of the flood of foreign students, especially Chinese; film footage showed Chinese-looking students, with the implicit comment that they must be foreigners. In the resulting uproar, university officials pointed out that the program's statistics on foreign students were inaccurate. 'W5' said that 100,000 foreign students, mostly Chinese, were enrolled in Canadian universities. But the real figure was fewer than 20,000, 22 per cent from Hong Kong and Taiwan (*Toronto Star*, 23 July 1983). A libel and slander suit was filed against CTV and 'W5' by five students from the Chinese Students Association of the University of Toronto, and a committee of Chinese Canadians against CTV and 'W5' was formed (see Gordon 1982, and Thomas and Novogrodsky 1983: 103). The end result was an apology by the president of CTV, who said in part that the critics had been correct: the program was racist, albeit unintentionally. There is no reason to doubt that statement; unintentional racism, as we shall soon see, is characteristic of the most basic kind: the institutional variety.

BEFORE THE SECOND WORLD WAR

Could the cases described above be dismissed as random incidents uncharacteristic of the country in general? Or, perhaps, weren't they simply unfortunate evidence that the 'American virus,' so alien to Canadian institutions, had temporarily crossed the border? To answer these questions, we must trace the country's record for racial tolerance over the decades.

Canada emerged out of the experience of colonization, and like that process everywhere, the major victims were the Native peoples. As Valentine (1980: 47) has pointed out, as a result of successive government strategies to dominate and control Native peoples, today they 'have the lowest incomes, the poorest health, and the highest rates of unemployment of any single group in the country.' They also are overrepresented in jails and underrepresented in the educational system. In some cases, such as the now extinct Beothuk of Newfoundland in the eighteenth century, Native peoples were the victims of outright slaughter (Hill 1977: 7).[4] While most Canadians are probably aware of the massive discrimination against Native peoples, it is possible that not everyone realizes that Canada was once a centre of slavery. The first slaves were Indian captives sold to traders (Greaves 1930: 9). Eventually blacks replaced them. The first black slave in Canada was brought to New France in 1608; by 1750 their numbers exceeded 4,000 (Frideres 1976: 137). In Nova Scotia there were slave sales and newspaper advertisements for runaways (Jones 1978: 82). Slavery actually lasted longer in Canada than in the northern United States, and rather than having always been a refuge for runaway slaves, Canada was the point of departure for many fugitive slaves who escaped to New England (Winks 1968: 288).

With the passing of the Emancipation Act by the British Parliament in 1833, slavery was abolished in Canada, but other expressions of racism remained and expanded. Segregation in schools was legalized in Ontario in 1849 (Head 1975: 12). The first race riot in Canada apparently occurred in 1907 in Vancouver when whites attacked Japanese and Chinese sectors (Ward 1978; Sugimoto 1972). More than 15,000 Chinese (Thomas and Novogrodsky 1983: 57) were brought to Canada by 1885 to work on the Canadian Pacific Railway, and when it was completed in 1885 a head tax of $50 was established to discourage further Chinese immigration (Bolaria and Li 1985: 86). By 1903 the tax had increased to $500 (Kallen 1982: 140). Then there was the infamous episode concerning the *Komagata Maru*, a ship that arrived at Vancouver in 1914 with about four hundred Sikhs. After waiting for two months in the harbour, because immigration officials would not admit the passengers, the ship set sail; only twenty-two people on board, all of whom had previously lived in Canada, were allowed ashore (Reid 1941; Ferguson 1975).

4 For recent analyses of the racist oppression of Native peoples and the Métis, see the chapters by Frideres and Adams in Bolaria and Li (1985). Part 1 of Elliott's reader (1983) also is devoted to Native peoples, and Kallen's *Ethnicity and Human Rights* (1982) is a constant source of sound analysis and insight as regards Native peoples and other oppressed sectors of Canadian society.

A dominant theme in *Saturday Night* at the turn of the century was racial purity. Canada, as the magazine explained, was a white man's country. Stephen Leacock, one of Canada's few genuine heroes, and a regular contributor to *Saturday Night*, wrote in 1911 that non–Anglo-Saxon immigrants were 'fit objects indeed for philanthropic pity, but indifferent material from which to build the Commonwealth of the future' (Wolfe 1977: 29). In the early days of the Ku Klux Klan in the United States, not all whites were desirable – only those who were Anglo-Saxon Protestants. Among those of 'indifferent material' in Canada were immigrants from Eastern and Southern Europe who in the first quarter of the twentieth century were regarded as 'dangerous foreigners' (Avery 1983). In the 1930s there was a prize in Alberta for the grade-twelve student obtaining the highest academic standing. One year an Indian girl won, but was told Indians did not qualify (Hill 1977: 9). In that same decade a black student was refused a scholarship that she had won, on the assumption that no opportunities would be subsequently presented to her (Tunteng 1973: 231; Potter 1968: 48). In 1929 when the World Baptist Conference was held in Toronto, coloured delegates were denied rooms in hotels (Greaves 1930: 61).

In 1858 (Howay 1939) about four hundred blacks immigrated to Vancouver Island from California. The governor of Vancouver Island then was James Douglas, an illegitimate child born in British Guiana, whose father was a Scot and mother, a Creole. Blacks seemed at that time (Killan 1978: 147) to be favoured over the Chinese by whites. Ironically, Douglas, who was knighted in 1863, himself once remarked about Asian immigrants: 'They are certainly not a desirable class of people, but are for the present useful as labourers' (Ward 1978: 25).[5] While one might think that a shared history of suffering would bring different ethnic groups together, the more usual pattern is dissension among them. This reflects a more general phenomenon: the tendency of subjected people to direct their hostilities at one another, rather than at the much more difficult target: their oppressors.

Although there was a growing movement in Canada against slavery in the early 1900s, inspired partly by anti-Americanism, once slavery was abolished Canadians seemed to lose interest in the plight of blacks. By the middle of this century blacks constituted less than 2 per cent of the Canadian population (Tunteng 1973) and for all intents and purposes were a superfluous people, sociologically invisible, ignored or underrepresented

5 For further analysis of attitudes in British Columbia towards Asian immigrants, see Roy (1980).

even in scholarly works as exhaustive as Porter's *The Vertical Mosaic* (1965). In this context, the title of Henry's study on Nova Scotian blacks, *Forgotten Canadians* (1973), is appropriate. Part of the problem, as I remarked in the previous chapter, appears to have been that blacks in Canada were divided among themselves, and did not constitute a homogeneous community. In Nova Scotia alone, there were at least four distinct categories of blacks: Loyalist blacks, Maroon blacks from Jamaica, Refugee blacks, and fugitive black slave descendants; the last named occupied the lowest rung on the ladder even among other blacks. In recent decades, with a growing black population from the West Indies and the United States, the degree of fragmentation has been even greater, with considerable resentment among native-born blacks towards the sophisticated, highly educated West Indian immigrants (Brown 1968) who tend to regard them as country bumpkins (Jones 1978: 94).

As time went on, prejudice and discrimination began to resemble the American model. Until 1951, for example (Winks 1968: 288), in Windsor, Ontario, there was separate sections in bars called 'jungle rooms.' In one respect, the character of racial prejudice in Canada may have been different than its counterpart in the United States: its formlessness. As Winks (1971: 325) has written: 'In London the mayor supported Negroes in bringing a suit against a restaurant that refused to serve them; in Dresden, fifty miles away, they could not eat with whites. In Windsor Negroes were not admitted to the Boy Scouts or to the Y.M.C.A. and so organized their own; in Toronto they joined both freely. In many small towns, Negro musicians were welcomed into the life of the community; in Owen Sound they had to establish their own orchestra. In Sherbrooke a Negro was a jockey; in Windsor blacks could not ride and interracial boxing was forbidden.'

In nineteenth-century Ontario the reaction of Gentiles towards Jews appears to have been rather benign. Wrong (1959: 46), for example, indicates that Christians contributed to the building fund for Toronto's first synagogue in 1875. At that time intermarriage between Christians and Jews was prevalent. One explanation for acceptance of Jews then was probably a matter of numbers: in 1846 there were only 12 Jews in Toronto, in 1849 only 39, and in 1875 only 350 (Speisman 1979: 15–16).[6] Another factor concerns the origin of Jewish settlers. Most of the nineteenth-century Jewish immigrants came from Britain or the United States, and language and cultural

---

6 By 1911 the Jewish population in Canada had grown to nearly 75,000; at the end of the First World War it was more than 120,000, and by 1971 about 300,000 (Rosenberg 1971: 38 and 205).

barriers with non-Jews were minimal. However, there was a dramatic change with the advent of East European Jews at the turn of the century. In terms of culture, language, and tradition Jews no longer were invisible, and not only were they discriminated against by Gentiles, but as Wrong has remarked (1959: 48) the established Toronto Jewish community also saw them as a threat to the harmonious relations that had been established with non-Jews. By the end of the 1920s, Jews were barred from some college fraternities and some clubs, and Gentiles refused to patronize Jewish doctors. In the Balmy Beach area of Toronto, membership was closed to Jews in tennis and golf clubs, and professions such as teaching and nursing were out of bounds unless a Jew was prepared to change his name, pass as a Christian, or at least have a Gentile spouse (Kayfetz 1975: 10–11). Referring to the 1930s, Wrong (1959: 53) has stated: 'The social atmosphere of upper middle class Toronto, while genteel in tone, was thoroughly anti-Semitic.'

Quebec, the province where the *achat-chez-nous* movement and Arcand's Fascist organization took root, was also fertile ground for anti-Semitism. Although the Jewish community there in the early part of the twentieth century was small, it still was the largest of any province in the country; anti-Semitism, encouraged by the Catholic clergy and the élite (Glickman 1984: 7), moved beyond the level of innuendo to accusations of a world conspiracy perpetrated by the killers of Christ. One sign of the pervasive anti-Semitism was reflected in the admissions policy at McGill University where Jews, until 1942 were required to have an average of 65 per cent, while non-Jews needed only have 50 per cent (Draper 1983: 281). Elsewhere, such as in Alberta, anti-Semitism (Palmer 1982: 153) existed in the 1930s, but was weak and unorganized. The exception concerned the fringe element in Aberhart's Social Credit party. Aberhart, it is true, publicly condemned anti-Semitism and made it clear that it was not intrinsic to Social Credit policies, but apparently his own ambivalent attitude towards Jews was part of the problem (Palmer 1982: 151–8).

THE SECOND WORLD WAR: JEWISH REFUGEES AND JAPANESE INTERNS

It is of no little irony that as organized expressions of Aryan superiority such as Arcand's Fascist party dissipated at the advent of the Second World War, a particularly pernicious form of anti-Semitism and racism emerged within the Canadian government itself, involving Jewish refugees and Japanese Canadians. The story of the way in which the government systematically and continuously thwarted efforts to relocate Jews in Canada has been poignantly told by Abella and Troper (1982). Canada, the authors argue persuasively, had possibly the worst record of all countries in the Western world in providing sanctuary to European Jewry. *None Is Too Many* documents in chilling detail the unrelenting efforts of Canadian government officials, some of them blatantly anti-Semitic, to keep Canada's doors closed to Jews, despite their desperate situation and the world's growing realization of Hitler's genocidal policy. Even three years after the war was over, and the full truth of what had happened to Jews became universally known, Canada had only accepted a trickle of Jewish refugees. *None Is Too Many* firmly explodes the myth of Jewish economic and political power. Torn by internal dissension, and faced with indifference at best and barely concealed anti-Semitism by government officials, the Jewish community could only stand by and lament its failure. As Abella and Troper remark (1982: 284), Canadian Jews, believing in the goodness of mankind, assumed that the civilized world would come to the rescue of the refugees, but they were wrong.[7]

Sunahara's *The Politics of Racism* (1981) is a companion book for *None Is Too Many*. Again, this time involving Japanese Canadians, it is clear that the major culprit was the government. Sunahara tells the story of how in 1942 the federal cabinet ordered 22,000 Japanese on the Pacific Coast to be expelled, stripped of their property, and confined to detention camps.[8] That these acts were unjust can be best illustrated by comparing the treatment of Japanese Canadians with that of German Canadians. At the outbreak of the First World War, the attitudes of Canadians and the government towards German Canadians was distinctly negative, and many of German descent actually anglicized their names to avoid persecution (Wagner 1981: 3). As Palmer wrote (1982: 47), the Germans in Alberta at the turn of the century, 'who formerly had been counted among western Canada's most desirable citizens, now became the most undesirable.' In Calgary, in 1916, mobs tore apart a restaurant that allegedly had dismissed returned war veterans and hired Germans in their place. During the First World War, 8,500 German and Austrian enemy aliens were interned by the Canadian government (Wagner 1981: 134).

---

7 Ironically, Canada did provide a home to some Jewish refugees, but they consisted of 'enemy aliens' who had been packed off to this country from Great Britain to live in internment camps. For details on this episode in Canadian history, as well as the remarkable educational atmosphere in the camps, see Draper (1978, 1983).

8 Interestingly, Sunahara (1981: 87) indicates that often the only people who would employ or provide accommodation to Japanese Canadians were Jews.

During the Second World War, not only Japanese aliens, but also German and Italian aliens, were under order to register with the RCMP. Yet only 840 German nationals and 60 naturalized Canadians of German origin were interned (Wagner 1981: 134). That was all the more remarkable in the context of the significant pro-Nazi sympathy and activity in Canada at the outbreak of the Second World War. In the Praire provinces, five out of seven German-Canadian weeklies (Wagner 1981: 114) sympathized with the Nazi cause. Moreover, Hitler supporters had founded the Deutscher Bund Canada in 1934, with a membership of about two thousand in 1938, almost one hundred of whom were members of the German Nazi Party. It is true that by that year many German Canadians, faced with the gathering hostility among English Canadians to Nazi Germany and its Canadian sympathizers, began to denounce Nazism and declare their allegiance to Canada, and an anti-Nazi German-Canadian organization (the German-Canadian League) existed. Yet if there was a threat to national security at all, and that is highly debatable, the apparent evidence points to the German Canadians. In 1944, for example (Sunahara 1981: 117), Prime Minister King acknowledged that not a single act of sabotage had been committed by a Japanese Canadian. Yet it was the Japanese who were dispossessed of their property and interned; even after the war was over, the government persisted in its program to deport Japanese Canadians. The conclusion would seem to be unavoidable: at the root of the treatment of the Japanese Canadians was cold-blooded racism.[9]

AFTER THE SECOND WORLD WAR

Almost all of the cases mentioned so far occurred prior to or during the Second World War. Could it be that endemic racism was a thing of the past, happily suffocated by a new era of enlightenment among Canadians? Well, in British Columbia class-rooms in the 1950s and 1960s, grade-four students still used a workbook called *Ten Little Niggers* (Killan 1978: 164). As late as 1973 (*Vancouver Sun*, 6 January 1973) there was a residential section in

---

9 Many Canadians might think that during times of war there is no alternative but to lock up nationals of the enemy camp, and some of them might ridicule the efforts of Japanese Canadians to gain reparation payments for the past treatment. However, it is not simply the internment that is involved in the reparation claims; more acutely, it is the fact that the internment was racially motivated that justifies the claims for reparation. There are, in addition to Sunahara, a number of important studies of the internment of the Japanese Canadians, such as Adachi's (1976).

Vancouver, established by British Properties before the Second World War, in which it was stipulated on each property deed that no person of Asiatic or African ancestry could stay on the premises overnight unless he or she was a servant. The law authorizing segregated schools was only removed in 1965. In Red Deer, where the Alberta Klan leader boasted that he had twenty-six members, three fires in shapes of crosses were set on the lawns of homes belonging to a Japanese family, an East Indian family from Tanzania, and an East Indian family from England, although police believed teenagers not connected with the Klan were responsible.[10] The Okanagan Valley has been the scene of exceptional racial tension, directed at migrant farm workers, mostly Francophone. One researcher stated: 'It's the worst racism I've ever seen. It is institutionalized at every level of the community. The hostility and tension are incredible. The local people are just choking themselves on hate' (*Vancouver Sun*, 30 August 1983). In 1976 letters were sent by the fictitious Canada Council for Commonwealth Relations to Toronto residents saying they had been selected to accommodate a Pakistani family on a cultural-exchange program. The letter went on to say that the family would include the father, mother, nine children, wife's brother, husband's grandmother, and her sister. The host family was advised to rent a mini-bus to collect the family at the airport.

Betcherman (1975: 147) concluded her study of Fascism in Canada prior to the Second World War with the statement: 'Fascist movements and racism did not vanish, but withdrew to await a more welcoming climate.' Certainly that was true as regards anti-Semitism. In 1960 anti-Semitic slogans were painted on buildings in Montreal and carved on an object at the Royal Ontario Museum in Toronto (*Canadian Jewish News*, 8 January 1960). In 1983, a Scarborough golf course trying to upgrade its status apparently was refusing Jewish members (*Toronto Star*, 23 July 1983). In that same year, unsolicited material denying the Holocaust was sent to the University of Winnipeg and the University of Brandon. A study focusing on Winnipeg (Driedger and Mezoff 1981) found that perceived discrimination was higher among Jews than among any other ethnic group; Jews reported receiving the most verbal abuse, hate literature, and physical attacks.

In chapter 2, it was shown that organized anti-Semitism was less prevalent in Quebec than in Ontario after the Second World War. Nevertheless, twenty-five of sixty-three incidents in Canada in 1982 occurred in Quebec (*Review of Anti-Semitism in Canada* 1982). Some observers, like

---

10 For an anlysis of several racist incidents in Alberta involving East Indians, see Bowerman (1980).

journalist Larry Zolf (*Toronto Star*, 20 December 1976), have contended that anti-Semitism pervades contemporary Quebec nationalism, which means in particular the Parti Québécois (PQ). Waller and Weinfeld (1981: 423) have flatly rejected that charge: 'Let it be said clearly that the Parti Québécois has given no evidence whatsoever of overt anti-Semitic tendencies or influences.' Elsewhere, however, Weinfeld (1977: 28) refers with concern to former premier René Lévesque's personal opinion that the establishment of Israel was 'an incredible political blunder' and that the Palestinian cause 'is and remains just.' The other side of the coin is the alleged Jewish lack of sympathy for Québécois aspirations. Perhaps the most visible sign was a widely reported comment by industrialist Charles Bronfman about the disastrous consequences for Canada and the Jewish community if the PQ was victorious at the election booth (Weinfeld 1977: 22). Finally, I have in my possession some curious materials implying a link in Quebec among advocates of natural medicine, natural health food, right-wing ideologies, and socio-biology, in which the Celtic-Nordic race is defended against yellow and black peoples and Jews.

STRUCTURAL RACISM

No matter whether the dimension is time, place, or social class, racism has been endemic in Canada. It has stretched from the early slavery at the nation's dawn down through the Fascist phase prior to the Second World War to the Paki-bashing of recent years. It has reached from the Pacific to the Atlantic, taking different forms according to the local ethnic composition, targeting Asians in Vancouver, blacks in Nova Scotia, and Jews everywhere. It has been represented in corporate and government boards and among manual labourers at construction sites. And it has appeared both visibly in the form of violent attacks and covertly in the form of variations in wages and employment opportunities based on racial criteria.

Many observers might want to argue that what racism does exist in Canada has simply been the sad product of deviant individuals, or a temporary problem brought on by unemployment or some other crisis. Yet the degree, scope, and persistence of the phenomenon lead to a single conclusion: racism in Canada has been institutionalized. Some writers give the impression that institutional racism means covert racism, and remark that in recent years blatant racism has gone underground or become 'institutionalized.' But this is wrong. Institutional racism means racism that is intrinsic to the structures of society. It may be overt or covert, expressed formally in the laws of the land, or less visibly in patterns of employment and the content of school textbooks. Apartheid in South Africa is an example of overt institutional racism, the counterpart of which in Canada, as Carstens (1971) has made clear, has been the reservation system for Native peoples. It is, therefore, erroneous to state that simply because racism has become less visible it has finally become institutionalized. More precisely, only one aspect – its overt manifestations – has tended to disappear. My contention, indeed, is that since the Second World War racism has polarized: it has become simultaneously more overt and more covert; more overt in the sense that numerous individuals have emerged as committed and public advocates of Aryan superiority; more covert in the sense that ordinary white Canadians are much more cautious about appearing to be racists. What is significant about institutional racism, whether open or hidden, is not only that differential advantage along racial lines is embedded in society itself, but also that it prepetuates itself over time, for that is the nature of the institutional framework: independent of individual volition, relatively unconscious and unmotivated, it reproduces itself. Effort is not required to maintain it; instead, effort is required to diminish it. In other words, institutional racism is almost synonymous with 'the way things are.' Coterminous as it is with immemorial custom, habit, and bias, there is little to take notice of or to ponder about. No wonder it is usually argued that institutional racism is the most significant variety of all, as well as the most difficult to eradicate.

OVERT INSTITUTIONAL RACISM

Among the most readily discernible examples of institutional racism are those that have been formalized into laws. Paul Winn, a black civil-rights activist in Vancouver, has asserted (personal communication) that there was more racist legislation in British Columbia than in any other province. One example was that British Properties convenant against Asians and blacks in one sector of Vancouver. In that same city there formerly were laws specifying where Chinese Canadians could live, work, and travel, and whom they could employ. The head tax introduced in 1885 curtailed the entry of Chinese immigrants. In 1923 a new Chinese Immigrant Act prohibited the entry of all Chinese except 'students, merchants, children born in Canada, diplomats and persons in transit.' Only three Chinese entered the country between 1924 and 1930 (Thomas and Novogrodsky 1983: 63). In Saskatchewan a law prevented white women from working for Asians. Then there was the law, established in 1908, that prohibited all immigrants from entering Canada unless they arrived from the country of their birth or citizenship by a continuous journey. That law was aimed at East Indians and Japanese who lived in Hawaii, and since there were no direct ships from India, and the Japanese in Hawaii were ineligible, both groups were effectively barred from Canada (Ward 1978: 76). Finally, there was the selective denial of voting rights. East Indians were not given the franchise until 1947; until then they were banned from obtaining Canadian citizenship (Ramcharan 1982: 23). Chinese Canadians also got the franchise in 1947, and Japanese Canadians became full citizens in 1949 (Sunahara 1981: 165). While the Inuit had the federal vote, it was only in 1962 that they were given the right to participate in provincial elections. Status Indians were denied the franchise until 1960 (Kallen 1982: 131). Being denied the right to vote meant that one could not join the public service, hold public office, or enter professions such as law and pharmacy.

COVERT INSTITUTIONAL RACISM

This variety can take the form of racism that is deliberately concealed, such as the efforts of Canadian immigration officials to deny entry to Jewish refugees during the Second World War, with the rationale that it was in their best interests not to enter Canada since their arrival would simply trigger anti-Semitism (Abella and Troper 1982: 80). What we usually mean by covert institutional racism, however, is unconscious, non-deliberate racism, racism which is hardly recognized by the racist himself; racism which only occasionally, and then usually accidentally, seeps out of the structure. A typical example concerns the practice of police stopping blacks who drive luxurious cars (Head 1975: 64), or asking blacks how long they have been in Canada, assuming that all of them are recent immigrants from the West Indies. When the late Tom Mboya, renowned as an enlightened political leader in Kenya, was a clerk in a public office, a white woman once approached his office and peering around him asked if anyone was there. That was social invisibility in action, and I witnessed a case of it much closer to home. As I followed an immaculately dressed black man into a university restaurant, the maître d' craned his neck around the distinguished scholar and asked me how many were in my party. A more generally known case concerns comments made by a radio announcer for Toronto's CKFM when he assumed he was off the air. This man, an authority on jazz, was overheard referring to Toronto's Caribana parade as 'four million niggers jumping up and down' (*Currents*, vol. 1, no. 2, Spring 1983: 21).[11] Another

11 One response to this case was the formation of the Committee against Racism Within the Media (CARM).

example in the media that we discussed earlier was the 'W5' program on the alleged invasion of Chinese foreign students in Canadian universities. Even Cardinal Carter, a renowned opponent of racism in the country, reportedly regaled an audience of policemen with Jewish jokes, and Secretary of State Gerald Regan was said to have referred to Ontario's agent-general in Paris as 'that Chinese girl' (*Toronto Star*, 23 July 1983). Finally, there is the case of a black lady who requested an appointment with the mayor of a large Canadian city in the 1970s. The mayors excutive assistant wrote on his Message Form: 'This is a coloured lady which believes she is being discriminated against. I think she wants to believe this. She is full of hatred.' In case there is any doubt that the tone of this message would not be music to the mayor's ears, I have a copy of a letter written by him a few years earlier in which he states that he formerly was in favour of adopting the Caribbean Islands as part of Canada until he discovered while on a holiday there that the people were immoral, irresponsible, and indolent.

IMMIGRATION

I now shall consider the potential racist nature of several institutions, beginning with immigration. As Kallen (1982: 140) has stated: 'A racist immigration policy is one of the most invidious techniques utilized by those in power to guarantee their ethnic ascendency in any society.' She goes on to point out that Orientals and blacks have usually been the targets of Canadian immigration restrictions. Indeed, until 1953 'climatic suitability' was formally included in the Immigration Act, and used to bar people from non-Western countries, supposedly for their own good. By 1964 there were thirty-two immigration offices located in twenty-one countries, but only four of those offices were in non-white countries (Ramcharan 1982: 15).

In recent decades, three specific years stand out as significant in terms of immigration policy: 1962, 1967, and 1975. Until 1962 Canada had an explicit and formal racist immigration policy (Frideres 1976: 137; Corbett 1957). In that year all previous national ethnic references and restrictions were abolished (Richmond 1975), which opened the door to non-white immigration (Thomas and Novogrodsky 1983: 66). In 1967 a points system based on education, professional, and occupational criteria replaced the previous ethnic and national criteria. Dramatic changes in the national and ethnic origins of immigrants were not long in coming. In 1966, there were 6,593 immigrants from China, Pakistan, and India (3.4 per cent of the total number of immigrants). In 1975, 25,475 immigrants (or 13.6 per cent of the total number) came from these three countries (Li 1979: 70). Wood (1978:

551) stated that whereas in 1967 about 80 per cent of Canada's immigrants originated from Europe, by 1974 fewer than 40 per cent did so. By 1976, Asia, West India, and Africa provided Canada with 59 per cent of her immigrants (Pitman 1977: 37).

The definition of who constitutes a desirable immigrant has undergone changes over the decades, and has been intrinsically related to economic conditions, manpower needs, and sometimes sheer bigotry, such as the Orange Order's opposition to Catholic immigration (Corbett 1957: 32). After 1896 the proportion of immigrants from northwestern Europe declined and that from southern and eastern Europe increased. These new immigrants were thought to be alien to the Canadian way of life, and incapable of adapting and assimilating (Corbett 1957; Avery 1983). During the depression era of 1907–8, signs appeared in Canada stating 'No English Need Apply.' Indeed, of 1,800 people deported in 1908, about 1,100 of them (or 70 per cent) were British (McCormack 1981: 41). Obviously, then, Canada's restrictive immigration policy has not been limited to Third World peoples, but the fact remains that the latter have been the prime target; by 1909, for example, with the depression passed, British immigrants again headed the list of desirables. New immigrants are ready scapegoats for a range of societal ills. In the early 1930s in Alberta (Palmer 1928: 128), immigrants were blamed for unemployment in much the same way as they have been in recent years. Often it is claimed that immigrants have a higher crime rate than the established population. Yet some studies (Richmond 1974–5: 16) indicate that exactly the reverse is true. Indeed, a report prepared for the secretary of state in 1974 found that the crime rate for new Canadians was only about one-half that for native-born Canadians (Thomas and Novogrodsky 1983: 87). Another criticism is that Third World immigrants, and especially Jews, tend to avoid the hinterlands where they are needed. Yet as Palmer (1982: 66–7) has pointed out, British immigrants go directly to the city and nobody cares.

The removal of conditions that favour Anglo-Saxon entry, and the sharp increase in Third World immigration, have been strongly opposed by both the radical and the fringe right, who contend that coloured immigrants will bring a racial problem to Canada. Curiously, some people who are themsleves totally opposed to racist organizations take a similar position when the question concerns immigration. As Head (1975: 63) has reported, some blacks in Toronto have themselves been wary of a more open, non-racist immigration policy. They fear that a sharp influx of blacks will make whites in Canada as aggressive and hostile towards them as are whites in the United States. In 1975 Art Phillips, then the mayor of Vancouver, reportedly warned (Toronto *Sun*, 12 November 1981) that groups from 'a dramatically different cultural background' could create a racial problem. As he apparently said: 'It is laudable to have non-discriminatory policies but it is a mistake if they lead to racial violence.' A demographer remarked to me that no matter how unpalatable, the scientific facts must be accepted: Third World immigrants cause racism. He claimed that most demographers share his views but are reluctant to say so publicly for fear of being labelled racists. Quite a different perspective has been provided by Walker (1978: 52): 'Racism has existed in Canada since its foundation. The immigrants merely present new opportunities for discriminatory behaviour.' If there is a problem, he continues, it is located in mainstream society, and it is there that one's analysis should focus, not on the immigrants themselves.

The Green Paper on Immigration, brought out in 1975, had the stated purpose of evaluating trends since the 1967 legislation. Whereas Mackenzie King had long ago declared that Canadians did not want 'to make a fundamental alteration in the character of our population,' the authors of the Green Paper urged Canadians to have 'clear perceptions of the type of country' they wanted, and expressed concern about the nations's capacity to absorb large numbers of people with 'novel and distinctive features.' In the estimation of some critics, such as Gordon (1975, 1982), the Green Paper was a racist document that would enable the government to drastically reduce non-white immigration.[12] His sharp criticisms appear to have been justified in view of the ensuing legislation which contained more stringent economic criteria, favouring in effect immigrants from industrialized Western societies.

EMPLOYMENT

In what can be described as a landmark study, Frances Henry (1978) reported that 16 per cent of the population of Toronto was extremely racist and 35 per cent somewhat racist. Subsequent studies such as *No Discrimination Here* and *Who Gets the Work*, produced by the Urban Alliance on Race Relations and the Metro Toronto Social Planning Council, demonstrated what should be obvious: such racist tendencies show up clearly in the occupational realm. Visible minorities, as it is often said, are the last to be hired and the first to be fired. In one city with a large non-white population,

---

12 Wood (1978: 564) denies that the new Immigration Act that followed the Green Paper was a racist document, and added that in no other country could new ethnic minorities have had such a profound influence in shaping immigration policy.

a fire department of 1,100 had only two non-whites; another city with numerous non-whites had only one non-white police officer; in three northern communities only two Native persons were counted among more than five hundred bank employees (*Currents*, vol. 2, no. 1, 1984: 17). A report done by two sociologists found that West Indian men earned $2,400 less annually than the average Metro Toronto resident, and West Indian women $3,800 less; also, unemployment was twice as high for East Asians as for the average citizen (*Toronto Star*, 3 February 1982). As M.P. Daudlin publicly observed (*Guelph Mercury*, 27 February 1984), structural inequality along racial lines flows from factors such as the old-boy network. Other biases built into the institutional framework are unnecessary height and weight regulations, the demand for Canadian experience and a Canadian educational diploma, and even IQ and personality tests; of course, these tests have come under heavy fire in recent years because of the cultural and class biases built into them, but the very attempt to measure the intellectual level of new immigrants or of people whose native language is other than English may itself be an instance of institutional racism (see *Currents*, vol. 2 no. 1, 1984: 22).[13]

A particularly vicious type of job discrimination has existed in some employment agencies. In 1980 a survey conducted in Halifax, Toronto, Winnipeg, and Vancouver by the Canadian Civil Liberties Association revealed that seventeen of twenty-five randomly selected employment agencies were willing to provide employers with whites only (Kallen 1982: 136). A similar inquiry into Ontario real estate agencies in the late 1970s came up with the same conclusion: of thirty agencies tested to see if they would accept a request to sell houses to whites only, twenty-seven agreed (*Toronto Star*, 10 January 1977). Elsewhere Head (1975: 57) reported that one employment agency had noted on its files that an employer wanted only 'peaches and cream' workers – a euphemism for whites. On one occasion (*Toronto Star*, 20 October 1977),apparently the Toronto General Hospital was ordered to pay $1,700 in damages to a black woman who was refused a job interview three times, while three other less-qualified women were hired. The employment supervisor eventually left the hospital and established his own employment agency. Even when visible minorities do find employment there is some evidence that they have to out-perform whites to prove that they are suitable for the positions (Head 1975: 57), just

---

13 Some readers may dismiss this claim as nonsense; yet how many English-speaking Canadians, with a smattering of highschool French, would welcome the opportunity to measure their IQs in a test composed in the French language?

as black students may have to perform better than white students to get the same grades.

Any lingering doubt that discrimination in employment exists in Canada has been laid to rest with a recent study conducted by Henry and Ginzberg (1985). The authors used two types of testing. First, teams of white and black job applicants carefully matched as regards age, sex, and educational and employment histories applied for a total of 201 jobs. Of 36 job offers received, the white applicant was hired 27 times and the black applicant 9 times. In addition, differential treatment of the white and black applicants occurred 38 times, such as telling the applicant that the job was already taken when it wasn't, or treating the applicant rudely; in 37 of these 38 instances, it was the black applicant who was treated unfavourably. The second type of testing was by telephone. Four job seekers – a West Indian, an Indo-Pakistani, a white 'ethnic' immigrant, and a 'majority' white Canadian – telephoned 237 prospective employers. Over one-half of the employers discriminated against at least one or more of the callers. The Indo-Pakistanis were told that jobs were closed or no longer available in nearly 44 per cent of the cases, the black West Indians in 36 per cent of the cases, the white immigrant Canadians 31 per cent of the cases, and the white majority Canadians in only 13 per cent of the cases. Combining the results from both tests, the authors were able to construct a ratio of discrimination, showing that whites have three job prospects to every one for blacks. These two direct tests in this carefully planned and executed study demonstrate beyond all doubt that employment discrimination on the basis of race does indeed exist in Canada.

EDUCATION

Over and over again it has been claimed that the quick solution to racism is education. Numerous studies (Henry 1978: 1; Li 1979: 71; Quinley and Glock 1979: 24) have reported that the higher one's education, the less one is prejudiced. In a more popular forum (Toronto *Sun*, 16 June 1978), a Toronto journalist, McKenzie Porter, claimed: 'Among educated people, black, brown and white, there is no such thing as racial prejudice. Only at the lowest economic and intellectual levels of society does skin color evoke animosities.' Yet I remain dubious. While it is reasonable to suggest that education can inhibit racist inclinations to some degree, it makes much less sense to regard education and racism as mutually exclusive. As the Cohen Report put it (1966: 28): 'it must be recognized that education alone does not and cannot eliminate prejudice. Even highly-educated people can be extremely prejudiced.' If there is a difference along educational lines, it may be that well-educated people are simply more adroit at concealing their prejudices. The fact is that there is ample evidence to show that racism and the educational system, from the elementary grades to the university level, can and do coexist.

In a study of the attitudes of white elementary-school children (Ijaz 1981) towards blacks and East Indians in Scarborough, Ontario, it was found that racist views abounded among fifth and sixth graders. A report financed by the secretary of state (*Toronto Star*, 14 January 1977) indicated that 64 per cent of 255 Toronto students harboured bigotry.[14] Several studies, neatly summarized by Kallen (1982: 39), have stressed the pronounced degree to which the educational system is based on the norms and values of the dominant urban, middle-class, white society.[15] The amount of racism in the university community also is substantial. Several centres of higher learning have been the scene of anti-Semitic outbreaks. Nigerian students at the British Columbia Institute of Technology were subjected to threatening telephone calls, the home where they resided was sprayed with racist slogans, and garbage was dumped on the lawn (McAlpine 1981: 16–17). On a building at York University the words 'Extinct a Chink' were scrawled. Then, too, the amount of racist graffiti in university wash-rooms is staggering, especially concerning Asian students. Shimomura (1984), reflecting on media reports of the success of Asian Americans in the class-room, particularly in science, comments on the subtle message behind the praise: a new 'Yellow Peril' may be on the way. From my own experience I am fully aware of the negative manner in which some teachers in Canadian universities regard foreign students from Asia, claiming that they pull the standard down and that they tend to work together rather than individually. The contradictory attitudes towards Asian students, praising their marvellous academic performance while at the same time regarding it as somehow tainted, had its counterpart in the treatment of the Japanese-Canadian community before the Second World War. The Japanese were defined as inferior and therefore received lower wages than British Canadians for the same work; yet they also were considered to be unfair

14 In view of the tendency for some schools to ignore racial issues, is must be pointed out that the Toronto Board of Education produced two impressive booklets on how to deal with racism: *Final Report of Sub-Committee on Race Relations* (1979) and *Facilitators' Handbook for Camp Kandelore* (1983).

15 This is essentially the conclusion that Glickman and Bardikoff (1982) arrived at in a study that found the treatment of the Holocaust in Canadian history and social-science textbooks decidedly inadequate.

competition because they worked longer hours and had higher productivity then white workers (Sunahara 1981: 10).

A related issue concerns the degree of racism among prominent people – well-educated individuals whose influential positions render their bigotry especially pernicious. One does not have to search the literature very hard to discover qualified cases. In a House of Commons speech in 1882, Sir John A. Macdonald, Canada's first prime minister, remarked that 'a Mongolian or Chinese population in our country ... would not be a wholesome element for this country' (Sher 1983: 33). In Mackenzie King's report on East Indian immigration in 1908, he stated (Ward 1978: 83): 'It was clearly recognized in regard to emigration from India to Canada that the native of India is not a person suited to this country, that accustomed as many of them are to the conditions of a tropical climate, and possessing manners and customs so unlike those of our own people, their inability to readily adapt themselves to surroundings entirely different could not do other than entail an amount of privation and suffering which render a discontinuance of such immigration most desirable in the interests of the Indians themselves.' Reflecting on the atomic bomb, Mackenzie King wrote in his diary (Sunahara 1981: 15): 'It is fortunate that the use of the bomb should have been upon the Japanese rather than upon the white races of Europe.' After a visit to Germany in 1937, King described Hitler as sincere, sweet – a good man. Abella and Troper (1982) point out that while at times King's anti-Semitism seemed to soften, in the end he listened to the political polls which indicated that there would be no benefit to the Liberal party in allowing Jewish refugees into the country.

A number of politicians of lower rank also have been implicated in Canada's racist policies. Sunahara, for example (1981: 16, 31), refers to Halford Wilson, a Vancouver alderman before the Second World War, as a racist whose anti–Japanese-Canadian rantings were astounding. She also tells the story of Ian Alistair Mackenzie, who was a Vancouver MP and a minister in King's government. Blatantly anti-Asian, Mackenzie was a major impetus behind the Liberal party's treatment of Japanese Canadians. Palmer (1982: 158) refers to two MPs, Norman Jacques and John Blackmore, who served under Aberhart in Alberta, and were known to be anti-Semites; there also was the case of Earl Ansley, said to be a firm believer in the Jewish conspiracy (*Edmonton Sun*, 29 March 1983), who had been Aberhart's minister of education. Comparable cases in more recent years also can be found. According to Gordon (1982), David Blake, a Manitoba Conservative MLA, remarked during a legislative debate in 1978 about fees for foreign students that the universities 'were only educating niggers and chinks, anyways.' Another politician, Dan McKenzie, became a hero to the right wing after a visit to South Africa. He stated publicly that blacks are still primitive and uncivilized, and not ready for self-rule. As C-FAR's *Newsletter* (no. 69, 14 February 1982) observed after the politician was rebuked by Prime Minister Clark, 'No one quite said that McKenzie was factually wrong, just that he had no right to say what he had.' The Klan's *Spokesman* (vol. 1, no. 1) suggested that rather than being a Conservative back-bencher, McKenzie should be that party's leader. Apparently McKenzie once was a guest speaker at Fromm's Alternative Forum, addressing the issue of discrimination against English-speakers in the federal civil service.

Occasionally the racist inclinations of politicians have been backed up by influential civil servants. Abella and Troper (1982: 9) describe Frederick Charles Blair, director of the immigration branch of the Department of Mines and Resources during the Second World War, as a narrow-minded bureaucrat whose contempt for Jews was enormous; Blair played a major role in keeping Jewish refugees from entering Canada. According to Abella and Troper (1982: 178), his efforts were complemented by those of Vincent Massey, the Canadian representative to the Intergovernmental Committee on Refugees. Massey, who had been Canada's high commissioner in London during the Second World War, associated with a pro-German and anti-Semitic group in that city, and argued against admitting Jews to Canada partly on the grounds that to do so would simply contribute to anti-Semitic sentiments (Abella and Troper 1982: 48). According to Glickman (1985), Goldwin Smith, a professor of law and modern history, and 'the revered mentor of Mackenzie King,' was 'a virulent racist and anti-Semitic.' Then there is the case of a Montreal radio broadcaster and writer, who was a Conservative candidate in a Quebec by-election in 1977. This man, according to media reports, equated Zionism with Nazism and racism, and authored a book in which he claimed that fewer than one million Jews were killed by Nazis, and that Anne Frank's diary is a work of fiction.

Let us not sensationalize these examples of racist inclinations among high-profile people. The number of individuals to whom I have referred is ridiculously low. Of course, we could easily swell their ranks, pointing to other politicians and civil servants, and to clergymen who have stated a perference for Hitler over Trudeau or labelled Jews the cancer of the Western world. Yet even if we could come up with a hundred cases, or five hundred, they would merely be a drop in the bucket as regards the nation's population. However, that is not the point. What is significant about the racist inclinations of prominent people is their potential impact on wider society. It is one thing to have a disgruntled member of the Western Guard sound off in a public park. It is quite a different story to listen to authority figures promote the Aryan line.

Finally, the educational solution carries with it the assumption that racists are poorly educated and irrational if not crazy. It is true that emotion can readily trump reason in a crisis. However, that holds for all people, university professors and store clerks; racists, non-racists, and anti-racists. Canada's committed white supremacists, as it has been often stressed in this study, are not for the most part poorly educated. Nor are they necessarily less rational than the average citizen. As Fawkes (1980: 8–9), an aggressive opponent of the Ku Klux Klan, has written: 'It is too easy to write off people who join and become active in the Klan as "crazy"; this is just not true, they are not "crazy." It is because they are not crazy that they are dangerous. They have a well thought-out plan. They are prepared to move slowly but steadily towards their established goal, and they have every chance of success.' Cashmore and Troyna (1983: 233) observed that racism 'for the working class is an almost rational response to changing social circumstances.' Horton (1981: 9) argues that 'right tendencies are always inherent in capitalism in crisis and are certainly not the product of a frustrated lunatic fringe, as media propaganda would like us to believe.' Spoonley (personal communication), who has written widely on the New Zealand right wing, has expressed dissatisfaction with Lipset and Raab's portrayal (1970) of Fascist groups as 'unreasonable.' Spoonley contends that the goals and ideologies of the right wing are highly rational to its members, and that to treat Fascism as abnormal and irrational is to distort one's analysis. The conclusion that I draw is as follows: to dismiss all racists as poorly educated madmen, and conversely to promote education as the one-punch victor over prejudice, is to mystify the phenomenon of racism and therefore encourage it.

THE MEDIA

If members of the media listened to what both the racists and the anti-racists said about them, they would end up with a headache. The right wing regards the media as part of the enemy. Ross, for example, in *Web of Deceit* (1978) devotes an entire chapter to the media, contending that they are an integral part of the international Jewish conspiracy. Andrews remarked (*Nationalist Report*, issue 46) that while white nationalists can't do without media attention, they must realize 'that the media is the System's most potent tool of trickery and political distortion.' In an earlier issue (28), he expressed some doubts about the value of television and radio coverage. The fifteen second film-clip exposure, he remarked, is set up by the Zionists and their stooges to show how violent, crazy, small, and weak organizations like the Nationalist Party are. Anti-racists, however, see the media as working hand in hand with the white supremacists, giving them free advertising, seduced by the sensational story. Sometimes it is said (Pitman 1977; Head 1975; *Equality Now!* 1984) that the media promotes the image of white Canada, especially in advertising, one of the only places in which visible minorities are invisible. If we look to the literature farther afield, what we find is the consistent argument that the media are to some degree implicated in the world's racial problems. As Troyna has reported (1982), members of Britain's National Front claimed they were continuously vilified by the media, but the press actually saw the organization as rich in news value, and faithfully reported its headline-grabbing actions. Bagley(1973) found that the press in Britain had a profound and negative influence on race relations. Hartmann and Husband, in *Racism and the Mass Media* (1974: 146), contend that the media have not merely reflected public attitudes or consciousness regarding racial matters, but have significantly shaped them, thus increasing rather than decreasing white hostility towards non-whites.[16]

The media's position, let it be stressed, is a difficult one. If they ignore organizations like the Klan, are they not guilty of the avoidance syndrome referred to earlier? If the media fail to report on racist outbreaks, how will the populace know what is going on, and prepare its counter-attack? Without the media, could there *be* a counter-attack? Perhaps the most persistent criticism of the media is that they permit themselves to be manipulated by the racists. Individuals like McQuirter are allowed to give their spiel, often without accompanying editorial comment, or without inviting representatives of anti-racist organizations to provide a rebuttal. Even student newspapers on various Canadian campuses were guilty in this respect at the height of McQuirter's impact. For example, *The Ubyssey* (27 November 1981), the University of British Columbia's organ, reported on an interview on campus with the Klan leader: 'Alex McQuirter looks like somebody you'd meet in a disco. Or maybe a commerce class. He has the aura of a confident, bright young man on the road to success. He hardly looks like one of Canada's leading racists.' The writer went on to report McQuirter's claim that there were more than twenty Klan members on the campus. There was no editorial comment or evaluation. The negative reaction was soon to come. A letter was printed (*Ubyssey*, 7 January 1982) from

16 See *Currents* (vol. 1, no. 2, Spring 1983) for an analysis of minorities in the media.

a student criticizing the newspaper for providing McQuirter with a propaganda platform, and not including an accompanying evaluation of the organization's history and goals. A week later (15 January 1982) another contributor repeated the criticism. In that same issue, the author of the original article on the Klan tried to make things right by identifying himself as a 'solid leftist student journalist' and by referring to McQuirter as 'the most hateful, dangerous and cruel person you've ever talked to in your life.' Yet, as another contributor observed (*Ubyssey*, 19 January 1982), although the student had asked for the reader's sympathy, he had brought on his own problems by simply allowing the Klan leader to say his piece. There is every reason to believe that the staff members of *The Ubyssey* were exceptionally disturbed by the interview with McQuirter, and even intimidated. Indeed, when I talked to some of them several months after the interview they still were partly in shock. It was that reaction to the Klan leader, I suspect, that led them simply to state the facts that McQuirter set before them. However, if one is constrained from placing organizations like the Klan in perspective, from editorializing and evaluating the content of their beliefs and goals, probably no coverage is better than some.

All of this suggests that the critical dimension in the treament of racism is perspective. Merely to report on the antics of white supremacists, which often are deliberately aimed at the media's eye, is tantamount to promoting their cause. Yet even explicit attempts to denounce organizations such as the Klan can backfire. In 1921, the liberal New York *World* ran a series of articles exposing and condemning the Klan. To the newspaper's astonishment, public reaction was one of intrigue and interest in the men and women in white hoods (Alexander 1965: 9). As Calbreath has remarked (1981), a comparable but more recent exposure of the Klan in the Nashville *Tennessean* was apparently applauded by Klan leaders, one of whom said he was flattered and impressed by the coverage. Similarly, when a Toronto newspaper ran an exposé on the Western Guard, representatives of the group expressed delight, claiming the article had resulted in a number of inquiries from potential members. Any kind of media coverage, even the most negative, Calbreath has pointed out, often was welcomed by the white supremacists. Yet my own view is that it is too facile to dismiss all media attention as counter-productive. First, while media coverage – even the most critical and negative – may well attract new recruits to racist organizations, it may equally stiffen the opposition to them among the general populace. To overlook the latter possibility is to distort the picture. Second, if the aim is to contain and suppress racism, some media promotion of such organizations may be an unavoidable cost. The alternative is to do nothing, or to apply the quarantine technique, which may carry even more risk. The litmus test concerns the stage of development of the racist organizations themselves. If they only consist of a handful of vocal individuals, reporting on them may backfire. But if they are organized, numerous, and expanding, and show signs of reaching the ears of part of the wider population, the insulation technique has outlived its usefulness. [17]

THE POLICE

From the viewpoint of visible minorities, policemen are often regarded as part of the enemy. Cardinal Carter (1979: 16) observed in his report on tensions between the police and minorities in Toronto: 'Perhaps nothing in all my research was more universal than a sense of frustration about real or fancied injustice or harassment at the hands of police officers.' As Charles Roach (1980: 27) has pointed out, racial prejudice among policemen is a much more serious problem than among citizens at large, because the police possess the legitimate power and force to act out their prejudices on innocent victims. Wilson Head, in an article printed in *News and Views* (vol. 31, no. 14, February 1981: 13), the Toronto Police Association's magazine, observed that while in his opinion policemen were no more hostile than other citizens to racial minorities, it would be naive to assume that all of them were free of racist inclinations. *News and Views* itself provides some insight into the mentality of the police. In one issue (vol. 31, no. 12, December 1980), Sergeant Ed Pearson, the former head of Metro Toronto's Ethnic Squad, remarked that policemen, including himself, find it difficult to recognize individual black people. [18] This represents the 'they all look alike' syndrome, comparable to the former colonial situation in which a new white arrival supposedly was mistaken for his predecessor of an earlier decade or two, and my initial reaction is to dismiss it as so much duplicity. Nevertheless, I myself can recall my early experiences in the class-room while with CUSO in Nigeria. For the first few days I only noticed black faces.

17 It is easy to come up with polar-opposite examples of the media's orientation towards racism. A Regina radio station, CKRM, was charged by the Canadian Radio-Television and Telecommunications Committee with broadcasting racially abusive material (*Globe and Mail*, 4 June 1977). However, there was the remarkable in-depth investigation of racism aired in March 1981 by Radio CKWX in Vancouver over a period of almost two weeks and published as a report entitled *Focus on Racism*.
18 There are now special ethnic squads in several Canadian cities. I had occasion to meet some of their members, and my evaluation is divided. One policeman whom I talked to was sensitive and sophisticated, but another man in a different city impressed me as naive, prejudiced, poorly trained, and incompetent for the job.

But after a couple of weeks colour suddenly vanished; all that I saw thereafter were individuals. All of this might be taken as support for Pearson's point, but I am sceptical. First of all, the sheer number of blacks in Canada today surely had rendered passé the syndrome in which they all look alike. Second, the syndrome itself can be a manipulative tool. Cardinal Carter (1979: 16), for example, referred to a policeman who said if the black man whom he was harassing lodged a complaint, he would simply claim that the man's description fitted that of a wanted person.

What is significant is that despite the concern, no doubt much of it justified, on the part of racial minorities about unfair police treatment, the police have played a major role in containing the radical right. Undercover police agents and hired infiltrators have provided a constant surveillance of the principal organizations. As I eventually realized, there was very little that I learned about the right wing (in terms of facts, if not analysis) that was not already known by the country's various intelligence agencies. In one province, I was told, the police had the Klan ducking for cover partly as a result of borderline strong-arm tactics of dubious legality. It was the legwork of the police, it must be recalled, that led to the successful legal prosecution of a number of right-wing enthusiasts: Beattie in the 1960s, Andrews in 1976, Taylor in 1979–80, McQuirter in 1982, and Zundel and Keegstra in 1985.

A related issue concerns the number of individual policemen in right-wing organizations. Sergeant Pearson reportedly remarked (*Toronto Star*, 17 July 1981) that the rigid right includes senior police officers. An intelligence officer in British Columbia pointed out to me that non-reflective policemen are inclined to agree with much of the right wing's conservative platform, without questioning the implied racist message. No doubt the police ranks are peppered with highly conservative individuals. But that does not mean that they have rushed out to join the various right-wing organizations. On the contrary, what has been remarkable about Canada is that so few policemen have been formal members of the right wing. The ones I learned about are as follows: a former RCMP officer who was a member of Arcand's Fascist organization before the Second World War; Pat Walsh, Gostick's subaltern, who apparently had been an RCMP undercover informer or agent; four members of the Royal Canadian Artillery who were members of the Fascist Canadian Nationalist Party in Ontario before the Second World War; on the sidelines there have been others such as the chief of police in Oakville in the 1920s who threw his support behind members of the Klan after they had staged a parade on the main street, and an RCMP constable who sang the praises of Keegstra, his former teacher.

Any effort to understand the police's role as regards the right wing and racism must consider two important issues. First, policing by its very nature is conservative, an instrument to maintain the status quo. Attempts by the police to contain and eradicate the radical right do not necessarily reflect a deep-root opposition to the far right. Instead, the police are opposed to all sectors of society that upset the applecart, including the extreme right and the extreme left. As Sergeant Pearson once stated, life for policemen would be a lot easier without the loony left and the rigid right. The second issue concerns a deep contradiction not just within the police's role, but also within the state more generally: official sectors of society flawed by racist inclinations that have been institutionalized over the decades, while simultaneously participating in eradicating them, responding to liberal values that have outgrown the social fabric. A great deal of the ambiguity surrounding the police's relationship to racism is a product of that contradiction.

THE STATE

Our last remarks lead us directly to the state. On the face of it, the state's record in confronting racism looks reasonably sound. There was the Cohen Report on hate groups in the 1960s, the effort to rid immigration policy of its most blatant bigotry, and the prosecution of prominent anti-Semites. In one government report, *Equality Now!* (1984), it was recommended that in cases of racially motivated criminal acts, an additional consecutive sentence should be imposed. In another report, *National Strategy on Race Relations* (n.d.), direct reference is made to the institutional nature of racism; indeed, it is stated that only by changing the structures of society can racism by combated. The implications of that statement are dramatic. There would appear to be no other interpretation than to assume that what is being recommended is a transformation of society along socialist lines, for what other kind of massive institutional change is even theoretically capable of addressing the phenomenon of racism? At this point, one can be excused for wondering just how serious the government is. Are such far-reaching recommendations meant simply as tranquillizers? Is the underlying assumption that to verbalize the problem is to shelve it? Not a few experts in the field of race relations, themselves recipients of numerous government research grants, contend that the government is playing a game. For example, while it is generally conceded that the various human rights commissions have served a purpose, they also are known to be severely limited, partly because they are complaint-based, dealing with each case on an individual basis, and partly because as government agencies they are restrained in investigating state-linked complaints.

Numerous critics also have found the country's policy of multiculturalism wanting. As Moodley (1981: 13) put it, the charter-group ethnics in Canada, after having gained control over the nation's institutions, 'can now afford to stress ethnicity as an ornament for ceremonial purposes.'[19] Peter (1981: 59–60) has declared that the government's bilingual policy was nothing more than an effort to appease Quebec and contain its political aspirations, and that multiculturalism served to prop up the dominance of the ruling English-speaking élite in the face of threats from Quebec and from increasingly aggressive ethnic groups. Kallen (1982: 165–9) concluded her critique of multiculturalism by stating: 'Intentionally or not, the multicultural policy perserves the *reality* of the Canadian ethnic hierarchy – the Vertical Mosaic of ethnic inequality – rooted in long-term discrimination and denial of human rights.' Elsewhere (*Currents*, vol. 2, no. 1, 1984: 14) it is suggested that multiculturalism, limited to the cultural realm (folk dances etc.), fails to confront the real structural, social, economic, and political barriers to full participation in Canadian society; it is even argued that multiculturalism actually promotes divisiveness, as different ethnic groups compete among themselves for funds. Burnet (1975: 39), while expressing strong support for the policy of multiculturalism, nevertheless wonders whether it will inadvertently 'foster the retention of ethnic and racial animosities and adverse ethnic and racial stereotypes.'

What is one to make of all these criticisms? Is the government serious about tackling racism, or is it only pretending to do so? The answer, I believe, is both. The explanation again concerns the notion of a deep-set contradiction in the state and its principal apparatuses. The state is intrinsically flawed by racism by virtue of the latter's institutionalization, benefits from it in terms of maintaining the existing balance of advantage and disadvantage, but is part of the active forces to eradicate racism, which means changing the state itself. State policy, conditioned as it is by the two sides of the contradiction, flip-flops back and forth between openly opposing and quietly condoning racist expression, providing grants to people like myself to tackle racism, but hoping that our research conclusions will be innocuous.

19 Bob Rae, Ontario NDP leader, also reportedly has accused the government (Toronto *Sun*, 3 November 1981) of 'folkloric multiculturalism ... urging ethnic groups to get together, have dances and write about their history and language, but still conform to Anglo-Saxon ways.'

CONCLUSION

The persistent message in this chapter has been that racism in Canada has been institutionalized, a conclusion which merely echoes the pioneering work of Hughes and Kallen (1974: 214), who observed that racism in this country is as deeply rooted as that in the United States. This point brings us to two contentious issues. The first concerns the relationship, if any, between such institutional racism and the white supremacism and anti-Semitism of the ultra-right. It would be unjustified to conclude that it has been proved that the former has caused the latter, or the converse. However, they are logically compatible phenomena, and it is plausible to suggest that the racism embedded in the wider society has provided an environment in which the radical right has been able to take root. Organized racism, in other words, would appear to represent a more overt and extreme version of weaker impulses beating within the heart of the larger social organism.

The second issue is even more controversial: whether the racist ideology of the far right and the milder forms embedded in the nation's institutions have a common source. Many Marxists would assert that they do, contending that both are related manifestations of efforts by the rich to divide the poor and in that way sustain patterns of privilege. Before dismissing this perspective as ideological dribble, we would do well to remember the contradiction built into the state: its diligent and even courageous attempts to redress racism, partly handcuffed by its own (unrecognized) racist character, the legacy of decades of institutionalized prejudice and discrimination. Moreover, as I remarked in chapter 1, and as I shall argue more elaborately in the next chapter, racism is foremost an instrument of power. If that is indeed the case, the relationship of all forms of racism – overt and covert, blatant and mild, conscious or otherwise – to power and privlege should at least be entertained. [20]

20 Implicit in these remarks are the quite different interpretations of racism embraced by the Western state and by Marxists. From the state's perspective, racism appears to be regarded as a regrettable but atypical social problem, located, when it does occur, among the ranks of the ignorant masses. The role of the enlightened state is to use its forces, including the police, the courts, and media instruments, to protect minority members from the vile assaults launched by deviant members of society. Many Marxists, in contrast, would trace racism back to the interests of the state itself, dismissing state intervention as so much duplicity, and contending that even if the majority of people share the state's interpretation of racism, that merely indicates the unfortunate efficacy of its ideology.

If it is no longer incomprehensible how so many right-wing organizations and members could exist in Canada, it remains puzzling how Canadians have been able to maintain a reputation for tolerance and harmony. What has characterized Canada, Moodley (1981: 15) has observed, has been 'an ostrich-like denial that a significant problem of racial hostility exists at all.' One explanation, I think, has been the absence of large influxes of Third World immigrants until after 1967; the tolerance of Canadian citizens simply was not tested before, especially since Native peoples and various other minority groups were well under control. A second reason concerns the Canadian proclivity to do things quietly; the country's racism, like its foreign policy, is low-keyed; as one Canadian black woman observed, racism in Canada is like a hair you can feel but not see. A third reason has to do with the reaction of victims. Race victims, as Sunahara has remarked (1981: 1), are like rape victims; they remain silent, ashamed to talk about what has happened to them. Moreover, the newcomers among them have not wanted to rock the boat, at least until recently. Finally, there is again the peculiar role of the state. Conventional wisdom, even academic wisdom, suggests that in comparison with that of the United States, Canada's history has been harmonious and placid, and relatively free of racism. The ready explanation concerns the greater political and economic control in Canada, and the associated values of tolerance, order, and respect for authority. All this accounts for, according to Clark (1954), the greater number of radical social movements, presumably including racist ones, below the border in comparison with the Canadian scene. Quite a different perspective has been offered by McNaught (1970). Not only does he contend that Canada's non-violent image is belied by its history, but he also identifies the peculiar nature of violence in Canada: the much greater degree, in comparison with the United States, to which violence has been linked to the state, to which it has been intrinsic to the operations of the political system itself. In other words, what distinguishes Canada from the United States is that violence in the former has tended to be more official than private, which means it has been more masked. With the history of the country's immigration policy in mind, as well as the treatment of the Japanese and Jews during the Second World War, and not least of all the proud but disputable reputation for tolerance, perhaps the same can be said about the nation's racism.

12

Deeper Questions

In the previous chapter we dealt with the following question: *how* can the right wing, and racism specifically, exist in Canada? In this chapter we turn to a different question: *why* does the right wing exist? This question can be conveniently broken down into two parts. First, why does the right wing exist from the perspective of the members themselves? Second, why does it exist from the perspective of the investigator? The initial question brings us face to face with a dominant theme throughout this study – the God-is-a-racist theme. No doubt individual right-wing members are motivated by a range of factors such as a lament for the idealized past, job insecurity, and hostility towards communism. Yet there is an overriding dimension that knits all the issues together: the presumed decay of Western Christian civilization, the identification of Western culture and white people with Christianity. From the viewpoint of members of the right wing, the language of their movement is the language of the Bible; its goals are Christian goals. The paramount importance of Christianity in the right wing introduces an additional problem. Before the nineteenth century, racism was rationalized by religious determinism. Yet the prevailing assumption among scholars, both regarding racism in general (Rex 1973: 191) and anti-Semitism in particular (Trachtenberg 1943: 219; Laqueur 1972: 29; Beloff 1982: 9), is that religious determinism has been replaced by biological determinism. In other words, scientific racism has supplanted theological racism. As far as the Canadian right wing is concerned, there is indeed a great deal of evidence of scientific racism, but it is overwhelmed by the religious variety. My argument will be that from the perspective of the right winger's mentality, theological racism constitutes the deeper explanation.[1]

---

1 Some writers might restrict racism to the scientific or biological variety. Ruth Benedict (1960: 187), for example, stated: 'Race prejudice isn't an old universal "instinct." It

SCIENTIFIC RACISM

Are white people inferior? As Harris has pointed out (1971: 510), if judged by all but the last 1,000 of the past 12,000 years, Northern Europeans would be included among the world's most retarded peoples. At the time when civilization thrived in Mesopotamia and the Indus Valley, Europeans had only barely settled into village life. Recall, too, the achievements of China at the beginning of the Christian calendar, and Songhay's Timbuctoo, with its university, palaces, and armies. Ironically, Cicero, after Britain was defeated by Julius Caesar, remarked (Leiris 1961: 207) that the British were too stupid to make good slaves, and advised his friends not to buy any of them. None of this is intended to disparage peoples of European origin, but simply to balance the radical right's claim of white superiority.

Racists assume a high correlation among biological, cultural, and intellectual development and that the white 'species' is far out in front, the least ape-like of all human populations; they rest their analysis on observable physical criteria (phenotypes) such as skin colour, amount of hair, and body stature. Yet one could easily point out that both Caucasoids and Mongoloids have thin lips, like those of an ape, but Negroids have thick lips, and in this respect can be said to be the most excessively human (Boas 1962: 39). Or one could observe that Caucasoids and Australoids have much more body hair than Negroids and Mongoloids, which again places Aryan closer than blacks to the ape. The point is, of course, that attempts to define and rank the perceived racial types in terms of such physical criteria are both obsolete and meaningless. Today physical anthropologists and human biologists operate with genotypes, and the consistent conclusion is that a taxonomy of human populations determined by genetic compostion contains virtually no overlap with that corresponding to phenotypes. Indeed, as Bohannan has wittily commented (1963: 192), rather than dividing the world's population into categories such as Negroid, Caucasoid, Mongoloid, and Australoid, it makes just as much sense to employ a beverage classification: milky white, café au lait, chocolat chaud, and weak tea.

There exists in the right-wing literature a virtual liturgy of famous names, repeated references to authority figures who have innocently or

---

is hardly a hundred years old. Before that, people persecuted Jews because of their religion – not their "blood"; they enslaved Negroes because they were pagans – not for being black.' Yet the religious variety was equally deterministic, and its targets were identifiable populations – blacks and Jews. Thus, in my view it makes eminent sense to talk in terms of both scientific and theological racism.

otherwise made racist-like statements. Toynbee, Churchill, Kipling, Pound, Bryon, Ford, Leacock – and even Lincoln and Jefferson – are eulogized as confirmed white supremacists or anti-Semites. Sometimes academic work, such as that focusing on racial strains, is ripped out of context to prove that the different races cannot live together; or studies indicating racial harmony are dismissed as phoney, their underlying purpose being to flash a green light to further Third World immigration. The fact is, however, that there is little need for the white supremacists to resort to distortion: a sizeable body of scientific racist literature is readily at hand.[2] Burt (1966) and Jensen (1969) have concluded that whites are a distinctive, advanced, intellectually superior race; the reported lower IQ scores among blacks, they claim, are due to genetics rather than environment. The latest fads in scientific racism are socio-biology and historical revisionism; the first supposedly explains why different races can't coexist; the second supposedly proves that the Holocaust is a myth, and implies the existence of a Jewish conspiracy. As Montagu has observed (1980: 13), socio-biology has proved a godsend to the extreme right wing. Montagu added that to his knowledge no socio-biologist has bothered to repudiate the misuse of that scholarly framework by organizations such as the Ku Klux Klan. Martin Webster, formerly a leading figure in Britain's National Front, remarked (Billig 1979: 9) that Jensen's work on IQ differences between blacks and whites provided racists with a tremendous source of self-confidence. In an article entitled 'Psychology and the Legitimation of Apartheid,' Colman (1972: 9) pointed out that former South African premier Dr H.F. Verwoerd was a professor of psychology, and that Jensen's famous article 'was ecstatically reviewed by psychologists in South Africa, as "proving scientifically"what white South Africans had known all along.'

The Western Guard's Taylor has referred to anthropology as the queen of the sciences. In one of that organization's documents it is stated: 'for a few thousand years now the most important science of mankind has been its anthropology.' Of course, Taylor had physical anthropology in mind. Social and cultural anthropology, in his view, are little better than sociology; all of them, he contends, erroneously promote environment over heredity, class over race, and egalitarianism over hierarchy – the legacy of Boasian anthropology. Taylor cites academic work to demonstrate that Europeans are naturally repulsed by the odour of Africans. In the Western

---

2 There is, of course, a large body of anti-scientific racism literature (Montagu 1942 and 1963; Comas 1961; Dobzhansky 1963), but it rarely penetrates the radical right's consciousness, and when it does it is dismissed as liberal pablum, promoted by white race-traitors or Jews.

Guard's 'Green Paper on Immigration' it was stated that most white people feel a natural revulsion at the mere physical appearance of the African race. Direct reference was made there to the work of the anthropologist Carlton Coon (1962). The Northern League, which caters to the interests of the Teutonic nations (Billig 1979: 7), was founded by a British anthropologist, Roger Pearson. Elsewhere (*Washington Post*, 30 May 1978) there is an account of Pearson's links to William Carto's Liberty Lobby (a Washington-based anti-Semitic organization), and to the World Anti-Communist League. Occasionally right-wing members in Canada indicated they knew Pearson, or at least his writings. As Billig (1978: 164) has pointed out, for the past three centuries Western science has been a consistent source of racist mythology; to dismiss racism as a prejudice embraced only by the uneducated, as incompatible with science and knowledge, he argues, is erroneous and unjustified. That was precisely my point in the previous chapter.[3]

THEOLOGICAL RACISM

In the 1920s in Canada, a prospective member of the Ku Klux Klan had to declare that he was 'a loyal white Protestant ... believing in the tenets of Christianity.' In *The Thunderbolt* (vol. 1, no. 5, 20 August 1937), published by the Canadian Union of Fascists, it was claimed that Christianity and Fascism cannot be separated. Arcand portrayed Hitler as the champion of Christianity, just as several comtemporary white supremacists have remarked that the Nazi leader has been the greatest Christian to appear on earth since Christ. God is a racist – the source of the title of this book – appeared in several places in *Straight Talk*, in *Aryan*, and in Taylor's recorded telephone messages. One such message (12 January 1977) stated: 'God is a racist. The seventh commandment means no race mixing ... Had God wanted coffee-coloured mongrels, He would have made us that way.' The Western Guard has portrayed itself as 'the patriotic Christian right.' Andrews once remarked (Johanson 1974): 'Religion is a racial thing and white people's religion is Christianity.' McQuirter contended (McAlpine 1981: 4) that the Ku Klux Klan is an expression of 'positive Christianity' and that race-mixing is 'evil and unChristian.' David Duke, while still with his American Klan organization, said he wouldn't accept an atheist as a member. The fringe right has been equally animated by religious concerns.

---

3 See the special issue entitled 'Racism in Science' in *Science for the People* (vol. 14, no. 2, March/April 1982).

The *Canadian Intelligence Service* was dedicated to the defence of Christian values. In the Alberta branch of the federal Social Credit party, fundamentalist Christianity and politics were entwined. Keegstra was the living example of the fusion of right-wing principles and Christian theology. Some organizations regarded homosexuality, foreign aid, fluoride, and centralized government as anti-Christian.

It would be easy to add substantially to these examples, but to do so would be redundant, for the Christian orientation of the right wing in Canada has been alluded to repeatedly throughout this study. Some organizations, however, have not been adequately described, such as Tradition, Family and Property (TFP), known in Canada as Young Canadians for a Christian Civilization. TFP was founded in Brazil in 1960. It is an anticommunist Catholic movement concerned to protect free enterprise and Western Christian civilization. In Brazil it has fought against land reform. In Canada it has levelled its attack against the 'Marxian-oriented' Canadian Catholic Organization for Development and Peace. In Spain it actively opposed legislation to make divorce easier to obtain. TFP, which sends volunteers in caravans around the countryside, apparently is well-funded. On one occasion, for example, it placed a six-page advertisement in *The Globe and Mail*. The two TFP representatives whom I met (they actually came to my office to interview me!) avowed that the organization was not racist or violent, and indeed it has been the fringe right in Canada that has regarded it as an ally. Urbonas, for example, spoke enthusiastically about TFP, and several years ago in the Edmund Burke Society's organ (*Straight Talk*, vol. 4, no. 4, January 1972) TFP was described as 'militants for a Western Christian civilization ... While maintaining that their strongest weapon is prayer, TFP militants are, nevertheless, well trained in self-defence.' As far back as 1971 there were TFP branches in Montreal and Toronto. During the Kosygin crisis involving Geza Matrai that year, a TFP representative paid a visit to the Edmund Burke Society headquarters (*Straight Talk*, vol. 4, no. 2, December 1971).

Chick Comic Books, a California-based organization founded by Baptist, Jack T. Chick, is also worthy of mention. Its Canadian branch is called Christ Is the Answer, Inc. Both anti-Semitism and anti-Catholicism figure prominently in the Chick publications. 'Support Your Local Jew,' for example, begins by saying that Egypt, the most advanced, powerful nation on earth, was the envy of the world, but it didn't support its local Jews and thus was ruined. In Rome the Jews were mistreated, and the Roman Empire disintegrated. Various African countries that have suffered from famine and drought, the publication observes, had all previously broken diplomatic ties with Israel. Even the British Empire is said to have fallen apart because Britain failed to give Israel all of Palestine. The story ends sarcastically: 'If you are already a true believer in Christ ... then pray for Israel and support your local Jew. God will bless you for it.' In 1981, Chick Comic Books containing an anti-Catholic message were distributed in Moncton, New Brunswick (*Moncton Times*, 7 November 1981). In 1984, two of its anti-Catholic publications, 'Alberto' and 'Double Cross,' appeared in Winnipeg, Manitoba (*Globe and Mail*, 20 April 1984). In 1981, Canada's customs and excise department banned 'Double Cross' and 'The Big Betrayal.' However, the importer appealed that verdict, and in August 1982 in Milton, Ontario, he won the court case.

ALTERNATIVES TO CHRISTIANITY

On one occasion during an interview with a wealthy supporter of the far right, he voiced the opinion that Christianity may not be an adequate force to counter the white man's enemies. If the battle for white society and Western civilization is to be won, he said, an alternative to Christianity must be found – a religion, he added, that could be as powerful and effective as Judaism has been for Jews. In this section I describe four religious alternatives to Christianity that have emerged in right-wing circles.

Odinism

In Norse mythology Odin is the supreme being, god of art, culture, war, and the dead; it is identified with the chief Germanic god Woden. Followers of Odin regard Christianity as an alien religion, a despotic religion, which preaches submission, universal brotherhood, and equality – all of which are seen as antithetical to folkish, tribalistic Aryans. In an article (unattributed, n.d.) entitled 'An Introduction to Odinism,' it is contended that Marxism is the 'secular gospel of Judeo-Christianity.' Odinism is referred to as 'Aryan religious philosophy.' The hope of Odinists is that folkish, tribalistic Aryans will overcome their generous and compassionate nature, which had made them vulnerable to unnatural Christianity, and embrace their religion, Odinism. While Odinism has not been a significant movement in Canada, there nevertheless have been some adherents. Back in the Beattie-Stanley era of the early 1960s, there were Odinists in Toronto, and according to *Countdown* (vol. 2, no. 1, 1973), a group of Odinists met four times per year in that city in the early 1970s. Andrews once remarked (Crysdale and Durham 1977: 15) that there were Odinists in the Western Guard around that time. One Odinist who was active in Toronto in the 1980s had been associated with fringe-right organizations since the Edmund Burke Society days.

Creativity

Creativity is a sect based in Florida. Connected to it is the Church of the Creator. This sect contends that Christianity has poisoned the white man's mind, and must be replaced by a sound racial religion. Creativity doesn't believe in a hereafter or in a Supreme Being. Yet in one document it insists that it is a religion, based on natural law: 'Our religion is rooted in race, and based upon the Eternal Laws of Nature. We are therefore a racial religion and a natural religion.' In that document it is stated that one of its tenets is to hate Jews, blacks, and other coloured peoples: 'if you love and want to defend those whom you love – your own family, your own White race, then hate for your enemies comes natural and is inevitable.' Reference is made to the 'suicidal' teaching of Christianity, specifically the tenet 'love your enemies.' Creativity's own golden rule is that that which is good for the white race is the highest virtue, and that which is bad for it is the ultimate sin. Jews are considered to be the white race's most deadly enemies, followed by all the other 'mud' peoples who compete for food and living space on this limited planet. Creativity spokesmen state that its program is similar to Hitler's, but point out that Hitler's mistake was to confine his interest to Germans. Creativity, in contrast, aims its message at the entire white race, regardless of national boundaries. There is not much evidence of Creativity's presence in Canada, although its emphasis on natural order is reflected in Taylor's erstwhile organization that went by the same name, and in the periodic remarks in the Western Guard, the Nationalist Party, and the Ku Klux Klan about the natural (i.e., healthy) distrust and hatred that one race has for others. One Canadian, with past activity in several white-supremacist groups, who has been associated with Creativity has indulged in an interesting sideline. From time to time he dresses up as a priest and goes door to door soliciting funds.

Black and Red Front

In Toronto in 1982 a new organization emerged. While it was dedicated to destroying Jewry, what was significant about it was its socialist and religious programs. The Black and Red Front, which to my knowledge only consisted of a handful of members, was established to promote the cause of 'revolutionary racial-socialists.' It is anti-capitalist, and contends that Hitler failed because he betrayed the socialist part of National Socialism; in this context direct reference is made to Gregor Strasser and his famous clash with Hitler over the socialist dimension. As far as religion is concerned, a spokesman for the Black and Red Front, who had formerly been involved with some of Canada's most extreme racist organizations, contended that Christianity has been manipulated and contaminated by Jews: 'We declare ourselves anti-Christian and against everything for which established Christianity stands.' He went on to say: 'We propose a new religion ... The core of this religion is our belief that since we have not been able to find God, we must become God ourselves.' That statement, of course, sounds not just a little like Marx, and one wonders to what extent the overlap was appreciated by the members of the new organization.

British Israel and Identity

The basic belief of British Israel is that the true people of Israel in the Bible are not Jews, but instead Anglo-Saxon and kindred peoples, including those in Canada and the United States. The movement began in the 1800s in Britain. The Anglo-Israel Association was founded in 1874, and the British Israel Identity Corporation in 1880. British Israel people are thought to be the lost tribes of Israel. The royal family, it is believed, is the head of British Israel; Christ will soon return to earth and occupy the British throne, preserved for him by Queen Elizabeth II. Members of the movement live in hope that the queen will soon make a public statement to that effect.

British Israel has a headquarters in Toronto (in Vancouver the movement apparently is known as the Associated Covenant People) in an old house bearing the painted sign 'British-Israel World Foundation.' The man in charge, about fifty-five years old, a former farmer with a high-school education, said that the movement is interdenominational; a member of British Israel for twenty-eight years when I met him, he himself is an Anglican. Meetings are held on the second Sunday of every month. There is a regular publication, *The Prophetic Expositor*, that stresses conventional right-wing issues such as the threat of communism. In one pamphlet, it was suggested that Canada may actually be the centre of 'the Kingdom of God on Earth,' a contention often made by John Ross Taylor. In 1984 the theme at one British Israel meeting in Toronto was 'Our Royal Traditions.' The organization also has a regular radio program. According to the Toronto representative of British Israel, the movement is only mildly right wing, and, he regretted, not politically active. Beattie used to belong to the organization, but was forced to resign because of his Nazi views. The representative did refer very positively to Gostick's Canadian Intelligence Service, to which he formerly belonged. More significantly, during our interview in walked no other than Taylor himself. The two men, according to the representative, were good friends, but he added that Taylor was not allowed to promote the Western Guard while at British Israel. Taylor, by the way, told me later that British Israel was distributing the 'Protocols' forty years ago.

The movement known as Identity, and sometimes referred to as the Gospel of the Kingdom, Kingdom Identity, or Christian Israel, evolved out of British Israel, taking root in North America in the late 1800s.[4] Identity today is a loosely knit movement consisting of several different groups but having no precise central organization. It constitutes an umbrella for white-supremacist, Nazi, and survivalist groups. It is part of a racial theological movement in North America that tries to make racism acceptable to ordinary citizens by revealing biblical proof of white supremacy.

Identity, one of its Canadian members told me, means exactly that: who they are. The answer is the people of Israel, God's chosen people. Like its British Israel predecessor, Identity's basic belief is that Jesus was not a Jew: instead, he was an ancestor of British, Germanic, and Scandinavian peoples. Identity believes that the white race is descended from Adam; that the black and yellow races were created before Adam, and thus have no direct connection with God; and that Jews are descended from Satan, who seduced Eve, resulting in the birth of Cain, the father of the Jewish 'seedline.' The belief that Adam was not the first man on earth, but instead the first white man, helps to clear up a confusion that often is apparent in the public utterances of racists. Sometimes, with Coon's thesis in mind that blacks evolved into *Homo sapiens* 200,000 years after whites, the white race is said to be the oldest on earth. Yet from the Identity perspective, it is the youngest. Finally, Identity followers believe that white men are fundamentally distinctive: God, they claim, gave white man a body, soul, and spirit, while all other races (and animals!) have no soul. Because Identity remains Christ-centred, it may be argued that it does not constitute a definite alternative to Christianity. Yet Christianity has been redefined to such an extent that it has little in common with its conventional manifestations.

Not all members of Identity preach racism and violence. Herbert W. Armstrong, the founder of the Worldwide Church of God, was an Identity member. His monthly publication, *The Plain Truth* (established in 1934, containing no advertising, distributed freely, and printed in five languages), ran articles on current political events, divorce, drug abuse, Britain's decline, and creationism versus evolutionism. Armstrong also had a radio

---

4 See 'The "Identity Churches": A Theology of Hate.' ADL Facts, vol. 28, no. 1, Spring 1983.

program called 'The World Tomorrow,' and was associated with Ambassador College in California. The vast majority of organizations and individuals connected to Identity, nevertheless, very definitely fall into the radical-right camp. The Aryan Nations, which I described in chapter 7, is an Identity member, as is Posse Comitatus. The latter group, established in the United States in 1969, composed of loosely affiliated bands of vigilantes and survivalists ('posse comitatus' translates loosely as 'power to the county'), has gained a reputation for combining the power of the gun with devotion to God. In a taped radio broadcast, one of its members declared (see ADL Memorandum, 7 March 1983): 'it's time Christians quit being afraid of the Jews ... We're going to fight for Jesus Christ, and anybody who gets in the way is going to get wiped out.' Another member of Identity is Robert Miles, the Michigan Klansman who attended the Western Guard banquet in Toronto in 1972, and later was convicted for bombing school buses. Tom Metzger, a California Klansman who won the Democratic nomination for the San Diego area a few years ago, also belongs to Identity. In Canada, I met Identity members in British Columbia and Alberta, but while British Israel had a headquarters in Toronto, there was little evidence that Identity had even a modest following among Ontario's radical-right groups. Finally, there is the case of Colonel Jack Mohr, the man who once spoke in Toronto on behalf of the John Birch Society. Mohr, former war veteran and Baptist minister, apparently switched to the Identity movement about 1980.[5] He was a guest speaker at the League of Rights conference in Calgary in 1983. The topic of his speech was 'The Brainwashing of Christendom'! Among his main points were familiar ones that communism is basically Jewish, that white Christian civilization is under a combined attack by communists and Jews, and that only the white race has been receptive to Christ's message. The basic thrust of Identity, however, is anything but familiar. It doesn't merely accuse Jews of deicide, but goes much farther. It seeks to supplant Jews, to deny their very existence.

THE WIDER SOCIETY

One might think that the religious basis of anti-Semitism, Christian or otherwise, is confined to the right wing, but that is far from the truth.[6] As

5 See his booklet, *Know Your Enemies!* (Merricmac, Mass.: Destiny Publishers, 1982). There he quotes the famous words of Burke: 'All that is necessary for evil to succeed, is for good men to do nothing.'
6 Millett (1982), incidentally, has argued that not only have all the major churches in Canada been ethnically organized, but they also have operated to preserve ethnic identity long after that function ceased to occur in other institutions.

Glock and Stark (1966) contended, Christian teaching, especially the Christ-killer theme, is the single most important cause of anti-Semitism. Quinley and Glock (1979: 94–109) pointed out that to some extent anti-Semitism persists today in main-stream churches, not just in fundamentalist ones. Trachtenberg (1943: 6) argued that while anti-Semitism pre-dated Christianity, the deicide theme gave rise to the demonological character of Jews, which continued to shape people's views in the twentieth century. Kallen (1971: 23) contended that to some degree anti-Semitism exists in every Christian country in the world. As he concluded: 'If you can end this teaching that the Jews are enemies of God and of mankind you will strike anti-Semitism at its foundations.' More recently (*Globe and Mail*, 23 March 1985), a Church of England bishop stated 'that Christianity, more than any other of the world's major religions, has succumbed to racism and that much of the blame rests with anti-Semitism in the Bible.' Memmi (1971: 189) has alluded to the threat of Christianity to Jews, rather than the reverse: 'To the Jew who still believes and professes his own religion, Christianity is the greatest theological and metaphysical usurpation in his history; it is a spiritual scandal, a subversion and blasphemy.'

Memmi (1971: 40) also referred with surprise to the widespread anti-Semitism in Canada. In 1983, in direct response to the Keegstra affair, a seminar was held at St Jerome's Centre for Catholic Experience in Waterloo, Ontario. The centre's director stated (*Toronto Star*, 29 October 1983) that rather than being an outrageous exception, Keegstra's anti-Semitism was only one instance of a common problem built into the history of Christianity.[7] In 1971 (*Globe and Mail*, 6 December 1971) the Reverend Paul Smith of the Peoples Church in Toronto apparently commented during a radio broadcast that if given a choice in an election he would choose Hitler over Prime Minister Trudeau. A decade later, according to reports, the Reverend Paul Melnichuk (Toronto *Sun*, 5 and 8 February, 1982) of Faith Cathedral in Etobicoke, Ontario, branded Jews as 'the most unloveable people in the world' and described the Roman Catholic church as 'that great whore.' He eventually apologized for his remarks, but not before the attorney general had inspected his sermon and about fifteen members of the JDL had protested outside his church.

The United church, claimed by the right wing to be Marxian-oriented and infiltrated by Jews pretending conversion, would seem to be a poor candidate for anti-Semitic accusations. Nevertheless, probably the most publi-

---

7 As my study of the right wing was going to press, I received a copy of a highly relevant work recently published by a Canadian scholar and rabbi entitled *The Christian Problem* (Rosenberg 1986).

cized clash in recent years in Canada between Christians and Jews involved that denomination. Starting after the 1967 Arab-Israeli war, and lasting about seven years, a running battle persisted between Jews and the United church. Reverend A.C. Forrest, editor of the United church *Observer*, had come out strongly in support of the Palestinian Arabs, and in the course criticized the Israeli government's attitude towards them. Jews interpreted his remarks as barely concealed anti-Semitism, and thought they were representative of the views of the United church in general.[8] Before the affair had subsided, the Canadian Jewish Congress had condemned the 'racists and bigots' who paraded their 'hatred and venom' in the *Observer* (Glickman 1985). Forrest had published his book *The Unholy Land*, and a Canadian rabbi (Slonim 1977), with the inspired title, *Family Quarrel: The United Church and the Jews*, had tried to patch things up by pointing out the faults of both parties. My own view is that if one cannot express concern for all suffering peoples, including Palestinians, then something is amiss. Yet the gentlemen involved with the *Observer* should have known that any message supporting the Palestinian cause automatically carries with it a blanket condemnation of Israel; if that had not been their intention, that should have been made clear. As things stood, the United church provided propaganda material for the right wing. *The Unholy Land* was widely reviewed in right-wing publications, such as *Countdown* (vol. 1, no. 8, February 1973). In that same issue there was a letter from Forrest, thanking Fromm for reviewing his book.

Let us return to the puzzle set at the beginning: how to explain the persistence of religious racism and anti-Semitism in an era where scientific racism has supposedly displanted it. My argument is that while the two types of racist rationalization are complementary, religious racism provides a deeper explanation and justification from the point of view of the racists themselves. Scientific racism serves the racist's cause in at least three ways. First, to some extent it attempts to explain why blacks are supposedly inferior and lack a 'taste' for civilization, and why whites are supposedly superior. Relevant here is the racist-oriented academic work of people like Coon, Burt, and Jensen. Second, it documents rather than explains the supposed superiority of the white race and inferiority of the black race. This documentation characterizes the majority of references to science in the right-wing literature; racial differences are merely described. Third, it uses the language of the times; to be plausible and carry weight, one's arguments

---

8 Ages (1981: 392), with the Forrest affair in mind, bluntly accused the *Observer* of 'a systematic campaign of vilification against Israel.'

must evoke the authority of science; racists have not been slow to recognize that necessity. It is my impression that the second and third usages of scientific racism have greater meaning for the racists than does the first. Yet even if scientific racism does provide an explanation for their beliefs, it may not be nearly as powerful as a theologically based one.

Theological racism not only supposedly explains why whites are superior and non-whites are inferior (God made us that way), but it also has the capacity to accommodate all the other significant strands in the white supremacist's belief system: communism is anti-Christian, homosexuality is an abomination before God, and the white man's Western civilization is coterminous with Christian civilization. Furthermore, there is a specific strand in the white supremacist's belief system, intrinsically linked to Christianity, that is the most potent of all: anti-Semitism. Jews are said to be Satan's children, the killers of Christ. Interracial mixing, communism, drugs, abortion, social change in general – all of these are supposedly promoted by Jews, providing evidence of the insidious international conspiracy. As my research progressed, I began to realize that anti-Semitism constituted the radical right's theoretical system or paradigm. All thought and action could ultimately be accounted for within its parameters. Finally, theological racism contains a crucial dimension over and beyond explanation and rationalization: it enhances emotional commitment. As one man remarked to me, before he became a member of Identity he continuously doubted his involvement in the radical right. Identity brought him peace of mind, fused his beliefs and emotions, and sustained his commitment to the goals of the Aryan movement at the point where it was faltering.

EXPLAINING RACISM

We now move on to the second part of our question: how do we make sense of racism, anti-Semitism, and the right wing from a theoretical point of view? The relevant literature on these issues is enormous, important, complex, to some extent unsatisfactory, but clearly beyond the scope of this study. All that I shall attempt to do is to identify some of the basic problems and directions, and indicate briefly my own position regarding them.

Is racism endemic to mankind? In Kallen's view (1982: 22), the answer is yes, and indeed the evidence points in that direction. On one occasion, for example, I interviewed a Chilean refugee in Ontario who had been attacked on the street by white youths. The whole matter, he explained, had been a case of mistaken identity. The whites had thought he was a Pakistani. Ironically, he went on to say that Pakistanis and East Indians have only themselves to blame for being targets, because unlike Latins they have weak blood and lack the guts to fight back.[9] While writing up this study, I talked to a white woman whom I knew was very friendly with a Hindu family. Much to my surprise, she blurted out that she can't stand Sikhs. In France and in England I have sat around the table with storekeepers, farmers, engineers, and teachers; more often than not, whenever the subject turned to East Indian or North African immigrants, which it almost always did, the reaction was the same: they are taking over the country, soon there won't be any more real Frenchmen and Englishmen left. All around the world, from light-skinned Arabs in clash with dark-skinned peoples of Sudan to Chinese Malaysians lined up against the indigenous population, the facts seem to lead to a single conclusion: racism indeed is universal and perhaps natural. Yet that is wrong.

Snowden, in *Before Color Prejudice* (1983) and in *Blacks in Antiquity* (1970), demonstrated that the Greeks and Romans were distinctly free from colour prejudice. Other authors such as Banton (1977) and Stepan (1982) have shown that the idea of race has not been universal. The earliest record of the term in English (Banton and Harwood 1975: 13) was in a poem written in 1508 by William Dunbar. Its usage then indicated a class or category of things, devoid of biological connotation. Furthermore, the assumption that racism is natural and endemic confuses related but nevertheless distinct phenomena. Most of the world's supposed racial clashes are in reality ethnic clashes, and more often than not they are generated by underlying class conflicts having to do with competition for power and control of scarce economic resources. There is also, as I indicated in chapter 1, a significant difference between ethnocentrism and racism. The first, the tendency to regard one's in-group as superior, as 'real' people, and others as inferior, may well be ageless. But it does not constitute racism. Another source of confusion concerns reverse racism – the racism that racism produces. Black hostility towards whites and Jewish denial of Gentile entry into their golf and social clubs are examples. Yet these things have a different quality from racism per se, because they are occasioned by it. Of course, once brought into existence, reverse or reactive racism may persist on its own steam; thus, if racism as such were to suddenly disappear, its offspring might well carry on the tradition.

Racism, thus, does not go only one way, but coloured people and Jews are singled out. Moreover, racist treatment of visible minorities is not just a

---

9 Obviously he was poorly informed on the subject of the warrior-saint in the Sikh tradition.

one-generation problem (the immigrant analogy), something that will disappear by the time their children grow up, or when a new wave of immigrants replaces them. Skin colour alone dictates discrimination regardless of the depth of one's national roots. This leads us to the unparalleled racism of white (Christian) society. All around the world, whites as a category appear to be privileged and to have power. When I decided to undertake a study in the general area of race relations, I thought it would be interesting to examine the position of whites in a country where they were at the bottom of the heap. But I couldn't locate a single example. No doubt the members of the radical right would take that as evidence for the white man's intrinsic superiority. Yet that is quite definitely not the case. On numerous occasions in Africa I observed modestly talented whites lording it over blacks, and getting away with it simply because of the colour of their skin. One man, a British citizen, used to become furious in the company of one of his servants, who was all too evidently his intellectual superior. Even in independent African countries, despite the rhetoric of nationalism and black consciousness, a white skin often remains a resource that assures some degree of deference and advantage, regardless of the capacity of the individual.

If racism is neither natural nor universal, what is it, when did it begin, and why are whites in particular implicated? Racism, above all else, is a political phenomenon. As Baker (1978: 316) has stated: 'Race relations are essentially group power contests.' In Ruth Benedict's words (1960: 148): 'Racism remains ... merely another instance of the persecution of minorities for the advantage of those in power.' Hughes and Kallen wrote (1975: 105): 'Racism, in the context of majority-minority relations, is a political tool, wielded by the dominant ethnic group to justify the status quo and rationalize the disability to which the minority group is subject.' Racism as an ideology took shape with the advent of European colonialism, and was significantly boosted by the develpment of capitalism.[10] It is intrinsically related to international labour flows and immigration. While primarily a power phenomenon, and informed by the division of labour, racism over the last century has developed an extra-class dimension; in other words, it

---

10 Once again, we must ask whether racism is confined to capitalism, or whether it also exists in socialist countries. In this context, the viewpoint of at least some Marxists is interesting. In a pamphlet entitled 'Blame the Rich and Not the People for Racist Attacks!' (Norman Bethune Institute, Toronto 1978), it is stated: 'Racism is a feature of the whole capitalist-revisionist world. More specifically, it is a feature of all the capitalist countries in the West and the revisionist countries in the East. The champions of racism on the world scale are the Soviet Union on the one hand and the u.s. on the other.'

has grown beyond its original economic cage, with the result that its ideological and political dimensions have become relatively autonomous. In addition to its sociological and political nature, racism has been fostered by a range of factors such as the individual's need for scapegoats, the propensity for ethnocentrism, and the search for security, stability, and simplicity; in the latter regard, racism acts as a classificatory tool, carving up, categorizing, and thus simplifying the social universe.

The argument that racism cannot be explained entirely as an economic reflex is controversial. I have encountered Marxists who claim 'the people,' meaning the workers, are not racist – indeed, that racism doesn't really exist at all. It is that viewpoint, I believe, that turns many minority-group members away from the Marxist perspective. Even Cox (1948), a brilliant pioneer in the analysis of race relations, did not deny the taint of racism among the proletariat. His argument instead was that racism divides black and white workers, obscures class conflict, and erodes class consciousness – all for the benefit of the ruling white bourgeosie. In this context, racism among the workers is merely an expression of false consciousness, and to deny its effect is a very peculiar brand of Marxism indeed.[11] In recent years, a number of radical, but non-Marxian, scholars (Prager 1972; Blauner 1972) have argued that racism is to some extent a thing in itself, and not simply epiphenomenal to class. Even some Marxist writers such as Miles (1984) and Poulantzas (1979) have begun to recognize the relative autonomy of the political and ideological dimensions of racism, and to stress the particular proneness of the petty bourgeoisie (the small producers and merchants, etc., between the proletariat and the bourgeoisie) to racist-Fascist politics.

Nikolinakos (1973) has pointed out that capitalist countries that did not inherit a racial problem from their colonial experiences create one for

11 The Marxist assertion that 'the people' aren't racist is clearly expressed in a pamphlet produced by the Norman Bethune Institute (Toronto 1978) entitled 'The Proletariat Is at the Centre of the Struggle Against Racist Attacks.' There it is stated: 'We are not talking about racist attacks against whites and blacks. There is no such thing in Canada.' Before dismissing this point of view as rubbish, however, it would be wise to understand the reasoning behind it. When Marxists claim that 'the people' aren't racist, what they mean is that they are not intrinsically or naturally so. Instead, racism is an ideological mechanism reflecting the interests of the rich and powerful. What Marxists object to is the assumption that racism is a problem rooted among ordinary people, to be overcome by the enlightened state. As long as it is recognized that regardless of its source, racism does indeed pollute the proletariat and that skin colour more often than not is the racist's central criterion, my personsl opinion is that there is a great deal to be said in favour of the Marxist position.

themselves. He also has contended that colour is purely accidental as regards racism. The first point is insightful, and reaffirms the links between racism and the capitalist system. The second point is very much in error, for it ignores the degree to which visible minorities are the usual targets of racism. In one sense, there *is* an accidental dimension to skin colour, which brings us back to the peculiar involvement of whites in the field of racism. Colonialism and capitalism had their origins in European cultures. [12] Had the peoples of Asia and Africa been light-skinned, and those of Europe dark-skinned, it is probable that the same patterns of racism, generated by colonialism and capitalism, would have emerged. Ironically, had that been the case, today we would be insensed about massive discrimination against whites!

The power dimension of racism helps to explain a phenomenon that drives racists to distraction: the supposed privileges afforded to minority groups. One might well wonder about the reported existence (*Vancouver Province*, 29 May 1981) of cheaper flights to Hong Kong from Vancouver for Chinese Canadians on Canadian Pacific and Japan Air Lines. But what the racists usually have in mind is the freedom of non-white peoples to express racial pride and to establish their own organizations. Why, they ask, can the National Association for the Advancement of Coloured People or the National Black Coalition of Canada exist, but not the Ku Klux Klan? How can there be a Chinatown if white-only districts are out of the question? [13] In my view, the simple answer concerns disproportionate power. White supremacists are attempting to buttress existing privilege; blacks, Asians, etc., are trying to overcome structural disadvantage, and the overwhelming psychological damage that makes them doubt their own worth. From a moral point of view, one can't argue for the defence of one's 'impoverished' position, as do white supremacists, if one is a member of the privileged sector of society.

One last question: why is racism such an emotional, volatile topic? A dispassionate analysis of South Africa would suggest that with one exception it is not more vicious or totalitarian than some other countries. It is its

12 Of course, religion, particularly Protestantism, was also involved. As it sometimes is said, the missionaries went first to the colonies, paving the way for the traders. As for the links of Protestantism to the development of capitalism, there is an important literature on the subject, dating back to the brilliant, if controversial, work of Weber (1958).

13 The racists' question, of course, assumes that Chinese Canadians *want* a Chinatown, whereas its origin probably has to do with the racist pressures from the wider society. Moreover, as Anderson and Frideres (1981: 166) have pointed out with regard to Toronto, only a minority of Chinese Canadians in that city actually live in Chinatown.

apartheid system that marks it as uniquely despicable. To call a person a racist would seem to be a much worse insult than to accuse a person of being an élitist or a class snob. Why? Part of the explanation probably concerns the central goals of Western capitalist society; if properly socialized, people devote their lives to accumulating material goods, striving for the economic summit, and then converting their wealth into status and prestige. In a peculiar sense, to be called a class snob is to be paid a compliment. But there is more than that to the puzzle. Anthropologists are only too well aware of the widespread symbolism in various societies that has the purpose of distinguishing culture from nature, or human beings from animals. Not only does racism run counter to notions of fairness and equality, but it denies its victims their humanity, relegating them to the animal world. Blacks and Jews, from the point of view of the extreme right, are not human beings at all.

EXPLAINING THE RIGHT WING

Throughout the Western world during the past two decades there has been a resurgence of right-wing, neo-Fascist activity. Dozens of right-wing organizations have existed in Britain, the best known of which has been the National Front (Billig 1978; Edgar 1977; Fielding 1981; Walker 1977). An organization with that same name can be found in France; indeed, its leader, Jean-Marie Le Pen, who advocates deportation of North African workers, received more than two million votes (11 per cent) in the 1984 elections for the European parliament, a consultative body for the European Common Market.

How do we account for the swing towards the right wing? There is some overlap between the explanations of racism and the right wing, but in terms of organization the latter is a more specific phenomenon, while in terms of issues it is a more general one. The right wing, of course, is not necessarily confined to concrete organizations; some writers would include the entire state apparatus of capitalist societies under that rubric. A further tricky problem concerns the definition of Fascism or neo-Fascism. To some extent that term has become a label to brandish against the bad guys, who ironically can be on both the right and the left. On numerous occasions during this project, not only did left-wing spokesmen label groups like the Edmund Burke Society and the Western Guard Fascist, but often the same label was pinned on far-left groups such as CPC-ML, and even on middle-of-the-road organizations like BCOFR. For a couple of reasons, it doesnt't help much to turn to the scholarly literature on classical Fascism, involving the German and Italian cases. That literature is itself shot through with ambiguity, contradiction, and widespread disagreement among specialists; in Payne's opinion (1980), Fascism is the vaguest of contemporary political terms. Even if that were not so, the applicability of the literature on classical Fascism would remain dubious. Organizations such as the Western Guard, the Nationalist Party, and the Ku Klux Klan clearly and definitely constitute Fascist phenomena. Even their spokesmen confirm that status. However, none of the Canadian organizations has achieved any degree of power, or progressed beyond the incipient stage of development. It would therefore be erroneous to regard those organizations as Fascist parties, and it is probably even imprecise to describe them collectively as a Fascist movement. Perhaps they can simply be called Fascist groupings; or, to turn the tables on the right wing's delight in using insect and animal metaphors for its victims (swarms of Third World parasites and roaches, teeming hordes of immigrants who breed like flies), let us label them Fascist amoeba.

More relevant to the contemporary Canadian scene is the more confined literature specifically aimed at the resurgent right wing. A now dated but influential interpretation was provided by Lipset and Raab. As they stated (1970: 484): 'Extremist movements are not primarily the product of extremists. The critical ranks in extremist movements are not composed of evil-structured types called "extremists," but rather of ordinary people caught in certain kinds of stress.' Elsewhere Lipset (1971: 113) described Fascism as extremism at the centre, as 'a middle-class movement representing a protest against both capitalism and socialism, big business *and* big unions.' What right-wing people are protesting against, according to Lipset and Raab, are changing times, with its accompanying ambiguity and relative or absolute status deprivation. Writers like Lipset (1964: 315) and Bell (1964: 47) have pointed out that periods of prosperity can give rise to social strains and protest movements. Yet as Wolfe (1981: 9) has observed, the right wing has actually become stronger as prosperity and economic growth have dwindled.

As a low-level descriptive statement of the right wing, the interpretation provided by Lipset and Raab is adequate enough. But it doesn't penetrate very deeply. Holding it back is the emphasis on status politics rather than class. Just as an analysis of racism cannot get very far without entertaining class factors, the same is true about the right wing. The consistent and plausible contention in the recent literature (Dixon 1981–2) is that the resurgence of the right wing in core capitalist countries has been a direct response to a world crisis in capitalist accumulation. This argument has been refined by Poulantzas (1979), who identifies the petty bourgeoisie at the centre of the storm. As a declining class segment or class fraction, incapable of reproducing itself in an era of the large corporate state, and lacking political power, the petty bourgeoisie, or what Lipset and Raab (1970) refer to as the deteriorating middle class, is diverted to a reactionary direction; no doubt it is sustained by pockets of support in both the upper and lower classes – what Lipset and Raab (1970: 429) have described as a marriage of interest, a symbiosis, between upper and lower economic strata. What is most significant in Poulantzas's perspective is the argument that the petty Bourgeoisie can itself be an authentic political force, the direction of which is Fascism.

Finally, let us return to the comparative scene. Two countries – New Zealand and Australia – have special significance for Canada in terms of the right wing. As in Canada, there is an Australian Nazi Party, A New Zealand Nazi Party, a National Socialist Party, and even an Odinist presence. More significantly, in both countries the League of Rights and Social Credit are active; moreover, they have direct connections with their counterparts in Canada, with visits by leading members back and forth. The League of Rights in Australia, founded in 1946, grew out of that country's Social Credit movement, and then spread to Canada, Britain, and New Zealand. New Zealand's organization was founded in 1970. In 1972 the Crown Commonwealth League of Rights was established. As in Canada, there are *On Target* publications in these other countries.

The founder of the Australian League of Rights was Eric Butler, described by Epstein and Forster (1967: 23–32) 'as one of Australia's leading anti-Semites.' Prior to the Second World War (Spoonley 1983), Butler wrote articles supporting Nazi interests, and in 1947 he published *The International Jew – The Truth about the Protocols of Zion*. In 1964 he toured Canada under the sponsorship of Gostick's *Canadian Intelligence Service*. In 1979 he published an article in one of Gostick's periodicals in which he traced the roots of communism back to the Second World War, described by him as 'a type of civil war between Christian European peoples.' Butler attended the League of Rights convention in Calgary in 1983, by which time his son Phillip had become deputy director of the Canadian organization. Others from 'down under' at the convention were David Thompson and Bill Daly, past and present directors, respectively of the New Zealand League of Rights. In 1981, Jeremy Lee, born in Kenya and deputy director of the Australian League of Rights, gave a series of lectures in Canada on the theme 'The Destruction of Western Civilization' (he has also published material in Gostick's *Canadian Intelligence Service*). Gostick, on his part, toured Australia for four weeks two years earlier.

Spoonley, who has written widely about the New Zealand case, and to some extent Australia's (1981, 1983, 1984), has described seventy-one right-wing organizations that existed between 1961 and 1981 in New Zealand alone. Like its counterpart in Canada, the League of Rights organizations in these two countries have become more circumspect in recent years about expressing racism and anti-Semitism. Yet as Spoonley 1984, points out, there are code words that cover the same ground like 'One Worlders,' 'International Finance,' 'Integrationists,' and 'Zionists.' As in Canada, both the Social Credit movement and the League of Rights in New Zealand draw their support from the rural areas and provincial towns, people who tend to fall within the petty bourgeoisie. If there is a difference between Canada and New Zealand, it concerns the latter's difficulty, in view of the low profile of its Jewish community, in persuading people to realize Jews are dangerous. As we have seen, no such obstacle has confronted the right wing in Canada.

EXPLAINING ANTI-SEMITISM

As Moodley (1981: 6) has remarked, if a person is prejudiced against one minority group, the chances are that he or she will be prejudiced against others as well; thus, to some extent the explanation of racism and anti-Semitism overlap. But there are differences. Recall the dictum that whites want blacks in their place, but want Jews to cease being Jews. Then, too, there is the Christ-killer theme, a peculiar source of anti-Semitism. As Cohn (1966: 40) has stated: 'It is often assumed that all ethnic prejudice is very much of a kind – that, for instance, hatred of Negroes must have precisely the same emotional roots as hatred of Jews; yet the assumption is certainly mistaken.' Cohn went on to argue, somewhat fancifully in my opinion, that Jews are the victims of unconscious negative projections among Christians who see them as the bad son and the bad father.

Just as we saw that racism has not always been with us, the same is true about anti-Semitism. For about 2,000 years (Cohn 1966: 35) there were Jewish settlements in India and China without accompanying anti-Semitism. Nevertheless, anti-Jewish sentiments are very ancient indeed. According to Trachtenberg (1943: 6), they actually pre-dated Christianity, and can't entirely be explained in terms of Christian animosity. Zionism, the movement to establish a Jewish homeland, gave rise to further such sentiments. The term 'Zionism' first appeared in the 1890s, and as Laqueur (1972: 384) has observed, opposition came from both non-Jews and Jews.[14] While anti-Zionism does not inevitably imply anti-Semitism, there is no

14 For a history of Zionism and anti-Semitism respectively, see Laqueur (1972) and Poliakov (1975).

doubt that the former often is a cover for the latter. In some quarters, it is believed that Zionism is colonialistic, racist, and expansionist. Zayid (1980: 29), for example, contends that racism is inherent in Zionist ideology, and that the concept of the Jewish chosen race is synonymous with Nazism's Aryan chosen people. Yet as more dispassionate scholars such as Dandeker and Troyna (1983: 29) have pointed out, while it is useful to inquire about parallels between some aspects of Nazi ideology and Zionism, as well as some features of Israeli foreign policy, any attempt to pin the Fascist label on Israel ignores her parliamentary institutions and legal system. Hobsbawm (1980) has argued that the establishment of Israel, and its demonstrated capacity to defend itself, has brought about a new respect for Jews and a decrease in anti-Semitism. In contrast, Ettinger (1982: 22) has referred to Israel's loss of prestige and stature following the war in Lebanon, and has remarked that Jews in power may behave as basely as everybody else in power. Some of the hostility towards Israel, Raab (1975: 54) has acutely observed, is not anti-Semitism at all, for if an Amish state instead of a Jewish one had been established in the same locality, the reactions of Arabs would have been much the same.

As far as Jewish power – especially economic power – is concerned, the literature on the subject is clear: it is mostly a myth. Had it been otherwise, it is quite improbable that fully six out of seven of all Jews in Europe would have been killed during the Second World War (Laqueur 1972: 559). In Gordon's (1984) authoritative study, it is shown that while Jews in Germany never exceeded 1.09 per cent of the population, they nevertheless were visible because they were concentrated in large cities and had distinctive occupational characteristics. They were overrepresented in business, commerce, banking, the stock market, and the public and private service, but underrepresented in agriculture, industry, and domestic services; they were also more highly educated and had higher incomes than non-Jews. However, none of this meant they controlled the German economy. As Gordon (1984: 16) observes, Jews in Germany were not the captains of industry; instead they were mostly middlemen, financiers, and members of professions such as law and medicine. In an earlier era, Jews were pioneers in trade and money-lenders in agricultural societies, living partly segregated from the surrounding population. But as Cohn (1966: 35) points out, in that respect Jews have been similar to numerous others such as Indian traders in Africa and Chinese traders in Java, all of whom have attracted the same kind of hostility.

A wide range of explanations in addition to deicide and Cohn's psychoanalytic speculations have been suggested as the cause of anti-

Semitism. Arendt (1958: 9) contended that modern anti-Semitism is closely related to the development of the nation-state, with Jews symbolizing the passing of the old ways. According to Rose (1971: 44), what Jews symbolize is the hated city life; country life, the bucolic past, is seen as devoid of Jews. As far as the apparent increase in anti-Semitism in the last decade or so is concerned, three factors are often singled out: economic malaise, sympathy for the Palestinians, and distance in time from the Holocaust. The last factor appears to be the critical one. As Elezar (1982: 16) bluntly put it, what we see today is 'the demise of the taboo against Jew hatred.' In the end, the quickening of anti-Semitism in the Western world, both within and beyond the organized radical right, has little to do with Jewish personality or behaviour; indeed, anti-Semitism and racism more generally are quite capable of surviving even in the absence of their targets. As Moodley (1981: 6) has pointed out, the particular characteristics or actions of minority members are largely irrelevant to the person who discriminates. Changing the behaviour of Jews or blacks will not eradicate anti-Semitism and racism. There is not a Jewish or black problem, but instead a white one.

Turning to Canada specifically, I assume that the widespread anti-Semitism in the country, from the 1930s up to the present, requires no further documentation. But there remain one or two subsidiary issues. The Canadian Jewish community, from its relatively impoverished beginnings at the turn of the century to its economic security today, has obviously gained ground, but in the process it has changed. As Salutin (1982) has vividly argued, Canadian Jews, once left-leaning and working-class, have become solidly conservative members of the middle class. In May 1985, several letters to the editor of *The Globe and Mail* took exception to a study reported in that newspaper (3 May 1985) about the influence of religious affiliation on income level. The study had found that Jewish males in Canada earned more than Protestant and Catholic males. The author of the study, an economist who had published his work on the subject in leading academic journals, must have been surprised by the public reaction. One man joked (*Globe and Mail*, 10 May 1985) that his non-Jewish colleagues were bugging him about his apparent high salary; on the same page, but in quite a different tone, another man said he found the article insulting, and implied it contributed to racism and anti-Semitism. A few days later a different writer observed (*Globe and Mail*, 14 May 1985) that it was 'remarkable' that such a study had been undertaken in the first place, and 'even more incredible' that it had been reported on in the newspaper's front page. Yet another writer (*Globe and Mail*, 21 May 1985) complained about the policy of Statistics Canada in releasing the data on which this study was based, and went on to say that in the next census he would withhold all information about his religion and income.

The report about Jewish income obviously touched a nerve, but one thing was certain: the economist's conclusions were consistent with those in many other studies, both in Canada and in the United States. Weinfeld (1977: 23), for example, remarked that Jews are 'by far the most affluent of Quebec ethnic groups.' Driedger (1980: 72) stated: 'Economically, the Jews who were originaly of lower socio-economic status, have risen to the highest status in Winnipeg.' In the face of the evidence that Jewish males top the income heap, one can almost hear the sigh of relief with the discovery that in both Canada and the United States there are a greater number of Jews who live in abject poverty. As Torczyner (1981: 183) pointed out, while an estimated one out of every five Canadians was poor, a Montreal-based study found that one out of six Jews was as well. Had any other minority group, subjected to discrimination over the years, become a similar success story, its achievements would have been applauded. Tragically, Jews can't seem to win. They are either fighting for survival, or, when historical circumstances provide them with a breather, and they 'make it,' they live in apprehension of being accused of having a stranglehold on the nation's finances.

If concern among some Jews about being affluent seems to be peculiar, the same can be said about the worry that Canadian society, despite its ingrained anti-Semitism, has been too hospitable. Jews in Canada, according to Medjuck and Lazar (1981: 241), have 'to struggle to remain an identifiable ethnic group.' The issue of intermarriage is especially sensitive. Rosenberg (1971: 83) expresses concern that because Jews have become increasingly accepted, they have the choice of opting out, marrying Gentiles, and in the process ceasing to be Jews. Weinfeld (1981: 381) too alludes to the danger of assimilation. All this might seem very strange, especially when one remembers that it was not too many years ago that intermarriage used to be brandished as the weapon to kill off racism, and when one recalls that one of the ultimate tests of racial tolerance is whether one would allow and welcome one's offspring to marry someone of a different racial origin. Nevertheless, as in the case of income, there is a sound reason for Jewish concern. As Plaut (*Globe and Mail*, 3 January 1984) has persuasively argued, intermarriage for Jews, given their small numbers (scarcely more than 1 per cent of the country's population), constitutes a real threat to their existence as a people. Intermarriage for Gentiles does not have the same consequences. If pockets of Protestants or Catholic marry Jews, and even convert to Judaism, Protestantism and Catholicism will not wither away.

The reverse is not true. When liberals such as myself take the position that intermarriage is admirable, what in effect we are advocating is that Jews become like ourselves, absorbed into the dominant Christian setting.[15]

RIGHT VERSUS LEFT

In 1982 I stood beside a prominent Marxist in Vancouver as a group of roughly-dressed young members of the Ku Klux Klan taunted the communists who arrived to demonstrate against them. Rather than dismissing the Klan members as idiots and racists, the Marxist remarked bitterly that those young people were exactly the type who *should* be committed believers in his own brand of revolution. That incident is significant because it concerns a much larger issue: the battle being fought between the radical right and the radical left for control over the assumed imminent revolution in the country. Human behaviour contains a degree of indeterminism. Because of a range of factors such as an individual's choice-making capacity and personality differences, two people with roughly the same social background and life experiences may end up at polar-opposite positions on the political continuum. As Hobsbawm (Healey and Hobsbawm

---

15 Trudeau, as leader of the opposition in 1979, apparently remarked (*Toronto Star*, 24 October 1979) that by pressuring the federal government on the Middle East conflict Canadian Jewish leaders had 'opened the way to growing anti-Semitism.' The following day it was reported (*Toronto Star*, 25 October 1979) that Philip Givens, who had served under Trudeau as a back-bencher, was outraged at Trudeau's accusation. I have no special knowledge about the strength of the Jewish lobby, and I certainly lack the credentials to comment authoritatively on the Middle East situation. However, this may be the place to clarlify some of my personal views. That anti-Semitism is widespread and deep-rooted is incontrovertible. I did not decide to undertake this study in order to focus on anti-Semitism. The fact that the research, rather than my preconceived ideas, led me to the theme of anti-Semitism lends all the more credibility to the conclusion that it is the key dimension in Canada's racist organizations. Yet it would be wrong to interpret this study as anti-Arabic in any shape or form. If ever a people needed and deserved a homeland, it was the Jews; but that does not mean that the Palestinian cause is unjust or that an acceptable (and moral) solution is not urgent. I have never been to Israel, but I have visited every country in North Africa, a couple of them repeatedly, and always with great pleasure. Moreover, I have no doubt that a companion study to this one could be written about prejudice and discrimination in Canada directed towards people of Arabic origin. In the end, the goal of eliminating discrimination against one people is not likely to be realized by transferring it to another. My remarks here merely echo those of Elie Wiesel, who, on the occasion of accepting the 1986 Nobel Peace Prize, reportedly opposed the methods (i.e., violence) of the Palestinians, but recognized their suffering, and called for action to resolve their plight (*Globe and Mail*, 11 December 1986).

1982: 123) has stated: 'There is nothing which says that if you have a particular social position, that God or destiny has decided that you're going to
end up on the revolutionary left or on the ultraright. It depends upon the
situations, and it depends on what you do to mobilize people and to
organize them.'

From the days of the Edmund Burke Society to the quickened Klan
activity in the early 1980s, the one constant feature has been the continuous
confrontation between the right and the left. The Western Guard could hold
a demonstration in downtown Toronto without being opposed by more
than a handful of blacks, East Indians, and Jews, but almost certainly the
CPC-ML and other left-wing groups would be there to greet them. Ironically,
however, several writers have stressed the similarities between the far left
and far right. Hoffer (1951: 84), for example, contends that fanatics of all
kinds share the same position on the political continuum. Committed racists
and committed communists, according to Hoffer, do indeed despise each
other, but it is the hatred of brothers. Often the relationship between the
fanatical left and the fanatical right is portrayed as a circle, with the two
parties almost touching at the joined ends. Sometimes it is claimed that both
the left and right are devoid of rational goals, motivated by nothing more
than the ecstasy of confrontation, the sheer delight in violence for its own
sake. In recent years terms like 'left wing fascism' (Horowitz 1981) have
crept into the academic literature, reflecting an image of the left wing as
mystical, élitist, and above all anti-Semitic.

That some degree of overlap exists between the left and the right is
indisputable. Each is inclined to violence and totalitarianism, and fuelled by
different versions of conspiracy theories; in the one case it is the machinations of the capitalist state (O'Toole 1977), in the other the international
Jewish design for world control. Nor do supposed differences in terms of
intellectual orientation and unity hold water. The radical left often is said to
be intellectual and utopian, guided by Marx's elaborate vision, and the
radical right non-intellectual and pragmatic. Yet the latter draws from a
large body of literature, some of it conventional treatises on race – scientific
racism – and some of it underground literature made available outside the
normal distribution networks. This literature is continuously pushed at
members of the right wing partly because it is a source of revenue, partly to
educate members about the right-wing philosophy, and partly to keep them
from backsliding. The far left is notorious for its internal divisions, generated to some extent by conflicting interpretations of Marxism. The far
right, as we have seen, is equally divided, but for different reasons. The
obvious one concerns the tendency for personality to overshadow

philosophy in the right wing, with individual leaders vying with one another for the position of top dog. A further, more profound, reason may be related to the essential nature of the far right – its overwhelming negativity. The proclivity to despise half the world's population, to be anti-this or anti-that, can turn upon itself, leading white supremacists and anti-Semites to assume the worst about each other.

Lending credibility to the presumed overlap between the radical left and right is the supposed ease with which a person can switch from the one to the other. As Hoffer (1951: 84) contends, it is much easier for a fanatical communist to be converted to Fascism than to become a liberal. There is, indeed, the case in which an entire organization, previously left wing, switched en masse to the right. That was Lyndon H. La Rouche's U.S. Labor Party, now known as the National Caucus of Labor Committees (NCLC), which apparently has units in Canada (ADL Facts, 1982; King and Radosh 1984). [16] Formerly a member of a Trotskyist group, La Rouche, a millionaire who has run for president of the United States, helped to organize a faction of the socialist-oriented Students for a Democratic Society in the 1960s. Today the NCLC is explicitly anti-Semitic and 'enjoys close ties to the Ku Klux Klan' (King and Radosh 1984: 15). There has been nothing quite that dramatic in Canada, yet one of my surprises in this project was to meet so many white supremacists who previously had been left-wing–oriented.

Despite all this, in my judgment only at the most superficial level can the radical right and the radical left be equated. The supposed ease, for example, in which a person can flip-flop from one extreme to the other is almost entirely a one-way street – from radical left to the radical right. While I learned about numerous individuals who had done just that, I never came across a single instance of the reverse process. What is curious is that white-supremacist, Fascist organizations welcome former Marxists and socialists with open arms. One man once said to me that it was entirely normal to be a socialist when young – indeed, perhaps one was flawed if one had not gone through that phase. It was as if a socialist background was a necessary prelude to 'the truth,' or perhaps evidence that the individuals in question were prone to politicization and hence had the makings of good right wingers. The attitude of the radical left to former Fascists is quite a different matter. I suspect that one reason that conversion in that direction rarely occurs concerns notions about eradicable moral pollution. Despite

16 In Canada, the organization also is known as the Party for the Commonwealth of Canada and Le Parti de la république du Canada.

the radical left's belief in the fundamental influence of environment and in the potential goodness and perfectability of the intrinsically malleable individual, it would seem that from its perspective prior involvement in racist organizations forever stamps a person as tainted, corrupt, and evil. [17]

Among the more apparent differences between the radical right and left are the following. The right is preservationist; it wants to maintain the status quo, or return to a (mythical) golden age; the left is revolutionary rather than reactionary; it seeks to transform society, to realize the potential perfection of mankind. The right is élitist, in favour of narrowing the lines of privilege; the left is egalitarian, in favour of broadening the lines of privilege, or, more accurately, of eradicating them. The right is racist, and its vision of privilege and quality is predicted on the presumed superiority of the white race; the left is non-racist (in principle), and unlike the right it centres its analysis on social class rather than race and nation, or blood and soil. The right assumes that human nature is fixed, and that social institutions that defy nature inevitably flounder; the left regards mankind as malleable, capable of creating social institutions that enshrine the higher values. The far right is almost always anti-Semitic; the far left sometimes anti-Zionist. The former is usually religion-oriented, linking Christianity to Western civilization and Aryan aspirations; the latter is usually secular. The right makes a distinction between good (productive) and bad (financial or speculative) capitalism, and favours private enterprise and the small businessman over monopolistic organizations; the left by definition is anti-capitalist in general. Finally, and perhaps most significant of all, while the left stands opposed to the capitalist state, the right tends to benefit from a degree of complicity with it, shoring up the power and privilege of the dominant-class fractions, or more simply the élite.

Let us return to the confrontation between the extreme right and left. Before embarking on this project, I naively assumed that the principal alternative to capitalism in the Western world was socialism. It is apparent, however, that also lurking in the background is Fascism. Indeed, one could say that whenever formally organized racist groups appear, the potential for Fascism has correspondingly increased. That situation is probably not appreciated by most citizens, but it certainly is by the radical left, which is why it challenges the right wing at all corners. As racial strife increases in the Western world, which appears probable, the confrontation between the

---

17 There also, of course, is the age factor. It appears that the older one becomes, the more conservative one becomes, which makes it less probable that right-wing people will eventually switch to the left.

right and the left will intensify. However, the left will have the longer distance to run because of the right's complicity with the state. Where does all this leave ordinary citizens, the vast majority of whom would seem to regard both the extreme right and left as nuts? The middle position may well appear to be more sane, but one thing is certain: it is not neutral. Instead, it is part of the status quo, with its institutionalized inequality. The big question is whether, in the crunch, the middle position is morally defensible.

CONCLUSION

Canada is unexceptional in both its right-wing tendencies and its tolerance. The organized right wing is substantial, but not out of proportion with that in other countries; nor is the radical right's racist thrust incompatible with the nation's wider setting and institutions. There is a significant religious basis to Canada's right wing, but probably not more so than elsewhere. There is nothing natural about anti-Semitism and racism. The former, while pre-dating Christianity, and informed by a multitude of sources, including state-level political interests, has been inexorably shaped by the Christ-killer theme; the latter, its roots in the era of empire-building, has been intrinsically related to power. The right-wing resurgence in recent years is an expression of social and economic problems (some of them linked to a crisis in capitalist accumulation), a reaction against the steady leftward drift of the Western world since the Age of the Enlightenment, a cry of anguish about social change in general, and a sign that Jew-baiting has once more become fashionable. The right wing may not consist entirely of the ignorant, uneducated idiots that are the stuff of the media. However, its solutions for the world's problems degrade humankind. The right wing, especially the far right, under the guise of both scientific and religious justification, and on the premise that liberalism in the face of human nature is unworkable, advocates that the world be rebuilt on the lines of natural law, which means in part recognizing the supposed animal-like inferiority of non-white peoples. Yet by denying the human capacity to create moral systems composed of higher values, manifested in the universal truths of art and literature and theology, and by promoting a blueprint resting on our 'true' (base) nature, the right wing's philosophy, more than other, collapses the differences between people and nature. It could appropriately be called the animal philosophy.

List of Organizations Since the Second World War

RADICAL RIGHT

Aryan Nations
Black and Red Front
British Canada Party
British Israel
British People's League (and Party)
Canadian Action
Canadian Anti-Soviet Action Committee (CASAC)
Canadian National Party
Canadian Nazi Party
Canadian Youth Corps
Christ Is the Answer, Inc.
Christian Defence Council
Christian Fellowship Assembly
Christian Mutual Defence Fund
Church of Creativity
Committee for Free Speech in Canada
Concerned Parents of German Descent
Direct Action
Ezra Pound Institute of International Studies
German Freedom Fighters
German-Jewish Historical Commission
House of Freedom (and Free Speech)
Hungarian Freedom Fighters Federation
Identity
KKK: Canadian Knights of the Ku Klux Klan

KKK: Invisible Empire, Knights of the Ku Klux Klan (British Columbia branch)
KKK: National Knights of the Ku Klux Klan (Ontario)
KKK: Imperial Knights of the Ku Klux Klan (British Columbia)
KKK: Confederate Klans of Alberta
National Advancement Party
National Association for the Advancement of White People (NAAWP)
National Citizens Alliance
Nationalist Party of Canada
National Socialist Alliance
National Socialist Liberation Front
National Socialist Movement of Canada
National Socialist (Nazi) Party
National Socialist Party
National Socialist Party of Canada (Quebec)
National Socialist Underground
National Social Party
National Unity Party
National White Americans Party
Natural Order (and Faith)
North American Labor Party
Odinism
Party for the Commonwealth of Canada
Realist Party
Samisdat Publishers Ltd
Social Credit Association of Ontario, Inc.
Union of Fascists (Canada)
United Anglo-Saxon Liberation Front
Western Guard
Western Guard Universal
White Canada Council
White Canada Party
White Canada Christian/Patriots Rights Association
White Legion
White Nationalist Revolutionary Army
White People's Vigilantes

FRINGE RIGHT

Action Canada
Alliance for Christian Laymen

Alliance for the Preservation of English in Canada (APEC)
Alternative Forum
Anti-Bolshevik Youth League
Campaign Life
Campus Alternative
CAFE (1): Canadian Alliance for Free Enterprise
CAFE (2): Canadian Association for Free Expression
Canadian Anti-Communist League
Canadian Crime Fighters Association
Canadian Defence League
Canadian Ex-Servicemen for One Canada
Canadian Friends of Free China Association
Canadian Institute of Guardianship
Canadian Intelligence Service
Canadian League
Canadian League of Rights
Canadian Liberty League
Canadian Loyalist Movement
Canadian Party of Ontario
Canadians for One Canada
Canadian Unison Society
Canadian Unity and Freedom Federation
Catholic Registrar
Catholics against Terrorism
Christian Action Movement
Christians Against Terrorism
Christian Nationalist Party
Church Watch
Citizens for Foreign Aid Reform (C-FAR)
Civilized Family Life Committee
Coalition for Life
Committee to Stop Bill 7
Confederation of Church and Business People
Cornerstone Alliance
Edmund Burke Society
Family and Freedom Foundation
Frazer Institute
Freedom Council of Canada
Friends of Rhodesia Association
Human Action to Limit Taxes (HALT)
Ideal Party

John Birch Society
League against Homosexuals
Libertarian Party
Major C.H. Douglas Society
McGill Magazine
The Michael
Moderate Majority
Moonies
National Citizens' Coalition
National Foundation for Public Policy Development
New Right
New Right Coalition
Orange Order
Positive Parents of Canada
Pro-Family Coalition
Pro-Life Party of Canada
Province of Toronto Society
Renaissance (several branches)
Right to Life Association
Social Credit (several small branches)
Speak-Up
University of Toronto Magazine
Western Canada Concept Party
Western Socialist Workers' Party
Women Alive
Young Americans for Freedom (YAF)
Young Canadians for a Christian Civilization

Bibliography

Abella, I., and Troper, H. 1982. *None Is Too Many*. Toronto: Lester and Orpen Dennys, Publishers

Adachi, K. 1976. *The Enemy That Never Was*. Toronto: McClelland and Stewart

ADL Facts. 1982. 'The La Rouche Network: A Political Cult.' 27 (no. 2): 1–14

Ages, A. 1981. 'Antisemitism: The Uneasy Calm.' In M. Weinfeld, W. Shaffir, and I. Cotler, eds., *The Canadian Jewish Mosaic*, pp. 383–95. Toronto: John Wiley and Sons

Albares, R. 1968. *Nativist Paramilitarism in the United States: The Minutemen Organization*. Centre for Social Organization Studies. Chicago: University of Chicago

Alexander, C. 1965. *The Ku Klux Klan in the Southwest*. Lexington: University of Kentucky Press

Anderson, A., and Frideres, J. 1981. *Ethnicity in Canada: Theoretical Perspectives*. Toronto: Butterworths and Co.

Anon. 1928. 'The Ku Klux Klan in Saskatchewan.' *Queen's Quarterly* 35: 592–602

Anti-Defamation League of B'nai B'rith. 1982. *Hate Groups in America: A Record of Bigotry and Violence*. New York, NY

Arcand, A. 1938. 'Does Canada Need Fascism?' *Country Guide*, July: 11, 44

Ardener, E. 1953–4. 'Some Ibo Attitudes to Skin Pigmentation.' *Man* 53–4: 71–3

Arendt, H. 1958. *The Origins of Totalitarianism*, 2nd ed. London: George Allen and Unwin, Ltd

Avery, D. 1983. *Dangerous Foreigners*. Toronto: McClelland and Stewart

Ayre, J. 1970. 'A Case of Paranoia Meeting Paranoia.' *Saturday Night* November: 20, 22

'Background on the Ku Klux Klan.' Nova Scotia Human Rights Commission (no author attribution or date)

Bagley, C. 1973. 'Race Relations and the Press: An Empirical Analysis.' *Race* 15 (no. 1): 59–89

Baker, D. 1978. 'Race and Power: Comparative Approaches to the Analysis of Race Relations.' *Ethnic and Racial Studies* 1 (no. 3): 316–35

Banton, M. 1970. 'The Concept of Racism.' In S. Zubaida, ed., *Race and Racialism*. London: Tavistock Publications

– 1977. *The Idea of Race*. London: Tavistock Publications

Banton, M., and Harwood, J. 1975. *The Race Concept* New York: Praeger

Bell, D. 1964. 'Interpretations of American Politics.' In D. Bell, ed., *The Radical Right*, pp. 47–73. New York: Anchor Books

Beloff, M. 1982. In 'Antisemitism Today: A Symposium.' *Patterns of Prejudice* 16 (no. 4): 3–53

Benedict, R. 1960. *Race: Science and Politics*. New York: Viking Press

Bercuson, D., and Wertheimer, D. 1985. *A Trust Betrayed: The Keegstra Affair*. Toronto: Doubleday

Betcherman, L. 1975. *The Swastika and the Maple Leaf: Fascist Movements in Canada in the Thirties*. Toronto: Fitzhenry and Whiteside

Billig, M. 1978. *Fascist: A Social Psychological View of the National Front*. London: Academic Press

– 1979. *Psychology, Racism and Fascism*. Birmingham, England: A Searchlight Booklet

Blauner, R. 1972. *Racial Oppression in America*. New York: Harper and Row

Boas, F. 1962. *Anthropology and Modern Life*. New York: W.W. Norton

Bohannan, P. 1963. *Social Anthropology*. New York: Holt, Rinehart and Winston

Bolaria, B., and Li, P. 1985. *Racial Oppression in Canada*. Toronto: Gramond Press

Bowerman, J. 1980. 'East Indians in Alberta: A Human Rights Viewpoint.' In K.V. Ujimoto and G. Hirabayashi, eds., *Visible Minorities and Multiculturalism: Asians in Canada*, pp. 181–91. Scarborough, Ont.: Butterworth

Bredvold, L., and Ross, R., eds. 1977. *The Philosophy of Edmund Burke*. Ann Arbor, Mich.: Ann Arbor Paperbacks

Brown, G. 1968. 'Community Tensions and Conflicts among Youth of Different Ethnic and Racial Backgrounds in Wards 3, 4, 5 and 6 in Downtown Toronto.' Report submitted to the Ontario Human Rights Commission

Burnet, J. 1975. 'Multiculturalism, Immigration, and Racism: A Comment on the Canadian Immigration and Population Study.' *Canadian Ethnic Studies* 7: 35–9

Burt, C. 1966. 'The Genetic Determination of Differences in Intelligence: A Study of Monozygotic Twins Reared Together and Apart.' *British Journal of Psychology* 57: 137–53

Calbreath, D. 1981. 'Kovering the Klan' *Columbia Journalism Review*, March/April: 42–5

Calderwood, W. 1973. 'Religious Reactions to the Ku Klux Klan in Saskatchewan.' *Saskatchewan History* 26 (no. 3): 103–14

– 1975. 'Pulpit, Press, and Political Reactions to the Ku Klux Klan in Saskatchewan.' In S. Clark, J. Grayson, and L. Grayson, eds., *Prophecy and Protest*, pp. 153–78. Toronto: Gage

Campbell, K. 1975. *Tempest in a Teapot*. Cambridge, Ont.: A Coronation Publications Copyright

Carmichael, S. 1971. 'Black Power.' In D. Cooper, ed., *The Dialectics of Liberation*, pp. 150–74. Harmondsworth: Penguin Books

Carstens, P. 1971. 'Coercion and Change.' In R. Ossenberg, ed., *Canadian Society*, pp. 126–45. Scarborough, Ont.: Prentice Hall

Carter, Cardinal Gerald, Emmett. 1979. 'Report to the Civic Authorities of Metropolitan Toronto and Its Citizens,' mimeo

Cashmore, E., and Troyna, B. 1983. *Introduction to Race Relations*. London: Routledge and Kegan Paul

Cerar, M. 1982. 'The Canadian Knights of the Ku Klux Klan.' Unpublished paper

Chalmers, D. 1981. *Hooded Americanism: The History of the Ku Klux Klan*. New York: Franklin Watts

Clark, K. 1971. 'Candor about Negro-Jewish Relations.' In Leonard Dinnerstein, ed., *Antisemitism in the United States*, pp. 116–24. New York: Holt, Rinehart and Winston

Clark, S.D. 1954. 'The Frontier and Democratic Theory.' *Transactions of the Royal Society of Canada* XLVIII, sec. II: 65–75

Cohn, N. 1966. 'The Myth of the Jewish World-Conspiracy.' *Commentary* 41: 35–42

– 1969. *Warrant for Genocide: The Myth of the Jewish World-Conspiracy and the Protocols of the Elders of Zion*. New York and Evanston: Harper Torchbooks

Collins, D. 1979. *Immigration: The Destruction of English Canada*. Richmond Hill, Ont.: BMG Publishing Ltd

Colman, A. 1972. 'Psychology and the Legitimation of Apartheid.' *Science for the People* 4 (no. 3): 7–10

Comas, J. 1961. ' "Scientific" Racism Again?' *Current Anthropology* 2 (no. 4): 303–40

Coon, C. 1962. *The Origins of Race*. New York: Alfred A. Knopf

Corbett, D. 1957. *Canada's Immigration Policy*. Toronto: University of Toronto Press

Cox, O. 1948. *Caste, Class and Race*. Garden City, NY: Doubleday

Crysdale, J., and Durham, N. 1978. 'White Power: An Analysis of the Western

Guard Party Ideology.' Unpublished MA thesis, Department of Sociology, York University

Csanji, I. 1981. 'The Emerging Shadow: The Klan in Canada, Fact or Fiction.' Unpublished document

Dandeker, C., and Troyna, B. 1983. 'Fascism: Slogan or Concept?' *Patterns of Prejudice* 17 (no. 4): 19–30

Dixon, M. 1981–2. 'World Capitalist Crisis and the Rise of the Right.' *Contemporary Marxism*, no. 4: 1–10

Dobzhansky, T. 1963. 'Possibility That Homo Sapiens Evolved Independently 5 Times Is Vanishingly Small.' *Current Anthropology* 4: 360–7

D'Oyley, V., ed. 1978. *Black Presence in Multi-Ethnic Canada*. Vancouver: Faculty of Education, University of British Columbia; and Toronto: Ontario Institute for Studies in Education

Draper, P. 1978. 'The Accidental Immigrants: Canada and the Interned Refugees.' *Canadian Jewish Historical Society Journal* 2: parts 1 and 2

– 1983. 'Muses behind Barbed Wire: Canada and the Interned Refugees.' In J. Jackman and C. Bordens, eds., *The Muses Flee Hitler. Cultural Transfer and Adaptation 1930–1945*, pp. 271–81. Washington: Smithsonian Institution Press

Driedger, L. 1980. 'Jewish Identity: The Maintenance of Urban Religious and Ethnic Boundaries.' *Ethnic and Racial Studies* 3 (no. 1): 67–88

Driedger, L., and Mezoff, R. 1981. 'Ethnic Prejudice and Discrimination in Winnipeg High Schools.' *Canadian Journal of Sociology* 6 (no. 1): 1–17

Edgar, D. 1977. 'Racism, Fascism and the Politics of the National Front.' *Race and Class* 19 (no. 2): 111–31

Edwards, F. 1938. 'Fascism in Canada.' *Maclean's*, 15 April: 10, 66, 68; and 1 May: 15, 30

Elezar, D. 1982. In 'Antisemitism Today: A Symposium.' *Patterns of Prejudice* 16 (no. 4): 3–53

Elliott, D. 1985. 'Anti-Semitism and the Social Credit Movement: The Intellectual Roots of the Keegstra Affair.' *Canadian Ethnic Studies* 17 (no. 1): 78–89

Elliott, J. 1983. *Two Nations, Many Cultures*. Scarborough, Ont.: Prentice-Hall Canada Inc.

Epstein, B., and Forster, A. 1967. *The Radical Right Report on the John Birch Society and Its Allies*. New York: Random House

Equality Now! 1984. Report of the Special Committee on Visible Minorities in Canadian Society. House of Commons, Issue no. 4

Ettinger, S. 1982. In 'Antisemitism Today: A Symposium.' *Patterns of Prejudice* 16 (no. 4): 3–53

Fawkes, T. 1980. 'Conspiracy of Hate.' *B.C. Labour News*, pp. 1–11

Ferguson, T. 1975. *A White Man's Country*. Toronto: Doubleday Canada

Fielding, N. 1981. *The National Front*. London: Routledge and Kegan Paul

Forster, A., and Epstein, B. 1965, *Report on the Ku Klux Klan*. Anti-Defamation League of B'nai B'rith

- 1974. *The New Anti-Semitism*. New York and Toronto: McGraw-Hill

Freyre, G. 1963. *The Masters and the Slaves*. Trans. by S. Putman. Second English-language ed., revised. New York: Alfred A. Knopf

Frideres, J. 1976. 'Racism in Canada: Alive and Well.' *The Western Canadian Journal of Anthropology* 6 (no. 4): 124–45

Fromm, P., and Hull, J. 1981. *Down the Drain?* Toronto: Griffin House

Fromm, P., and Varey, R., 1983. *Sociobiology: Blueprint for Survival*. C-FAR Canadian Series 3

Garrity, J. 1966. 'My Sixteen Months as a Nazi.' *Maclean's*, 1 October

Glickman, Y. 1981. 'Jewish Education: Success or Failure?' In M. Weinfeld, W. Shaffer, and I. Cotler, eds., *The Canadian Jewish Mosaic*, pp. 113–27. Rexdale, Ont.: John Wiley and Sons Canada Ltd

- 1985. 'Antisemitism and Jewish Social Cohesion.' In J. Goldstein and R. Bienvenue, eds., *Ethnicity and Ethnic Relations in Canada*, 2nd ed., pp. 263–84. Toronto: Butterworths

Glickman, Y., and Bardikoff, A. 1982. *The Treatment of the Holocaust in Canadian History and Social Science Textbooks*. Downsview, Ont.: League for Human Rights of B'nai B'rith, Canada

Glock, C., and Stark, R. 1966. *Christian Beliefs and Anti-Semitism*. New York: Harper and Row

Gordis, R. 1971. 'Negroes Are Antisemitic Because They Want a Scapegoat.' In L. Dinnerstein, ed., *Antisemitism in the United States*, pp. 132–7. New York: Holt, Rinehart and Winston

Gordon, D. 1975. In *Minutes of Proceedings and Evidence of the Special Joint Committee of the Senate and of the House of Commons on Immigration Policy*. Queen's Printer, Issue no. 40, 17 June

- 1982. 'Manifestations of Racism in High Places.' *Contrast*, 19 and 26 March

Gordon, S. 1984. *Hitler, Germans and the 'Jewish Question.'* Princeton: Princeton University Press

Greaves, I. 1930. *The Negro in Canada*. Montreal: McGill University Economic Studies

Groberman, R. 1980. 'The Foreign Student Experience in Canada Today.' In K.V. Ujimoto and G. Hirabayashi, eds., *Visible Minorities and Multiculturalism: Asians in Canada*, pp. 151–62. Scarborough, Ont.: Butterworth and Company Ltd

Hamilton, R. 1982. *Who Voted for Hitler?* Princeton: Princeton University Press

Harris, M. 1971. *Culture, Man, and Nature*. New York: Thomas Y. Crowell Company

Hartmann, P., and Husband, C. 1974. *Racism and the Mass Media*. London: Davis-Poynter Ltd

Head, W. 1975. *The Black Presence in the Canadian Mosaic*. Ontario Human Rights Commission

Healey, D., and Hobsbawm, E. 1982. 'Arriving at Truth.' *Socialist Review* 12 (no. 66): 115–24

Henry, F. 1973. *Forgotten Canadians*. Don Mills, Ont.: Longman, Canada Ltd

– 1978. *The Dynamics of Racism in Toronto*. Toronto: York University

Henry, F., and Ginzberg, E. 1985. *Who Gets the Work: A Test of Racial Discrimination in Employment*. The Urban Alliance on Race Relations and the Social Planning Council of Metropolitan Toronto

Henson, T. 1977. 'Ku Klux Klan in Western Canada.' *Alberta History* 25 (no. 4): 1–8

Hill, D. 1977. *Human Rights in Canada: A Focus on Racism*. Canadian Labour Congress

Hobsbawm, E. 1980. 'Are We Entering a New Era of Anti-Semitism?' *New Society*, 11 December: 503–5

Hoffer, E. 1951. *The True Believer*. New York and Evanston: Harper and Row

Holter, E. 1934. *The ABC of Social Credit*. Vancouver: Institute of Economic Democracy

Horowitz, I. 1981. 'Left-Wing Fascism: An Infantile Disorder.' *Transaction/Society* 18: 19–24

Horton, J. 1981. 'The Rise of the Right: A Global View.' *Crime and Social Justice*, Summer: 7–17

Howay, F. 1939. 'The Negro Immigration into Vancouver Island in 1858.' *British Columbia Historical Quarterly* 3 (no. 2): 101–13

Hughes, D., and Kallen, E. 1974. *The Anatomy of Racism*. Montreal: Harvest House

Hull, J. 1982. *The Canadian Lifeboat*. Toronto: C-FAR Canadian Issues Series 1

Ijaz, M. 1981. 'Study on Ethnic Attitudes of Elementary School Children toward Blacks and East Indians.' Report submitted to the Scarborough Board of Education

Jensen, A. 1969. 'How Much Can We Boost I.Q. and Scholastic Achievment?' *Harvard Education Review* 39: 1–123

Johanson, N. 1974. 'Guarding Whose Christian Moral Values.' *United Church Observer* June: 22–4

Jones, B. 1978. 'Nova Scotia Blacks: A Quest for a Place in the Canadian Mosaic.' In V. D'Oyley, ed., *Black Presence in Multi-Ethnic Canada*, pp. 81–96. Vancouver: Faculty of Education, University of British Columbia; and Toronto: Ontario Institute for Studies in Education

Jordan, W. 1968. *White over Black*. Chapel Hill: University of North Carolina Press

Kallen, E. 1982. *Ethnicity and Human Rights in Canada*. Toronto: Gage Publishing Ltd

Kallen, H. 1971. 'Christianity and Antisemitism.' In L. Dinnerstein, ed., *Antisemitism in the United States*, pp. 17–23. New York: Holt, Rinehart and Winston

Kayfetz, C. 1975. 'Only Yesterday.' *Congress Bulletin*, September: 10–11

Killan, C. 1978. *Go Do Some Great Thing*. Vancouver: Douglas and McIntyre

King, D., and Radosh, R. 1984. 'The La Rouche Connection.' *The New Republic*, 19 November: 14–25

King, W. 1980. 'The Violent Rebirth of the Klan.' *New York Times Magazine*, December

Kirk, R. 1962. 'Your Social Credit Questions Answered.' Ottawa: Social Credit Association of Canada

Kotash, M. 1984. 'Eckville, Alta. The Agony of a Small Town.' *Chatelaine*, February: 51, 154, 156, 160

Kyba, P. 1964. 'The Saskatchewan General Election of 1929. MA thesis, Department of Economics and Political Science, University of Saskatchewan

– 1968. 'Ballots and Burning Crosses – The Election of 1929.' In Norman Ward and Duff Spafford, eds., *Politics in Saskatchewan*, pp. 105–23. Toronto: Longmans, Canada, Ltd

Lapajne, B. 1983. *CUSO and Radicalism*. Toronto: Citizens for Foreign Aid Reform, Inc.

Laqueur, W. 1972. *A History of Zionism*. London: Weidenfeld and Nicolson

Lasry, J. 1981. 'A Francophone Diaspora in Quebec.' In M. Weinfeld, W. Shaffir, and I. Cotler, eds., *The Canadian Jewish Mosaic*, pp. 221–40. Toronto: John Wiley and Sons

Leiris, M. 1961. 'Race and Culture.' In Unesco, *Race and Science*, pp. 181–218. New York: Columbia University Press

Le Riche, W. 1983. *Overpopulation and Third World Immigration*. Toronto: C-FAR Canadian Issues Series 7

Levy, H. n.d. 'A Preliminary Report on the Edmund Burke Society.' ADL Basic Documents

Li, P. 1979. 'Prejudice against Asians in a Canadian City.' *Canadian Ethnic Studies* 11 (no. 2): 70–7

Lipset, S. 1964. 'The Sources of the "Radical Right." ' In D. Bell, ed., *The Radical Right*, pp. 307–71. New York: Doubleday

– 1971. 'Fascism as the Extremism of the Centre.' In G. Allardyce, ed., *The Place of Fascism in European History*, pp. 110–20. Englewood Cliffs, NJ: Prentice-Hall

Lipset, S., and Raab, E. 1970. *The Politics of Unreason: Right-Wing Extremism in America, 1790–1970*. New York, Evanston, and London: Harper and Row

McAlpine, J. 1981. *Report Arising out of the Activities of the Ku Klux Klan in British Columbia*. Presented to The Honourable Minister of Labour for the Province of British Columbia

McCormack, R. 1981. 'Cloth Caps and Jobs: The Ethnicity of English Immigrants in Canada 1900–1914.' In J. Dahlie and T. Fernando, eds., *Ethnicity, Power and Politics in Canada*, pp. 38–55. Toronto: Methuen

McDougall, B. 1981. 'The Canadian Right: A History and Perspectives.' International Socialist Document Series, no. 1: 1–15

McMurtry, J. 1984. 'Fascism and Neo-Conservatism: Is There a Difference?' *Praxis International* 4 (no. 2): 86–103

McNaught, K. 1970. 'Violence in Canadian History.' In J. Moir, ed., *Character and Circumstance*, pp. 66–84. Toronto: Macmillan of Canada

Medjuck, S., and Lazar, M. 1981. 'Existence on the Fringe: The Jews of Atlantic Canada.' In M. Weinfeld, W. Shaffir, and I. Cotler, eds., *The Canadian Jewish Mosaic*, pp. 241–58. Toronto: John Wiley and Sons

Memmi, A. 1971. *Portrait of a Jew*. Trans. E. Abbott. New York: The Viking Press

Mertl, S., and Ward, J. 1985. *Keegstra: The Trial, the Issues, the Consequences*. Saskatoon: Western Producer Prairie Books

Miles, R. 1984. 'Summoned by Capital: The Political Economy of Labour Migration.' In P. Spoonley, C. Macpherson, D. Pearson, and C. Sedgwick, eds., *Tauiwi*, pp. 223–43. Palmerston North, NZ: Dunmore Press

Miller, J. 1971. 'The Attack on Kosygin Worked out Very Well for the Edmund Burke Society, Anyway.' *Canadian Magazine*, December: 24–5, 27–8

Millett, D. 1982. 'Defining the Dominant Group.' *Canadian Ethnic Studies* 13 (no. 3): 64–79

Montagu, A. 1942. *Man's Most Dangerous Myth: The Fallacy of Race*. Cleveland and New York: The World Publishing Company

– 1963. *Race, Science and Humanity*. Toronto: Van Nostrand Reinhold Company

– 1980. *Sociobiology Examined*. London: Oxford University Press

Moodley, K. 1981. 'Canadian Ethnicity in Comparative Perspective: Issues in the Literature.' In J. Dahlie and T. Fernando, eds., *Ethnicity, Power and Politics in Canada*, pp. 6–21. Toronto: Methuen

Nader, L. 1972. 'Up the Anthropologist – Perspectives Gained in Studying a Politically Sensitive and Deviant Community.' *Social Problems* 14: 357–66

National Strategy on Race Relations. n.d. Ottawa: Multiculturalism Canada

Nikolinakos, M. 1973. 'Notes on an Economic Theory of Racism.' *Race* 14: 365–81

O'Toole, R. 1977. *The Precipitous Path: Studies in Political Sects.* Toronto: Peter Martin Associates

Overstreet, H., and Overstreet, B. 1964. *The Strange Tactics of Extremism.* New York: W.W. Norton and Company, Inc.

Palmer, H. 1982. *Patterns of Prejudice.* Toronto: McClelland and Stewart

Patel, D. 1980. *Dealing with Interracial Conflict: Policy Alternatives.* Montreal: the Institute for Research on Public Policy

Payne, S. 1980. *Fascism.* Wisconsin: University of Wisconsin Press

Petchesky, R. 1981. 'Antiabortion, Antifeminism, and the Rise of the New Right.' *Feminist Studies* 7 (no. 2): 206–46

Peter, K. 1981. 'The Myth of Multiculturalism and Other Political Fables.' In J. Dahlie and T. Fernando, eds., *Ethnicity, Power and Politics in Canada*, pp. 56–67. Toronto: Methuen

Pitman, W. 1977. *Now Is Not Too Late.* Submitted to the Council of Metropolitan Toronto by Task Force on Human Relations

Poliakov, L. 1975. *The History of Anti-Semitism*, vol. III. London: Routledge and Kegan Paul

Porter, J. 1965. *The Vertical Mosaic.* Toronto: University of Toronto Press

Potter, H. 1961. 'Negroes in Canada.' *Race* 103: 39–56

Poulantzas, N. 1979. *Fascism and Dictatorship.* Trans. Judith White. London: Verso Editions

Prager, J. 1972. 'White Racial Privilege and Social Change: An Examination of Theories of Racism.' *Berkeley Journal of Sociology* 17: 117–50

Quinley, H. and Glock, C. 1979. *Anti-Semitism in America.* New York: Free Press

Raab, E. 1974. 'Is There a New Anti-Semitism?' *Commentary* 57: 53–5

– 1983. 'Anti-Semitism in the 1980s.' *Midstream* 32 (February): 11–18

Ramcharan, S. 1982. *Racism: Nonwhites in Canada.* Toronto: Butterworths

Redekop, J. 1965. 'Billy James Hargis' Perception of the American Constitution, Government, and Society.' *The Journal of Church and Society* 1 (no. 1): 1–22

Reid, R. 1941. 'The Inside Story of the Kamaguta Maru.' *British Columbia Historical Quarterly* 5: 1–23

Report of the Special Committee on Hate Propaganda in Canada. 1966. Ottawa: Queen's Printer

Rex, J. 1970. *Race Relations in Sociological Theory.* New York: Schocken Books

– 1973. *Race, Colonialism and the City.* London: Routledge and Kegan Paul

Richmond, A. 1974–5. 'The Green Paper – Reflections on the Canadian Immigration and Population Study.' *Canadian Ethnic Studies* 6–7: 5–21

- 1975. 'Black and Asian Immigrants in Britain and Canada: Some Comparisons.' *New Commentary* 4: 510–16
Roach, C. 1980. 'Minorities and Police Racism.' *Prometheus*, no. 2 (Winter): 27–32
- n.d. 'Blacks and Jews: Collision Course or New Relationships?' Unpublished manuscript
Rose, A. 1971. 'Antisemitism's Root in City Hatred.' In L. Dinnerstein, ed., *Antisemitism in the United States*, pp. 41–7. New York: Holt, Rinehart and Winston
Rosenberg, S. 1971. *The Jewish Community in Canada*, vol. 2. Toronto and Montreal: McClelland and Stewart, Ltd
- 1986. *The Christian Problem: A Jewish View*. Toronto: Deneau Publishers
Rothbard, M. 1969. 'Listen, YAF.' *The Liberation Forum* 1 (no. 10): 1–2
Roy, P. 1980. 'The Illusion of Toleration: White Opinion of Asians in British Columbia, 1929–37.' In K.V. Ujimoto and G. Hirabayashi, eds., *Visible Minorities and Multiculturalism: Asians in Canada*, pp. 81–91. Scarborough, Ont.: Butterworth and Company Ltd
Salutin, R. 1982. 'The Converstion of the Jews.' *Saturday Night*, January
Samuels, F. 1969–70. 'Color Sensitivity among Honolulu's Haoles and Japanese.' *Race* 11: 203–12
Sartre, J. 1948. *Anti-Semite and Jew*. Trans. by G. Becker, New York: Schocken Books
Schwartz, B., and Disch, R., eds., 1970. 'Introduction' to *White Racism*, pp. 1–66. New York: Dell Publishing Company, Inc.
Shaffir, W. 1981. 'Chassidic Communities in Montreal.' In M. Weinfeld, W. Shaffir, and I. Cotler, eds., *The Canadian Jewish Mosaic*, pp. 273–86. Toronto: John Wiley and Sons
Sher, J. 1983. *White Hoods: Canada's Ku Klux Klan*. Vancouver: New Star Books
Shimomura, F. 1984. 'Academic "Yellow Peril"?' *New Canadian*, 22 June: 2.
Snowden, F. 1970. *Blacks in Antiquity: Ethiopians in the Greco-Roman Experience*. Cambridge, Mass.: Harvard University Press
- 1983. *Before Color Prejudice: The Ancient View of Blacks*. Cambridge, Mass.: Harvard University Press
Speisman, S. 1979. *The Jews of Toronto: A History to 1979*. Toronto: McClelland and Stewart, Ltd
Spoonley, P. 1981. 'New Zealand First! The Extreme Right and Politics in New Zealand, 1961–1981.' *Political Science* 33 (no. 2): 99–126
- 1983. 'The Political Expression of White Ethnicity: Racism and the New Zealand League of Rights.' Paper delivered at the New Zealand Sociological Association Meeting, Auckland, May

- 1984. 'The Politics of Racism: The New Zealand League of Rights.' In P. Spoonley, C. Macpherson, D. Pearson, and C. Sedgwick, eds., *Tauiwi*, pp. 68–85. Palmerston North, NZ: Dunmore Press, Ltd

Stein, M. 1973. *The Dynamics of Right-Wing Protest*. Toronto: University of Toronto Press

- 1975. 'Social Credit in the Province of Quebec: Summary and Developments.' In S. Clark, J. Grayson, and L. Grayson, eds., *Prophecy and Protest*, pp. 347–65. Toronto: Gage

Stepan, N. 1982. *The Idea of Race in Science*. London: Macmillan

Sugimoto, H. 1972. 'The Vancouver Riots of 1907: A Canadian Episode.' In H. Conroy and T. Miyakawa, eds., *East across the Pacific*, pp. 92–106. Santa Barbara: American Bibliographical Center

Sunahara, A. 1981. *The Politics of Racism: The Uprooting of Japanese Canadians during the Second World War*. Toronto: James Lorimer and Company

Sypnowich, P. 1964. 'My Weird Weekend with the Hate-Mongers.' *The Canadian Weekly, The Toronto Daily Star*, 13 June

Thomas, B., and Novogrodsky, C. 1983. *Combatting Racism in the Workplace*. Toronto: Cross-Cultural Communication Centre

Torczyner, J. 1981. 'To Be Poor and Jewish in Canada.' In M. Weinfeld, W. Shaffir, I. Cotler, eds., *The Canadian Jewish Mosaic*, pp. 177–91. Toronto: John Wiley and Sons

Trachtenberg, J. 1943. *The Devil and the Jews*. New Haven: Yale University Press

Troyna, B. 1980. 'The Media and the Electoral Decline of the National Front.' *Patterns of Prejudice* 14 (no. 3): 25–30

Tunteng, P. 1973. 'Racism and the Montreal Computer Incident of 1969.' *Race* 14: 229–40

Ujimoto, K.V., and Hirabayashi, G., eds., 1980. *Visible Minorities and Multiculturalism: Asians in Canada*. Scarborough, Ont.: Butterworth and Company Ltd

Valentine, V. (assisted by I. Taylor). 1980. 'Native Peoples and Canadian Society: A Profile of Issues and Trends.' In R. Breton, J. Reitz, V. Valentine, eds., *Cultural Boundaries and the Cohesion of Canada*, pp. 45–135. Montreal: The Institute for Research on Public Policy

Wagner, J. 1981. *Brothers beyond the Sea: National Socialism in Canada*. Waterloo, Ont.: Wilfrid Laurier University Press

Walker, J. 1978. 'Historical Study of Blacks in Canada: The State of the Discipline.' In V. D'Oyley, ed., *Black Presence in Multi-Ethnic Canada*, pp. 51–70. Vancouver: Faculty of Education, University of British Columbia; and Toronto: Ontario Institute for Studies in Education

Walker, M. 1977. *The National Front*. London: Fontana

Waller, H., and Weinfeld, M. 1981. 'The Jews of Quebec and "Le Fait Français," ' In M. Weinfeld, W. Shaffir, and I. Cotler, eds., *The Canadian Jewish Mosaic*, pp. 415–39. Toronto: John Wiley and Sons

Ward, W. 1978. *White Canada Forever*. Montreal: McGill-Queen's University Press

Weber, M. 1958. *The Protestant Ethic and the Spirit of Capitalism*. Trans. Talcott Parsons. New York: Charles Scribner's Sons

Weiman, G., and Winn, C. 1986. *Hate on Trial: The Zundel Affair, the Media, and Public Opinion in Canada*. Oakville, Ont.: Mosaic Press

Weinfeld, M. 1977. 'La Question Juive au Québec.' *Midstream* 23: 20–9

– 1981. 'Intermarriage: Agony and Adaptation,' In M. Weinfeld, W. Shaffir, I. Cotler, eds., *The Canadian Jewish Mosaic*, pp. 365–82. Toronto: John Wiley and Sons

Westin, A. 1964. 'The John Birch Society.' In D. Bell, ed., *The Radical Right*, pp. 239–68. New York: Anchor Books

White Racism in the 1980s. n.d. A report from the pages of *The Tennessean*

Winks, R. 1980. 'The Canadian Negro: A Historical Assessment – Part I.' *The Journal of Negro History* 53 (no. 4): 283–300

– 1969. 'The Canadian Negro: A Historical Assessment – Part II.' *The Journal of Negro History* 54 (no. 1): 1–18

– 1971. *The Blacks in Canada*. New Haven: Yale University Press

Wolfe, A. 1981. 'Sociology, Liberalism, and the Radical Right.' *New Left Review* 125–30: 3–27

Wolfe, M. 1977. 'Purity: The Struggle for WASP Supremacy.' *Saturday Night* 92 (December): 26, 29, 30

Wood, J. 1978. 'East Indians and Canada's New Immigration Policy.' *Canadian Public Policy* 4 (no. 4): 547–67

Wrong, D. 1959. 'Ontario's Jews in the Larger Community.' In A. Rose, ed., *A People and Its Faith*, pp. 45–59. Toronto: University of Toronto Press

Zayid, I. 1980. *Zionism: The Myth and the Reality*. Indianapolis, Ind.: American Trust Publications

Index